waves of
RANCOR

waves of RANCOR

TUNING IN THE RADICAL RIGHT

Robert L. Hilliard and **Michael C. Keith**

M.E. Sharpe
Armonk, New York
London, England

Copyright © 1999 by M. E. Sharpe, Inc.

All rights reserved. No part of this book may be reproduced in any form
without written permission from the publisher, M. E. Sharpe, Inc.,
80 Business Park Drive, Armonk, New York 10504.

Library of Congress Cataloging-in-Publication Data

Hilliard, Robert L.
Waves of rancor : tuning in the radical right / Robert L. Hilliard and Michael C. Keith.
p. cm. — (Media, communication, and culture in America)
Includes bibliographical references and index.
ISBN 0-7656-0131-1 (hardcover : alk. paper)
1. Broadcasting—Political aspects—United States. 2. Talk shows—United States.
3. Conservatism—United States. I. Keith, Michael C. II. Title. III. Series.
PN1990.6.U5H49 1999
302.23´0973—dc21   98-45397
CIP

Printed in the United States of America

The paper used in this publication meets the minimum requirements of
American National Standard for Information Sciences—
Permanence of Paper for Printed Library Materials,
ANSI Z 39.48-1984.

BM (c)   10   9   8   7   6   5   4   3   2

Standing, as I do, in the view of God and eternity I realize that patriotism is not enough. I must have no hatred or bitterness towards anyone.

—Edith Cavell

The most convenient way to organize recent American cultural life is to visualize a dominant conservatism.

—Robert M. Crunden

Congress shall make no law respecting an establishment of religion, or prohibiting the free exercise thereof, or abridging the freedom of speech, or of the press; or the right of the people peaceably to assemble, and to petition the Government for a redress of grievances.

—The First Amendment to the U.S. Constitution

Dedicated to the memory of
Kim Cavallero

Table of Contents

Foreword

The M.E. Sharpe book series "Media, Communication, and Culture in America" is designed to explore the massive transformations that have occurred as a consequence of the changes in communication technology and the enlarged role that communication has played in American life. The emphasis is on communication, but the series attempts to examine the interstices of media and culture and to explain the broader patterns of communication in everyday life.

The diversity of topics that fall within the domain of communication continues to grow. The topics frequently are interdisciplinary. The issues focus upon a world now being reconfigured by the revolution in communication and where the speed and variety of communication transactions promise to open up a "new frontier" in American life. These changes allow us not only to imagine a future that is shaped by communication; we also are able to reexamine the past and reassess the distinctive role that communication has played in our cultural heritage. The objective of the series is to convey communication's diversity, to analyze its past, and to forecast its unfolding revolution.

The first book in the series is *Waves of Rancor: Tuning In the Radical Right* by Robert L. Hilliard and Michael C. Keith. One of the more durable aspects of American democracy is that individuals and groups who feel disenfranchised have been able to join together to articulate their discontent. Sometimes these social movements have become a religious crusade; sometimes they have developed a psychological stance that borders on what historian Richard Hofstadter has called "the paranoid style of American politics." Typically, the groups identify villains and scapegoats, level attacks against unscrupulous and scheming leaders, and bolster their own patriotism by depicting a vision of a glorious millennial era attached to some bygone period in American history. What is distinctive about these groups in the 1990s is their use of modern media—radio, television, cable, and the Internet—to convey their message.

Hilliard and Keith have written a significant book. They have unearthed sources and documentary evidence that had been unknown. This is a study based primarily on original source materials. The authors examine the current embodiments of the Radical Right from the congenial faces of Rush Limbaugh and the Christian Coalition to the extremist groups that openly advocate terrorist tactics to obtain their objectives. Hilliard and Keith provide us with a counterintuitive observation about the "rancor of the right" that is penetrating and insightful: Modern media have not created a homogeneous society. Rather, they have permitted the Right to use the by-products of modern communication to legitimize their activities and to unite members who previously would have encountered substantial barriers to communication.

This is a groundbreaking book. It is clearly written, it is well researched, and it tells an engaging story. Hilliard and Keith discuss the Oklahoma City bombing as the high tide of right-wing rancor. But the story that the authors convey indicates that the movement has the ability to reinvent itself and that the power to persuade has increasingly gained adherents for splinter groups on the Right. Hilliard and Keith are strong supporters of the First Amendment. They provide us with astute glimpses of the code words, hate speech, and escalated levels of intimidation that flow from right-wing activists. In *Waves of Rancor,* Hilliard and Keith construct a compelling account of an important social phenomenon in American life where culture, communication, and media converge.

Donald Fishman
Boston College

Introduction

In 1940 on a Brooklyn, New York, street corner a preteen argued vociferously with another preteen. "You killed Christ," the first youth cried passionately. "You Jews killed Christ and now Germany is punishing you for it. You deserve to be punished."

"I didn't kill anybody," the Jewish youth answered. "Why are you blaming me? Why should the Jews be punished?"

"Because Father Coughlin said so," came the response. "I heard it on the radio. We know all about you Jews from Father Coughlin. My family listens to Father Coughlin on the radio all the time."

In 1952 a student in a radio programming college course on Long Island confronted a teacher who had assigned students several talk and news shows to analyze for the class. "Are you a communist, sir?" the student demanded. "You want us to listen to different talk shows on the radio, including the Barry Gray show on WMCA, and he's a communist. I don't want to listen to any communist propaganda."

"What makes you think he's a communist?" the teacher asked. "He's had guests who have spoken out against McCarthyism, but I've never heard any pro-communist rhetoric on his show."

"Of course he's a communist," the student replied. "Walter Winchell says so. Walter Winchell calls him 'Borey Pink.' Whatever Walter Winchell says must be true. We always listen to Walter Winchell at home on the radio."

In 1993 in New Orleans a white girl told an African-American girl that she couldn't play with her anymore.

"Why not?" the African-American girl asked.

"Because you're a mud race. Because you're inferior to me. Because you don't have enough intelligence to play with white kids. And besides, pretty soon all of us whites will have to fight all you coloreds to keep you from taking over the world with the Jews."

"I never heard that before," the African-American girl said. "What makes you say all that?"

"Because we heard it from David Duke on the radio. My folks listen to David Duke all the time."

In 1994 in downtown Boston an elderly woman was picketing a rally for a national health insurance bill at which Hillary Rodham Clinton was the principal speaker. "Rush Is Right," her picket sign said. "This health insurance business is a communist-socialist plot," she eagerly told any passersby who would listen. "The Clintons are trying to destroy our country. They're really communists." How did she know that? "I know that it's true because Rush Limbaugh says so," she loudly proclaimed. "I listen to Rush on the radio all the time."

In 1995 in Oklahoma City a neighbor told a grieving mother that her child died in the bombing of the Murrah federal building because President Clinton killed her. "We heard it on the radio in the 'Mark from Michigan' program yesterday. He told us how the government bombed the building themselves to make the militias look bad so Clinton could ban guns and take over the United States for the 'New World Order.' We listen to 'Mark from Michigan' all the time on the short-wave."

In 1997 in Detroit a man turned to his friend as they sat at a bar and whispered the suggestion that they make some pipe bombs and leave them by the doors of some federal government offices in the city. "We've got to teach those niggers and Jew commies who run the Zionist Occupied Government in Washington that we whites won't stand for their bastardizing our race."

"Yeah, I listen to Chuck Baker on the radio, too," his friend said. "I agree with you and Chuck. We've got to teach them a lesson. But how do we make the bombs?"

"No problem. Just listen to Kurt Saxon's radio program. He tells you where to get the material and how to make them."

In 1998 a college student confronted his history professor. "Sir, it's time you stopped filling us with lies about World War II."

"What do you consider lies?" the professor asked.

"All that garbage about a Holocaust. There was no Holocaust. There were no gas chambers and death camps. Millions of Jews didn't die. The whole thing was fabricated by the international Jewish bankers to squeeze sympathy and money out of the rest of the world. Those gas chambers you see in photos were built by the Jews after the war for their blackmailing purposes."

"And where did you learn all this?" the professor asked.

"From the Zundelsite. On the Internet. Thousands and thousands of people log in every day to learn the truth about the Jews and the Holocaust."

What do these stories—only the tip of the iceberg—prove? Not that the commentators referred to are necessarily right or wrong—you will judge for yourself as you read this book—but that those who have access to the media have a powerful influence over the minds and hearts of the listeners and viewers they reach. Radio and, more recently, the Internet have had enormous impact on the political and social actions, mores, and progress of our society, in the United States and throughout the world. And none have had more influence than those commentators, talk show hosts, and Web-site operators who represent the right-wing political spectrum, the ultraconservatives who have the talent, ability, and opportunity to appeal to the large number of people who are dissatisfied with one or more aspects of the world they are living in and believe that the solution is not to move forward but to negate social change and move backward to what they feel was a more stable, safe, and righteous time.

That is what this book is about: how the radical right media personalities and programs have affected American society, what their motivations and purposes are, and how they personally perceive their contributions to the world. They have not done so subtly or, in most instances, with sensitivity. They have done so, by and large, with anger, falsehoods, and vituperation. They have used the media to transmit waves of rancor.

waves of
RANCOR

Chapter 1

The Genesis of Bitter Air

Who stilleth the raging of the sea, and the noise of his waves, and the madness of the people.

—Prayer Book, 1662

Radio and television are the most powerful forces in the world today affecting the minds and emotions of their viewers and listeners. In virtually every country in the world, with the exception of those poverty-stricken nations where television is available only to the rich, and radio sets are in short supply, most people spend more time viewing television or listening to the radio than they devote to any other endeavor except working (if, in fact, they have a job that takes up more than thirty-five hours of their time each week) and sleeping (if, in fact, they sleep more than an average of seven hours per day).

In the United States, for example, the average television set is on twenty-eight hours per week and the average radio is tuned in two and one-half hours a day. It is not surprising, then, that whenever there is a rebellion or revolution in a country, the first thing fought for is not the treasury, not the government buildings, not the universities, not the shops, not even the airports—but the radio and television stations.

For the last decades of the twentieth century, radio has been the most pervasive medium, simply because of its economic and technological availability to more people. In 1975 Julian Hale wrote:

> Radio is the only unstoppable medium of mass communication. It is the only medium which reaches across the entire globe instantaneously and can convey a message from any country to any other. Combined, these qualities of radio ensure that it plays an indispensable role in international communications and keeps its place as the most powerful weapon of international propaganda.[1]

During the quarter-century since this was written, other media—television, cable, satellite, and the Internet—have become important additional factors.

3

As cyberspace use expands, the Internet is quickly joining the older media as a controller of people's hearts and minds. In one sense, the Internet is even more powerful than radio and television insofar as it permits any one individual to reach out to literally millions of other individuals. Even though there may be millions who log on to any single Web site, the process affects participants as if it were one-on-one communication. As this is written, at the end of the second millennium, it is expected that not far into the new millennium the economic and technological availability of computers will spread rapidly to all parts of the world, expanding and strengthening cyberspace's role as a communicator and persuader.

Dictators, charlatans, and even random opportunists know that whoever controls the media of a country controls its political processes. Even without outright ownership or physical control of a station, any individual or group can influence public beliefs and affect public policy. In the United States, for example, with few exceptions, the candidate who spends the most money on television advertising wins the political race. A television or radio station owner who provides a candidate more free air time on news and public affairs programs than the opponent greatly enhances that candidate's chances. (The Equal Time provision of the Communications Act of 1934 was vitiated in 1984 during the Reagan era of deregulation, allowing stations to interpret what public affairs programming consists of and permitting stations to air public debates with candidates of their own choosing, excluding those they do not support. Thus, they can strengthen the candidacies of those they support and those who have the most money for television advertising, and effectively cut short the candidacies of those they oppose by removing them from public view.)

With the development and availability of new communications media, the opportunities for influencing the public's attitudes, feelings, and actions increased. The Internet especially opened the door for interactive influence, providing immediate feedback and follow-up for the few who would control the many.

The United States, arguably the world's leading democracy, is not immune to favoritism in the media. Michael Parenti writes in *Inventing Reality: The Politics of News Media* that the media in the United States are the "products of many forces, involving the dominant political culture and powerful economic and government institutions—all dedicated to maintaining an ideological monopoly, controlling the flow of information and opinion in ways that best advance their interests."[2] According to Parenti, "the CIA runs the biggest news service in the world with a budget larger than those of all the major wire services put together."[3]

The most susceptible viewers and listeners are those who (1) are dissatisfied with their life and seek to blame it on an outside party such as a government or a group or a few individuals, or (2) lack sufficient education to judge either the truth or the impact of media materials upon them, succumbing as media illiterates to emotional appeals, or (3) are sufficiently psychologically disturbed to seek support from what they consider alternatives to conventional attitudes, no matter how destructive those alternatives may be.

These viewers/listeners/Internet participants are easy prey for those who believe that their religious beliefs are the only correct ones, that their political attitudes are the only acceptable ones, that their social behavior is the only justifiable one. Those who would create hate and chaos to forward their personal agendas of power and superiority are avid users of the media to achieve their goals.

In his book, *Inside Talk Radio,* Peter Laufer points out that "groups throughout the spectrum of ideas are fast learning how to manipulate talk radio"[4] and that "the talk show demagogues are adept at manipulating anger and turning righteous resentment into fearful hatred of the oppressed."[5] Laufer agrees on the power the media give the controller and user: "The power is real, not just as a money-making force, but also as a political force."[6]

Michael Parenti is concerned that the right wing is making such effective use of the media. He writes: "Many call-in shows enable us to hear directly from listeners and provide opportunities for the brief airing of dissident viewpoints. Many of these talk shows, when running at prime time, are dominated by right-wing hosts or mainstream centrists, who show only a limited tolerance for leftist call-ins. . . . such meager accommodations are designed to create the impression of an open communication between media and public where one does not exist."[7]

Laufer expresses similar concern: "Talk radio continues to attract real crackpots as hosts, many much further over the edge than the controlled and calculated rants and raves of a Limbaugh or a Stern";[8] "Hate, scapegoating and stereotyping fill the airwaves."[9]

As Frank Rich pointed out in the *New York Times,* the bombing of the Alfred P. Murrah federal building in Oklahoma City in 1995 didn't occur in a vacuum: "Timothy McVeigh didn't come from nowhere but was an exemplar, however extreme, of a diverse, violent right-wing fringe, ranging from neo-Nazis to gun-absolutists to Christian Identity white supremacists."[10] Rich notes that since the 1995 Oklahoma City terror, bombings have increased throughout the United States, many of them attributed to right-wing militia organizations.

It is not a coincidence that the militias and militia-related or supporting organizations are prolific users of radio, television, and the Internet to convey their messages of hate and violence and to influence and recruit people to implement their goals of terror and chaos and ultimate control of their immediate, then larger societies. Their justification is a defense against a purported Jewish-controlled UN-implemented New World Order that they believe is about to take over the United States. Timothy McVeigh was an avid listener and viewer of right-wing radio and videos.

A look at Web home pages on the Internet, promoted by organizations through newsletters as well as through the media, reveals such sites as "White Nation: Our Salvation," "The New World Order," "The Holocaust Never Happened," "Christian-Race Conscious," "Ku Klux Klan," "Aryan Pre-Christian Religion," "Join the Militia: Prevent Tyranny," and "Skinheads."

In fact, what might be termed the "newer" media, such as shortwave radio and the Internet, have become the principal tools for far-right propaganda, replacing what is often thought of as the mainstream dissemination source, traditional radio stations. One specialist in the study of extremist groups stated: "I have mixed emotions about the level of bigotry on talk radio, but I'm more worried about short-wave radio and the Internet. That's where the fringe groups are the most active, and it's very frightening."[11]

Talk radio in the United States is dominated by those who support the aims of militias, white supremacists, and ethnic purists. Most people think of Rush Limbaugh when they think of right-wing radio. Compared to most right-wing hosts, Limbaugh is hardly radical. Frequently bracketed with talk show hosts such as Oliver North and G. Gordon Liddy, Limbaugh does not push, as they sometimes do, to the edge of extremism. And North and Liddy even appear moderate when compared to far-right and extremist-right media personalities such as Pete Peters, Kevin Alfred Strom, David Duke, William Pierce, Chuck Baker, Chuck Harder, Kurt Saxon, Ernst Zundel and a host of others. Limbaugh's is probably the most widely heard of all radio talk shows in the United States, with an estimated reach of more than 20 million listeners daily on more than 600 stations. His principal influence shows itself through the ballot box, inasmuch as some estimates suggest that over 90 percent of his listeners vote, as compared to a nationwide total of only about half that number.[12] Interestingly, Rush Limbaugh's listeners "rated themselves as 'superior' in their knowledge of history and current events,' but scored lowest in simple tests in both categories."[13]

Although some analyses of his programs show he has consistently given false information in order to forward his political agenda, Limbaugh generally remains within the political spectrum that comprises the Republican Party. In fact, some extremist right-wingers have even called for Limbaugh's execution on the grounds that he is hurting the real right wing by being too moderate. Unlike many right-wing talk show hosts, he does not advocate terror and murder to accomplish his political goals. However, he does not hesitate to use epithets and insult to describe those he disagrees with, in many ways similar to the language used by further-right personalities. Two of Limbaugh's favorite terms, for example, are "Femi-Nazis" and "Environmentalist-Wackos."

By contrast, station KVOR in Colorado Springs features Chuck Baker in a three-hour stint following Limbaugh's daily program. Baker has advocated and endorsed his callers' advocacy of such actions as bringing in private militia soldiers to kill members of Congress whom Baker and his supporters consider traitors, and to mount an armed revolution against the government.

One of his influenced listeners, Francisco Duran, did what Baker advocated and went to Washington and fired a couple of dozen bullets at the White House. Duran "was a fan of right-wing radio talk shows. He was active in the militia. And he hated Janet Reno and President Clinton. . . . Duran picked up his semi-automatic rifle and went to Pennsylvania Avenue. He fired about 30 shots . . . at the White House, trying to kill the president . . . [H]e reportedly was a big fan of Rush Limbaugh and of a far-right talk show host named Chuck Baker. One day Baker went on the air and talked about the need for an armed revolution to take out the 'slimeballs' in Congress."[14]

No one was killed that time. When a caller to Baker's show suggested that militia members and other "patriots" embark on an armed intervention in Washington, Baker replied: "Am I advocating the overthrow of this government? . . . I'm advocating the cleansing. . . . It's provided for in the Constitution, . . . it's well within my right under free speech."[15] (A couple of years later, in 1998, a deranged gunman from Montana, likewise inspired by hatred of the government, killed two policemen in an assault on the nation's Capitol. A radio was found in his remote cabin.)

Other far-right and extremist-right radio hosts who have had a marked effect on American politics and who, in the minds of many people, pose increasing threats to public safety are discussed in greater detail in subsequent chapters of this book. One of the best known is Mark Koernke, whose program "The Intelligence Report" has been on and off the air, depending on how far the right-wing radio stations that carry him think he has gone in fomenting violence. Researcher and writer on far-right groups Daniel Levitas has said: "Koernke is not a radio personality. What Koernke is is a leader of a paramilitary right wing movement who is using communications technology to advance the militant violent objectives, to recruit and communicate."[16] Another example is William Cooper, who, after the Oklahoma City federal building disaster, told his radio listeners that he knew who had really been responsible for the bombing: "Who has the expertise and the experience to pull off such a precision bombing? Who has the resources and power to cover it up, and who, in fact, is covering it up? We all know the answers to that and it has nothing to do with the militia. This is the Reichstag all over again."[17] Another key right-wing user of the airwaves is Kurt Saxon, who not only justifies violence, but informs his listeners how to go about it. On one program he told his audience in detail how to "build a bomb with materials from local stores." On another program one subject was a call-in inquiry on "what the best weapon was for picking off

Martians at 300 feet." "Martians" is a euphemism used by right-wing militants for minorities.[18]

Despite Limbaugh's distancing himself from such extremist advocacy of violence, he, like all right-wing talk show hosts, bristles when his program is accused of fomenting harmful effects on society. For example, not long after the bombing of the federal building in Oklahoma City, President Clinton said, "We must stand up and speak against reckless speech that can push fragile people over the edge beyond the bounds of civilized conduct and take the country into a dark place. I say no matter where it comes from . . . If people are encouraging conduct that will undermine the fabric of this country, it should be spoken against whether it comes from the left or the right, whether it comes on radio, television or the movies." Rush Limbaugh and a number of other conservative—although not necessarily far-right-wing—talk show personalities interpreted those comments as aimed at them and joined the extremist commentators in angry denunciation of Clinton.[19]

Authors Jeff Cohen and Norman Solomon cite a number of right-wing talk show hosts' advocacy of violence and even murder. G. Gordon Liddy, whose show is syndicated by one of the country's largest radio program distributors, Westwood One, "told listeners how to kill Federal Bureau of Alcohol, Tobacco and Firearms agents . . . 'head shots, head shots' . . .'kill the sons of bitches.' " He also described for his listeners how to construct a bomb using ammonium nitrate, diesel fuel, and dynamite, adding "that would do enormous work . . . take out a wall of a quarry, or take out that building."[20] Note, again, that Liddy is not considered as far radical right as many others on the air. On Phoenix's KFYI, talk show host "Bob Mohan declared that gun control advocate Sarah Brady 'ought to be put down.' " On San Francisco's KSFO, listeners can hear talk show hosts advocate " 'lynching a few liberals' and encourage listeners to 'shoot illegal immigrants who come across the border.' "[21] On radio stations in various parts of the country, including short-wave station WWRC (Worldwide Christian Radio), listeners have heard "Pastor" Pete Peters assure his audience that the Bible sanctions killing gays and lesbians, Kurt Saxon explaining how to kill people with dry ice and hardware parts, and "militia commander" Linda Thompson calling for an armed militia attack on Washington, among other exhortations.[22]

These are only a few of the kinds of persuasive rhetoric found on radio in the United States; they are, as will be evident in later chapters in this book, just the smallest tip of the iceberg, just as radio as most people know it is only a small part of the airwaves used by the right. With an estimated over 1,000 right-wing or so-called "patriot" groups in the United States in 1999, including more than 400 known armed militia organizations, and with many state attorneys general reluctant or unable to take any action against these groups, twenty-four hours a day one can hear and see programs on radio, television, and the Internet advocating racial purity ("ethnic cleansing"), militant insurrection, and action against Jewish and liberal conspiracies.

The crowded domestic AM and FM radio spectrum, the limited frequency space and numbers of stations, and the rapid expansion of right-wing hate groups in the past few years have led to the increased use of shortwave radio to reach people across wide geographical areas of the globe. Some of the names of these short-wave stations are indicative of their orientation: Liberty Lobby, America First Radio, Radio Free America, USA Patriot Movement, Another Voice of Freedom, and, not facetiously, Almost Heaven. Programs on right-wing shortwave radio include the following topics: Jewish bankers are behind the attacks on Pat Buchanan; the story of possible life on Mars is a hoax designed to destroy Christianity; Freemasons are taking over the country; history of the Ku Klux Klan; Vince Foster's murder cover-up; the Roman Catholic Church is a tool of Satan; U.S. sovereignty is relinquished to foreign troops on U.S. soil; welfare reform is a giveaway to the poor; learn to defend yourself—buy survivalist products; U.S. Taxpayers Party reports; income tax is illegal; drivers licenses are unconstitutional; thirteenth and fourteenth amendments (abolishing slavery and giving citizenship to freed slaves) were unconstitutional and harmful to the country; militias must get ready to fight the existing world socialist government; free speech allows the right wing to show that Jews are Satan's spawn and Blacks are subhuman; gun ownership is a key right; abortion must be stopped at all costs; gays and lesbians must be destroyed.

With an explosion of right-wing Web sites, subjects such as these have proliferated. Much of the programming promotes specific militia groups and extols their leaders. With the sheer volume of programming on standard AM and FM radio, on traditional television (as well as low-power television—LPTV) and cable, on shortwave and "pirate" micro-radio stations, and on the Internet, large numbers of vulnerable citizens are being reached and convinced. In fact, since the Oklahoma City bombing—an act that revealed the true nature of many militias and turned most citizens against such groups— the number of so-called hate groups and militias has dramatically increased. Some estimates suggest that since—and to a degree the result of—the Ruby Ridge shoot-out at the Weaver compound, more than 400 new militia groups have come into existence.

Most critics—both those who oppose the right-wing groups and those who support them—agree that there is a direct correlation between the rise of right-wing radio and the increased number of murders, bombings, and other hate crimes. Of course, one set of critics takes a negative view of this development while the other set supports such cause and effect. Joseph T. Roy Sr., director of the Klanwatch/Militia Task Force project of the Southern Poverty Law Center, says: "Make no mistake about it, these people are at war with this country,"[23] a sentiment echoed by many leaders of militias and other right-wing groups. James Latham, station manager of Radio For Peace International, which operates a service that monitors right-wing media, has written, "As the militant right forces turn up as perpetrators of more and more violence, including murder, intimidation, bombings, and attempted bombings, the question is often asked: Is there a connection between these hate crimes against humanity and the rise of far-right programs on short-wave [radio]?"[24]

Shortwave radio broadcasting nationwide has made it possible for far-right-wing beliefs and purposes to be disseminated without drawing community attention to their immediate source. "They can reach all of their potential supporters without arousing the attention of the community in a local station's broadcast area. One can now hear programs about 'racialism,' militancy, and/or 'conspiratology' nearly 24 hours a day."[25] Chip Berlet, an expert on right-wing activities for Political Research Associates, writes,"The success of the political and religious right in shaping public debates is in part due to the network of right-wing institutions that package and disseminate their propaganda using diverse modern technologies." Berlet notes the increasing use of new technologies by the "hard right" in the 1990s, including online computers providing instant global outreach, home satellite reception of audio and video materials, fax networks (taking a cue from Ross Perot's use of such networks in his 1992 presidential campaign), mail order videos and audiotapes, syndicated satellite programs, and local cable systems, including cable access channels, as well as shortwave, AM, and FM radio, and broadcast television.[26]

Many people tend to dismiss "radical right" or "far right" or "hard right" or "extremist right" radio and television talk shows and Internet site hosts as "kooks," "idiots," "weirdos," and "sickos." That is a mistake. Whether one who advocates hate, violence, even murder, is psychologically disturbed is not the point here. What is the point is that these radical right purveyors are, in many cases, well educated, articulate, sincere, serious, and highly effective in recruiting people to their points of view and even influencing some adherents to take physical action—sometimes seriously harmful—on behalf of their causes. To call them "neo-Nazis" or "racists" or "white supremacists" or "anti-Semites" as if such appellations will embarrass them or make them feel beyond the pale is shortsighted and unrealistic. These appellations describe, to them, what they sincerely believe in, and are not terms of derision but in fact descriptions of honor. They believe as strongly and fervently as any believer in any cause that their causes are just. They believe that their ethical goals in life are to forward those causes. And, importantly, they believe that most people, once they learn the nature of their beliefs and causes, will support them and join them in achieving their goals.

The right-wing-media purveyors believe that they are fighting a repressive overclass, reflecting the concept that "talk radio is the province of proletarian discontent, the only mass medium easily available to the underclass."[27] Their cynicism about government justifies, for them, their extreme attitudes, based on their "belief that government is unresponsive to citizen needs."[28]

While some right-wing radio hosts resort to flagrant inflammatory rhetoric that becomes not only quickly transparent to, but easily rejected by, listeners who are not already committed to the beliefs or causes espoused, many right-wing radio hosts convey the same messages using what appear to be reasoned, logical arguments. An example of such a host is Chuck Harder, heard internationally via satellite, and operating under the rubric of People Network Inc. out of Venice, Florida. His programs are frequently categorized as "hate radio." But he provides examples to back up each of his illustrations or arguments, avoiding the ranting and raving that characterizes many hate programs, enabling him to get his points across more effectively than many far-right talk show hosts with the same agenda. (See Harder's interview and personal statement in chapter 7.)

Some critics are not convinced that there is such a thing as "hate" radio. Michael Harrison, editor of *Talkers* magazine, a publication for talk show producers and hosts, believes that "hate radio as a genre doesn't exist." He states that when it does pop up, the stations, the advertisers and the community get rid of it immediately. The extent of hate in talk radio, he says, is sporadic, usually in random outbursts of a caller. For example, Harrison notes that although Chuck Harder is a conspiracy theorist, he hasn't heard him advocate violence or say any hateful things about a particular group. He also states that Chuck Baker, although a strong gun supporter and devotee of survivalism and extreme nationalism, has had a lot of what he says taken out of context. "He's a nice guy," Harrison says. Harrison also contends that G. Gordon Liddy is a "benign entertainer." Harrison's conclusion: "I don't want to be a defender of hate radio, but these people don't seem to be as dangerous as depicted. They just deal with a lot of issues that are favorite issues of those who are that radical." Harrison says that in the last few years there's been less political talk, and more entertainment, lifestyle exploration, and just fun on mainstream media talk shows.[29]

To understand not only the nature of right-wing-media use, but also its impact on society and, if one is opposed, how to deal with it, it is necessary to understand its nature as more than a far-out fringe movement, but instead as a serious, well-organized movement led by many people of intelligence, dedication, and substance.

Some take a less benign view of talk radio. In his book, *Hot Air,* Howard Kurtz writes "Talk radio spread[s] wild theories, delicious gossip, and angry denunciations with gleeful abandon."[30]

Walter Cronkite states:

Talk radio is a phenomenon which is of fairly recent date. There was a program way back in the late 1920s called "Vox Populi," Voice of the People, that was an early example of talk radio. But it bears little resemblance to the talk shows out there today with these hosts and hostesses who are the "stars" of their programs. The talkers seek controversy, I think, rather than discussion. Talk radio, when it is conducted with anything like a sense of responsibility, can be a very important form of communication, and there are a few such programs, I think, out there. That is really about where radio stands as a culture today, rather vapid, I'm afraid.[31]

Steve Allen expresses serious concern about the trend of talk radio. Allen writes:

Let us quickly dispose of a specific form of dumbth presently common, the perception that the American media, by and large, has a liberal bias. Has no one noticed that—at least the last time I checked—approximately 600 radio stations were carrying the Rush Limbaugh show?

Is nobody in an informed position doing demographic studies that reveal the incredible dominance, on American radio, both AM and FM, of the most extreme presentations of the case for conservatism? I have long thought, written and said that a sane political society needs both a responsible Right and Left. After all, the record of history as to what happens when one party—any party at all—has near-total control of the levers of government is sobering enough. But we are now presented with clear evidence that a great many on the Right—perhaps even a majority—actually prefer the rude, sarcastic and often poorly-informed saloon loudmouth rhetoric of a Rush Limbaugh to the more admirable support of the case for conservatism that we expect from our George Wills, William F. Buckleys and Brent Bozells. These spokesmen—though one may differ with them on one public question or another—are gentlemen, and communicate as such in the present intellectual climate. However, it's a small wonder that such intellectuals are not only much admired by millions on the Right but are, in fact, often spoken of derisively by those so far gone down the road of conspiracy theory that they spend a surprising amount of their time and energy in attacking such obviously conservative organizations as the FBI, the CIA, the Army, the Navy, the Marines, the U.S. Congress and local police officials.[32]

The proliferation and impact of right-wing radio, television, and Internet sites in recent years appear to some to be a phenomenon of the 1990s. While it is true that right-wing media growth in the nineties has been almost phenomenal, it is not new and not recent. Use of the media by those who wish to use hate and violence to create chaos and a vacuum to facilitate their own seizure of power goes back to the very beginning of the use of the airwaves for communication.

So-called "hate radio" and "hate television" prompt many people to ask why the United States government doesn't do something to stop such activity, which tends not only to harm target groups and individuals, but to tear the fabric of democratic tolerance and co-existence that has been the principle—though history shows us not necessarily the hallmark—of the American constitutional and social system. Tell these hatemongers to either prove what they are saying or to get off the air, many people demand. As a scarce national resource, the airways belong to the people and, as such, are regulated in the public interest, convenience, or necessity by the agency representing the people—the United States government and its communications regulation office, the Federal Communications Commission (FCC). Congress is responsible for creating the communications laws, which must be signed by the president or passed over a presidential veto, that in turn are implemented by the FCC. It is important to remember that under the Communications Act of 1934 As Amended, which governs the regulatory actions, censorship by the government is specifically forbidden.

Historical and Legal Bases for Freedom of Speech on the Airwaves

We have often heard angry citizens say: "Appeal to their logic. Ask these right-wing hate purveyors to explain why they want to hate and hurt people, and if they can't give a logical explanation, throw them off the air." First, it's important to understand that there is not a logical reason for hate. Hate needs only an emotional feeling, and for those who hate and at the same time believe they are intelligent human beings with informational motivation, only a rationalization need be added.

Second, it is also important to remember that in our democratic society, the freedom to preach hate is just as inviolate as the freedom to preach love. Our First Amendment rights—which many political radicals would deny to others in the belief that only they are right and everyone else wrong—are the basis for the freedom of speech and press that enables the majority to resist the dictatorship of a minority, and presumably, the minority to resist the dictatorship of the majority.

Often throughout U.S. history attempts have been made by government to silence speech that was considered politically objectionable or subversive. Most of the time the federal courts have rejected such attempts at censorship.

Prior restraint of political speech goes back even before the establishment of the federal republic. At one time any criticism of a public official or any information derogatory to a public official was considered seditious libel—even if the allegations were true. That principle still is the law in many countries, enabling those in power to retain their position by keeping the truth of their actions from the public by declaring that anything critical of the government—true or false—undermines the government and is therefore a crime. The first successful challenge to that principle in America, establishing truth as a defense against punishment for libel or sedition—occurred in 1735 when the publisher of the *New York Weekly Journal,* Peter Zenger, was put on trial for his criticism of New York Governor William Cosby. Zenger was charged with "printing and publishing a false, scandalous and seditious libel, in which . . . the governor . . . is greatly and unjustly scandalized, as a person that has no regard to law nor justice." Zenger's attorney, William Hamilton, asked the jurors to do something unheard of at the time: to acquit Zenger if they found his statements about Cosby were true. He did this in opposition to the judge's instructions to the contrary. The jury acquitted Zenger and established a new principle that was incorporated into the practices of the new nation more than forty years later and, with occasional exceptions, still governs libel and sedition trials today. False statements about a person are actionable. However, court decisions over the latter half of the twentieth century have made it extremely difficult for a plaintiff to win a libel case. The plaintiffs not only must prove that the allegations are false, but also that they are harmed by the assertions and that the person making the statements acted with reckless disregard for the truth. Public figures have an even more difficult task to prove libel. They must show, in addition, that the false statements were made with deliberate malice.

An early case in the new nation, however, reinforced the imposition of restrictions on freedom of speech and press guaranteed by the First Amendment of the U.S. Constitution. In 1798 Congress enacted the Alien and Sedition Act, which provided for a fine or jail sentence for anyone convicted of "any false, scandalous and malicious writing or writings against the government of the United States . . . with intent to defame the . . . government, or either house of . . . Congress or the . . . President as to bring them, or either or any of them, into contempt or disrepute." A Thomas Cooper was put on trial under the Alien and Sedition Act for publishing a list of what he considered to be mistakes by the president, John Adams. The presiding judge told the jury, "All governments punish libels against themselves. If a man attempts to destroy the confidence of the people in their officers, their supreme magistrate, and their legislature, he effectively saps the foundation of the government." This is precisely what many right-wing groups have openly and avowedly used the media to try to do in the 1990s. Two hundred years ago Cooper was found guilty. A couple of years later, however, Thomas Jefferson became president, and, with the strong support of a public that opposed the Alien and Sedition Act, he pardoned those who had been convicted under it.

At times of crisis—in more recent America right after World War I and World War II—insecure governments have passed similar acts and jailed or deported people whose political ideas the government found unacceptable. The Smith Act, part of the pre– and post–World War II cold war, resulted in the conviction of alleged communists whose rhetoric and proposals were not as radical or violent as that of some of the right wing today. Several presidents, including Richard Nixon and Ronald Reagan, tried to muzzle the media, believing that the media (although mostly Republican-owned) were biased against them, and claiming that criticisms of them as presidents were false and undermined the country. But the strength of the First Amendment prevailed and they were unable to apply any law that would result in the silencing of the media. Certainly, if some of the early restrictions on freedom of speech and press were applicable in recent years, the party in power—the government— would have had to jail a large number of media outlets every presidential election year. Certainly, the vilification of President Bill Clinton and his wife, Hillary Rodham Clinton, would not have been permitted.

The earlier court decisions formed the bases for judging the First Amendment freedoms of radio and television in more recent years. The first regularly scheduled radio station did not go on the air until 1920 and the regulation of the airwaves (except for naval and experimental requirements) did not occur until Congress enacted a Federal Radio Act in 1927, establishing the Federal Radio Commission, which were supplanted by the Communications Act of 1934 and the Federal Communications Commission. Recognizing the power of the airwaves and committed to diversity in ownership and, consequently, hoped-for diversity in the views expressed on the air, the FCC attempted, at first, to discourage and even suppress the presentation of only one side of an issue by a radio or TV station. In 1941, as part of its report on renewing the license of a station that had been challenged by a competing applicant, the Mayflower Broadcasting Company, the FCC ruled that a station may not editorialize on the air. To prevent a station owner's given point of view—which could be considered radical right by some and radical left by others—from dominating, the FCC said, "A truly free radio cannot be used to advocate the causes of the licensee . . . the broadcaster cannot be an advocate."[33] This Mayflower Decision, as it was called, clearly prevented free speech on the air in the interest of preventing only one side of free speech from being heard. This was hardly a democratic solution and in 1949 the FCC modified the Mayflower Decision to allow a station to editorialize, provided it made air time available for "balanced presentation of all responsible viewpoints on particular issues." The FCC reaffirmed that "radio be maintained as a medium of free speech for the general public as a whole rather than as an outlet for the purely personal or private interests of the licensee. . . . that the public has a reasonable opportunity to hear different opposing positions."[34]

This is considered to be the beginning of what became known as the "Fairness Doctrine." It was not designed to guarantee any given philosophy or advocacy access to the airwaves; it did, however, result in opening up the airwaves to an increasing number of diverse viewpoints. In effect, it strengthened the First Amendment by extending freedom of speech and press to more and more people over the public airwaves, that is, the airwaves owned by the public. Through court cases and FCC Reports and Orders, the Fairness Doctrine could be applied when a station broadcast only one side of an issue that was controversial in its community of service, and then refused to honor requests of responsible citizens or groups to present opposing viewpoints. Upon complaint of the refused party, the FCC could investigate and, if it found the station in violation of the doctrine, could require the station to provide comparable air time—not equal time, which applies only to political candidates—to that party.

The Fairness Doctrine was further refined in 1969 in the Red Lion case. In 1964, in a syndicated recorded program carried by some 200 radio stations throughout the country, right-wing commentator Rev. Billy James Hargis personally attacked writer Fred Cook, who had written an article critical of Senator Barry Goldwater, Republican candidate for president. Most of the stations honored Cook's request under the Fairness Doctrine for time to reply. WGCB, in the town of Red Lion, Pennsylvania, licensed to right-wing Rev. John M. Norris, refused, despite an order from the FCC to do so. The case ultimately reached the U.S. Supreme Court, which decided that "it is the right of the viewers and listeners, not the right of the broadcasters, which is paramount. . . . it is the purpose of the First Amendment to preserve an uninhibited marketplace of ideas in which truth will ultimately prevail. . . . it is the right of the public to receive suitable access to social, political, esthetic, moral, and other ideas and experiences."[35]

The Fairness Doctrine lasted until 1987. In 1985 a conservative FCC under the Reagan administration got its chance to eliminate the doctrine when it was forced by the facts of law to support the Syracuse Peace Council's Fairness Doctrine complaint against television station WTVH, which had refused the council's request to reply to false statements by the station promoting a nuclear power referendum. The station's appeal was upheld by a U.S. Court of Appeals, which found that the doctrine is not a statute law and the FCC was not obligated to enforce it. In 1987 Congress overwhelmingly passed a Fairness Law on the grounds that in its thirty years of existence the doctrine had "enhanced free speech."[36] President Reagan, however, vetoed it and the Senate override count fell just short of the two-thirds required. The FCC thereupon eliminated the doctrine, stating that it "chills free speech and . . . contravenes the First Amendment."[37]

Ostensibly this put no limits on any ideas, philosophies, or other political matter a station might wish to advocate. In reality, it swung the tide of radio and television political advocacy to the right. By the very fact of being wealthy enough to own a radio or TV station and by dint of the position and influence of the station in any given community, owners by and large are part of a structure that by its very nature of power, wealth, and success believes that the status quo is as far left as they would like to see society go. Moderate to right-wing thinking reflects their beliefs, and their stations, in the absence of the requirements of the Fairness Doctrine, surged in that direction. The elimination of the Fairness Doctrine restored full freedom of speech—including hate speech—essentially to the political right, without a requirement that other views be offered. The increasing proliferation of right-wing talk shows on radio and television in the last decade of the twentieth century is to some degree one of the results of the abandonment of the Fairness Doctrine. Whether this was an anticipated by-product of Reagan's veto is not clear.

Full freedom of speech has been modified by the courts according to the tenor of the times, and in some cases restraints on freedom of speech by the private sector have been upheld by the courts as a reflection of public opinion of the given time. Presumably, a 1937 Supreme Court opinion delivered by Chief Justice Charles Evans Hughes in a case involving a man accused of criminal conduct by conducting meetings under the auspices of the Communist Party established a modern basis for freedom of speech in general. Hughes stated: "The greater the importance of safeguarding the community from incitements to the overthrow of our institutions by force and violence, the more imperative is the need to preserve inviolate the constitutional right of free speech, free press and free assembly in order to maintain the opportunity for free political discussion."[38]

It is this principle that right-wing radio and television today legitimately invoke when accused of preaching hate and violence. Historically, rarely has right-wing speech been stifled. On the other hand, left-wing speech, moderate to liberal speech, and even speech that may simply disagree with or question right-wing beliefs or actions, frequently have been stifled. The most flagrant example in U.S. broadcasting history was during the so-called McCarthy era of the 1950s. It was only necessary to accuse someone of being a communist (or, by implication, of being subversive by calling them a "pinko" or "fellow traveler" or "commie dupe") to blacklist them from radio and television, as well as from Hollywood films. A key case in point was that of John Henry Faulk, the Johnny Carson of early talk radio, whose homespun philosophy was far from politically provocative. But he was an officer of the broadcast performers union, then the American Federation of Radio Artists (AFRA), which condemned blacklisting, and he, in turn, was accused of being leftwing and was blacklisted. Unlike most blacklisted performers, who hoped the fascist aura that was dominating American thought would soon end and they would be able to reenter their profession, Faulk sued the principals who had convinced the broadcast networks to cooperate in the blacklisting. Faulk won, helping to bring an end to the blacklist, although his career and future remained destroyed. It was not that Faulk purveyed left-wing advocacy of hate and violence; it was that he refused to cooperate with the right wing in its purveying of hate and violence. Today, to a degree, with no Fairness Doctrine and the means of communication owned largely by conservatives, it should be no surprise that right-wing philosophy and practice dominate the airwaves.

Early Waves of Rancor

Was it always thus? The answer is partly yes and partly no. Beginning in the early 1920s, shortly after the first regularly scheduled radio station went on the air, a number of radio programs were filled with philosophical and political rancor. Pioneer radio critic Ben Gross wrote, "Tailors, preachers, loan sharks, swamis, and physical culture men, merchants, nostrum dispensers, and frenzied advocates of odd ideas, such as Colonel Henderson of Shreveport, Louisiana, who combined primitive theology with hatred of chain stores, indulged in a saturnalia of 'free speech.' "[39]

However, despite historic case law protecting free speech in print, the designation of the airwaves as a scarce national resource whose diversity should be protected, plus the fact that at that time station licenses had to be renewed every six months (as compared with every eight years as mandated by the Telecommunications Act of 1996), the Federal Radio Commission could—and did—act to deny license renewal or even to cancel the license of any station it believed was presenting programming not in the public interest. In most cases the programming that the FRC considered inimical to the public interest was stopped or ameliorated through negotiation or, if necessary, FRC threats. However, some of the stronger actions taken by the FRC at that time likely would not have stood the test of a court case in later years and certainly not in the talk show era of the present day.

One outstanding example of such action was the FRC's refusal to renew the license of KGEF, Los Angeles, because of the airing of a Rev. Dr. Shuler's vitriolic personal attacks on people he disagreed with. While Shuler's apparent purpose was to crusade against what he considered corruption in local government, his hate diatribes influenced large audiences against other targets as well.

One of the first nationally successful and what many consider one of the most influential uses of the airwaves to spread a political philosophy was the program of a Catholic priest, Father Charles E. Coughlin, in the 1930s and 1940s. While Coughlin was even more vitriolic than Shuler and had greater influence as a hatemonger, the FRC and, subsequently, the FCC did not curtail his freedom of speech on the airwaves. Because Coughlin and other right-wing preachers and purveyors on radio did not own stations, but purchased time for their programs, the commission could not lift their personal licenses, as in the Shuler case.

In 1926 Coughlin began his radio career with a regional broadcast from his Shrine of the Little Flower in suburban Detroit. In 1930 he began a regular series of programs over CBS. At first he supported the ostensibly blue-collar-interest policies of people like—and in particular—Franklin D. Roosevelt. Within a few years Coughlin was the country's leading talk-media star. He received an average of 80,000 letters a week, more than did the president of the United States, and in a 1933 national poll Coughlin was voted the "most useful citizen of the United States."[40]

By 1930 Coughlin had established the format and approach that right-wing media personalities of seventy years later strive for. He "had broken down the barriers between political opinion molding and celebrity. By fusing his talent and training in the thespian arts with an entirely new medium of communication [Coughlin] transformed radio broadcasting, and thereby public discourse, in American society."[41]

After Franklin Roosevelt's 1932 election to the presidency and his implementation of policies that Coughlin disagreed with, Coughlin turned against Roosevelt and, in fact, began labeling the president a communist. The rise of fascism in Italy and Nazism in Germany fueled Coughlin's fire. Similar to some televangelists today, his approach was to target certain groups in order to obtain the support of other groups and to garner, through his radio talks, millions of dollars in donations. He railed against Jews, against labor unions, against immigrants, against racial minorities, stirring and reinforcing resentment and hate against these competitors for jobs and social status in prewar Depression-ridden America. At the same time he widened his constituency by including other targets such as Wall Street and big business. As World War II grew closer he supported Mussolini and Hitler and blamed the Jews for the world's ills. He called for an "America whose people would control the economy and preserve their Christian values"[42]—identical language to that used by far right radio personalities currently. Coughlin was a forerunner of the Holocaust-deniers and neo-Nazis of today. After America entered the war he became an embarrassment to his Republican friends and supporters and gradually disappeared from the airwaves. CBS disowned him and he established a network of stations for his syndicated shows, but those stations also gradually abandoned him.

Before his rhetoric became so extremist and beyond the pale for most Americans—who supported the war against Hitler and Nazism—Coughlin developed an approach and a style in his broadcasts that were highly successful in attracting audiences and that were mirrored by several commentators after his popularity waned and are found even today in Rush Limbaugh's shows. Coughlin enticed his listeners with half-truths and suspense, sometimes with outright falsehoods. He was like a gossip columnist, playing up what was titillating and even outrageous; however, he did it with biting political comment, appealing to the fears and dissatisfactions of his listeners. He had an additional technique: as a priest he frequently added soothing organ music and spiritual homilies to his talks.[43] In his book on Father Coughlin, *Radio Priest,* Donald Warren quotes an admirer of Coughlin's technique: "He [used] a walking stick, in which he demonstrated that by staying back from the microphone and shouting and then moving close, for conveying an intimate voice, the dramatic effects he desired could be attained."[44]

Many people think of Walter Winchell, arguably the best-known commentator of the 1930s–1950s era, as a patriotic reporter. He was not labeled a kook or a radical, but was considered by many an objective moderator. Winchell was the forerunner of the Rush Limbaughs of today. He made anticommunism a cornerstone of his patriotism and was reportedly a close friend and confidante of one of his strong supporters, J. Edgar Hoover. His radio show, begun in 1932, was ostensibly a gossip program. But he expanded it into right-wing political commentary, excoriating as a "pinko" or "commie" anyone who disagreed with him or, in the late 1940s and early 1950s, with McCarthyism. His shows had a huge, loyal audience and he could affect national policy and make or break an individual's career with a few seconds of commentary on the air. He spread rumors; set styles; forged national opinion; built some careers and ruined others; popularized books, plays, and movies; changed the language; waged feuds; excoriated some politicians and promoted the programs of others; he articulated the public mood.[45]

The use of radio—and other media—in the United States for political propaganda purposes had as one of its models its use by the fascist governments in Europe in the 1920s and 1930s. Even as he seized power in Italy in 1922, Benito Mussolini understood the power of the brand-new medium, radio, and he began to use it as soon as it was electronically possible in his country. Some years later he was quoted as saying, "If it weren't for radio, I wouldn't have the power over the Italian people that I have." In Nazi Germany Joseph Goebbels became a master of using all available media to solidify the German people's dedication to the principles espoused by Adolf Hitler. It is neither ironic nor surprising that in the United States today the domestic neo-Nazis are using radio in the same way to espouse the same ideology that the Nazis did in Germany in the 1930s and 1940s. Nazi Germany set the precedent. "Propaganda by radio was largely an invention of the Nazis, who saw the potential of the medium more clearly than their enemies and used it with unequaled force."[46]

As early as 1932 the British used shortwave radio to broadcast their ideology to their various colonies and partner countries throughout the world, to keep their civil servants abroad connected to the mother country, and to strengthen British culture in those far-off lands.[47] Italy was a pioneer in broadcasting propaganda in the language of the people being propagandized. In 1934, Radio Bari in Rome began an Arabic language service to North Africa, in a challenge to British domination there. A few years later, in 1937, the British government authorized the BBC to begin a similar Arabic language service.[48] Soon many countries saw the two-pronged value of using radio for international propaganda purposes: first, to solidify their influence over countries in which they already had a foothold, and second, as World War II approached and the conflagration began, to attack their enemies even as they trumpeted their own philosophies.

The BBC and the United States' "Voice of America" were key players in the propaganda efforts of World War II. Germany's shortwave programs beamed at the Allied countries were equally effective, playing on the psychological fears of its enemies. Germany knew how to use programming to attract listeners, lure them into acceptance through pleasurable entertainment, and then inject them with totalitarian ideas. One of its most effective programs featured sultry-voiced Mildred Gillars, an American who had moved to Germany. Called Axis Sally by the Allies, "she would play popular music, interspersed with commiseration for the GIs listening on how their wives and sweethearts back home were undoubtedly having affairs with the men who were smart enough to evade Army service. Her comments, between musical numbers, appealed to the prejudices of the listeners, unhappy and frightened as they risked their lives so far from home. 'Damn Roosevelt! Damn Churchill! Damn all Jews who made this war possible. I love America, but I do not love Roosevelt and all his kike boyfriends!' "[49]

Japan used shortwave radio in a similar fashion. At one time Japan was estimated to have twenty-seven female disc jockeys on programs reaching the Allied troops in the Pacific.[50] Iva Ikuko Toguri d'Aquino, a first-generation Japanese-American, was visiting a relative in Japan when she was pressed into service by the Japanese to broadcast anti-American propaganda. She became known as "Tokyo Rose." After the war it was revealed that she apparently used whatever methods she could to lessen the impact of the material she was required to present and in some cases was even able to distort it.[51]

World War II saw the growth of commentators, concomitant with the growth of broadcast news itself. The country's main source of immediate news was radio. Although commercial television stations had been authorized by the FCC in 1941, the onset of the war resulted in a freeze on new stations, on major expansion of old stations, and on the manufacture of radio and TV sets in order to utilize for war purposes the parts and materials that otherwise would be used for transmission and reception. Relatively few people had TV sets at that time, but virtually every home had at least one radio receiver. And because almost everyone had a relative or friend in the armed forces, people listened assiduously to radio reports and comments on the progress of the war.

Although the war by and large unified America, there was still a great diversity of opinion on radio. When the United States entered the war there were an estimated twenty network commentators on the air; the number increased during the war, and in 1947 there were an estimated 600 commentators on the networks and on local stations throughout the country.[52] Opinions varied, but even though the country was considered relatively politically liberal during the war and supported Roosevelt and the New Deal, conservative commentators dominated. In 1945 a survey by *Variety* magazine of thirty network commentators classified four as moderately liberal, ten as middle-of-the-road, five as conservative, six as reactionary, and ten as unclassifiable.[53] They could and did influence the public before, through, and after the war. Irving Fang writes, "Radio commentators regularly picked over the day's events to find corroboration for their continually voiced beliefs."[54]

On the international front after the war, shortwave radio continued what it had begun in World War II—only this time the rancor was principally between former allies, the United States and the Soviet Union. The cold war saw the intensification of "anti-capitalist" propaganda on one side and "anti-socialist" propaganda on the other. The BBC, the Voice of America, and Radio Moscow were joined by Radio Free Europe, sponsored by the United States to beam anti-Soviet propaganda throughout eastern Europe. Its mission was described as follows:

> In the initial stage its purpose is to prevent, or at the very least to hinder the cultural, political and economic integration of the target area within the Soviet Union. In a later stage it may prove useful as a means of inviting or of stimulating positive and effective action. For the time being the programs of Radio Free Europe are designed to keep hope alive among our friends, and to confuse, divide and undermine our enemies within the satellite states.[55]

Another U.S. radio station beamed to the Soviet Union was Radio Liberty, aimed principally at changing the beliefs of Russian citizens. Both of these systems, RFE and RL, carried hard-line anti-Communist propaganda designed to stir up discord in the Soviet countries, frequently by direct attacks on individual leaders in those countries. One of their projects was to foment a revolution in Hungary; they succeeded, but the Hungarians, who consequently expected assistance from NATO forces, were left hanging and the revolution was crushed. RFE later played a key role in encouraging the growth of the Solidarity movement in Poland. Although both stations—RFE and RL—operating from Munich, Germany, claimed from time to time that they were independently financed, the funding came from the United States and the stations were generally judged to be under the control of the Central Intelligence Agency.

The differences between so-called left and right radio commentators became more pronounced in the late 1940s when Senator Joseph R. McCarthy, a Republican from Wisconsin, began to exploit the cold war and exercised great influence on American thought and action, throwing fear and obeisance not only into the media industries—principally film, radio, and television—but also into leaders and opinion-makers of the country, including Presidents Truman and Eisenhower, neither of whom was able to stand up to him. Almost all commentators either supported McCarthyism or, out of fear of being blacklisted, were afraid to criticize him or his methods. A few did. Edward R. Murrow was most effective in doing so, risking his career to produce with his producer/writer partner, Fred W. Friendly, a two-part television program on McCarthy, in which McCarthy's own words played an important role in revealing himself to the American public and eventually bringing about his downfall. Another respected commentator, Elmer Davis, who had headed the U.S. government's Office of War Information during World War II, was not afraid to declare that McCarthy was a greater danger to the country than communism. Davis said, "I shall not speculate on his [McCarthy's] motives, being neither a psychoanalyst nor an inspector of sewers."[56] Over the years there were a few others who were considered liberal, including Raymond Gram Swing, who supported the postwar One World concept (initially popularized by 1944 Republican nominee for president Wendell Willkie); Swing was denounced by McCarthy as a communist. Dorothy Thompson was considered liberal for her support of women's rights on the air over many years and, by some, for her support of Arab rights after the end of the war.

But most commentators in the pre- through postwar era were more like Fulton Lewis Jr., considered by some the predominant right-wing commentator of that time, to whom Rush Limbaugh is often compared. Lewis supported McCarthy's contention that the U.S. government was infiltrated by communists and that secret plots were being hatched by communist secret agents throughout the United States.[57] Lewis's influence was great; he not only reflected, but stimulated and helped form through his use of the airwaves, what appeared to be the consensus of American public opinion for some years. Most top commentators, however, expressed no opinions on events and issues of the time. Most popular reporters and news anchors, such as David Brinkley, Chet Huntley, Walter Cronkite, and Charles Kuralt, as informative as they might have been, rarely took a stand on anything critical. (When Cronkite finally did take a stand in 1968 on the war in Vietnam, his influence was such that his negative comments about the United States's role allegedly convinced President Lyndon Johnson, who was pursuing the war relentlessly, not to run for another term.)

The 1950s were a time of suppression, and only after McCarthy's censure by the Senate and his death shortly afterward did some commentators come out of hiding and venture an opinion or two. Most commentators continued as they had before—as reflectors of conservatism and the status quo. Anything that wasn't pro-McCarthy and, after his demise, pro-American, was considered communistic. Discussion of any serious topic or political issue was open to misinterpretation. "Any political association made sponsors nervous. . . . anything political raised the specter of being accused of Communist sympathies. . . . any serious realistic programming went into decline, a trend that contributed to the stations having little interest in other serious programming, including more serious talk TV."[58]

After McCarthyistic suppression and punishment was no longer a concern to the media, and the counterculture of the 1960s began to emerge, the media reinstated some elements of free speech, including some news and public affairs shows that dealt with controversial issues, and more talk shows. "News producers flocked to create new forms of talk TV in a more socially conscious age."[59] In fact, "increasingly, talk TV became a source of news as well."[60] It was not until after full-service radio networks disappeared and specialized limited-time networks consisting mostly of music took their place—along with community-targeted narrowcasting, also mostly music, on local stations—that talk show hosts with set opinions emerged in force. Call-in shows grew as disc jockeys elicited sexual comments and admissions from bored and frustrated housewives. Expressing categorical opinions, even without adequate knowledge or background, many of these DJs metamorphosed into talk show personalities, the talk increasing and the music decreasing. Ratings went up and these kinds of shows proliferated. Personalities like Jerry Williams, Alan Burke, Long John Nebel, and Larry Glick became household names. Glick was one of the few left-of-center hosts, a precursor of the outrageous right-and-left libertarian opinions of a later Howard Stern.

The far right understood more fully than the middle or the left the power of talk radio, and quickly deluged stations with calls and opinions and stimulated a demand for, as some put it, loud-mouthed right-wing talk show hosts.[61] One such host was Joe Pyne, who became one of the most popular talk personalities in the country with glib, biting, and unabashedly opinionated comments such as "go gargle with razor blades" and "take your teeth out, put them in backwards, and bite your throat."[62] One co-author of this book recalls appearing as an interviewee on one of Joe Pyne's programs in 1953. Even before he could sit down at the microphone, Joe Pyne began regaling him and the audience at large with great happiness and laughter. He was ecstatic because "we finally burned Julius and Ethel Rosenberg tonight." He went on to excoriate the Rosenbergs as "commie pigs," saying that electrocution was too good for them. His guest was constantly interrupted during his interview by Pyne's gleeful interjections about roasting the Rosenbergs. A number of hosts, such as Bob Grant, later became famous by using Pyne's approach. Grant often referred to African-Americans as "savages" and used expletives about other targets freely. Grant attributed his reputation to show-business techniques, not bigotry. "The positions I take are honest. I was always a right-winger," he said. "[My opinions] are just stated in more colorful terms. This is entertainment."[63] Ira Blue, who hosted a talk show in San Francisco in the 1960s, stated that "the principal ingredient of any successful hot-line show is the personality of the host, and often the more opinionated the better."[64]

As the 1950s and 1960s progressed, many right-wing talk show programs and hosts became more subtle, using twisted logic rather than blatant vituperation to persuade their audiences.

The conservative-to-right-wing ownership of the media attempted to reprise their McCarthy-era suppression of opinion other than their own in the late 1960s and early 1970s when millions of Americans marched on the Capitol in Washington, D.C., and on state capitols all over the country to protest American involvement in the war in southeast Asia. Once again, anyone who protested the government's political stance on Vietnam was labeled a communist. The media supported the U.S. war in Vietnam virtually without question and propagandized the concept that dissenters and critics of the government were obviously subversives. Commentators throughout the country overwhelmingly followed the right-wing dictum. There was little place on radio or on network television for other viewpoints. The networks, however, though willing to suppress and censor, didn't want to be accused of reviving McCarthyism. Although a "graylist" continued sub rosa from the 1950s—anyone publicly attacked as leftist was considered controversial and was either not hired or their show dropped for spurious reasons (as CBS did to Ed Asner's "Lou Grant")—an overt blacklist was not reimposed. Dissent found its way into television through non-news programs: entertainment, drama, and sitcoms. A prime example was "The Smothers Brothers Comedy Hour." The Smothers brothers dealt frequently with political issues, including Vietnam, and their irreverence got them into trouble with CBS censors. NBC had similar problems with "Saturday Night Live." Some advertisers backed out of both programs. The Smothers brothers' show often featured anti-Vietnam-War guests like Pete Seeger, and CBS dropped the show abruptly in May 1973.[65]

Writer-producer Norman Lear probably was most effective in offering an alternative—that is, left of center—viewpoint on television. Through his characters in a number of series, including "All in the Family," "The Jeffersons," and "Maude," he was able to reach people with liberal views on racism, abortion rights, immigration and immigrants, poverty, education, and war, among other vital issues of the day. In that respect, he was probably more effective in influencing public opinion than the right-wing commentators who dominated both television and radio.

Right-wing rancor on talk shows went in two distinct directions. As the means of distribution proliferated, including more radio and television stations on the air, the growth of cable networks, and the still-growing Internet, more opportunity existed for fringe advocators. Ranters and ravers, some affiliated with organizations dedicated to violence, had their access to the airwaves. Soft-spoken intellectuals dispensing the same bottom line also had their access. Two examples were William Buckley's "Firing Line" and Martin Agronsky's "Agronsky and Company." The former came across as a conservative, although he frequently espoused further-right viewpoints; the latter came across as a moderate, although he purveyed conservative viewpoints. They understood that there was little point in preaching to the believers and not much chance to win over the hard-liners on the other side. They wooed those in the middle, on the political fence. And they did so quite successfully by appearing to be nonthreatening, logical, and in the "middle" in their appeals. Buckley reinforced the appearance of objectivity by debating well-known opponents of his philosophies, ranging from George McGovern to Germaine Greer.

The 1980s saw a huge increase in the popularity of national television network talk shows with the rise of charismatic personalities as hosts. Phil Donohue set the pace for content-based talk shows, with his orientation on the liberal political side. "I'm convinced you don't solve problems by repressing inflammatory ideas," Donohue has said.[66] Oprah Winfrey became, and at this writing, still is, the most influential talk show personality on television. She, like Donohue, began by dealing with controversial issues, her orientation also liberal. Geraldo Rivera's early talk show career was also marked by concern for important issues and ideas, including political attitudes and advocacy. He, too, was considered liberal. There were a few others who also defied conventional practice and became successful with talk programs that took a compassionate view of the human condition. As of this writing Donohue has retired and some others who started out to deal with human issues have deteriorated into scandal, titillation, and exploitation as competition prompted them to move away from serious subjects to pure entertainment, both fluff and bizarre.

Interestingly enough, many conservative and right-wing talk hosts on television have not similarly succumbed. Two of the most prominent and successful are Rush Limbaugh and Morton Downey Jr. Like their local radio and Internet counterparts, they take different paths to accomplish similar philosophical goals. Downey has followed the path of outrageousness, baiting his guests and orchestrating physical confrontation on his shows. His manner has been loud, threatening, and obnoxious. Limbaugh, conversely, portrays, on both television and radio, the role of a serious, low-key expert, using his wit and wiles rather than bombast and chaos to make his points. The chairman of the American Conservative Union, David Keene, credits talk shows with "revitalizing and refueling the conservatives and Republicans at the grass roots."[67]

The U.S. government has rarely restricted any opinions over the airwaves, with the notable exceptions of times of national frenzy when superpatriotism resulted in the stifling of unpopular views and even the incarceration of some of those who expressed them (as previously noted, for example, under the Smith Act of 1949 when members of the Communist Party of the USA were sent to jail for speech that allegedly advocated the overthrow of the government by force and violence. Later court decisions ruled that in the absence of any evidence of any actual force and violence, such speech is not prosecutable). Ironically, the far-right talk show purveyors who advocate force and violence and the incarceration or execution of anyone who espouses what they believe are communist ideas are the ones now protected as a result of Communist Party members' ordeals.

But it was a different kind of First Amendment restriction that threw a chill over free speech and press in the United States in the early 1990s. As a condition of covering the Gulf War, the Department of Defense required all correspondents—radio, television, and print—to sign an agreement permitting the military full censorship of the correspondents' movements and their reports to the American public. This valentine gift of the Pentagon to the American people on February 14, 1991 was ostensibly because "information should not jeopardize operations and endanger lives." In fact, there was little danger of that happening. Correspondents in previous wars had conscientiously avoided filing any stories that could aid the enemy. What was behind the Pentagon's action was the lesson it had learned in the Vietnam war. When the media finally began to report back to the American people the truth of what was happening in Vietnam, including U.S. atrocities and revelations of continual lies the Pentagon had been feeding the public in an effort to keep political opinion on the side advocating continuation of the war, the public reacted strongly and angrily. Political opinion about the conduct of the war turned against the government and the Pentagon, and resulted in America's finally having to end its role in southeast Asia. In subsequent military actions the Pentagon limited press freedom. It did not permit the press to cover the first day of its invasion of the small island of Grenada, where its purpose was not, as stated, to protect Americans but to oust a government it deemed leftwing, nor did it permit the press full access to what was happening in the first several days of its invasion of Panama. To this day many unanswered questions about the Panama action remain. It feared another Vietnam reaction in the Gulf—political attitudes contrary to the public support it wanted for its military endeavors. Few commentators questioned America's goals or conduct in the Gulf War at first, just as with Vietnam. But the more the government stopped correspondents from getting the full truth to the American people in order to control political opinion about the war, the more correspondents rebelled, and a number filed a court challenge to what they believed was a violation of their First Amendment rights. However, the war ended before the case came to trial and it was declared moot. Radio and television talk—as well as print reports—had been stifled because of the ban on news reaching the people.

As powerful as radio and television talk shows had become, a new phenomenon in the 1990s provided an even greater forum, a worldwide one, for those who would use the media to air their rancor and provoke the rancor of others: cyberspace. Literally thousands of Web sites all over the world are used for political propagandizing, some by left-wing groups, most by right-wing groups.

In the United States, at the beginning of 1999, an estimated almost 200 hate-group Web sites were in operation, an increase of about one-third from the year before. Don Black, a former grand dragon of the Alabama Ku Klux Klan, who has been credited with initiating the use of the Internet as a medium for right-wing extremist organizations, states, "We are able to reach millions of people that we never had access to in the past. The Internet is becoming an alternative news medium for those who have an alternative point of view."[68]

A number of countries have attempted to stifle what they consider "hate" speech, usually as a corollary of national laws or regulations prohibiting such speech on the grounds that it incites violent action or threatens the security of the government. The United States is one of the very few countries where government has not censored such political speech, although some members of Congress have proposed doing so.

The closest the United States came to censorship on the Internet was the Cyberspace Decency Act of 1996, passed in tandem with the Telecommunications Act of 1996. The Cyberspace Decency Act prohibited, in vague terms, materials that might be considered "indecent." The Act was declared unconstitutional by the United States Supreme Court as a clear violation of the First Amendment. "Hate" speech on the Internet in the U.S. has been addressed by private groups, including organizations concerned with specific content and targets, and by Internet connection providers. The Anti-Defamation League of B'nai B'rith protested to America Online (AOL) the presence of a Ku Klux Klan Web site on AOL. AOL replied that "we have been in touch with ADL and we obviously agree that what the KKK represents is reprehensible," but it would not close down the KKK site unless and until it believed that the transmissions were actually inciting to violence.[69]

Hate Web sites don't fare so well in much of the rest of the world. Considered by some the most notorious hatemongering Web site is that of Ernst Zundel, an extremist activist who has been arrested on several occasions as a suspect in bombings and whose diatribes feature anti-Semitic, antiliberal, and anti-Zionist themes. His Web page is one of the leading Holocaust-denier sites on the Internet. While his Web site has been banned in many countries, the home site emanating out of California is operating with no government interference or restriction. Zundel himself claims "a 38-year record of non-violent, peaceful and democratic advocacy."[70]

Germany, in an attempt to prevent democracy from being destroyed along with people, as happened under the Third Reich, has ironically been most zealous in banning hate speech. In 1996 it banned access to a left-wing site, *xs4all,* which originated from The Netherlands.[71] Great Britain established an Internet Watch Foundation in 1996 to filter postings on Web sites, an outgrowth of the government's previous requirement that Internet providers censor "illegal" materials transmitted by so-called news sources.[72] Singapore, in keeping with its heavy-handed repression of free political speech, established a government-controlled Internet server, SigNet, as the only access to the Internet for its citizens. Sites were banned that, in the government's opinion, might lower morale, negatively affect races or religions, or threaten government security.[73] Throughout the world more and more countries are reacting to what they consider threats to their political, moral, religious, and economic policies and beliefs by devising ways to ban or censor transmissions and receptions on the Internet.

There are many who believe that far-right and extremist talk radio, Internet sites, and television programs contribute directly to hate, violence, and even murder. But in the United States, many or most of those who find the right-wing rhetoric and incitement despicable generally defend the right to be heard of those they disagree with. For example, G. Gordon Liddy, the convicted Watergate burglar, has overtly advised listeners on how most effectively to shoot at and kill federal law enforcement agents. Some have suggested, some are certain, that shows like Liddy's contribute to the paranoia that resulted in the Oklahoma City bombing. But journalist Sydney Schanberg, while stating that there may be some truth in "rabid" speech having fed the "nihilistic rages of the bombers," argues that "shutting up the radio spewers won't solve anything, except to make martyrs out of them."[74] Ellen Ratner, White House correspondent for Talk Radio News Service, wrote, "Talk radio is the ultimate arena for free speech. Blaming talk radio for the bombing in Oklahoma City is condemning the Constitution for guaranteeing the right to speak freely."[75]

Appendices to Chapter 1

Three White House Press Releases

(downloaded from the "White House Virtual Library" Web site)

Appendix 1
Three White House Press Releases

(downloaded from the "White House Virtual Library" Web site)

Appendix 1A: March 29, 1997

RADIO ADDRESS OF THE PRESIDENT
TO THE NATION

THE PRESIDENT: Good morning. Spring is a season of renewal, not just of the world around us, but of the ideals inside us -- those that bind us together as a people. Millions of families will come together to celebrate Easter this weekend and Passover in the coming weeks, to reaffirm their faith in God and their commitment to our sacred values.

And in this season of renewal, I ask all Americans to reaffirm their commitment to this central ideal -- that we are many people, but one nation, bound together by shared values, rooted in the essential dignity and meaning of every American's life and liberty. That is the root of the American idea of a community of equal, free, responsible citizens and the American Dream to build the best possible future for our children.

The divide of race has been America's constant curse in pursuit of our ideals. The struggle to overcome it has been a defining part of our history. Racial and ethnic differences continue to divide and bedevil millions around the world. And as we become an ever more pluralistic society with people from every racial and ethnic group calling America home, our own future depends upon laying down the bitter fruits of hatred and lifting up the rich texture of our diversity and our common humanity.

We're not there yet, as we often see in the tragic stories in the news. Just last week in Chicago, a 13-year-old boy, riding his bike home from a basketball game, was brutally attacked and almost beaten to death -- apparently for no other reason but the color of his skin. Lenard Clark is black; the young men accused of attacking him are white. This weekend, I hope all Americans join Hillary and me in a prayer for Lenard and his family.

There is never an excuse for violence against innocent citizens. But this kind of savage, senseless assault, driven by nothing but hate, strikes at the very heart of America's ideals and threatens the promise of our future -- no matter which racial or ethnic identity of the attackers or the victims. We must stand together as a nation against all crimes of hate and say they are wrong. We must condemn hate crimes whenever they happen; we must commit ourselves to prevent them from happening again. And we must sow the seeds of harmony and respect among our people.

And let's be honest with ourselves: racism in America is not confined to acts of physical violence. Every day, African Americans and other minorities are forced to endure quiet acts of racism -- bigoted remarks, housing and job discrimination. Even many people who think they are not being racist, still hold to negative stereotypes, and sometimes act on them. These acts may not harm the body, but when a mother and her child go to the grocery store and are followed around by a suspicious clerk, it does violence to their souls.

We must stand against such quiet hatred just as surely as we condemn acts of physical violence, like those against Lenard Clark.

At the same time, black Americans must not look at the faces of Lenard Clark's attackers and see the face of white America. The acts of a few people must never become an excuse for blanket condemnation -- for bigotry begins with stereotyping, stereotyping blacks and whites, Jews and Arabs, Hispanics and Native Americans, Asians, immigrants in general. It is all too common today, but it is still wrong.

In Chicago, we see leaders of different races and political philosophies coming together to decry the crime against Lenard Clark. That is good and it is reason for hope.

The holidays of this season teach us that hope can spring forth from the darkest of times. Those of us who are Christians celebrate a risen God who died a painful, very human death to redeem the souls of all humanity without regard to race or station.

So as families come together to celebrate Easter and Passover, as parents reunite with their children, their brothers and sisters, and friends with each other, let us all take time to search our souls. Let us find the strength to reach across the lines that divide us on the surface and touch the common spirit that resides in every human heart.

And let us also remember there are some Americans who feel isolated from all of the rest of us in other ways -- sometimes with truly tragic consequences like the events just outside San Diego, which have so stunned us all this week. Our prayers are with their families, as well.

In this season of reflection, we must find kinship in our common humanity. In this season of renewal, we must renew our pledge to make America one nation under God. In this season of redemption, we must all rise up above our differences to walk forward together on common ground, toward common dreams.

Thanks for listening.

END

Appendix 1B: April 30, 1997

STATEMENT BY THE PRESIDENT

I applaud the leadership of Senator Baucus, along with Senator Burns and all members of the United States Senate who have joined together to designate today as a National Day to Erase the **Hate** and Eliminate Racism. America is the world's most diverse democracy, and the world looks to us for leadership in building on that diversity, and showing that it is our greatest strength. Today's Resolution shows that the Senate is determined to reach across party lines to help achieve that promise.

We must do all we can to fight bigotry and intolerance, in ugly words and awful violence, in burned churches and bombed buildings -- including efforts such as today's resolution. The only way we can meet our challenges is by meeting them together -- as one America -- and giving all of our citizens, whatever their background, an opportunity to achieve their own greatness.

Appendix 1C: May 3, 1995

TO THE CONGRESS OF THE UNITED STATES:

Today I am transmitting for your immediate consideration and enactment the "Antiterrorism Amendments Act of 1995." This comprehensive Act, together with the "Omnibus Counterterrorism Act of 1995," which I transmitted to the Congress on February 9, 1995, are critically important components of my Administration's effort to combat **domestic** and international **terrorism**.

The tragic bombing of the Murrah Federal Building in Oklahoma City on April 19th stands as a challenge to all Americans to preserve a safe society. In the wake of this cowardly attack on innocent men, women, and children, following other terrorist incidents at home and abroad over the past several years, we must ensure that law enforcement authorities have the legal tools and resources they need to fight **terrorism**. The Antiterrorism Amendments Act of 1995 will help us to prevent **terrorism** through vigorous and effective investigation and prosecution. Major provisions of this Act would:

o   Permit law enforcement agencies to gain access to financial and credit reports in antiterrorism cases, as is currently permitted with bank records. This would allow such agencies to track the source and use of funds by suspected terrorists.

o   Apply the same legal standard in national security cases that is currently used in other criminal cases for obtaining permission to track telephone traffic with "pen registers" and "trap and trace" devices.

o   Enable law enforcement agencies to utilize the national security letter process to obtain records critical to **terrorism** investigations from hotels, motels, common carriers, storage facilities, and vehicle rental facilities.

o   Expand the authority of law enforcement agencies to conduct electronic surveillance, within constitutional safeguards. Examples of this increased authority include additions to the list of felonies that can be used as the basis for a surveillance order, and enhancement of law enforcement's ability to keep pace with telecommunications technology by obtaining multiple point wiretaps where it is impractical to specify the number of the phone to be tapped (such as the use of a series of cellular phones).

o   Require the Department of the Treasury's Bureau of Alcohol, Tobacco, and Firearms to study the inclusion of taggants (microscopic particles) in standard

explosive device raw materials to permit tracing the
source of those materials after an explosion; whether
common chemicals used to manufacture explosives can
be rendered inert; and whether controls can be imposed
on certain basic chemicals used to manufacture other
explosives.

o   Require the inclusion of taggants in standard
    explosive device raw materials after the publication
    of implementing regulations by the Secretary of the
    Treasury.

o   Enable law enforcement agencies to call on the special
    expertise of the Department of Defense in addressing
    offenses involving chemical and biological weapons.

o   Make mandatory at least a 10-year penalty for
    transferring firearms or explosives with knowledge
    that they will be used to commit a crime of violence
    and criminalize the possession of stolen explosives.

o   Impose enhanced penalties for terrorist attacks
    against current and former Federal employees, and
    their families, when the crime is committed because
    of the employee's official duties.

o   Provide a source of funds for the digital telephony
    bill, which I signed into law last year, ensuring
    court-authorized law enforcement access to electronic
    surveillance of digitized communications.

These proposals are described in more detail in the enclosed
section-by-section analysis.

The Administration is prepared to work immediately with the
Congress to enact antiterrorism legislation. My legislation will
provide an effective and comprehensive response to the threat of
terrorism, while also protecting our precious civil liberties. I urge
the prompt and favorable consideration of the Administration's
legislative proposals by the Congress.

                        WILLIAM J. CLINTON

THE WHITE HOUSE,
    May 3, 1995.

Chapter 2

For Which They Stand

I am American bred, I have seen much to hate here—much to forgive.
—Alice Duer Miller

The so-called right wing (and its use of radio, television, and cyberspace) does not consist of one homogenous group of advocates with one identifiable common purpose. While there is a common thread of dissatisfaction with government and, frequently, a targeting of specific groups as scapegoats for what is perceived to be wrong with society—exactly as Hitler consciously and carefully did with the Jews—there are many disparate right-wing groups with individual agendas and, depending on the intensity of their beliefs and feelings, they each have their own approaches toward accomplishing their goals.

Chip Berlet, an expert researcher and writer on the right wing, categorizes the hard right, epitomized by the so-called "Patriot" organizations; far right, as exemplified by the "armed militias"; and ultra-right, represented by "neo-Nazi" and "Skinhead" groups. There are, as well, the "conservative" groups, beginning from politically right of center across a spectrum that approaches the hard right. The Rush Limbaughs and their stated philosophies, for example, would fall somewhere in the middle of that spectrum, contrary to many Americans' belief that the Limbaughs are purveyors of the far right. It is precisely because he is not at either extreme of the right wing—that is, neither at what would be considered a moderate Republican conservative stance reflecting the center of American politics and including conservative Democrats, nor at the violence-begetting ultra-right—that Limbaugh has been able to influence so many Americans. He reaches into the mainstream of the right wing. His followers generally act with their votes. In no small measure were the Rush Limbaughs responsible for the democratically achieved ballot box victories for the Republican Party in the congressional elections of 1994 and 1996 and the right wing dominance that orchestrated the House impeachment of President Clinton in 1998. While many in the hard to the ultra-right as well as the moderate right, vote Republican, it is because they see no other choice. The Democrats are perceived as evil—communists, Zionists, traitors—while the Republicans are closer to the radical right's beliefs and even have as leaders individuals whom the radical right considers very close to its own ideals. In this book we most often use three categories: right-wing, which encompasses the moderates; far right, which includes those who are openly racist, anti-Semitic, and anti-government; and extremist right, which refers to those groups that advocate violence to accomplish the goals embraced by the far right and, in many cases by the moderate right wing.

The Right Ideas

The American political right-wing practitioners—like all dedicated political factions—are ideologues. They believe that they alone have the correct answers. There is no compromise. Everyone else is wrong. Like dedicated ideologues everywhere, they would impose their beliefs and way of life on all others, believing, as fundamental religious groups do, that everyone else, whether they think so or not, will be better off for it. Dissent is simply wrong and impermissible.

In large measure, it is the very voices that the right wing would stifle—such as the American Civil Liberties Union (ACLU) and other civil liberty organizations—that make it possible for the right-wing dissidents and radicals to make their voices heard. There is no attempt to apply logic to their belief that only their words are the words of truth and therefore they should be free to proclaim their ideas without interference, but that those who disagree with them should be censored. It is no accident, therefore, that many of these right-wing ideologues use the church and religion as bases for their proclamations, bypassing reason by relying on the I-believe-because-I-believe and blind-faith-is-your-guide dicta.

Even those right-wing groups that are not overtly and consciously neo-Nazi frequently adopt the same approaches used by the Nazis. *"Gott mit uns"* provides the rationale for the better-than-thou superman justification of denigrating and, if necessary, eliminating all others who do not have the same God-given superiority and are therefore inferior and literally dispensable and disposable. While many churches and religious groups object to what they consider such misuse of religion, history shows time and again that even the mainstream churches of any given era—sometimes quite eagerly—support or condone or, at the very least, do not object to the use of religion as justification for subjugation and even genocide of designated groups of people. Certainly the European Crusaders murdering and pillaging in the Middle East, and the refusal of the Catholic Church to condemn Germany's deliberate genocide against Jews, Gypsies, homosexuals, and others in World War II—and even cooperating in it by its silence—provide bases for the beliefs and calls to action of many current religious right organizations. A PBS documentary in 1996 summed up the rise of the religious right in the program's title, "With God on Our Side."

While many right-wing religious programs on radio, television, and the Internet are moderate in tone, seeking principally to proselytize for their particular denomination or sect, many others use the religious base for reinforcing their brand of hate among their audiences. One "Christian television" broadcaster, for example, is Bob Enyart. He states: "I am Bob Enyart, America's most popular, self-proclaimed, right-wing, religious fanatic, homophobic, anti-choice talk show host." He is advertised as "one of the greatest people on television today . . . a Born Again Christian who knows right from wrong." And to make certain that his audience is aware of the religious base for his presentations, he is further described as "a Rush Limbaugh with a twist of Christianity."[1]

The right-wing religious groups do not fall easily into categories. Indeed, some may be white religious hate groups that attack Blacks; and some may be Black religious hate groups that attack whites. Essentially, however, the right-wing hate movement encompasses several key across-the-board beliefs: racist white superiority, anti-Semitism, hatred of government, and fear of a New World Order. In 1997 the Southern Poverty Law Center's Intelligence Project identified 911 chapters of hate groups, including "racist Christian Identity ministries [and] black separatists with racist platforms, including the Nation of Islam."[2]

The term "religious right" is clearly a catchall for many right-wing groups, most of which subscribe to a fundamental or narrow (i.e., exclusive) religious base. Some of the religious-right groups do, in fact, orient their goals and processes around specified religious principles; others simply encompass or include religion as a subfactor.

The Horace Mann League, which describes itself as "patriotic and educational"[3] and would be considered "liberal" by right-wing standards, issued a guide for public school administrators entitled "The Religious Right: Beliefs, Goals, Strategies."[4] The guide included some of the following beliefs, as compiled by the League from literature published by religious-right organizations:

- There can not be morality (right or wrong) without the Bible.
- Christians can more effectively apply Biblical principles to government because they read the Bible and trust its teaching.
- The nation's founding fathers built laws and standards for society on Biblical principles.
- There is only one law—God's—and only one source to get it from—the Bible.
- Books in classrooms and libraries that include "anti-Biblical" language or any reference to the occult should be banned.
- The Bible empowers Godly Christians with the right to supervise the teaching of children.

- For America to be saved, the people have to return to patriotic and conservative domestic policies (i.e., ban abortions, conditionally reinstate school prayer, maintain military strength, outlaw pornography).
- "Secular humanism" and other "anti-God" philosophies must be replaced with God-centered morality.
- It is the Lord's plan to bring public education back under the control of the Christian community.
- The religious right must win elections to gain majorities on every city council and school board.
- One day, by serving God, the Christian right will rule and reign along with their sovereign, Jesus Christ.
- The Pentecostal perspective predicts a second harvest unleashing the wrath of God; drought, famine, earthquakes, epidemics, wars, and nuclear terror as well as widespread demonic activity will occur in the near future (a key tenet of the Survivalists).
- The world is divided between the saved and the unsaved and between good and evil (only Christians are saved and good, a key tenet of the Christian Identity groups).

The religious right does not operate in a vacuum, it applies its beliefs actively in the political arena, which explains its domination of the Republican Party during the 1990s. One 1993 report referring to education, but encompassing the general area of politics, is an example:

> This year, 1993, is the most critical year of the next four years of a liberal Congress and a liberal president. They can pass any liberal bill they choose to pass. You and your children must then live under that yoke of bondage which could destroy not only what you believe in, but could totally alienate your own children from you, through your school's liberal, socialistic indoctrination.[5]

While many think of the Christian right as overt hate-mongers or, as with Christian Identity groups, not only racist and anti-Semitic but conspiracy theorists as well, a number of Christian-right groups, by avoiding inflammatory rhetoric, appear to be moderate and unthreatening. One such group is the fledgling Promise Keepers, a Christian men's organization that in the 1990s began holding large rallies in various parts of the country and, in October 1997, held a huge march in Washington, D.C., to demonstrate its strength. Having recruited many otherwise apolitical American men into its ranks, it appears politically innocuous—other than the sexist nature of its principles and practices—and, in fact, strongly insists that it is apolitical. However, its stated goal is "taking back

America for Jesus," the same exclusionary rhetoric used by the acknowledged far-right Christian religious hate groups; and some of its leaders have been identified as being affiliated with far right and extremist groups. At this writing the mainstream media have not yet delved into the operations and detailed agenda of the Promise Keepers or its leaders.[6] It is not clear whether the Promise Keepers will become the multiracial counterpart of Louis Farrakhan's Nation of Islam and its comparable Million Man March, whose racist, sexist, and anti-Semitic views have been virtually identical to those of some of the white far-right hate groups (except that white hatred has been substituted for Black hatred). One right-wing-watch organization, Political Research Associates, made the following comment about the Promise Keepers:

> Attracting 70 men to its first rally in 1990, Promise Keepers now [1997] holds rallies in stadiums across the country that attract an average of 40,000 men. These stadium events now allow Promise Keepers to claim a following of over 1 million men. The organization's operating income rose from $1.5 million in 1991 to $96.4 million in 1996. A huge rally called Stand in the Gap, held on the Washington Mall this past October [1997], was a clear success for both Promise Keepers and its right wing founder Bill McCartney. Promise Keepers is the softer, kinder face of the right—the face that can effectively recruit within Christian communities of color, an explicit Promise Keepers goal. By self-censoring its more revealing rhetoric, such as calls for women to "submit" to their husbands, and statements admitting that its goal is simply racial reconciliation and not racial justice, Promise Keepers may be the most effective recruitment arm yet developed for the Christian right. If so, it could lead to further solidification of the Christian right's power within the Republican Party . . . the Promise Keepers' courtship of pastors through huge training and revival meetings (such as one held in Atlanta attended by 39,000 pastors) assures continuing influence within many churches, including churches of color.[7]

The dedication and practical participation of Christian-right adherents in the political arena resulted in the election of a Republican-controlled conservative Congress the following year, 1996. The Christian right, from moderate to radical, has been turning its fears into action.

The Intelligence Project's *Report* listed 474 different "hate group" organizations that participated in documented hate activity such as crimes, marches, rallies, and leafleting. The real extent of the existence of hate groups is punctuated by the fact that the Project report did not include so-called Patriot groups such as militias or organizations that exist only on the Internet, representing in most cases only individuals or relatively small groups who have managed to establish personal Web sites.[8]

The *Report* divided the active hate groups into the groups' major self-described affiliations or function-category: Ku Klux Klan, Neo-Nazi, Skinheads, Christian Identity, Black Separatist. Those that did not fall clearly into the listing—political groups such as the America First Party, nationalistic groups such as the Confederate Society of America, publishers such as the Celtic Cross Press, and racist groups such as the National Association for the Advancement of White People (with its dozens of chapters across the United States), are listed under Other.[9] (See Appendix A at the end of this chapter.)

The report confirmed findings released by the FBI several months earlier, which noted "further decline in traditional left-wing domestic extremism and an increase in activities among extremists associated with right-wing groups and special interest organizations." The report states that right-wing extremist recruits "feel displaced by rapid changes in the U.S. culture and economy, or are seeking some form of personal affirmation."[10]

It was not surprising that one of the white supremacist right-wing groups, the New Order, had planned to bomb the Southern Poverty Law Center's headquarters and to kill its head, Morris Dees. The New Order's leaders, including a former KKK officer, were arrested before they could carry out their mission.[11]

Even Democratic fund-raising efforts use right-wing religious groups as a "bête noire." A 1998 mailing asks the reader to donate to the Democratic Senatorial Campaign Committee as an affirmation of the following: "I will not stand by while highly organized and lavishly financed right-wing groups (like the Christian Coalition) attempt to take control of the United States Senate."[12] A map enclosed with the mailing states, "The Christian Coalition is dominant in Republican parties in 18 states and substantial in 13 more." (See Appendix B at the end of this chapter.)

In the Name of What's Right

Most designations of right-wing hate groups are limited to those that are easily identifiable as activist organizations that, in the judgment of society as a whole, are causing or intend to cause blatant physical or psychological harm to that society. Many designations, however, include organizations that at first appear to be within the accepted political spectrum of the United States, but which, upon closer examination, are perceived as dangerous to the common weal. Chip Berlet and Margaret Quigley, in *Eyes Right! Challenging the Right Wing Backlash,* state that the resurgent right consists not only of "the militant anti-government populism of the armed militia movement and the murderous terrorism of the neonazi underground," but also "the electoral activism of the religious fundamentalist movements ... the best known sector of the hard right ...

often called the 'Religious Right.' It substantially dominates the Republican Party in at least 10 (and perhaps as many as 30) of the 50 states."[13]

Berlet and Quigley add to this "theocratic right" movement others as advocates of "regressive populism": patriot, armed militia, and white supremacy groups, the "overtly racist far right" organizations such as the "Ku Klux Klan, Christian Patriots, racist skinheads, neonazis and right-wing revolutionaries . . . promoting in various combinations and to varying degrees authoritarianism, xenophobia, conspiracy theories, nativism, racism, sexism, homophobia, anti-semitism, demagoguery, and scapegoating."[14]

Dr. Jean V. Hardisty, director of Political Research Associates, defines the principal goals of the right wing as "white supremacism, preservation of individual wealth in a setting of free market capitalism, preservation of rigidly traditional religious and family structures, and defense of US military hegemony."[15]

It is important, however, not to stereotype all organizations or movements of the far right with identical aims, or to stereotype all members of those organizations with common motives and goals—although those members and organizations tend to stereotype individuals, groups, and institutions they disapprove of with a broad brush. Chip Berlet and Matthew N. Lyons have noted, for example, that while some militias have emerged from old "hate-race" groups, not all militia members are racists or anti-Semites. Many members are drawn to militias not on the strength of traditional hate agendas, but more on the strength of dissatisfaction with the existing government as an entity in itself. To stereotype every militia member as a "Nazi terrorist" is wrong. Such stereotyping of militias, Berlet and Lyons say, "dismisses out of hand every political grievance they have, and it denies the social roots of the militia movement." They note that some of the grievances cited by militia members are, in fact, real.[16]

That does not ameliorate, however, the actions based on belief of many militia members. While the Oklahoma City bombing appears to have militia roots for its conspiratorial and implementational aspects, other less dramatic activities have marked militia concerns. Many militia members base their dedication on the principles that guide many Christian Identity adherents, that "Jews, Blacks, Communists, Homosexuals, and race-traitors have seized control of the United States. They refer to Washington, D.C. as the Zionist Occupational Government (ZOG)."[17]

While estimates of armed militia members in the country range from 10,000 to 5 million, it is impossible to arrive at an accurate measurement. Especially after Oklahoma City, many militias began forming into smaller groups, similar to the communist cells of an earlier era. Some militias consist of only a few people meeting clandestinely in someone's living room, while other boast of hundreds of heavily armed members practicing maneuvers in preparation to fight a war. According to the FBI, which issued a nationwide alert in April

1996, the militia extremists were in fact planning to "wage war on the government" if the Freemen were attacked, and were prepared to " 'shut federal operations down' by targeting military fuel depots, federal satellite centers, senior federal law enforcement officials and others."[18]

While there are many descriptions of and justifications for the militia movement available from all the media, one striking example is an Internet analysis distributed in 1996.[19] The material was entitled "The Rise of the Militia Movement," with a subheading, "This Information is Presented as a Service to the Patriots of the Republic of The United States and Concerned Citizens Everywhere." The report was designed to "clarify the reasons and purposes of the Militia Movement which is rising Worldwide."[20]

The report asserts that the roots of current militia movements are the underground movements in Europe to overthrow Mussolini's fascists and the German armies [Nazism is not mentioned], the slave rebellions of Roman times, and the Christian movements in ancient Israel and Rome—which, the report asserts, have been forgotten. "The rise of the Militia movement is the natural response of ALL free men everywhere, Sovereign Citizens, the Children of God, to the oppression and the tyranny of government." The report stresses the right to sovereignty of every individual citizen, as opposed to the sovereignty of feudal lords, royalty, and other oppressive governments. The report states that when the United States was founded, citizens yielded some rights, but essentially retained individual sovereignty to enjoy and defend "life and liberty, of acquiring and protecting reputation and property, and, in general, of attaining objects suitable to their condition, without injury to another [and] the responsibility for maintaining these same rights for all other Citizens, the Defense of Liberty."[21]The report continues: "Unfortunately, as a result of the citizenry not being attentive to the machinations, fraud and deceit of the politicians and bankers, the government of the United States . . . has once again devolved to a feudal system . . . statutory laws and regulations, which have in effect suspended the Constitution of the United States. It is in defense of the Constitution and the Sovereign rights of all Men that the Militias are instituted, for the very same reasons that Jesus was motivated to speak out in defense of the inherent rights of All Mankind." Following quotes from the Bible to support the Biblical analogy, the report states that "the Pharisees and Scribes and Moneylenders of Jesus' time are the Politicians and Lawyers and Bankers of today." The report concludes that "the Internet is a marvelous tool never before available to the mass of Mankind in our search for the Truth, the Oneness, and the Unity of ALL Mankind, of whatever nationality, race, or creed."[22]

While some militias do not actively preach violence, others do. Some take a philosophical "us and them" approach, as stated by Bob Fletcher of the Militia of Montana: "We have to forget about right-wing, left-wing. We have good guys and bad guys, that's it."[23] Others, like Norm Olson of the Michigan Militia, go a bit further in identifying the opposition, while maintaining a defensive rationale, "If this country doesn't change, armed conflict is inevitable. Who is the enemy? Anyone who threatens us."[24] Others are more direct in their advocacy, not only threatening violence in general, but naming specific targets. Bo Gritz, a survivalist leader, said: "The tyrants who ordered the assault on the Weavers and Waco should be tried and executed as traitors."[25] Sam Sherwood of the United States Militia Association said: "Go up and look legislators in the face, because some day you may have to blow it off."[26] And Mark Reynolds of the Unorganized Militia of Stevens County, Washington, stated: "The reason the Second Amendment was put into the United States Constitution . . . [was] so that when officials of the federal and state and local government get out of hand, you can shoot them . . . eventually people like Janet Reno will be . . . summarily executed."[27]

Righteous Rationale

The logic and passion are broad, the justifications encompassing a spectrum of beliefs and concerns. The explanations suggest the reasons for the many and varied groups, some with conflicting goals, that find their way under the large militia tent.

The militia supporters almost invariably cite the Second Amendment of the U.S. Constitution as their guide and justification, and follow it with a lesser known excerpt from the United States Code. They quote Title 10–Armed Forces, Subtitle A–General Military Law, Part I–Organization and General Military Powers, and Chapter 13–The Militia, as follows:

   a) The militia of the United States consists of all able-bodied males at
      least 17 years of age and, except as provided in section 313 of title 32,
      under 45 years of age who are, or who have made a declaration of in-
      tention to become citizens of the United States and of female citizens
      of the United States who are members of the National Guard.
   b) The classes of the militia are:
      1) the organized militia, which consists of the National Guard and the
         Naval Militia; and
      2) the unorganized militia, which consists of the members of the militia
         who are not members of the National Guard or the Naval Militia.[28]

It is the latter provision that militia members argue legally guarantees them the rights and status they have claimed.

The militias' general philosophy is reiterated succinctly in a response to House Concurrent Resolution 206, which was placed in the *Congressional Record* by Rep. Jackson-Lee of Texas with the following remark: "a sense of

Congress that expresses the threat to the security of the American citizens and the U.S. government by armed militia."[29] The right-wing issued New World Order Intelligence Report countered with the following description of the armed militias:

> that the militia has constantly advocated a peaceful return to the Constitution and Bill of Rights . . . that the militias are composed of men and women of every colour, creed, ethnic background and profession, bound together by a common love of liberty and Constitutional government is smeared . . . by the accusation that it is a 'white supremacist', racist movement. . . . That terrorism by the government itself—notably at Waco and Ruby Ridge—drove large numbers of the population to form, again, Constitutional militia. . . . The founding Fathers and the U.S. Code sanction and legitimize the militia, but it is Janet Reno and ilk who have been the most powerful motivating forces in its modern re-birth.[30]

There are other common and, in some cases, unifying factors for the militia movement. One is Liberty Lobby, a highly influential radical-right group that provides encouragement, information, propaganda, and support for the militias. It is also one of the older modern far-right organizations, founded in 1955 by Willis Carto, still judged to be its head. In the 1950s Liberty Lobby considered Senator Joseph McCarthy to be a great hero and anyone to his left, including conservative President Dwight D. Eisenhower, to be an enemy of the country.[31] Liberty Lobby's goals have been described as "to rehabilitate Hitlerian National Socialism and agitate on behalf of a neo-Nazi movement in the United States."[32] Among Carto's past statements, indicating the orientation of Liberty Lobby, is the following: "Hitler's defeat was the defeat of Europe. And of America . . . The blame, it seems, must be laid at the door of the international Jews . . . If Satan himself . . . had tried to create a permanent disintegration and force for the destruction of the nations, he could have done no better than to invent the Jews."[33] Liberty Lobby states: "We fought on the wrong side with the Communists and International Bankers in World War II. Now fight on the RIGHT side."[34] Liberty Lobby also supported South Africa's apartheid.[35]

Liberty Lobby has spawned several additional radical-right groups, including the Populist Party, established in 1984 as its political action group and which was the banner under which David Duke ran for president of the United States in 1988. Liberty Lobby has also established materials centers, such as the Institute for Historical Review, thought to be the principal source in the world for Holocaust-denial material. It should be noted that both the Populist Party and the Institute have broken with Liberty Lobby in a fight over who would control the respective budgets and funds.[36]

Liberty Lobby publishes a weekly newspaper, the *Spotlight*, which reaches an estimated 100,000 right-wing activists, including militia members. Liberty Lobby also broadcasts to countless listeners over its Sun Radio Network. So radical are its messages that even conservatives such as William Buckley and Robert Bork have criticized Liberty Lobby's anti-Semitic propaganda.[37]

In the mid- and late 1990s Liberty Lobby appears to have concentrated heavily on fueling militia group beliefs and actions. the *Spotlight* has stressed stories supporting conspiracy theories regarding the federal government that directly pertain to militias and has strongly supported militia groups' major concerns such as opposition to national and international gun control, the loss of national sovereignty, and the conspiracy of the United Nations to take over the United States.[38]

Liberty Lobby's philosophy reflects, as well, the anti-global ideology of most right-wing groups, which they use to justify their violence in protection of what they believe are individual American citizen sovereign rights that are allegedly being stolen by the federal government. They see themselves as "modern-day minutemen, citizen-soldiers prepared to defend their liberties against the depredations of federal agents and international elites."[39] They deeply believe that they are at war with the federal government, in an effort to prevent it from being taken over by the United Nations through a conspiracy between federal officials and foreign powers. They see themselves as patriots who believe that their duty is to go to war against the federal government, thus justifying, to many militia members, the bombing of the federal building in Oklahoma City. They believe that they must arm themselves so that, if necessary, they can preempt the inevitable coming of federal agents to arrest or kill them.[40]

While some believe that this fear is purely paranoia, it is important to note that other sources, moderate and left-of-center, have criticized national, state, and local police forces in a manner similar to the criticism of the right wing, although for vastly different reasons. The far-right groups are anti-Black, anti-gay, and anti-drug use (specifically, they are against the use of marijuana, but, hypocritically, are generally not against the use of tobacco, which has been cited for far more serious effects), and do not object to police action against those designated enemies; conversely, some liberal and left-wing groups object to what they consider excessive police force against those targets. While the "white" right wing has not raised a furor over police brutality and concentration on minority neighborhoods, for example, some other entities—including African-American right-wing organizations as well as moderate and left-wing groups—believe that "increasingly, America's neighborhoods, especially within minority communities, are being treated like occupied territories."[41] The right-wing objects to police action against right-wing lawbreakers, but supports stronger police action against minority law-breakers.

In the past twenty-five years, "police agencies have organized paramilitary units . . . in battle dress uniforms with automatic assault rifles, percussion flash-bang grenades, CS gas and even armored personnel carriers. . . . Within the police, the elite highly militarized units have fueled a culture of violence and racial antagonism."[42] One oft-stated belief is that, philosophically, America has arrived at this threshold [a flashpoint of armed citizen resistance] through "its own militarism, its pathological puritanism, and its unshakable racism."[43]

Perhaps more than any other single event, the storming and destruction of the Branch Davidian compound at Waco, Texas, in February 1993, by agents of the federal government's Bureau of Alcohol, Tobacco and Fire-arms spurred the growth of right-wing extremist groups. "The episode has given rise to myriad conspiracy theorists, inspired anti-governments groups to defend their declarations of independence from the United States in armed standoffs with federal authorities, and fueled the growth of ultra-right-wing militia organizations."[44]

It is important not to dismiss the followers of the philosophy of armed defense against government. Mark Rupert states in his Internet "Virtual Tourists" Web site that "according to the media, the political far-right is popu-lated by paranoids and crazies, denizens of the 'lunatic fringe.' . . . [P]eople with political views which at first glance we find hard to understand might not necessarily be crazy or irrational. Rather, they may be trying to make sense of a complex and changing world in terms of the ideas and information available to them. [We should] take a closer look at the political belief system—or ideol-ogy—which motivates far-right political activists."[45]

Within the militias themselves there is disagreement about how far is too far. Since the Oklahoma City bombing, the militias have been vilified by most of American society as "a gun-toting and conspiracy-crazed lot, their ranks riven with Klansmen and neo-Nazi racists."[46] While the Oklahoma City event triggered an increase in militia enlistments by those dedicated to violent action to forward their beliefs, some militia leaders tried to avoid being tarred with the "far-right-crazies" brush, concerned that some of its members who are more interested in defense rather than offense might become disenchanted. Some began to denounce racism and terrorism, using the media to reach the general public. They attempted to create a gap between their operations and those labeled far-right fringe or extremist groups. They insisted that the militia move-ment was not dedicated to white supremacy or armed revolt, but primarily was concerned with what they believed was a government threat to their Second Amendment rights. They claimed their main purpose was to stop legislation such as the Brady Bill and the assault weapons ban. One of the militia leaders attempting to refurbish his group's reputation, Mike Vanderbrough of an Ala-bama militia, said that "this is a constitutional movement—this is not about race. . . . [T]he spontaneous militia that sprung up in the wake of Waco, Ruby

Ridge and the Brady Bill are primarily Second Amendment people who were convinced that conventional means of ensuring those rights weren't sufficient."[47]

While some critics believe that the "backing off from the revolutionary rhetoric" was sincere, others believe it was simply a public relations ploy, pointing to the continuing arrests of militia members throughout the country for terrorist or planned terrorist activities.[48]

The Freemen, a religious quasi-militia group of separatists (for example, the Republic of Texas group had a standoff with federal authorities in 1996 and there was a federal siege of the Freeman ranch in Montana in 1995) sincerely believe in their own supremacy, similar to the Nazi ideology. "The Freemen," wrote journalist James Ridgeway, "believe God placed the white Anglo Saxon, descendent of Adam, on earth as the true sovereign citizen. All others—women, minorities, especially Jews—are ranked beneath him . . . the Freemen's interpretation of the Bible and their subsequent reading of the laws, provides a foundation for their thinking."[49]

Some analysts suggest that religion-based organizations may be the most dangerous. Dr. Jerrold Post of George Washington University, an expert on bio-terrorism, states that "religious fundamental terrorists and right wing fanatics such as survivalist, racist and militia groups" post the highest threat of biological attack—similar to the use of biological weapons in the Tokyo subways and the threats posed by Sadaam Hussein of Iraq—partially because they feel no need to obtain public acceptance or even understanding for what they do. "The audience for a religious terrorist is God," Post states.[50]

For some time not as prominent as other groups, such as the militias, neo-Nazis, Christian Identity, and survivalists, the Skinheads in recent years have become a formidable force. Although their origin began with "punk" styles and social rather than political behavior in England, Nazi-type offshoots were formed to fight the increasing number of Britain's nonwhite immigrants. When the movement spread to America, the British styles were adopted but the political purposes were much stronger. The Skinheads are dedicated to ridding the United States of Jews, African Americans, and homosexuals. Composed of young people, as differentiated from the older members of the already established right-wing groups, the Skinheads are eager and ready to take physical action against those they perceive as their enemies—to provoke confrontation, if necessary. Their philosophies are essentially the same as those of the older organizations: white supremacy, anti-Semitism, struggle and survival against an imperialist government. Violence is as essential part of their everyday activity. One Skinhead stated that "none of the other Skinheads are going to respect you unless you go out and mess somebody up, and if they don't you get messed up." A former Skinhead explained the difference between the Skinheads and the previously established right-wing extremist groups: "The old guys, they were a buncha bench sitters. The Skinheads took it to the streets. It was a new resource to rejuvenate these organizations." Another Skinhead said that on "Judgment Day" the Skinheads will "annihilate everyone in our way." An interesting aspect of the Skinheads is that, unlike with most of the other groups with the same aims, females have been in leadership roles from the organization's very beginning. According to Klanwatch, women have "been out there in their Docs from the start, stomping people." The Skinheads consider themselves the "SS" of the right-wing movement in the United States. They even use the number 88 as a symbol, and sometimes greet each other with a "Heil Hitler."[51]

The Skinheads have been among the fastest growing of the right-wing extremist groups, spreading rapidly into communities across the country, urban, suburban, and rural, and becoming a rallying point for disaffected young people of both genders, even those barely into their teens. High school students are frequent targets of Skinhead recruiters, sometimes by their own classmates.[52]

Skinhead philosophy and goals are expressed in one of their "skinzines," their euphemism for magazine:

> We are everywhere, and we are nowhere.
> You fail to see us, but we are here . . .
> We are the predators in your urban jungles.
> And our time to strike is fast approaching.[53]

A Call to Arms

Some right-wing organizations predicate their existence on one major concern, such as pro-choice or abortion rights. In the 1990s there were an increasing number of bombings of family-planning or, as described by right-to-life groups, "abortion clinics" or "murder factories" and murders of physicians who legally performed abortions. Using the same basic passion and rationale as other right-wing militants (such as those who bombed the federal building in Oklahoma City), single-cause right-wing organizations organized such clinic bombings. It is estimated by the Bureau of Alcohol, Tobacco and Firearms that between 1983 and 1996 there were over 175 arson and bomb attacks on women's health centers in thirty-three states. It wasn't until 1998 that the anti-conspiracy RICO provision of the law was found by the federal courts to apply to right-to-life groups, thus legally, at least, limiting the violent hate behavior of such organizations.

Nevertheless, the anti-abortion movement continues to grow, serving as a common-ground rallying cause for otherwise disparate far right and extremist right groups. Sociologist Dallas Blanchard states "militia types have shown more and more interest in the abortion issue, while the anti-abortionists are becoming more and more militant and allying themselves with the militia movement." One example is Eric Rudolph, sought by authorities for alleged bombings at the 1996 Olympics, of a gay bar and a family planning clinic in Atlanta and another clinic in Birmingham. Survivalist Rudolph, who has been linked to right wing militias, disappeared into the North Carolina mountains and at the beginning of 1999 was still at large.[54]

A number of far right groups and individuals joined together into an organization they call the Army of God to spearhead bombings and other attacks on abortion clinics.

The Army of God issued a manual recommending sixty-five different ways to destroy abortion clinics and even included an illustrated description on how to make a fertilizer bomb—the kind used in the Oklahoma City bombing. The manual was described by the *New York Times* as a "Manual for Terrorists."[55]

Interestingly enough, the media could have played—but didn't—a key role in relation to the far right's terrorist bombings of abortion clinics. Michael Moore's "TV Nation" program, which was broadcast by NBC in December 1994, was to have included an interview in which a spokesperson for the Christian Action Group stated that assassinating Supreme Court justices would be justifiable homicide and that President Clinton was in "probable harm's way." NBC deleted that segment of the program. Shortly afterward two people were killed in the bombing of abortion clinics in Brookline, Massachusetts, by a bomber allegedly having ties to the Christian Action Group. Michael Moore said that if the segment had remained in the program, its revelations might have led to arrests that could have prevented the abortion clinic bombings. In commenting on the NBC censorship, Moore said, "It's a federal offense to say the President should be killed."[56] The segment was never shown in the United States, but was broadcast by the BBC in the United Kingdom.

In some cases the activities of one right-wing individual or group may spur similar activity by others. The Oklahoma City bombing is a case in point. Before the Oklahoma City terrorist act, the FBI reported, about 100 domestic terrorist bombings were being investigated; three years after Oklahoma City the FBI was investigating 900 cases. Federal counterterrorism squads discovered plots to kill judges, poison drinking water sources, bomb a gas refinery, and bomb the FBI's fingerprint identification center, among others. Excited and encouraged by the Oklahoma City attack, some fanatic groups were prevented by the federal authorities in their efforts to take such actions as attacking Holoman Air Force base in New Mexico because the German Air Force allegedly had quarters there, and bombing Fort Hood because Red Chinese troops allegedly were stationed there. Another group was arrested before they could implement a plan to murder key federal officials and establish a whites-only Aryan People's Republic.[57]

Activities uncovered and stopped by the FBI or local law enforcement authorities ranged from the arrest of two white supremacists in Little Rock on grounds of murder, racketeering, and conspiracy in their attempts to overthrow the government and replace it with an Aryan People's Republic to the arrest of a man in Philadelphia who left pipe bombs at a number of businesses and painted swastikas on the offices of local politicians. Comparable activities following the Oklahoma City bombing included bank robberies and the bombing of newspaper and Planned Parenthood offices in Spokane, Washington; a dynamite blast uncovering explosives stored by alleged local militia members in Yuba City, California; the arrest of twelve militia members in Phoenix who stored ingredients identical to those used to make the Oklahoma City bomb, as well as other arms and ammunition; a seven-state Midwest crime wave of pipe bombs and bank robberies by members of the Aryan Republican Army; the Army of God claiming responsibility for bombing the Centennial Olympic Park, gay bar, and abortion clinic in Atlanta; the arrest of an Oklahoma militia leader preparing to bomb civil rights offices, abortion clinics, welfare offices, and gay bars.[58] The list goes on and on.

The determination and the commitment of the right-wing extremists should not be underestimated. Writer Michael Reynolds participated in a meeting of right-wing extremist groups in Missouri under the banner of the Second Annual Super Conference of the International Coalition of Covenant Congregations—a lengthy but innocuous-sounding title. He reported that the general underlying theme was that of white Christian identity standing up to a trampling conspiratorial government, with a mandate to the attendees to take things into their own hands, to fight a "spiritual battle" against a government that "behaves as a beast," and that whoever bombed the Oklahoma City federal building simply assumed that "they can't rely on the Lord to take vengeance." The attendees were exhorted to follow God's order that Christians "get an assault rifle, or else." "Our backs are against the wall," they were told. In a conversation with a self-described Christian patriot complaining about the conspirators in Washington, D.C., Reynolds was told, "They've been taking this country from us piece by piece, for years. But we got a piece of it back in Oklahoma City."[59]

While most right-wing hate groups may have different agendas and different means for attaining their ends, studies have indicated that there appear to be two major concerns that cut across the entire right-wing spectrum and are basic to the philosophies of most such groups: a hatred of the federal government and a hatred of individuals and groups different from themselves, with an emphasis on racial, gender, lifestyle, and religious differences, the latter most specifically targeting Jews. One or more of these beliefs appear to cross the spectrum of the right wing, sometimes making it difficult to separate what appear to be mainstream conservative groups from the so-called lunatic fringe. For example, the National Rifle Association, which has in its membership people from all political spectra, nevertheless did not hesitate to equate federal agents enforcing the gun laws with the Nazi Gestapo. Some members of the U.S. Congress, rarely overtly racist or anti-Semitic, have nevertheless appeared on Radio Free America, which is sponsored by Liberty Lobby, known for its neo-Nazi, anti-Semitic stance.

Similarly, while many libertarians are sincerely concerned about what they perceive as excesses of government, some use the libertarian mantra for advocating the abolition, even the physical destruction, of the government. Political Research Associates, in analyzing "how much dimensional the right's message of intolerance" has become, cites the "increasing influence of libertarianism":

> On the surface, it would appear that libertarianism is simply a quirky ideology that offers no challenge to the Christian right's current ideological dominance. Though libertarians share with the larger right a vision of a completely unregulated free market, they are radical individualists whose largely secular social vision is anathema to the Christian right's family values. Libertarians are pro-gay, pro-choice, pro-drug legislation. While the Christian right's political success has led many commentators to think that *its* message has captured the American public, libertarians seem a marginal group that runs losing candidates under the flag of the small and scrappy Libertarian Party. . . . In the past, libertarians seemed to enjoy their status as ideological oddballs who stayed on the margin and prided themselves on being allegedly 'neither right nor left', but through two primary vehicles—the huge and increasingly influential Cato Institute in Washington, DC, and *Reason* magazine—libertarianism has gained increasing influence within the right.[60]

The names of many organizations appear to be innocuous or, at least, acceptably conservative. Yet, their rhetoric belies what might be perceived as acceptable or even desirable constitutional conservatism. Many people join or support these organizations on the basis of name impact, verbal emotion over the radio, and the print and visual materials they receive in the mail or over the Internet, without determining the true nature of the organizations. Some of these groups whose names make them seem different from what they really are, as listed by People for the American Way, are Accuracy in Academia, Accuracy in Media (which once even suggested that Democrats who supported Clinton were unpatriotic subversives and should be blacklisted from the airwaves), Alliance for America, American Center for Law and Justice, American Family Association, Americans for Tax Reform, Cato Institute, Catholic Alliance, Center for Education Reform, Citizens for a Sound Economy, Claremont Institute, Concerned Women for America, Heritage Foundation, National Association of Scholars, Progress and Freedom Foundation, and Young America Foundation.[61]

An example of one of these organizations that appears to be completely mainstream until its leaders and actions are examined is the Media Research Center in Alexandria, Virginia, which describes itself as a media watchdog organization. And, indeed, its principal activity appears to be analysis and exposé of what it considers to be dangerous left-wing material in the media. It takes aim at media personalities or participants whose comments disagree with its philosophy, implying that those commentators are un-American and even subversive—an echo of McCarthyism. Its chair is William F. Buckley's nephew, L. Brent Bozell III, and among its "experts" who judge the media personalities is G. Gordon Liddy.[62]

Some splinter organizations provide a rallying ground for relatively small groups of people with a common bond made manifest by a similar problem, experience, or occupation. For example, one such fringe group is the Kansas Territorial Agricultural Society, which sounds like a traditional grange association. Its major contention is that the state government of Kansas is invalid. Therefore, the society's members formed their own government with their own laws, including what they call a common law court and their own trial processes. Society members have openly confronted duly elected state officials as usurpers, threatening them with hanging.[63] In the late 1990s the "common law court" movement spread, with its adherents refusing to abide by the laws of their communities and ignoring any paper contracts they wished, such as paying of bills and loans, and threatening any civic employees or officials who tried to enforce local ordinances. These "common law separatists" have been among the most active of the patriot groups. "Thousands of people have been threatened, slapped with false liens against their property and 'convicted' of crimes such as 'treason' by these pseudo-legal, vigilante counterfeits of the real court system." By mid-1998 some twenty-seven states had passed or were considering laws to outlaw or strengthen existing laws against these groups' activities.[64]

The name Christian Identity, adopted by a growing movement in the United States, might seem to many like a religious organization composed of people peacefully and devoutly affirming their beliefs in the Christian faith. In fact, it is neither a denomination nor a sect. According to Michael Barkun, a professor of political science at Syracuse University and the author of *Religion and the Racist Right,* Christian Identity is "a movement composed of independent churches, Bible study groups, political organizations and communal settlements tied together by shared religious beliefs [and] has been identified as the theological underpinning of some of the extremist militia groups in the country."[65] Richard Agenes, who is the director of the Religious Information Center of Southern California, states that the Christian Identity movement has five major tenets: White people, or Aryans, are in reality the Old Testament's Israelites;

Jews literally are descendants of Satan; Adam and Eve were the first members of the white race; nonwhites descended from pre-Adamic races and are an entirely different species than whites; Armageddon is the war between the white and nonwhite races, and will soon be here.[66]

Barkun notes that most Christian Identity adherents are law-abiding, engaging principally in lobbying and electioneering to achieve their goals, but that some specified Identity groups are committed to "campaigns of terrorism and guerrilla warfare."[67]

Some right-wing groups deliberately recruit and cater to the most vulnerable members of society: young people. The Internet and rock music are two key attractions for youth. CDs and Web sites have presented young people with music mixed with advocacy of violence and racial separation. One Skinhead Web site uses a swastika to click on, then provides horror stories of government atrocities against Skinheads, at the same time presenting neo-Nazi rock bands. It works. Resistance Records, in Detroit, identified as a neo-Nazi music label, sells about 50,000 albums a year through its Web site. Mark Potok of the Southern Poverty Law Center states that "popular culture is being used to mask a new kind of barbarism . . . on the fringe you are finding a lot more hate sites on the Web with state-of-the-art graphics that are appealing to a broad variety of kids in the upper and middle class."[68]

The appeal of some right-wing groups seems so innocuous that they are able to recruit supporters who would, on reflection, find some of their ideas anathema. In a commentary in the Op Ed section of the *Tampa Tribune,* Jean Caldicott wrote that the distinction of "self" from "other" frequently results in the swaying "of ostensibly well-meaning individuals who may find racial bigotry intolerable but who think nothing of diminishing the value of or discriminating against persons with disabilities, persons with mental illness, gays and lesbian citizens or immigrants—both legal and illegal. Do we even recognize our own prejudices when they merely reflect opinions shared by so many of our peers?" she asks.[69] While many of us would reject outright the barefaced appeal of a candidly militant group, many of us are easy prey for groups that are more subtle in their approaches.

Left of Right is Right

Ironically, even groups that the right would generally label as being to the left sometimes echo the same hate-based prejudices as right-wing groups. In early 1998, for example, the Sierra Club, attacked by the anti-environmentalists and other right-wing groups as being too protective of the environment and, therefore, must be left-wing, split on whether to issue a resolution limiting the number of immigrants allowed into the United States—a policy strongly endorsed by right-wing groups, usually for racial and ethnic-bias reasons. The Sierra Club's rationale was that continued immigration tended to harm the environment. In a vote of the membership, this xenophobic proposal was rejected.

While some right-wing groups encourage the impression that they are respectable middle-of-the-road conservative organizations, others are overtly militant and appeal to the disenchanted whose frustrations need an active outlet—a group substitute and reinforcement for smashing one's fist into a wall. The armed militias fall into this category. Chip Berlet and Matthew N. Lyons describe the armed militias as the militant wing of the Patriot movement in the United States, which they estimate has about 5 million followers. They estimate the membership of the armed militias as high as 40,000 (some investigators have estimated it to be considerably higher, some as low as 10,000). The principal concern of the militias, Berlet and Lyons state, is that the federal government is becoming increasingly tyrannical. The militias particularly object to gun control, taxes, federal regulatory agencies, and what they believe are federal restrictions on constitutional liberties.[70]

It was, in fact, the government's excessive use of force against the Weaver compound in Idaho and against the Branch Davidian compound in Waco, Texas, that spurred the establishment of the armed militias as part of the Patriot movement. They felt they were left with no other choice but to prepare to use armed force against what they considered was illegal and unconstitutional armed force by the government against their Patriot colleagues.

Many militias also align themselves with the conspiracy theorists, who believe that a secret cabal, principally Jews, controls the government, the economy, and the country's culture, including its media. A variation on this conspiracy concept, also subscribed to by many militia members as well as other right-wingers, is that the government is part of a worldwide liberal plot to remove God from all of society and to impose a single government or New World Order on the globe under the United Nations. While these beliefs do not necessarily reflect a racist, white supremacist philosophy, they are easily moved into such amalgamation—something most of the far right and extremist groups, such as the Aryan Nation, the Posse Comitatus, and the Christian Patriots appear to be doing successfully.[71]

The Conspiracy Theorists sometimes have conflicting scapegoats. In the mid-1990s President Clinton was a prime target. Some of the Conspiracy Theorist groups maintain that he was a focal point for an Anglo-American conspiracy operated by the Council on Foreign Relations and the Trilateral Commission. This belief has been promulgated by some of the most popular right-wing radio commentators. Some Conspiracy Theorists concentrate principally on the traditional scapegoats: Jews and people of color. Plots to take over the world are attributed to international Jewish bankers, with reliance for proof on the long-since discredited hoax that Henry Ford promoted, *The Protocols of the Secret Elders of Zion.*[72]

Some scholars trace the Conspiracy Theory movement back more than two hundred years, when it was claimed that the Illuminati Society had infiltrated the Freemasons and with them had created a conspiracy to abolish the church and the state as the world knew it and establish a single global government.[73]

The Patriot movement is considered to be "moderate" by the John Birch Society and Pat Robertson's adherents, and considered more militant by farther-right groups such as the neo-Nazis and white supremacists, say Berlet and Lyons. That the armed militias appear to be moving more and more right is punctuated by their targets of violence: going beyond abortion clinics and practitioners, racial minorities, homosexuals, and Jews, they have openly threatened and planned destruction of government buildings and officials. In 1995, on the April 19 anniversary of the Waco disaster, it was expected that the militias, officially or by some of their individual members, would take some drastic action; few expected, however, that it would be as drastic as the murder of 165 innocent adults and children by bombing the Oklahoma City federal building.[74]

The bombing dismayed even many militia members, whose commitments did not include mass murder, and initially there was dissatisfaction within some of the militia organizations. But the militia's use of the media to convince its members of another scenario was successful, and shortly after the Oklahoma City bombing, militia memberships began to increase dramatically and continued to do so. A co-author of this book was in a remote part of Alaska shortly after the bombing and spent some time talking with a very pleasant man from the northern part of the Lower Forty-eight who had become part of an isolated Eskimo community but kept in touch with world events through television, short-wave radio, and the Internet.

When the subject of Oklahoma City came up, he told us confidentially but assuredly that the militias were not to blame. He had heard from certain quarters that all government employees working in the Alfred P. Murrah federal building were phoned the day before the bombing and told not to report for work the next day. It was quite clear to him, therefore, that the federal government had bombed its own building. This allegation became an important part of right-wing propaganda. Chip Berlet of Political Research Associates notes that there is frequently a grain of truth in such allegations. In this instance, Berlet explained, the government had been advised by a right-wing watch committee that it should be on guard for possible extremist violence on key dates, such as June 14 (Flag Day), July 4 (Independence Day), and April 19 (the beginning of the country's revolutionary war and the date of the destruction of the Branch Davidian compound). Accordingly, the GSA (Government Services Administration), which manages all federal buildings and services, sent a general memo to employees in federal buildings to be on the alert. Thus, the grain of truth is used as a basis for the story.[75]

One militia movement leader and radio personality, Mark Koernke, a janitor from Michigan, stated at the "Great Ohio Preparedness and Self-Reliance Expo of '96" in Columbus that the federal government itself blew up the Murrah Building in Oklahoma City as part of a plan to discredit the militia movement. While he presented no evidence, he said that "logic dictates" this conclusion. He said that because the federal government was increasingly being criticized for its excessive force at Ruby Ridge, Idaho (in 1992), and at the Branch Davidian compound in Waco, Texas, the following year, "they had no choice but to do a radical surgery to turn the patient around . . . beyond a shadow of a doubt, the government did it [bombed the Murrah building]."[76] He also accused the government of using operatives in the U.S. Postal Service to perform the highly visible post-office killings and of planning additional mass murders, all designed to discredit the militia movement. He said the only way to stop our "out-of-control" government is by revolution.[77]

No Rightful Apology

But, as noted earlier, the dedicated right-wing armed activists neither apologize for nor shy away from violence. Many feel they have been put into a position where they have no other choice. Over the years their threats have been bold and open. For example, one right-wing activist, Joe Holland, told the Montana attorney-general: "How many of your agents will be sent home in body bags before you hear the pleas of the people?" As noted earlier, the leader of the U.S. Militia Association, Samuel Sherwood, publicly advised his followers to "Go up and look legislators in the face, because some day you may be forced to blow it off." Ellen Gray, an Audubon Society official in Washington, was told, "We have a militia of 10,000, and if we can't beat you at the ballot box, we'll beat you with a bullet." Bill Ellwood, the acting chief justice of a self-proclaimed citizens' court in Columbus, Ohio, Our One System Court, summed up the feeling and the threat: "Yes, the militia are involved. They are the last resort of enforcement for the common-law courts."[78]

Berlet and Lyons lament the fact that despite mounting evidence of the militias' danger to the country, Congress has been reluctant to investigate and hold hearings on right-wing violence. "If there had been a movement set on violent confrontation with the U.S. government and consisting of 10,000 to 40,000 armed militia members who were African-Americans," Berlet and Lyons assert, "you can bet they would have been investigated months ago, with many members arrested."[79]

In some parts of the country, however, some legislators are concerned enough about a perceived danger to the public from militias to seek political repression of the groups. In Colorado, for example, Senate Minority Leader Mike Feeley introduced a bill similar to that proposed in seven other states, one that would declare two or more persons training with weapons as "unauthorized military organizations." Feeley said that "these people advocate nothing less than the dismantling, by force, if necessary, of the entire U.S. government and the repudiation of many of our constitutional rights."[80] Similarly, in Connecticut, State Senator Alvin W. Penn attempted to revise a Colonial-era law that permitted armed militias to form in that state and to legally train with weapons to oppose the state government if they believed it necessary.[81]

However, many individuals and organizations strongly opposed to the armed militias's ideology have defended the militias' rights to freedom of speech and assembly as constitutional rights. As noted in chapter 1, one of the strongest defenders of right-wing organizations' right to say what they wish, on the air and off, is the American Civil Liberties Union (ACLU), itself a target of right-wing attacks.

In 1995 Dr. Bruce Hoffman analyzed "American Right-Wing Extremism" in an article for *Jane's Intelligence Review.* His analysis included an overview of militias and commentary on several specific militia groups. While noting that "organized hate groups, embracing far-fetched conspiracy theories, such as the Ku Klux Klan and the John Birch Society, have existed in the USA for decades . . . the advent of extremist citizens' militias and other paramilitary groups oriented toward survival skills, guerrilla training and outright sedition are a more recent development." He describes the militias as especially attractive for those opposed to gun control and who believe in the conspiracy theories involving the United States leadership, President Clinton, and foreign powers. He states that militia members are part-time warriors who liken themselves to the early-republic patriots such as the minutemen and the patriots of the American Revolution. He believes that it is not coincidental that the Oklahoma City bombing took place on the same date that the American Revolution began in Boston 200 years previously.[82]

Hoffman describes the Michigan militia, with which convicted Oklahoma City bomber Timothy McVeigh was linked, as "paramilitary survivalist," using guerrilla warfare training to resist what it believes is the Clinton administration's plan to crush any opposition. Montana had the North American Volunteer Militia and the Almost Heaven survivalist compound, the latter led by Bo Gritz, a Vietnam Green Beret whose active political endeavors included a candidacy for U.S. president. These "patriots" believe that the "apocalypse" between good and evil is coming soon, requiring them to stockpile supplies and prepare themselves for guerrilla warfare. In Texas, the Big Star One militia claimed to have a force the size of an army division. The Indiana militias adhered to the traditions of the Ku Klux Klan and similar groups. Hoffman quotes its members as stating that they are "sick and tired of being raped and pillaged by the bunch of thieves that run the federal government" and that they intend to take matters into their own hands. Hoffman traces the militias back to the Posse Comitatus and its 1980s offshoot, the Arizona Patriots. He notes that the extremism in all these groups goes beyond anti-gun control and conspiracy theories, but encompasses a shared hostility to any government above the county level, a hatred of Jews and non-whites as "children of Satan," the goal of racial purification of the United States, a belief in a Jewish conspiracy that controls the U.S. government, the media, and the banks, and a commitment to overthrow the U.S. government—or ZOG (Zionist Occupied Government, as noted in chapter 1).[83]

Hoffman also notes the religious motifs dominating the far-right groups, including the assumption of clerical titles by the leaders of individual Aryan Nation, Ku Klux Klan, militia, and other groups. He further notes the Christian Identity movement belief that Jesus Christ was not a Jew, nor were the so-called Lost Tribes of Israel Jews, and that Anglo-Saxons, not Jews, were the "chosen people." He states that the Aryan Nation considers itself to be performing a function similar to the Palestine Liberation Organization (PLO), providing an umbrella for a number of resistance groups. He quotes from Aryan Nation literature: "We shall have a national racial state at whatever price in blood if necessary . . . the leadership of malicious, bastardizing politicians [in] modern, decadent America [where] millions of whites watch in abject dismay and hopelessness as their great culture, heritage and civilization evaporates in the steaming, stinking, seething milieu of so many alien races, cultures, and gods."[84]

Hoffman discusses the role of religion as a justifying basis for the terrorism that has very recently shaken the Middle East, the Far East, Europe, Africa, and even the United States. "Whereas secular terrorists generally consider indiscriminate violence immoral and counterproductive, terrorists motivated by this religious imperative regard such violence not only as morally justified but also as a necessary expedient for the attainment of their goals. Thus religion serves as a legitimizing force conveyed by sacred text or imparted via clerical authorities claiming to speak for the divine. . . . [This terrorism] is a characteristic of radical sects and religious movements everywhere and—much as Americans may have resisted admitting it—in the USA as well."[85]

As noted earlier, the differences among right-wing organizations are frequently blurred by their areas of similar concern and mutual goals. The Christian factor, usually coupled with white supremacy and anti-Semitic beliefs, cuts across most right-wing organizations. One of the most prominent representatives of Patriot, militia, neo-Nazi, and Ku Klux Klan groups in the early 1990s,

David Duke, heavily emphasized the Christian factor when he emerged in early 1998 after virtually disappearing from the public eye. He told his stunned supporters that he would not continue his "political crusade against government tyranny and his support of far right militia and Patriot movements."[86] Duke was quoted as saying on a radio show that "in the final analysis—and this is right from the Lord God Almighty when he visited me last summer—he said a lot of people think our problems are in Denver or Washington, DC, but those elected representatives are just a mirror of ourselves. Even if you could replace them, nothing fundamentally would change . . . the plain fact is that political solutions won't work. The problem with America is in our own heart, and when our heart changes . . . then America will change. and there's no easy way to do that except getting on your knees before the Lord God Almighty and saying 'Lord, tell me what I've done wrong.' " Duke later stated that there will be "a nationwide spiritual revival, and I will have a role in that."[87] Whether Duke's purposes include a stronger establishment of the Christian Identity concept as a base for the right-wing conglomerates or substitution of a religious basis for some of the far-right militant violence is not yet clear.

Historical Denials

Holocaust denial is a staple of virtually all of the far-right groups. Willis Carto's Institute for Historical Review, mentioned earlier, is a leading purveyor of this view. "The Holocaust-denial movement is the clearest expression of the anti-Semitic nature of white supremacy. Various institutions within the white supremacist movement are revising the history of Nazi Germany, claiming that the Holocaust against the Jews either did not happen or was greatly exaggerated."[88] One Internet site offered an archetypal approach:

Friends, the information in this section is simply THE most banned and unacceptable data in America today. You are not supposed to know these things. The sources here totally contradict what you have been taught in school or fed by the media. Have you ever heard the newsmedia referred to as the "Jewsmedia"? Or the USA as the "Jewnited States of America"? Or the New World Order as the "Jew World Order"? Or the federal government as Zog: the Zionist Occupational Government? . . . Why have Jews been expelled from every country they have ever inhabited? . . . There were NO gas chambers. Mass gassing is part of the myth. . . . There was no "Holocaust." Germany had no program of genocide. . . . The "Holocaust" is the biggest propaganda coup ever fabricated. It is a lie. The reason the "Holocaust" was created was to prevent ANY and all criticism of the Jewish theft of Palestine in the creation of Israel. . . . The Holocaust never happened.[89]

Perhaps the best-known Holocaust-denial source internationally is the "Zundelsite," operating on the Intenetout of Canada, but with perhaps hundreds of comparable sites worldwide spreading Ernst Zundel's philosophy. The Zundel Web site shares letters from people globally, virtually all attesting that the Holocaust either did not occur or that relatively few Jews were exterminated, and that the concentration camps, gas chambers, and crematoria were constructed after the war as a propaganda ploy by powerful and wealthy international Jews. At one time the Canadian government attempted to shut down the Zundelsite by arresting Zundel, but Canada's Supreme Court upheld his freedom to speak even false, hate speech. Ernst Zundel and the Zundelsite is discussed in greater detail in chapter 8 of this book.

At one time the John Birch Society was considered on the leading edge of right-wing extremist groups. By the 1990s it was heard of much less often than most of the other groups. However, it still maintains an outreach, with its members using the airwaves and its headquarters publishing a Web site newsletter. It appears, on the surface, to work principally as a political lobby, urging its members to support or oppose specific legislation pending in Congress. One of its key issues continues to be the United Nations; it urges U.S. withdrawal from the UN and, ultimately, dissolution of that body. It feels, as other groups do, that the Constitution has been usurped by those who control the government and by those in charge of our judicial system. Its recent public rhetoric has not included the threat or advocacy of armed violence.[90]

In the early part of the century, the leading "hate group" in the United States in terms of members, influence, and activity, was the Ku Klux Klan. While still active and growing in many parts of the South and Midwest, it has in recent years been displaced by the Patriot groups that have taken more immediately active roles in areas of violent action. In the mid-1960s the Ku Klux Klan was the largest of all the hate groups in the United States with a membership estimated at more than 40,000. A substantial portion of the KKK's white supremacist membership has joined groups such as Christian Identity, neo-Nazis, and Aryan Nation. That is not to say that the KKK is out of business; they continue to operate, with perhaps thirty different KKK groups in the United States, most, as in the past, still in the South. Offshoot organizations, such as the Knights of the KKK in Arkansas, have claimed greater militancy than the parent organization. Convictions of many Klan members in the 1990s for criminal activities resulted in a different public face for some Klan groups, with public disavowance of violence.[91] In fact, many of its chapters publicly espouse a banner of nonviolence. While the KKK still metes out physical harm to those it believes have transgressed against the moral beliefs it would impose on all of society, it is been recently known more for marches and rhetoric than overt violence, notwithstanding its past record of murder and beatings and court convictions and more recent violence by individual members. The North Georgia White Knights of the Ku Klux Klan describes itself as

> a patriotic, White Christian revival movement, dedicated to preserving the maintenance of White Pride and the rights of the White Race. These rights are rapidly being taken away on a daily basis by crooked politicians. We believe in using all legal means possible to rebuild our collapsing society on the principles of honor, duty, courage, brotherhood and patriotism. . . . Only those who can practice true Klanishness are allowed in our ranks. No person is allowed in our ranks who cannot pledge himself to the maintenance of White Pride and the preservation of the White Race. A person who cannot practice true brotherhood is not allowed into our organization. Every member is sworn to uphold the law and principles of justice and that he will not conspire with others to commit any unlawful or violent acts. Only White people of non-Jewish, non-Negro, non-Mexican, non-Asian descent, who are at least 18 years old and will pledge themselves to the maintenance of White Pride and the protection of the White Race, can enter into the North Georgia White Knights, Ku Klux Klan.[92]

Current and former Klan members, however, continue to be arrested for conspiring to commit violence and committing violence. For example, at about the same time the above description of one KKK group in Georgia was released, a one-time leader of the KKK in Illinois, Dennis M. McGiffen, was charged with planning a nationwide campaign of racial terrorism, including "assassinations and bombings financed by bank robberies." Drawings by McGiffen's children depicted "the hanging of black people with blood dripping down." Other allegations included the possible poisoning of water supplies in several large cities.[93] Also about the same time three men in Los Angeles were convicted of attempted murder and assault by shooting at African Americans after flashing Ku Klux Klan signs at their intended victims.[94]

Another common target of right-wing groups, based on Biblical interpretation and religious intolerance, are gays and lesbians. When individuals or small groups have been arrested for physical beatings or even wanton murder of gays and lesbians, affiliations with or influence by right-wing groups have usually been found to be a factor. An example of the tactics used by "gay-bashers" who stop short of physical violence is the activity of the Reverend Fred Philips, a Baptist minister in Topeka, Kansas. He and his followers, among other things, picket the funerals of AIDS victims with signs such as "God Hates Fags," "AIDS Cures Fags," and "Thank God for AIDS." His grandson runs an Internet Web site called "God Hates Fags."[95]

The degree of psychic violence and insensitivity emanating from the fanatic commitment of such anti-gay adherents was emphasized at the funeral in October 1998 of Matthew Shepard, the University of Wyoming student who was "abducted, beaten with a pistol while he pleaded for his life, robbed, and strung up on a fence in rural Wyoming in near-freezing temperatures," and with his skull bashed in, was left to die.[96] The horror was compounded when the Philips followers heaped further torture on his family and friends with their picketing of his funeral.

Psychologist Kenneth Morgen found that "45% of lesbians and 29% of gay men had suffered physical attacks because of their sexual orientation."[97] The *Intelligence Report* opines that "if 45% of whites had been attacked because of the color of their skin, there would be a hue and cry the likes of which this country has never seen. But in the case of homosexuals, other Americans have not risen in large numbers to the defense. The voices of outrage have been few, even as vilification of gays and lesbians has grown."[98]

While some right-wing groups advocate—overtly and covertly—corporal attacks on gays and lesbians, others concentrate on legal harassment or inequity as a means of control or punishment for those whose lifestyles they regard as ungodly and sinful. For example, an anti-homosexual video entitled "The Gay Agenda," was made by a former CBS sportscaster, Bill Horn, that purported to reveal hidden, unhealthy practices of the gay community. Thousands of copies were distributed to media personalities, members of Congress, and state and local government officials. The video received national television exposure. In the fall of 1992 some 10,000 copies were sent to voters in Colorado and Oregon just before the vote on antigay initiatives on the ballots in those states. Seventy-percent of the "yes" voters said their vote was influenced by the video.[99]

The right wing uses the strategy of localism—making it appear as though the antigay and -lesbian movement is locally based, although the organizing and supporting resources come from an outside national base. Dr. Jean Hardisty, director of Political Research Associates, has stated that one of the right wing's principal approaches has been "to make local anti-homosexual campaigns appear to be exclusively grassroots efforts when they are guided by major national organizations."[100]

While most homophobic right-wing groups go quietly about their business, the mainstream media, essentially catering to the perceived common-denominator prejudices of their audiences, disdain to reveal the real agendas and practices of these groups. Occasionally the public is given a glimpse of such groups' beliefs and activities. In 1997 Gil Alexander-Moegerle, a founder of Focus on the Family, a Christian organization, criticized the alleged leader of the organization in a book about its practices. "I apologize to lesbian and gay Americans who are demeaned and dehumanized on a regular basis by the false, irresponsible, and inflammatory rhetoric."[101]

Ironically, Barry Goldwater—"Mr. Conservative," perhaps the best known advocate of right-of-center philosophy of the second half of the twentieth century—offered a different attitude toward homosexuality than most of those who generally supported his views. Commenting on the U.S. Armed forces discriminatory policy against gays and lesbians, Goldwater said, "You don't need to be 'straight' to fight and die for your country. You just need to shoot straight."

Some right-wing groups have expanded from local or state concentration and beyond even their national affiliations. A number of organizations are increasingly international in their scope. In the United States some right-wing organizations have found it relatively easy to have Canadian links. For example, a group called the Heritage Front, ostensibly an isolated organization in Canada, has links with many other right-wing outfits, including White Aryan Resistance, Church of the Creator, Citizens for Foreign Aid Reform, Ernst Zundel's Holocaust-denial Web sites, and Skinhead groups.[102] While these are Canadian-based organizations, their outreach and connections go beyond the country's borders, finding common philosophical ground, information exchange, mutual propagandizing, and cooperative plans and projects with comparable groups in the United States.

The Internet has facilitated the rise of international hate organizations. One such Internet group headquartered in Canada operates the New World Order (NWO) "Intelligence Update" home page, and promotes the sale of books and other materials promoting the worldwide conspiracy theory and stressing a Christian base. One of its major disseminations is a detailed analysis of what it calls "FEMA—the U.S. 'Shadow Government,'" in which it describes a hidden West Virginia government retreat called Mopiti Weather. Here, the NWO asserts, is a small city, including underground complexes, containing replacements for all high government officials. It believes that this setup makes it possible that "the United States could experience an honest-to-God coup d'état posing as a national emergency."[103] NWO further claims that the Russians have a similar site, funded by U.S. money, with the implication that it might be used as base for a takeover of the United States.[104]

The NWO "Intelligence Update" clarified even further its conspiracy theory in one of its many noncyberspace media appearances, on the "Quinn in the Morning Show" on WRRK-FM, Pittsburgh, with subsequent broadcasts over Internet radio and on the "Quinn in the Morning Show" Web site. Jim Quinn interviewed John Whitley, editor of the "New World Order Intelligence Update," on the subject "Is the New World Order a Kook Theory or Mainstream News?" With lead-ins from Quinn such as "Rush [Limbaugh] tells me that if I believe any of this stuff I'm a kook! I don't think that [Gordon] Liddy believes in any of this stuff, yet I keep getting hit in the face with evidence that something's going on here," Whitley detailed his beliefs about the New World

Order conspiracy. He cited names and places to prove his allegations. "The whole idea is that you divide the world up into three governmental zones, and each one will have an enforcement army; and then you merge those government zones into one, and you merge those three armies into one. In essence, you get a threefold world state. And this has been the long-term plan of the Trilateral Commission, which is how it got its name."[105]

Whitley and Quinn went on to tie President Bill Clinton directly to the conspiracy, but also stated that the Chinese and Russians are planning their own "Marxist New World Order," which will dominate Clinton and turn over the entire world to the Marxists. Even former President George Bush was named as part of the conspiracy. Further, the environmental movement was linked to the United Nations plan to take over specified parts of the country under the guise of protecting the environment. In addition, according to Whitley, the conspirators would "unleash on us again starvation, disease, and a calamitous transfer of wealth, primarily through a stock market collapse, from the vast majority of the population to a small number of the elite, which will bring us once again under the control of oligarchy and tyranny."

"Until once again it's overthrown," Quinn suggested. And Whitley answered: "Exactly." Whitley made the point that "Americans grow up with a natural sense of patriotism which is born out of blood. They bought their freedom with a price . . . if you scratch hard enough and deep enough, the Constitution comes bubbling up. And that's the one thing that's the bedrock resistance to these people . . . the key is that we both have enough people on both sides of the border who understand on what basis our countries were founded . . . that they just can't impose overnight what they would like to do."[106]

A Trinity in Likeness

Christian Identity, Survivalists, and the Posse Comitatus are three faces of the right-wing that have common interests, goals, and motives. Chip Berlet states that these groups all appear to include white supremacist, anti-Jewish factors in their rationales. Some do so overtly and passionately. In order to survive what they say is a worldwide Jewish conspiracy to take over their churches and governments, some of these groups arm themselves, prepared for a showdown at any time with the representatives of Satan—most likely the government forces that they believe massacred the Weaver family and the Branch Davidians.[107]

The basic Survivalist philosophy, however, is just what it sounds like. While it grew out of the Christian Identity movement and retains some of the basic conspiracy and anticolor, anti-Jewish tenets of that movement, it essentially believes that the end of society as we know it is near at hand. Members, therefore, have stockpiled food and other necessities for their personal survival, and collected weapons and ammunition to prepare for what they expect to be the collapse of law and order and racial rioting. Not all survivalists adopt the white supremacist beliefs of the Christian Identity movement, but many, like Randy Weaver, do subscribe to those beliefs. One concise summary of the survivalist philosophy is presented on the Internet by an organization called Survival Enterprises, which offers rhetoric plus "the following products and services: 1. firearms sales, repair and refinishing service, 2. health products, 3. (and believe it or not) comic books for sale!"[108]

When you log onto the Web site you are told:

> If you hate and fear guns, if you feel the federal government and politicians are the saviors and guardians of our lives, if you feel people are just too stupid, dangerous, ignorant and dishonest to be trusted with their weapons, their jobs, their children and their country—you can go [off our Web site].
>
> If you're the kind of person who doesn't give-a-damn that the socialist liberal democratic party will call you an 'insensitive right-wing Christian extremist skin-head militia junk-gun & assault weapon toting intolerant homophobic women children and old folks hating extra 'Y' chromosomed union busting angry white male NRA member, *come on in!!*[109]

For some survivalists the year 2000 has prompted a so-called "millennium" philosophy: the belief that human history, as we know it, will end shortly into the new millennium. In his book, *Millennium Race: Survivalists, White Supremacists, and the Doomsday Prophecy,* Philip Lamy states that the Christian Identity movement's racism, anti-Semitism, and anti-government dedication provide a unifying theology for the Ku Klux Klan, Aryan Nation, Freemen, Skinheads, and neo-Nazis, helping to create a survivalist belief that extreme measures must be taken to prepare to survive the ultimate battle against the forces of evil. Evil is personified by those who do not fit into and subscribe to the beliefs of these extremist groups.[110] The Christian Identity view—one that generally pervades the other right-wing extremist groups—is that the new millennium's Armageddon will be essentially a race war between Aryans on one side and Jews and nonwhites on the other. That the Aryans—the Christian Identity—will win the war is guaranteed by virtue of their being the "true Israelites," the Biblical tribes that migrated from the Middle East to Western Europe. The Jews, they believe, are not descended from Israelites, but are "Satan's spawn," the result of sex between the devil and Eve in the Garden of Eden. This theological view permeates many of the other right-wing groups, including the KKK, the militias, survivalists, neo-Nazis, and others. It is the conspiracy of the Jews and nonwhites, representing the Devil, that have developed the threat against the white race that must be defeated in the upcoming Armageddon.[111] While some observers may view this as a science-fiction fixation on the year 2000, the belief and preparation are real. A leading (some say *the* leading) far-right talk show host, Chuck Harder, warned on his "For the People" radio show in mid-1998: "I must tell you the millennium bug is going to bite."[112]

White supremacy is not only the cornerstone of most right-wing groups but also the organizational identification of some of the groups. White supremacists not only are patently anti-Black, but in also subscribing to the conspiracy theory believe that the "yellow race"—more specifically the Chinese communists—will be in the vanguard of the United Nations armed takeover of the United States.[113] One of the key right-wing extremist groups based on racial and ethnic hate is the Aryan Nation. Its principal tenet is anti-Semitism. A state group coordinator stated it this way: "The Jew is like a destroying virus that attacks our racial body to destroy our Aryan culture and purity of our race."[114]

The Aryan Nation convenes frequent conferences, some called "World Congress of Aryan Nations," to solidify its commitments and recruit new members. Its recruitment targets include prison inmates. More than ten years ago, in 1987, it started a publication directed to prisons, "The Way," which connects the "outside" Aryan Nation with the "inside" Aryan Brotherhood, a network of prison gang members—many of whom are former Aryan Nation members who were convicted for crimes against society.[115] Two of the white supremacists arrested for lynching an African-American man in Jasper, Texas, in 1998 reportedly honed their hate in prison, both presumed to have become members of the KKK and its affiliate, the Confederate Knights of America, while serving a previous term in a prison where the white inmates were apparently ruled by the Aryan Brotherhood. One also joined the Christian Identity movement. Brian Levin, director of the Center on Hate and Extremism at Richard Stockton College, states that "even people who are not hard-core hatemongers when they go in get caught in the web of hatred and are stuck in it when they get out." And John R. Craig, a writer on white supremacy, said of one of the accused perpetrator's initial experience in prison, "He went in a street punk and came out a white supremacist. It was a complete metamorphosis."[116]

Not heard of as often as the Christian Identity and Survivalist movements, but more militant, is the Posse Comitatus. The Latin term literally means the power of the county (not country), but actually means "to empower the citizenry." Like the old Western posses, the movement's members believe it is their right to organize any group of citizens to carry out law enforcement functions. A concomitant belief is that the Constitution does not authorize any government law enforcement powers above the level of county marshal or sheriff. Any law enforcement above that level is, they believe, part of the conspiracy to deny them their basic rights as citizens. Many members also believe that the conspiracy is a joint venture of Jews, Blacks, homosexuals, and communists.[117]

Like other dedicated right-wing groups, Posse Comitatus tends to influence many who do not necessarily join the specified organization, but are attracted to and agree with its principles. For example, according to Klanwatch, which tracks and analyzes militia activity, Terry Nichols, the "second man" with Timothy McVeigh in the Oklahoma City terrorist bombing, used Posse Comitatus ideas, methods, and even language in his activities against banks and the U.S. monetary system, although there was no evidence that he was actually a member of the organization.[118] The leader of Posse Comitatus, James Wickstrom, vehemently denied Nichols' link to his organization, but did not disagree with Nichols' renunciation of the federal government as "illegitimate"—the same as his group's rhetoric.[119] A less publicized court case in 1996 dealt with a group founded on Posse Comitatus principles, calling itself Family Farm Preservation. It sold some $80 million in fake money orders from 1992 to 1995 in an attempt to destroy the country's monetary system—a key goal of Posse Comitatus.[120]

Chip Berlet sums up the general dogma that cuts across all the above movements as a reflection of the fundamental beliefs of the Christian Identity movement: white power and Aryan supremacy, inferiority of African Americans; anti-communism; jingoistic patriotism; mistrust of government and law officers; fear of Black pride and Black power, which is controlled by Jews from Tel Aviv and from Moscow; media are controlled by Jews and communists; armed defense is necessary for survival.[121]

But Christianity isn't the only religious base for intolerance. All major religions in the United States—Christian, including Catholics and Protestants; Jewish; and Islamic—have adherents who are intolerant of all other beliefs and denigrate persons whose religious beliefs are different from theirs. The difference is in the extremists who call for the subjugation and even annihilation (as practiced for centuries) of those they consider nonbelievers. Most often, the religious base for hate is coupled with racial hatred. While the overwhelming number of religious-racist hate groups are white, in 1997 there were an estimated twelve Black separatist groups in the United States, some of which were predicated purely on race, but a number of which included religion and were part of the Nation of Islam.[122]

It is, perhaps, the militia movement that has come to the fore amid all the furor surrounding the right-wing extremist groups in the United States. Part of the reason is the sensationalist aspect of an armed citizen army within the United States prepared to kill other citizens in an effort to seize power and control the country. That their plans and goals are based on sincere beliefs that the U.S. government is, as they often say, "homicidally out-of-control" and requires a revolution to restore constitutional guarantees of freedom does not appear to provide any greater justification for their existence and actions than did the similarly sincere beliefs of the National Socialist Party that took over Germany through a combination of politics and armed violence in the 1930s. It is also important to note that the German Nazis initially had no more—probably fewer—members than the combined militias have now. What they did have—and no charismatic leader has yet appeared to unify the far right in the United States—was Adolf Hitler. Although the David Dukes and Pat Buchanans and Pat Robertsons appear to aspire to that position, they have not yet shown the ability to become national fuhrers.

Since Oklahoma City, the militias have devoted much of their time to a defense of their efforts, although the available numbers indicate that Oklahoma City prompted a great increase in militia membership. Most of the militias, as noted earlier, have played down declarations of violence and played up the peaceful political, rather than terrorist, activities of their members. They've stressed the Second Amendment as a principal concern. They attack the media for what they say is a gross distortion of their aims and activities. As an example of the approach taken by most militias, the co-founder of the Montana militia, John Trochmann, told a survivalist convention that militias are essentially civil defense types of organizations that are guaranteed the right to bear arms under the Constitution. He attacked the media for not warning the American people of the United Nations' movement toward a one-world government and of its already having corrupted the world's banking systems. He stated that one of the strong critics of militias, the Anti-Defamation League of B'nai B'rith, was located in the same building as the UN (in fact, it is not.) He denied that the militias are white supremacists and even introduced an African-American, James Johnson, a former Ohio militia leader, who called Trochmann his mentor and said the militias were not racist, but dedicated only to the battle against an overbearing government and the world's elite who control it. Johnson said, "We don't preach overthrowing the government. We preach overhauling it." He also suggested, following the lead of many far-right leaders, that the government itself was behind the bombing of the federal building in Oklahoma City. He predicted that the government would stage a disaster at the Olympics (upcoming that year, 1996) in Atlanta so that United Nations troops in Atlanta could begin a takeover. "We've had one report from inside . . . that said Oklahoma gave you the anti-terrorism bill. Atlanta will give you martial law."[123]

Critics of the militias have taken different views, such as the ADL's Arthur Teitelman's statement that "most militia groups have a long and ugly history of mixing anti-government ideology with racism and anti-Semitism, and whenever you mix anti-government ideology, extremist rhetoric and the presence of guns, you have a dangerous and volatile mix."[124]

Some critics of the militias are concerned that the rise in memberships after Oklahoma City and the withdrawal from militias of some of the less extremist members has resulted—as stated by Sen. Carl Levin—in "the remnant [being] tighter, more fanatical and more dangerous."[125] Some state officials are concerned that the militias "have formed small, secret groups that operate independently to avoid detection and infiltration."[126] In Michigan, Wayne Country Sheriff Robert Ficano said: "What we're seeing is a real fringe element shake-out, clusters with a more extreme tendency toward violence."[127] McVeigh and Nichols, the two principals thus far in the Oklahoma City bombing, are alleged to have belonged to such secret militia cells, using encryption software on the Internet to communicate and organize. Crimes such as bank robberies, pipe bombings, assassinations of state troopers, and stealing of bomb ingredients, arms, and ammunition are frequently committed by persons who are traced to militia membership. Many critics of the militias believe that hard-line militants "are growing weary of doing the same old thing, and they're taking steps closer to the edge."[128]

Appendices to Chapter 2

Appendix 2A: Active Hate Groups in the U.S. in 1997

(from the *Intelligence Report*, Winter 1998; reprinted with permission of the Southern Poverty Law Center)

This list of active hate groups is based on information gathered by the Intelligence Project from hate groups' publications, citizens' reports, law enforcement agencies, field sources and news reports. Only organizations known to be active in 1997, whether that activity included marches, rallies, speeches, meetings, leafletting, publishing literature or criminal acts, were counted in the listing. Entities that appear to exist only in cyberspace are not included because they are likely to be individual web publishers who like to portray themselves as powerful, organized groups. This year, to provide more information, the list has been expanded to include all known chapters of hate organizations (the first listing in multi-chapter groups is the headquarters chapter, if that information is known).

Groups are categorized as Klan, Neo-Nazi, Skinhead, Christian Identity, Black Separatist and Other. Only racist Skinhead groups are included in the Skinhead tally. Because Skinheads are migratory and often not affiliated with groups, this listing understates their numbers. Christian Identity describes a religion that is fundamentally racist and anti-Semitic. Black separatist groups, a new category, describe organizations whose ideologies include tenets of racially based hatred. The "other" category includes groups and publishing houses endorsing a hodgepodge of hate doctrines.

A map on pages 30–31 indicates the location of groups and chapters. For further information, please contact the Intelligence Project.

KU KLUX KLAN

Alabama White Knights of the Ku Klux Klan
Semmes, AL
Little River, AL

America's Invisible Empire Knights of the Ku Klux Klan
Hartselle, AL
Cottonwood, AL
Crane Hill, AL
Cullman, AL

Bayou Patriots Knights of the Ku Klux Klan
Choudrant, LA
McDavid, FL

Bedford Forrest Brigade
Gainesville, FL

Bell Kounty Koon Klub
Bell County, KY

Christian Knights of the Ku Klux Klan
Mt. Holly, NC
Chicago, IL
Calvert City, KY
Decatur, IL

International Keystone Knights of the Ku Klux Klan
Johnstown, PA
Davie, FL
Bechtelsville, PA
Walston, PA
Enoree, SC
Laurens, SC

Invincible Empire Knights of the Ku Klux Klan
Wood River, IL
North Salem, IN
Louisville, KY
Iota, LA
Hyannis, MA
Hudson, MI
Waters, MI
New York, NY
Columbus, OH
Niles, OH
Porter, OK
Grants Pass, OR

New Order Knights of the Ku Klux Klan
Overland, MO
Garden Grove, CA

North Georgia White Knights of the Ku Klux Klan
Rossville, GA

Northwest Knights of the Ku Klux Klan
Tacoma, WA
Coeur D'Alene, ID
Great Falls, MT

Rome, GA

Alexandria, LA

Tulsa, OK

American Knights of the Ku Klux Klan

Butler, IN

Denver, CO

Bear, DE

Bradenton, FL

Rantoul, IL

Baltimore, MD

Bear, MD

Rising Sun, MD

Timonium, MD

Denton, NC

Elkin, NC

Pilot Mountain, NC

Mt. Sinai, NY

East Liverpool, OH

Wooster, OH

Pittsburgh, PA

Odessa, TX

Mercer, WI

Aryan Christian Knights of the Ku Klux Klan

Browns Summit, NC

Aryan White Knights

Jasper, AL

Louisa, KY

Charlotte, NC

Beaufort, SC

West Columbia, SC

Christian White Knights of the Ku Klux Klan

Gainesville, GA

Chesterfield, VA

Confederate Independent Klansmen

Holder, FL

Confederate Knights of the Ku Klux Klan

Henderson, NC

Lexington, KY

Forest, VA

Sandston, VA

Confederate White Knights

Clanton, AL

Covenant Knights

Jacksonville, FL

Florida Black Knights of the Ku Klux Klan

Micanopy, FL

Green Mountain Knights

Poultney, VT

Imperial Klans of America

Powderly, KY

Rocky Ridge, MD

Chambersburg, PA

Invincible Realm Knights of the Ku Klux Klan

Lakeland, FL

Invisible Empire, Pennsylvania Ku Klux Klan

Punxsutawney, PA

JWS Militant Knights

Valley Head, AL

Klay Kounty Klavern

Grandin, FL

Knights of the Apocalypse

Valrico, FL

Knights of the Forest

Silver Springs, FL

Knights of the Ku Klux Klan (Thom Robb's group)

Harrison, AR

St. Louis, MO

Waco, TX

Seattle, WA

Knights of the Ku Klux Klan (offshoot group)

Humansville, MO

Newport Beach, CA

Redan, GA

Hudson, FL

Falmouth, VA

Knights of the Ku Klux Klan

Kathleen, FL

Knights of the Ku Klux Klan

New Port Richey, FL

Knights of the Ku Klux Klan

Salina, KS

Knights of the Ku Klux Klan

Lodi, OH

Knights of the White Kamellia

Lafayette, LA

Winter Springs, FL

Arcadia, LA

Meraux, LA

Pine Prairie, LA

Ville Platte, LA

Howell, MI

Austin, TX

Canyon Lake, TX

Mauriceville, TX

Chesterfield, VA

Grafton, WV

Missouri Federation of Klans, Inc.

St. Louis, MO

National Knights of the Ku Klux Klan

South Bend, IN

Order of the Ku Klux Klan

Rockville, IN

California

Rangers of the Cross

Deland, FL

Royal Knights of the Ku Klux Klan

Deltona, FL

Southern Cross Militant Knights

Valley Head, AL

Southern Knights of the Ku Klux Klan

Monticello, FL

Templar Knights of the Ku Klux Klan

Port St. Lucie, FL

Tri-County White Knights of the Ku Klux Klan

Mt. Grove, MO

Tristate Knight Riders of the Ku Klux Klan

Florence, KY

True Knights of the Ku Klux Klan

Boyd, TX

US Klans Knights of the Ku Klux Klan

Camden, TN

(continued)

Appendix 2A (continued)

United Knights of the Ku Klux Klan
Fort Worth, TX
White Camellia Knights of the Ku Klux Klan
Cleveland, TX
White Shield Knights of the Ku Klux Klan
Parkersburg, WV
Winder Knights
Winder, GA

NEO-NAZI

Adolf Hitler Free Corps
Kirkwood, PA
American National Socialist Resistance
Bellevue, IL
Aryan Free Press
Champaign, IL
Aryan Nations/Church of Jesus Christ Christian
Hayden Lake, ID
Mesa, AZ
Jerome, ID
Orland Park, IL
Pekin, IL
Rock Island, IL

Hagerstown, MD
Midland, MI
Charlotte, NC
Elon College, NC
Raleigh, NC
Siler City, NC
Hewitt, NJ
Reno, NV
Bronx, NY
Dayton, OH
Parma, OH
Philadelphia, PA
Reading, PA
Austin, TX
Fort Worth, TX
National Socialist German Workers Party
Lincoln, NE
National Socialist Irish Workers Party
Bethlehem, PA
National Socialist Movement
Minneapolis, MN
National Socialist Resistance
Lake Worth, FL
National Socialist Vanguard
The Dalles, OR
National Socialist White Peoples Party

Redondo Beach, CA
Davie, FL
Ft. Lauderdale, FL
Ormond Beach, FL
West Palm Beach, FL
Chicago, IL
Peoria, IL
Rantoul, IL
Springfield, IL
Evansville, IN
Billerica, MA
Baltimore, MD
Detroit, MI
Raymond, MS
Missoula, MT
Superior, MT
Reno, NV
Binghamton, NY
Cortland, NY
Ohio
Pittsburgh, PA
Austin, TX
Salt Lake City, UT
Bremerton, WA
Sumas, WA
Tacoma, WA
Franklin, WI
Milwaukee, WI

Eastern Hammer Skins
York, PA
Fourth Reich Skins
Phoenix, AZ
Tucson, AZ
Springfield, MO
Future Fighters
Acworth, GA
Lebensbaum Project
Birmingham, AL
Master Players/All-American Boys
Rochester, MN
National Party
Los Angeles, CA
Northern Hammer Skins
Des Plaines, IL
Naperville, IL
Guilford, IN
St. Paul, MN
St. Louis, MO
Portland, OR
Hartland, WI
Oi Boys
Kenosha, WI
Peckerwoods
Antelope Valley, CA
Reich Skins
Orange County, CA

Association of the Covenant People
Ferndale, WA
Buckeye Educational Forum
Solon, OH
Christ and Country Church
Baltimore, MD
Christ's Gospel Fellowship
Spokane, WA
Christian Bible Ministries
Christiansburg, VA
Christian Conservative Churches of America
Flora, IL
Christian Crusade for Truth
Deming, NM
Christian Guard
East Ridge, TN
Christian Israel Church
Wayne, WV
Christian Israel Covenant Church
Colville, WA
Christian Research
Eureka Springs, AR
Christian Separatist Church Society
Kodak, TN
Christian Soldiers

Picayune, MS
Lexington, NC
Cincinnati, OH
New Vienna, OH
Medford, OR
Merlin, OR
Ripley, TN
Christian Defense League
Arabi, LA
Church of the Avenger
Tampa, FL
Euro-American Alliance
Milwaukee, WI
European American Educational Association
Eastpointe, MI
Fascist Action Group
Boca Raton, FL
German American Nationalist PAC
Pensacola, FL
National Alliance
Hillsboro, WV
Alleghany, CA
Pomona, CA
Orlando, FL
Tampa, FL
Arlington Heights, IL
Baltimore, MD

Charleston, SC
Palmetto, GA
Indianapolis, IN
Simpsonville, KY
Hyannis, MA
Collinsville, MS
Chapel Hill, NC
Toledo, OH
Portland, OR
Kirkwood, PA
San Angelo, TX
New Order
Milwaukee, WI
SS Enterprises
Fresno, CA
Volksfront
Portland, OR
Salem, OR
White Aryan Resistance
Fallbrook, CA
Catoosa, OK
White House Network
Harrisburg, PA
World Church of the Creator
Murphysboro, IL
Auburn, CA
Carmichael, CA
Monrovia, CA
Napa, CA

SKINHEADS

American Front
Portland, OR
San Diego, CA
Pittsburgh, PA
West Newton, PA
Arizona Hammer Skins
Phoenix, AZ
Army of Israel
St. George, UT
Aryan National Front
Prattville, AL
Aryan Reich Skins
Idaho
Bound For Glory
St. Paul, MN
Center Lane Skins
Levittown, NY
Clarksville Area Skinheads
Clarksville, TN
Confederate Hammer Skins
St. Petersburg, FL
Conflagration
Albany, NY
Corps
Tucson, AZ
Denver Skins
Denver, CO

Salt City Skinheads
Hutchinson, KS
South Side Skinheads
Chicago, IL
SS Boot Boys
San Francisco, CA
Texas Aryan Nationalist Skinheads
Baytown, TX
Tri-State Terror
Stroudsburg, PA
Waynesville Area Skinheads
Waynesville, MO
Western Hammer Skins
California
White Power Kids
Chicago, IL
White Survival
Springfield, MO

IDENTITY

America's Promise Ministries
Sandpoint, ID
Artisan Sales
Muskogee, OK
Aryan Nations/Church of Jesus Christ Christian
(See neo-Nazi listing)

South Dakota
Christians for Truth
Shawano, WI
Church of Christ in Israel
Munising, MI
Church of God
Anadarko, OK
Church of Israel
Schell City, MO
Church of Jesus Christ Christian
Harrison, AR
Church of True Israel
Polson, MT
Covenant Church of Our Redeemer
Monarch Beach, CA
Crusade for Christ
Little Rock, AR
Cyrus Ministries
Garland, TX
Destiny Publishers
Merrimac, MA
Destiny Research Foundation
Salem, OH
Elohim City
Muldrow, OK
Faith Baptist Church and Ministry
Houston, MO

(continued)

Appendix 2A (*continued*)

Fellowship of God's Covenant People
Burlington, KY
Gabriel's Enterprises
Albert Lea, MN
God's Remnant Church
Boring, OR
Gospel Broadcasting Association
Houston, TX
Gospel Foundation
Coarsegold, CA
Gospel of Christ Kingdom Church
Hayden, ID
Gospel of the Kingdom Mission
El Cajon, CA
Gospel Ministries
Boise, ID
Identity Christian Fellowship
Collinsville, IL
Identity Study Group
Franklin, IN
Israel Bible Society
Kenner, LA
JHM Baptist/Identity Church
Apple Valley, CA

Noah's Books
Lakeview, MO
Northpoint Tactical Teams
Topton, NC
Old Order Israelite Brethren
Mountain View, AR
Order of St. Michael
Las Vegas, NV
Our Savior's Church
Webster Point, AK
Gainesville, MO
Outreach
Worthville, KY
Proclaim Liberty Ministry
Adrian, MI
Remnant of Israel
Opportunity, WA
Restoration Bible Church
Berkley, MI
Restoration Bible Ministries, Inc.
Royal Oak, MI
Revelation Books
Staunton, VA
Sacred Truth Ministries
Mountain City, TN
Scriptures of America Ministries/Laporte Church of Christ

Your Heritage
San Diego, CA

BLACK SEPARATIST

House of David
Inglewood, CA
Atlanta, GA
Brockton, MA
New Bedford, MA
New York, NY
Nation of Islam
Chicago, IL
Los Angeles, CA
Miami, FL
Atlanta, GA
Boston, MA
Durham, NC
Philadelphia, PA

OTHER

14 Word Press
St. Maries, ID
ALPHA
Pennyslvania
America First Committee
Birmingham, AL
America First Party

National Association for the Advancement of White People
New Orleans, LA
Ardmore, AL
Selma, AL
Harrison, AR
Texarkana, AR
Meyer, AZ
Loyalton, CA
Torrance, CA
West Haven, CT
Atlantic Beach, FL
Avon Park, FL
Callahan, FL
Clay County, FL
Crescent City, FL
Eagle Lake, FL
Fort Lauderdale, FL
Gainesville, FL
Hilliard, FL
Hudson, FL
Jacksonville, FL
St. Petersburg, FL
Tampa, FL
Winter Haven, FL
Conyers, GA
Hogansville, GA
Honolulu, HI
Mocksville, NC
Omaha, NE
Gloucester City, NJ
Milford, NJ
Webster, NY
Brookfield, OH
Dayton, OH
Grove City, OH
Miamisburg, OH
Reynoldsburg, OH
Hellam, PA
Philadelphia, PA
Conestee, SC
Cross Anchor, SC
Darlington, SC
Murfreesboro, TN
Nashville, TN
Arlington, TX
Houston, TX
Colonial Heights, VA
Richmond, VA
Sandston, VA
Seattle, WA
Vienna, WV
Nationalist Forum
Los Angeles, CA
Nationalist Movement
Learned, MS
Occidental Pan-Aryan

Jubilee
Midpines, CA
Keys to the Kingdom Church
St. Augustine, FL
Kingdom Identity Ministries
Harrison, AR
Kingdom Ministry
Lawrenceville, GA
Land of Peace
Prattville, AL
Lord's Work
Austin, KY
Melchizedek Vigilance
Denver, CO
Ministry of Christ Church
Mariposa, CA
Mission to Israel
Scottsbluff, NE
Mystery of the Kingdom Ministry
Wausau, WI
New Beginnings
Waynesville, NC
New Christian Crusade Church
Metairie, LA
New Harmony Christian Crusade
Midpines, CA

Laporte, CO
Shepherd's Chapel
Sebring, FL
Solid Rock Bible Church
Smithville, OK
Son Light
Kearney, MO
Spiral Path Learning Center/Vision 20/20
Eclectic, AL
Spirit Ministry
Anchorage, AK
Stone Kingdom Ministries
Asheville, NC
Unifier
Olathe, KS
Verity
Markleeville, CA
Virginia Christian Israelites
Round Hill, VA
Virginia Publishing Company
Lynchburg, VA
Voice of Liberty
Decatur, GA
Wisconsin Church of Israel
Appleton, WI
Word of Christ Mission
Damon, TX

Palm Beach, FL
American Revolutionary Nationalist Nuclei
California
Army of God
Georgia
Aryan Book Center
Decatur, IL
Aryan Circle
Albermarle, NC
Carnegie, OK
Aryan Pride
Eugene, OR
Blood Bond
Waters, MI
CAUSE Foundation
Black Mountain, NC
Celtic Cross Press
Fort Lee, NJ
Confederate Society of America
Cincinnati, OH
Crusade Against Corruption
Marietta, GA
Day of the Rope Productions
Berlin, NJ
Fuknig
San Jose, CA
MSR Productions
Wheat Ridge, CO

Columbia, IL
Marissa, IL
Peoria, IL
Clarksville, IN
Shelby, IN
Paducah, KY
Belle Chasse, LA
Gretna, LA
Jena, LA
Pearl River, LA
Shreveport, LA
Slaughter, LA
Violet, LA
Sudbury, MA
Accokeek, MD
Dearborn Heights, MI
Garden City, MI
St. Paul, MN
Springfield, MO
Brookhaven, MS
Escatawpa, MS
Hazelhurst, MS
McComb, MS
Oxford, MS
Petal, MS
Philadelphia, MS
Sontag, MS
Union Church, MS
Booneville, NC

Crusader
Richmond, VA
Resistance Records
Detroit, MI
Separatist's Circle
Jackson, TN
Southern National Party
Memphis, TN
Sunset White Boys
San Francisco, CA
Truth At Last
Marietta, GA
United Southern Aryans
Bossier City, LA
Westboro Baptist Church
Topeka, KS
White Liberation Message Line
Mobile, AL
White Power
Gilbert, AZ
White Power
Marrero, LA
Wolf Pack
Minneapolis, MN
Wolf Pack Services
St. Paul, MN

Appendix 2B: Direct Mail Solicitation from the
Democratic Senatorial Campaign Committee

JAMES CARVILLE

Dear Mr Hilliard,

I like to think of myself as a warm and caring human
being.

But there are certain individuals -- mainly of the hard-
core right-wing Republican persuasion -- who think otherwise.

Those folks will tell you that I am a really bad guy...a pit
bull partisan and maybe even the devil's spawn -- and that's
when they are feeling charitable.

But there's one thing I know...these people scare me to
death.

And I think that you have good reason these days to be
every bit as scared as I am about what these right-wing
Republicans are doing to this country.

To illustrate, I am enclosing a map of the United States.
Please take a look at it.

The map shows in detail the extent to which a tightly-
organized and lavishly-financed right-wing group called the
Christian Coalition has taken control of the Republican Party.

Believe me -- that's frightening.

According to Pat Robertson, who is the Christian Coalition's founder and funder, that radical group now has major-to-decisive influence on the Republican Party in thirty-one states.

In eighteen of those states, says Robertson, the Christian Coalition is "dominant" within the GOP. And believe you me -- when Pat Robertson says "dominant," he means <u>dominant</u>.

In another thirteen states, the Coalition's influence on the Party is what Robertson calls "substantial." ("Substantial," the dictionary tells us, means "ample...of real worth or value.")

And the Christian Coalitionists are not standing still.

"We are only a portion of the way there," Robertson proclaims. "We must complete the job in all fifty states."

Now, what does it mean to "complete the job?"

For starters, it means eliminating what tiny little bit is left of the "moderate" wing of the Republican Party.

Mostly, that's been accomplished. If you look at the Republicans in the U.S. Senate -- now <u>there's</u> an un-pretty sight -- you will plainly see that many of them are so far out on the goofy right that a reasonable Republican like Dwight Eisenhower simply wouldn't be able to recognize today's GOP.

What you have now are prominent Republican Senators who sound like members of the Idaho militia.

But let's face it.

You and I know that when that hard right-wing crowd go after the so-called "moderate" Republicans, they're just practicing -- sharpening their teeth -- enjoying, perhaps, an <u>hors d' oeuvre</u>.

The right-wing extremist groups know full well that their <u>real</u> fight is not with some margarine "moderates" in the GOP.

It's with us -- the Democrats.

We're the folks who stand between these ambitious preacher-politicians and the political power they crave.

They want to sweep us out of the way. And even as you read this letter, that's exactly what they're trying to do.

What can we do about it?

We can -- and with the greatest urgency I hope that we Democrats will -- do the right thing, and that, of course, is giving our maximum support to the vital work of the Democratic Senatorial Campaign Committee.

Just think about it for a moment...think what's at stake.

1998 is an election year -- a critical one.

In November of this year, the Republicans and their ferocious right-wing allies are hoping to win for themselves the ultimate prize -- a filibuster-proof majority in the U.S. Senate.

If they succeed, Trent Lott, Phil Gramm and Jesse Helms will have the whip hand.

They will be in a position to enact whatever they want to enact -- and to repeal whatever they want to repeal.

They will be able to declare "dead-on-arrival" the program that President Clinton spelled out for the country in his State of the Union Address.

And most disturbing of all, the Senate Republicans will be in a position to pay off, with interest, the enormous political debt they owe to the religious right-wing.

Just think what that would mean for the separation of church and state...for a woman's right to choose...for public education.

These right-wingers mean business.

And whatever else we may want to say about them -- and I can think of plenty -- the fact is that these guys know a thing or two abut playing political hardball.

In 1998, the right-wing will go all out to strengthen their Senate power base.

They'll promise tax cuts. They'll denounce so-called "big government." And only later will we discover that the tax breaks are for the rich and that in GOP-speak, "big government" means Medicare, Social Security, school loans and environmental protection.

This time we've got to be ready for them.

What's their strategy?

We know for sure that at the top of every right-wing "hit list for 1998" are the names of three pro-choice Democratic women -- Senators Barbara Boxer of California, Carol Moseley-Braun of Illinois and Patty Murray of Washington.

We also know that they will pour their resources into defending arch conservative Republican incumbents like Lauch Faircloth of North Carolina (a Jesse Helms clone) and Alfonse D'Amato of New York (the man who daily gives new meaning to the word "chutzpah.")

All over the country in 1998, the far right groups will work -- and work some more -- to defeat our Democratic candidates for the U.S. Senate.

They will work to elect every Republican.

And unless we stand up to them and give <u>our</u> candidates the support they need, the Christian Coalitionists will win. And they will do to the country what they have already done to the Republican Party.

That is why I appeal to you today.

The Democratic Senatorial Campaign Committee, which is the major source of support for Democratic Senate candidates, urgently needs your help.

As we head into this crucial campaign season, we <u>know</u> that the Republicans will outspend us.

We know, too, that the Christian Coalition and the other right-wing groups will do everything they can to savage our Democratic candidates for the Senate.

But the fact is that we <u>can</u> fight back. We <u>can</u> win. And we <u>can</u> elect a Democratic Senate majority. <u>The polls show that in every section of our country today, a major Democratic trend is under way</u>.

That's good. But I myself would prefer a Democratic WAVE.

If you agree, please sit down right now and write to the DSCC the most generous check you can afford -- $500, if you can, or $100, $50, or even $35.

We can do this. Together, we <u>shall</u> prevail.

Sincerely,

James Carville

P.S.   A couple of years ago, I wrote a book called, <u>We're Right, They're Wrong</u>. This is what I said about the Republican right-wing: "If progressivism folds we will not have any right to go pointing fingers at the Republican Party...We will have only ourselves to blame. It will be our fault, and ours alone. It will mean that we were mute when we should have been defending what we believe."

These words are still true today.

So I have one last thing to say about how important it is for you to support the DSCC. Get moving! No one's going to do it for us.

Chapter 3

Lions of the Arena

Then he will talk, good God, how he will talk.

—Nathaniel Lee

As noted at the beginning of the previous chapter, it is the right wing that most often and most effectively uses the airwaves to proclaim its message. And it is the right-wing center—the Rush Limbaughs—who have been most successful in convincing the American electorate that audiences' fears and the commentators' solutions are both correct.

The left wing uses the airwaves, too, but to a much lesser degree. Part of the reason is that the media—including radio, television, and cable—are controlled by those who, by the very nature of owning stations or systems, are generally fairly wealthy, with status and power in their communities. Understandably, they believe that the status quo is the best of all possible worlds. The Democrats are perceived—not incorrectly, given the historical patterns of policy and legislation—as wanting to change the social and economic structure in such a way that more of the resources and power within small and larger communities would flow to the general public and away from the powerful and wealthy. The Republicans—also not incorrectly, given their legislative history—support policies that strengthen the rich and powerful, usually at the expense of the poor and middle class. Therefore, media outlets are more open to right-wing than to left-wing talk shows and personalities.

With the passage of the Telecommunications Act of 1996, Congress and the president made it more possible for the media conglomerates to own even more and more broadcast stations, by eliminating the antimonopoly multiple ownership rules that for a half-century had attempted to provide a diversity of ownership and opinion on the airwaves. Those who favor the status quo and support conservative and, in many cases, right-wing causes now have greater opportunity to influence American beliefs and policies. For example, Jacor Communications in Cincinnati, previously not in the same league with Westwood One and other groups that owned literally hundreds of radio stations, acquired a network of 140 stations along with EFM Media Management, which syndicates

86

Rush Limbaugh's programs, gaining the ability to distribute Limbaugh's views through "a vast national distribution arm."[1]

Whoever uses the airwaves has found that the nonprint media are increasingly more powerful in reaching and influencing the public. In the 1990s it was estimated that the average American read for a total of thirty minutes each day—and that time length included the back of the cereal box at breakfast. As stated earlier, the average television set is on approximately thirty hours per week, and the average radio is on about the same length of time. While the growth of Internet use has been advancing too fast to permit accurate measurement, those who have online computers are spending an increasing number of hours per individual on the Internet, sending and receiving materials via e-mail, chat rooms, and Web sites. In 1998 the U.S. government estimated that traffic on the Internet was doubling every hundred days, with some 70 million Americans using the global cyberspace network. The government report noted that the Internet was growing faster than all previous communication technologies have. It was just four years after the availability of the Internet that it had 50 million users, while it was thirty-eight years after radio came on the scene that it had that many listeners, and it took television thirteen years to get that many viewers.[2] Some estimates indicate that by the year 2000 some 350 million people worldwide will have access to the Internet.

With all these communications outlets available and the increasing purchase of equipment by the public, the number of groups—mainly right-wing—using these outlets dramatically increases year by year. Some of the most significant identifiable types of groups using the airwaves are spread throughout Chip Berlet's categories noted in chapter 2, including right-wing conservative radio talk shows; the general dissident voices heard on radio and the Internet, as exemplified in the National Alliance's programs entitled "American Dissident Voices," which claim to be "the only radio programs for White ["W" capitalized] men and women worldwide";[3] and the religious right described as follows by Vincent Coppola: "Among Identity Christians, meekness is no virtue. Turning the other cheek is pure cowardice. In this religion, blacks and minorities are 'pre-Adamic' mud races . . . far-right groups like The Order, Posse Comitatus, Ku Klux Klan, skinheads, and an increasing number of militias have woven Identity 'truths' into their nightmare scenarios for America. Racial identity is the thread that ties disparate crazies together, that turns hatemongers into crusading zealots."[4]

While one might seek categories for the types of use made by the right wing of the airwaves, it should not be assumed that such use is organized by distinct ideological factions or specific member groups. Much of the right wing media use is by individuals. Obviously, the Internet offers the greatest opportunity for the one-person dissemination of rancor. Any individual can establish her or his Web site and, depending on the title and orientation that can be found in the various Internet directories, can have hundreds, thousands, and even millions of "hits" (the number of times a specific Web site is consulted) on any given day. It is much more difficult to obtain air time on the more traditional media—radio, television, and cable—unless the outlets are owned and/or operated by an individual or group sympathetic to the particular right-wing viewpoint being aired.

Despite the ownership and control of U.S. media largely by conservative or right-wing entities and individuals, most right-wing groups insist that they have been denied access to the airwaves because the media, they say, are owned by Jews. The National Alliance published on its Web site its analysis of media control, prepared by the staff of *National Vanguard Magazine,* a right-wing journal. The article, capsulizing the attitudes toward the media of most right-wing organizations, recognizes the importance of the media's role in right-wing outreach. "The mass media form for us our image of the world and then tell us what to think about that image," the article states. It is concerned with "the heavy-handed suppression of certain news stories" and the "blatant propagandizing of history-distorting 'docudramas'" of the "opinion-manipulating techniques of the media masters."[5] The article, using examples of news stories and entertainment programs, further states:

> Most Americans fail to realize they are being manipulated . . . all of the controlled media—television, radio, newspapers, magazines, books, motion pictures—speak with a single voice . . . [the people] are presented with a single view of the world—a world in which every voice proclaims the equality of the races, the errant nature of the Jewish 'Holocaust' tale, the wickedness of attempting to halt a flood of non-White aliens from pouring across our borders, the danger of permitting citizens to keep and bear arms, the moral equivalence of all sexual orientations, and the desirability of a "pluralistic" cosmopolitan society rather than a homogeneous one. It is a view of the world designed by the media masters to suit their own ends.[6]

The article discusses television, the entertainment industry, radio, newspapers, magazines, and books, naming past and current executives in these fields who, according to the article, are Jewish. It concludes in each case that each medium is controlled by Jews:

> The Jewish control of the American mass media is the single most important fact of life, not just in America, but in the whole world today. . . . . [B]y permitting the Jews to control our news and entertainment media we are doing more than merely giving them a decisive influence on our political system and virtual control of our government; we are also giv-

ing them control of the minds and souls of our children. . . . [T]he Jew-
controlled entertainment media have taken the lead in persuading a
whole generation that homosexuality is a normal and acceptable way of
life; that there is nothing at all wrong with White women dating or marrying Black men, or with White men marrying Asiatic women; that all
races are inherently equal in ability and character—except that the White
race is suspect because of a history of oppressing other races; and that
any effort by Whites at racial self-preservation is reprehensible. . . . [W]e
must oppose the further spreading of this poison among our people. . . .
[T]o permit the Jews, with their 3000–year history of nation-wrecking,
from ancient Egypt to Russia, to hold such power over us is tantamount
to race suicide. . . . [W]e must shrink from nothing in combating this evil
power.[7]

   This argument not only emphasizes the right wing's understanding and use
of the power of other media, but reinforces one of the key tenets of almost all
far-right thinking: anti-Semitism. The use of the media as a cohesive factor for
right-wing groups is emphasized by Michael Barkun in *The Christian Century*.
Noting the overlapping membership of right-wing organizations, with faction-
alism and internal conflicts sometimes resulting, Barkun states that "whatever
cohesion this [right-wing] world possesses comes from its alternative system of
communications. Mail-order book services, computer bulletin boards, gun
shows, Bible camps, pamphlets, periodicals and short-wave radio broadcasts
knit the far right together. . . . [T]hese media suggest that the dominant
worldview is fraudulent, that things are not as they seem, that only the chosen
few within the movement really know what is happening and why."[8]
   Those in the far-right movements seek what they believe is the only truth
through right-wing media. One example of such sources is a radio program
received through the Internet, "Truth Radio." One of its programs plugged the
sale of a report entitled "Premonitions of an American Holocaust": "America is
due for judgment, and judgment begins at the house of God . . . [this report]
outlines the plans that the rulers of the darkness of this age are designing for
Christians and the resisters of Satan's Plan of the Ages to enslave mankind.
Will you be destroyed for lack of knowledge. Get this report . . . from Truth
Radio Network."[9]
   Another example of the kinds of media used by right-wing groups is noted
in the movement's "The Banned Media and Organization List," which includes
the following sources under the heading of "Broadcast: Radio, TV, Cable,
Satellite": American Dissident Voices; Radio Free America (Sun Radio Net-
work); "Truth for the Times" sponsored by Scripture for America on radio,
television, and satellite; Voice of Freedom on radio and television; People's

Radio Network, broadcasting twenty-four hours a day, with a notation that "the best program is Chuck Harder's 'For the People' "; and the Patriot Network, broadcasting twenty-four hours a day, naming as the best program Bo Gritz's "Freedom Calls."[10]

William Pierce, leader of the far-right National Alliance, summed up the right-wing movement's increasing use of multimedia to achieve its purposes. He stated in his organization's journal *The National Vanguard* in 1994 that because government agents "are too many for us to assassinate, the only feasible strategy for us is to develop our own media of mass communication and then use these media to make everyone painfully aware of the true meaning of the New World Order . . . [and to] fan that response into a revolutionary conflagration. . . . [I]t's a case of either we destroy them or they destroy us. . . . [This] almost certainly will not be done without a full-fledged revolution and much attendant bloodshed and suffering. Nevertheless, it must be done; otherwise we lose the future, and everything becomes meaningless."[11]

Among the prime targets of the right-wing media in the 1990s are President Bill Clinton and Hillary Rodham Clinton. Both have expressed concern over the impact of far-right communications upon the public. The president said: "We hear so many loud and angry voices in America today whose sole goal seems to be to try to keep some people as paranoid as possible and the rest of us all torn up and upset with each other. They spread hate. They leave the impression that, by their very words, that violence is acceptable. . . . When they talk of hatred, we must stand against them. When they talk of violence, we must stand against them. When they say things that are irresponsible, that may have egregious consequences, we must call them on it. The exercise of their freedom of speech makes our silence all the more unforgivable."[12]

In a C-Span interview in 1997 Hillary Rodham Clinton expressed a point of view about the media diametrically opposite to that of right-wing critics. She stated that it was the "right-wing, conservative" media control that influenced overall news coverage and presented no balancing liberal views. "So much of what passes for political commentary," she said, "is either dead wrong or out of date tomorrow or personally or politically or commercially motivated . . . you've got a conservative and/or right-wing press presence with really nothing on the other end of the political spectrum."[13]

The issue of free speech, as noted by President Clinton, versus the propagation of hate and even harm, divides many traditional supporters of First Amendment rights. While the ACLU continues to protect the speech of even those far-right purveyors who would destroy the ACLU, some others who previously had allied themselves with the protection of civil liberties find themselves advocating suppression of what they consider "hate" speech. For example, one of the most blatant, and popular, right-wing radio personalities is Bob

Grant, whose WABC, New York, show was generally considered racist and inflammatory. Shortly after the Disney company bought the American Broadcasting Company, which included its flagship radio station, WABC, it fired Bob Grant for what was described as racially insensitive speech. The Reverend Al Sharpton, sometimes associated with anti-white racism, supported the firing, stating that "we support freedom of speech, but no one has the right to profit from hatred." He was joined by the Reverend Jesse Jackson, long considered a leading advocate of civil liberties as well as civil rights, who also called for the firing of the station's program director "because he's the man who produced hatred." Another African-American leader, Rep. Charles Rangel, took a different view: "I don't have any bad feelings about Grant being kicked off the air. He's an obsessive racist. But does this mean that at some point I can't say whatever the hell I want?"[14]

Some activists and people phoning call-in shows advocated the firing of other talk show hosts they considered offensive, including Rush Limbaugh, Howard Stern, Ed Koch, and Curtis Sliwa. Others, however, were concerned that the Grant firing and threats against other on-air personalities, right or left or center, could have a serious chilling effect on freedom of speech for all.[15] Grant, incidentally, was immediately picked up by another station and his outreach, if anything, grew.

AM and FM Radio

Most people think of traditional radio, AM and FM, as the key media for right-wing use, principally because the most well-known right-wing commentators among the general public, such as Rush Limbaugh, Oliver North, G. Gordon Liddy, and others with national reputations, are heard on the most popular radio stations. Some not as well known among the general public, but with loyal listening audiences regionally or locally, also appear on AM and FM radio stations. Because of FM's better sound quality, it has become virtually all music, catering to a younger, pop-music-oriented audience. AM has become largely news and talk, the carrier of most of the right-wing talk hosts. In point of fact, short-wave radio has surpassed traditional radio as the largest purveyor of right-wing programming, and the Internet may now well exceed both in terms of volume.

As Michael Barkun points out, the media have become a point of cohesion for right-wing groups with disparate beliefs and agendas, cutting across the moderate conservative stance to the radical right. At the Republican convention of 1996, for instance, Oliver North interviewed Gary Aldrich on the latter's book that viciously vilifies Clinton, and then had Steve Forbes as a guest on his show; Bob Grant interviewed right-winger Armstrong Williams and then talked with Henry Kissinger; throughout the convention Republicans made full use of the political spectrum of talk radio to get their views across to the public, with special emphasis on using Christian radio networks.[16]

Most of the right-wing radio shows, however, are not interested in the moderate representatives of the right. Rush Limbaugh, considered by the general public to be the epitome of right-wing radio, is considered a traitor to the cause by many who are much farther right. For example, Chuck Baker has a three-hour show that follows Rush Limbaugh on radio station KVOR in Colorado Springs. Baker does not speak about the conservative movement as Limbaugh does; he speaks about the Patriot movement establishing guerrilla units to take out the "slimeballs" in Congress. While Limbaugh and others like him advocate political action, Baker and others like him advocate militias taking violent action, such as killing Senator Howard Metzenbaum, who supported the Brady Bill on gun control. "Put the dirt on top of the box, and say, 'I'm pretty sure he's in there'" Baker advised. Baker also has said: "Am I advocating the overthrow of this government? . . . I'm advocating the cleansing . . . why are we sitting here?" He has also called for an "armed revolution." As already observed, the point is that talk show personalities such as Baker are not the exception in right-wing radio, but more the norm. Baker, in 1997, was still a member of the advisory board of the National Association of Radio Talk Show Hosts.[17]

Some right-wing talk show hosts are carried by the larger radio networks, a number of them covering virtually the entire country. Some radio stations that feature right-wing talk shows are not part of a network, but are powerful enough (50,000 watts) to cover entire regions of the country. AM stations have even greater coverage after dusk, when the atmosphere makes it possible for an AM signal (unlike an FM signal, which radiates from point-to-point in a direct line) to "bounce" off the atmospheric layers and extend a thousand miles or more.

Many local stations provide highly cooperative outlets for right-wing radio, ranging from the Christian religious right to Limbaugh conservatism to far-right radical advocacy. As a case in point, in 1997 the *New Orleans Times-Pic-ayune* surveyed the orientation of New Orleans' seventeen radio stations. It described two as extremist stations, three more as Christian music stations with moderate to extremist talk show hosts, and four others as Christian radio with varying formats.[18]

Here are some examples of far-right syndicated talk shows representing Patriot groups, heard nationwide on AM and FM stations, with some of the stations that carry them: "The Jubilee" NewsLight program on KCCA-AM, Arizona, KDNO-FM, Delano, California, and WJYM-AM, Bowling Green, Ohio; anti-government host Bob Mohan's show on KFYI-AM, Phoenix; the home of the U.S. Patriot Network, KHNC-AM, Johnstown, Colorado; ardent militia supporter Chuck Baker's talk show on KVOR-AM, Colorado Springs; Identity and militia leader Mark Reynolds' "Love of Truth" on KCVL-AM, Colville, Washington; Pete Peters' "Truth for the Times" on WJCR-FM, Upton, Kansas; and Bo Gritz's program on WMKT-FM, Charlevoix, Michigan.[19]

One extremist group asks its followers on its Web site: "Would you like us to speak on your local talk radio show?" It goes on to say that "talk radio is one of the fastest and most effective ways of waking up large numbers of our fellow-citizens to the truth!" It notes talks on "the New World order, the elite's plans for global government, the draconian Wildlands Project, the attack on property rights, the link between environmentalism and the NWO, and the coming global famine" on talk shows on KGNW–Seattle, WOAI–San Francisco, KVET–Austin, Radio Liberty–California, WKDR–Vermont, KFAY–Arkansas, KKEY–Seattle, the Jeff Baker syndicated report, Jim Quinn's "Warroom," the Dan Gregory Show in Florida, Jeff Rence's "End of the Line" network program, and the Derry Brownsfield 110–station network. The Web site goes on to say: "If you are a radio talk show host and you'd like to introduce these current and critical topics to your listening audience, call us or fax us at the numbers listed above. . . . [W]e'll be glad to provide you with a knowledgeable and interesting interviewee. Or if you're an informed listener and you'd like to suggest that your favorite talk-show host call us, we'd be glad to work with him or her on this."[20]

The impact of these far-right talk shows continues to be debated. Although there have been many links of violent acts to the rhetoric and encouragement of right-wing radio, most radio hosts say that "talk radio does not lead, it follows."[21] Did talk radio contribute to the bombing of the Murrah federal building in Oklahoma City? Was talk radio responsible for the torching of dozens of churches in the south in the mid-1990s? Rev. Alfred Baldwin, the pastor of First Missionary Baptist Church in Enid, Oklahoma, which was burned down in 1996, said: "Whenever you have individuals sending out hate messages on radio and TV, somebody at the very bottom rung will take that as encouragement to do evil."[22] And the assistant U.S. attorney general for civil rights, Deval Patrick, said that conservative talk radio was an important factor in creating an atmosphere conducive to abhorrent behavior such as arson and bombing.[23] As Dusty Saunders, broadcasting critic of the Denver *Rocky Mountain News*, asked: "Where would bigots, often describing themselves as Christians, vent their hatred if talk shows didn't exist?"[24]

And as Al Brumley wrote in the *Dallas Morning News*, "Talk radio is clearly an important outlet for millions of people who feel left out of the process and are angry because of it. Many of these people believe that talk-show hosts are their only trustworthy news sources."[25]

Many politically oriented program purveyors seek out offshoots of the traditional media because of the lack of sufficient numbers of available stations, due in part to the fact that most of them are commercial enterprises dependent on advertising for their continued existence, thus relying on high-audience entertainment programs for their higher ad revenues. Where right-wing talk shows do attract such large audiences, they stay on the air. Where they do not, alternative outlets are sought. In some communities the extremism of some proposed programs discourages stations from airing them. In other communities the anger of the majority of the citizens at the hate and divisiveness of such programs makes it unwise and dangerous for the right-wing purveyors to live and broadcast in the given community, and they seek out alternative stations or media in other communities as their dissemination base.

Right-wing groups have gravitated over the years to so-called alternative media, in part because access to mainstream media is virtually impossible for any nonmainstream organization, and in part because the alternative media, by their very nature, espouse an aura of secretiveness, conspiracy, independence, dissidence, protest, and even subversion.

Chip Berlet stated in an interview with Grant Kester that "the electronic media have attracted the full range from conservatives to the far right." He noted that in addition to radio, the Internet, and short-wave, radio signals can be received through satellite dishes at home.[26] In a chapter entitled "Right-Wing Alternative Information Networks," prepared for an anthology titled *Who's Mediating the Storm?* Berlet noted that although some right-wing programs have mainstream distribution, such as Rush Limbaugh on radio and Pat Robertson's "700 Club" on cable television, "the vast majority of right-wing media ... seldom step from behind the curtain into the spotlight of mass culture."[27]

Shortwave Radio

Shortwave radio has been a significant outlet for right-wing individuals and groups. Shortwave radio has been around a long time—even before the first regularly scheduled radio station went on the air in 1920. Radio developed largely through the efforts of experimental operators or, as they later became to be known, "hams," who built and ran their own transmitters. Shortwave or ham radio was originally conceived as a person-to-person means of transmission internationally, and for emergency and safety purposes domestically. Shortwave operates on frequencies that cannot be accessed by regular AM and FM receivers. Shortwave stations are private—that is, operated by an individual who has received a license from the Federal Communications Commission. *VISTA,* the newsletter of Radio For Peace International, describes the current shortwave radio scene as follows:

> Historically, private U.S. short-wave broadcasters have had a long
> tradition of transmitting missionary style programming. The basic idea of

this programming is to convert some impoverished individual, possibly an indigenous person, with a simple short-wave receiver, living in a remote region. While the damage done by this conversion of indigenous cultures worldwide has long been debated, what we are witnessing today is the emergence of a different kind of programming altogether. Whereas as in the past U.S. private stations targeted remote areas, or Eastern bloc countries, today's far-right/hate broadcasts are aimed at listenership within the U.S. itself. Toll-free call-in shows are widely used as well as toll-free order lines for selling books, subscriptions, newsletters, and memberships. Unlike the missionary broadcasts of the past that used an assortment of languages, today's far-right programs are for the most part in English. It is clear that these far-right broadcasts are for U.S. domestic use.[28]

Shortwave radio has become identified with many right-wing extremist groups in the United States, including the militia movement and the Christian Right.[29] The cost of buying time on powerful right-wing shortwave stations such as the 100,000–watt WWCR (World Wide Christian Radio), Nashville, and substantial if less powerful stations such as WRNO in New Orleans and WINB in Red Lion, Pennsylvania, is only about $150 for a half-hour. That makes it possible for any individual, even from their home, to broadcast a program with an extensive reach and listenership, via a cassette tape, a satellite patch, or a telephone link. A good digital receiver costs about $200 and gives the listener access to shortwave stations throughout the world.[30] Even a $30 or $40 shortwave radio from Radio Shack makes it possible for anyone to pick up most worldwide shortwave broadcasts, including the many right-wing stations in the U.S. directed at U.S. listeners.

Many shortwave radio stations are operated by individuals as well as by groups. The cost of building and operating a shortwave radio station can be as low as a few thousand dollars, using second-hand equipment and requiring no staff. Many shortwave stations, including some that have developed national and worldwide exposure for their content and for their on-air personalities, operate out of a spare room in individual homes or apartments.

Shortwave talk radio has been described as "low-tech, but it serves much the same function as other alternative avenues of information such as the Internet, or even Court TV and C-Span, which, compared to the slicker, more packaged offerings of the traditional networks, give viewers a sort of unfiltered, as-it-happens sense of events."[31] As one listener put it, "I tune in to shortwave radio to get alternative information. . . . I feel like the mainstream media holds back things."[32]

One of the most important influences on the right wing's use of shortwave radio was "Radio Free America," a 1990 talk show sponsored by Willis Carto's

Liberty Lobby and hosted by Tom Valentine. Through this medium they very effectively spread Holocaust revisionism, conspiracy theories, and racism. The use of shortwave for recruiting and organizing has been a major factor in the growth of the Patriot movement, including the militias, in the 1990s. "Leaders learned from Willis Carto's experience that with one program on one station which broadcasts nationwide, they can reach all of their potential supporters without arousing the attention of the community. One can now hear programs about 'racialism,' militancy, and/or 'conspiratology' nearly 24 hours a day."[33] James Latham, cofounder of Radio For Peace International, reinforced this view: "Racist organizations find short-wave to work well for them. As their supporters are not concentrated within any one geographic area, AM/FM stations don't reach their disparate constituencies effectively. When one station can cover most of the country, however, the number of supporters they can reach is quite significant."[34] Latham has also stated that hate groups have used shortwave radio because it would be easier for angry communities and the Federal Communications Commission to find them if they were more easily locatable using AM/FM stations.[35] Latham also noted the cost factor. A program can be produced on a regular basis for an investment of about $1,000 in equipment, and air time can be bought for between $100 and $250 an hour on shortwave radio, reaching some 17 million shortwave radio receivers in the U.S. and more than 600 throughout the world.[36]

Latham clarified who makes most effective use of shortwave radio: "We're not talking about the Rush Limbaughs or Gordon Liddys. We're talking about the whole spectrum of the extreme far right—elements of the militia, neo-Nazis, John Birch Society, Ku Klux Klan, Posse Comitatus, Christian Identity, various White Aryan Nation people, survivalists and conspiracy theorists."[37]

The impact of shortwave radio on the far and extremist right is exemplified by the fact that it is a constant companion of the hard core. Timothy McVeigh was an avid listener, especially to William Cooper's "The Hour of the Time." He is not allowed a shortwave receiver in his prison cell, so he tunes in to two other favorites on the standard radio he is permitted, G. Gordon Liddy and Chuck Harder. Linda Thompson had been an avid shortwave listener; Cooper was also one of her favorites. When Commander Norm Olson of the Michigan Militia was interviewed on "60 Minutes," prominently displayed on a shelf in his gun shop was a shortwave receiver. The militias recommend a shortwave radio as an essential part of one's survival gear. James Latham has said, shortwave radio is an "umbilical cord to the brainwashing hatred of the Far Right leadership."[38]

Some of the specific shortwave radio right-wing programs and personalities indicate not only right-wing content but desired impact. Pastor Pete Peters, a former college professor, is a Christian Identity leader who makes effective use of shortwave radio. In the mid-1990s he hosted a show entitled "Scriptures for America," and devoted a show to "The Bible Says It's OK to Kill Homosexuals."[39] Peters uses theology as a base for anti-Semitism and racism, and includes feminists and "liberals" among his targets.[40]

"American Dissident Voices" (ADV) is a highly popular and effective far-right program on shortwave. In trouble with the FCC for allegedly using shortwave for domestic rather than for worldwide programming, contrary to its license, "American Dissident Voices" has been defended by its parent organization, National Alliance, which stated, that "It is now quite obvious that the activities of several Jewish and allied groups, which have acted on numerous occasions to have us taken off the air, that there is a determined conspiracy to deny us our freedom of speech on the public airwaves."[41] ADV stated that "We have always desired an international audience [and] we do in fact have one. . . . Our desired audience is every person of European descent on this planet, plus any other person who is interested in the issues we discuss."[42] Kevin Alfred Strom, a host on ADV, has been identified as a neo-Nazi who concentrates on revisionist, homophobic, and racist and anti-Semitic programming. He rails against "interracial breeding."[43] Kurt Saxon, a leading survivalist identified as a former American Nazi, uses his program to tell listeners how to build a shotgun and how to murder someone using dry ice while they are sleeping. When asked by a listener what to do with the body, he replied: "Throw it outside your house and when someone comes by asking about it, say the militia shot him."[44] Tom Valentine is a well known personality on "Radio Free America," sponsored by the Liberty Lobby. The show presents a conglomerate of far-right subjects, from conspiracy theories to gun control to cancer cures. On one program, following the suicide of deputy White House counsel Vincent Foster, Radio Free America devoted the show to "the uncovering of an alleged plot by Hillary Clinton and three Jewish scholars to murder Foster."[45]

So many rightwing shortwave radio stations went on the air in the 1990s, particularly after the Oklahoma City bombing, that Radio For Peace International (RFPI) established its own shortwave broadcasts (as well as publications and Internet outlets) just to monitor, analyze, and throw a spotlight on rightwing shortwave radio broadcasts. "Short-wave radio," wrote one columnist, "once used primarily by religious missionaries and government agencies such as the Voice of America, has become a vital tool of far right extremists in recent years."[46] Jeffrey A. Baker, managing partner of a right-wing shortwave radio network, said that shortwave "is now like FM was 25 years ago, an explosion waiting to happen."[47]

An "All Things Considered" report on National Public Radio in 1995 was titled "Hate Groups Use Shortwave to Rant, Rave, and Recruit." It made the point that "short-wave radio has been an inexpensive and powerful tool for organizing and recruiting within the militia movement. For just a few hundred dollars for an hour of broadcasting, [programs preaching hate] have been available almost every night." It pointed out further that "the new militia programs share the shortwave program with some of the most racist groups in America today," including White Aryans, neo-Nazi, and Ku Klux Klan organizations. "They reach a new audience as potential militia members, who do not trust the mainstream media, tune in to the shortwave broadcasts." While these stations were licensed for international broadcasting, reporter Deborah Amos stated, "some programs give out 800 numbers that are only accessible from the United States."[48]

William Pierce, chair of the National Alliance, who has been characterized as a leading neo-Nazi and anti-Semite, lauds the right-wing use of shortwave. He has stated that it is a cheaper alternative to commercial radio, has less government regulation, and is less susceptible to outside pressures. "Commercial networks," he says "are hesitant to take any politically incorrect views because they face a lot of pressure from Jewish groups. . . . Short-wave gives people a lot of different viewpoints, the chance to hear dissident voices."[49]

Another supporter of right-wing radio, Kerry L. Lynch, described his view of "The Importance of Short-Wave Radio Listening" in his Alternative News Center's "A Different Point of View." He believes that shortwave stations provide the most accurate news: "I have found that the type of people that provide the 'formatted' programs on many of the Patriot Networks are self-sacrificing, family, church-going people. Not NUTS like the mass media makes them out to be." He expressed concern that because of the Clinton administration's hatred of certain "politically incorrect" talk shows, on "January 1, 1997, all radio programming will come under special control/auditing by the White House.[50] This did not occur, of course. Under the Communications Act of 1934 the federal government may not censor (that is, exercise any prior restraint) over any programming, except under special wartime powers. In fact, the Federal Communications Commission has consistently protected right-wing speech, based on a 1985 decision not to take action against a station in Dodge City, Kansas, that was accused of attacking Jews, African-Americans, and other racial, religious, and ethnic minorities. And in 1995 the FCC also refused to act on a complaint against the stations that carried G. Gordon Liddy's instructions on how to kill federal agents, stating, "In the absence of evidence of clear and present danger of imminent violence . . . we are constrained to take any action."[51]

Not everyone supports the right-wing's regard for shortwave. One journalist wrote: "Short-wave radio, judging from some of the stories published since Oklahoma City, is one more shadowy cave filled with lunatics."[52]

Radio For Peace International has disseminated a list of some of the leading right-wing shortwave stations, along with brief descriptions of their programming approaches. The rationale: "With the Republican party being infiltrated and often dominated by Christian Conservatives; with the effects of Clinton's 'neo-liberal' economic policies (such as NAFTA) on the average American income; with a resurgence of nationalistic, ethnic, and religion-based conflict in countries around the globe; and with a general shift rightward on the political spectrum, it seems that hate speech, exclusionist principles, militancy, and good ol' fashioned white supremacy are enjoying a revival these days."[53] Here are some of their listings: "Scriptures for America Worldwide," Christian Identity leader Pete Peters, host, on WCR, WRNO, WRMI; "American Dissident Voices," America's Promise Ministries, hosted by David Barley, suspected of inspiring several bombings, on WHRI; Bo Gritz's "Freedom Calls"; Kurt Saxon, a survivalist who preaches that Armageddon is near, on WWCR; Jack McLamb, leader of Police Against the New World Order, on WHRI; Randall Terry, who founded Operation Rescue, on WWCR. Ernst Zundel's "Voice of Freedom" was dropped from a number of stations for being too outrageous even for far-right radio, but the Zundelsite on the Internet carries his anti-Semitic, Holocaust-denial message. The National Socialist White People's Party advises followers to "destroy [non-whites] completely, methodically, clinically, as if in a surgical operation." The Independent White Racialists urge immediate action on the part of "leaderless cells." The American Patriot Network and the American Freedom Coalition urge action. Other listings include groups whose main agenda is to cut off all immigration; those who accuse any who disagree with their ideals of being Communists; gun fanatics; and the extreme Christian right.[54]

WWCR, World Wide Christian Radio, is still considered to be the leading right-wing shortwave station. It was the first privately owned shortwave radio station in the United States, and in 1996 added a fourth 100,000–watt transmitter. It continues to carry the programs of the major far-right and extremist-right organizations and personalities, charging between $150 and $200 an hour to do so. WWCR was a key promoter of the Mark from Michigan "Intelligence Report." Mark Koernke is a leading proponent of militia action and his reputation spread after he promulgated the belief that the federal government itself was responsible for bombing its own building in Oklahoma City. Koernke's ties to active militias was such that he himself was under suspicion of possible complicity in the bombing.[55] Koernke's programs have left many listeners with the impression that armed conflict between the federal government and the militias is about to happen at any time. Koernke's remarks on Oklahoma City were considered so outrageous and inflammatory, even for his right-wing shortwave station owners, that in 1995 his show was dropped.[56] Another right-wing talk show host who joined Koernke in blaming the federal government for the Oklahoma City bombing, albeit in a different respect, is Richard Palmquist, owner of a Delano, California, station. Palmquist wrote to President Clinton: "If you are looking for the real thought leader behind Oklahoma City, look in the mirror. Then, turn inward and go after the ATF and FBI terrorists who are in truth responsible for Oklahoma City as well as Waco."[57]

Even more accusatory than Palmquist on Oklahoma City was William Pierce, whose National Alliance organization, considered strongly neo-Nazi, sponsors his shortwave broadcasts. "When the government engages in terrorism against its own citizens," Pierce said, referring to Waco, "it should not be surprised when some of those citizens strike back and engage in terrorism against the government. You [the government—especially Clinton and Reno] are responsible for this bombing, for the deaths of these children."[58]

WRNO (Worldwide Radio New Orleans) is also an important distributor of right-wing shows, and is a rival to WWCR. It was originally an FM station, but in 1993 became the first private shortwave station in the U.S. Its income comes mainly from selling air time for far-right and extremist programs such as the National Alliance's "American Dissident Voices" and the Kingdom Identity Ministry's "Herald of Truth."[59]

WHRI (World Harvest Radio in Indiana), was at one time essentially an evangelical station. In 1994, however, it began adding far right and extremist personalities such as Chuck Harder, Pete Peters, Jack McLamb, and Bob Enyart.[60]

In Colorado, radio station KNHC claims to have an audience of more than 3 million listeners in thirty-one countries for programming that includes extremist personalities such as Bo Gritz and Norm Resnick, emphasizing the coming holocaust to be perpetrated by the internationally Jewish-controlled, United Nations–implemented New World Order. Originally called the "USA Patriot Network," it changed its slogan to "American Freedom Network" after Patriots were linked to the Oklahoma City bombing. KNHC is itself not a shortwave radio station, but has an AM frequency. Like other AMs that carry right-wing programming, it feeds its signals to one of the shortwave stations—in this case WWCR—to get its message to the entire country and overseas.[61]

A shortwave station that went on the air in 1995 is WRMI in Miami, operated by Jeff White. At first principally oriented to anti-Castro broadcasts to Cuba and on programs for short-wave hobbyists, it soon began to carry the programs of right-wing extremists who advocate racism and violence, including Pete Peters, Mark Koernke, and Tom Valentine.[62]

In early 1999 WGTG was established in Georgia with a power of 50,000 kilowatts, and serves the far right with conspiracy theory materials and exhortations to cleanse the government.[63]

WINB in Red Lion, Pennsylvania, continues to go on and off the air, depending on its finances. Essentially a fundamentalist station, it nevertheless sells air time to far-right and extremist programs. Pete Peters's organization provided some financing for the station, which has given Peters direct input for its orientation and programming.[64]

Some lesser-known programs on shortwave are "The Mike Brown Show," which stresses the need to put power back into the hands of the people; "Blueprint for Survival," with Steve Quayle, which deals with ways to survive the future with special emphasis on trust in God; and David J. Smith's "Newswatch Magazine," which provides voluminous data to validate the conspiracy theories.[65] Another popular show has been William Cooper's "The Hour of the Time" on WWCR. One of Cooper's approaches is name-calling, attacking President Clinton as "that duck-hunting liar in the White House."[66]; Michael Callahan Jr., claiming that he is not affiliated with any group, has purchased time on several shortwave stations for his program, in which he stresses Bible-based attacks on the government. Callahan does not consider Rush Limbaugh a serious conservative: "I consider Rush Limbaugh infotainment."[67] Ted Gunderson is one of the mainstays of WWCR. A former FBI agent, Gunderson's guests generally represent far-right and extremist views regarding—as stated in a WWCR press release—corporate and government actions that "affect our freedom, constitutional rights and civil liberties."[68]

Leading short-wave stations are WRNO, WWCR, WYFR, WHRI, WWCR, WEWN, KTBN, WVHA, WGTG, WRMI, and KJES. More program titles and subjects heard on the Patriot Network, the American Freedom Network, and others are Rick Tyler's "Voice of Liberty," Mike Callahan's, "Protect Your Wealth," Derk Hainey's "Jungle Outfit," Bo Gritz's "Freedom's Call," E.C. Fulcher's "Truth House," Brother Stair's "The Overcomer," James Lloyd's "Apocalypse Chronicles," Bob Spear's "The Preparedness Hour," Kurt Saxon's "Survival Hour," Stan Johnson's "The Prophecy Club," Dr. Stan's "Radio Liberty," Dr. Dixon's "Sound the Trumpet," Chuck Allen's "America at the Crossroads," Sue Ellen's "Wake Up America," Larry Bates's "Unraveling the New World Order," Richard Palmquist's "To Free America," Ken Adams's "Take America Back," and numerous religious programs, virtually all Christian, from traditional gospel to anti-Semitic white racist exhortation. Brad Heavner of Radio For Peace International compiled a typical day's log, with annotations, of some of the far-right radio programs that can be heard on shortwave. See Appendix C at the end of this chapter.[69]

Perhaps the most descriptive phrase for the potential political impact of shortwave radio is the title of a pamphlet promoting its use as an alternative to the "ruling class" control over commercial and state radio: "Radio is our Bomb."[70]

Microstations

Many right-wingers, especially extremists, have taken to broadcasting over microstations, which operate without federal licenses. These stations have sprung up throughout the country during the past few years and have inspired the ire of commercial broadcasters, who fear any additional competition in the already saturated radio marketplace. But the microstations, although operating with very low power and reaching only a limited area—from a few miles to a 10– or possibly 20–mile radius—offer a free and unfettered opportunity for those with even the most outrageous messages and exhortations to reach the public. These stations have been referred to as "pirate" radio.

Pirate stations in themselves are nothing new and have presented a wide range of material, including far-right to far-left political programs; alternative music not generally carried by the standard stations in a given community; educational, informational, and cultural programming by groups such as racial and ethnic minorities not otherwise given access to the airwaves; programs with indecent, obscene, profane, or sexual content not heard on regular AM and FM stations.

These very low-power stations are essentially aimed at a designated community. They operate without FCC licenses, inasmuch as the frequencies they use are either not allocated for radio use or are co-frequencies of already licensed stations, thus likely to cause interference with existing signals of commercial or noncommercial stations or air, police, fire, and other official communications. In order to prevent chaos on the airwaves, which would render unintelligible many existing signals, the FCC permits licensing of stations only on frequencies that the commission determines will not create any interference. Because of limited spectrum space in high-population areas, frequencies are scarce or nonexistent—commercial operators quickly obtain licenses for available frequencies in areas where the number of potential listeners engenders profit-making advertising. Therefore, many groups and individuals who wish to use radio for political or social purposes cannot obtain access to the airwaves; thus, illegal pirate microstations. It should be noted that the FCC does crack down from time to time on unauthorized stations, and during the past five years a large turnover of stations has occurred. In 1997 the FCC shut down ninety-seven and in the first three months of 1998 closed sixty-five.[71] In all likelihood, stations referred to in this book may have already disappeared from the airwaves, and new ones not mentioned here may have taken their places.

The numbers indicate the problem; pirate stations are dramatically increasing. And the increase is due in large part to their use by right-wing extremist groups that find other radio outlets insufficient for their purposes. In early 1998 in Cleveland, Ohio, there were six pirate stations on the air, and in Miami twenty-two pirate stations can be heard along a ten-mile stretch of highway. With the AM and FM bands too congested, in mid-1998 the FCC was considering the authorization of legal low-power radio, one-watt stations where they could be fitted into the AM and FM bands without causing interference. While commercial broadcasters have expressed strong disapproval of that idea, many citizen groups, including both right-wing and left-wing individuals and organizations, have strongly supported it.[72] For less than $500 one can put a microstation on the air, while $100,000 is considered a low cost to get a regular power station on the air if a vacant frequency were found. Buying an existing radio station, depending on the market, costs from hundreds of thousands to millions to dollars. Some estimates put the number of pirate stations on the air nationally in early 1998 at well over 1,000.[73]

Microradio has brought the right-wing and left-wing together, not on the message, but on the messenger, in their advocacy of microstations. They claim that traditional stations don't serve the real needs of the community and that they alone truly represent the concerns and attitudes of the public. Both the Right and the Left, from moderate to radical, have challenged the Federal Communications Commission on its ban of microradio "pirate" stations. The following statement, attributed to Steven Dunifer, who operates "Radio Free Berkeley" and describes himself as a "long-haired Berkeley radical," indicates how close both the left and right are on the subject of micro pirate radio: "The band is crowded only in urban areas because of the mega power FCC has allowed big stations to use. If that power was brought down, community stations could coexist. . . . Our wonderful liberal friends at the Corporation for Public Broadcasting have spent the last ten years lobbying FCC to get rid of all the 10–watt community stations. . . . All we want is the right to create community radio."[74]

[In the interest of objectivity, it should be noted that one of this book's authors, when chief of the FCC's Educational (Public) Broadcasting Branch, fought unsuccessfully to keep 10–watt station authorization, and the other author of this book managed a 10–watt station.]

Denifer further stated that it is the alienated and disenfranchised who most need microstations to get their ideas to the public[75] —a sentiment echoed by right-wing advocates. The mission statement of microstation NLRN in Seattle expands Denifer's argument in terms of right-wing thinking:

[T]o deliver knowledge to the people in this area, that have been deprived of truth, Freedom, and the Original American way of life, through campaigns of propaganda, deception, coercion and stealthy encroachment by agencies of Government whose sole existence is to enslave ALL peoples, first by economic attrition, second, by total removal of God given Rights, and third, by the formation of a One World Government by Institution of Socialistic Democracy and Colorable Law.[76]

Both the Right and the Left have publicly stated that the mainstream media have become monopolies controlled by the rich. They promote access of their groups to media as the only alternative to the misinformation and disinformation they feel is normally disseminated to the public. There is a difference, however, between left and right: left-wing radio tends to be an operation of one or a few people, usually in urban areas where they believe the authorities are not adequately addressing civil rights, civil liberties, and the problems of the poor. Right-wing radio, on the other hand, tends to be a well-financed operation, usually under the auspices of a wealthy lobbying group, such as the National Alliance, with outreach to a number of domestic stations and, more importantly, nationally and internationally through shortwave transmission.

Microstation Radio Clandestino in Los Angeles broadcasts politically left Chicano material; Radio Free Bakersfield plays punk-rock bands generally ignored by commercial stations; Radio Free Bob includes readings from "Winnie-the-Pooh" books; and a fundamentalist pastor in Adrian, Michigan, wants a microstation that can air far-right leader Bo Gritz, especially his diatribes against the income tax.[77] One representative of rightwing microstations is Radio Tejas in Texas, although it is more moderate than the typical far-right station. Its founder, Keith Parry, was motivated by the siege of the Branch Davidian compound in Waco to establish his clandestine station. He carries programming from the American Freedom Network, a far-right radio group emanating from Colorado, from Republic Radio in Augusta, Michigan, and from other far-right outlets. Radio Tejas's power of 90 watts covers a radius of some fifteen miles.[78]

Radio Free America, which claims to be "the largest microradio network in the United States," lists affiliate microstations in Seattle (three stations), Albany (NY), Syracuse (NY), Tampa Bay (FL), and Eugene, Bend, and Portland (OR). Its statement of purpose includes the following:

> the people involved in micro radio . . . have a lot of things in common. We all are united in the fight to protect our first amendment rights at virtually any cost. . . . We are a group of American citizens that would stake nothing less than our life on the values this country is based on. . . . The FCC will not sell [sic] a broadcasting license to anyone in low wattage radio. . . . Small cities and areas that would not normally have a voice can have one with micro radio. . . . not allowing micro radio stations to exist at all in the United States is a crime against our communities, and against humanity.[79]

A description of a program entitled "Micro-Radio in the U.S.," on San Francisco Liberation Radio states that despite FCC sanctions, microradio stations "continue to broadcast to bring out the truth and a sense of reality about the world we live in that simply is not present in the mainstream media."[80]

The Federal Communications Commission doesn't know how many microstations are on the air and claims it doesn't have any totals of the number it has shut down. When it finds an illegal station—and because many of them use small portable transmitters and move from place to place, it is not always easy to locate them—it first issues a warning and, if the transmission continues, FCC field representatives will enter the transmitting site and shut down the station. Although the law provides for penalties for unauthorized use of the airwaves, rarely does the FCC impose a penalty, although it has the right to fine a violator up to $20,000. Some repeat offenders who refuse to comply with the regulation are arrested and charged. It makes no difference whether the pirate station is right-wing, left-wing, or apolitical. In early 1998, in a test case of the antipirate station criminal law against operating a station without a license (Title 17 of the U.S. Code), a case that could reach the Supreme Court, Arthur Kobres, a pirate station operator in the community of Lutz, Florida, was convicted by a federal court jury. The programming was principally religious and antigovernment Patriot movement material, representative of many right-wing microstations.[81]

Kobres based his programming on a number of right-wing concepts, including the following:

- "Our freedoms are granted by God and only protected by the U.S. Constitution.
- Forces of evil are conspiring to subvert the Constitution to the charter of the United Nations.
- Americans are being slowly stripped of their freedoms by unconstitutional treaties and laws.
- The establishment media is too entertainment-oriented to warn people about all this, and most people are too happy-go-lucky to realize it."[82]

A flyer put out by Lutz Community Radio told a more complete story, one exemplifying to a great degree the far-right and extremist stands of many of the microstations, including conspiracy, survivalist, anti-Semitic, Christian Identity, and militia viewpoints. Some of its more specific principles, delineated in the flyer signed by station operator Lonnie Kobres under the heading "A nonprofit, low-power Broadcast Station dedicated to the defense of God, Family, and Country," are cited here as an example of right-wing material put out on microstations:

- This information is for traditional Americans who are troubled that our original, God-centered republic is being transformed into a government-controlled police state.

- We have discovered that fundamental changes in our original American Common Law have been gradually and clandestinely instituted by government officials.
- Many of us previously believed (falsely) that individuals who have respect for our traditional American values would head government offices, major corporations, newspapers, television, movie, and music studios. Our trust is proving to be unwarranted.
- [T]he media has knowingly and willingly misinformed and distracted us. We have not been informed of the *un*-American alliance of government and financial leaders, or of the fact that these leaders have chosen as their faith secular humanism. . . . Humanists consider chaos as merely an opportunity to establish new order. . . . an example of their handiwork is the 1962 Supreme Court scheme of removing the Holy Bible's virtuous teachings from the children's formal learning experience.
- We know that World Government under an anti-Christ is prophesied in the Bible. The current elitists hope to have their version of Global Government in place very soon—by the year 2000. . . . Patriotic Americans are rising to that challenge from coast to coast. . . . To accomplish the task . . . we must get back to the rugged, independent, self-governing character that made America great.
- Do you realize that in 1913 Congress handed over our money to a private, for profit operation? The Federal Reserve Bank . . . 'Permit me to issue and control a nation's money and I care not who makes its laws'—Mayer Archibald Rothchild [sic] (founder of the Rothchild [sic] banking dynasty whose agents wrote and promoted the Federal Reserve Act).
- The remaining freedom we enjoy is made possible only because we are a heavily armed population . . . the US government has agreed to gradually disarm Americans, including our military. World Government requires only one military—the U.N."[83]

An attachment to the Lutz Radio flyer warns against the institution of any form of gun control, including the alleged "Communist Rules for Revolution: Cause the registration of all firearms on some pretext, with a view to confiscating them and leaving the population helpless." Gun control is cited as part of a communist plot to overthrow the U.S. government.[84]

The far right and extremist right alleges that the FCC's efforts to close down unlicensed mircostations is part of the conspiracy to turn the country over to a foreign power, specifically the United Nations. With the instability of microstations because of FCC monitoring, many individuals and groups have switched their rancor to an unregulated means of disseminating their views: the Internet.

As noted, microstations' range of content spreads across the entire political spectrum. For example, many stations are essentially religious in nature, forwarding the conservative to extremist-right message of the given sponsoring religious organization or the religious beliefs of the station owner, and not injecting political propaganda. One religious station shut down by the FCC was oriented to recruiting for a Christian church, using popular music with proselytizing lyrics to get the attention of young listeners. The station operator, Tom Scruggs, said: "This is great music with lyrics that point to hope, faith and relationship with our Creator. Secular music may have the same beat, but not the same message. . . . God led me to this show, and if He wants it to continue, in whatever form, I'm ready."[85]

Examples of several other short-wave and/or micro-station right-wing programs that have been aired in the United States in recent years (some have gone off the air, permanently or temporarily, and some are dealt with in greater detail in subsequent chapters of this book) are: Kurt Saxon's "Poor Man's James Bond" series, which explains how to make terrorist weapons at home, and was published in a four-volume set of books when the program went off the air; Linda Thompson, who proclaimed herself acting adjutant general of the Unorganized Militia of the United States, was taken off the air after she called for an armed march on Washington by militias; Dave Barley's national radio ministry of the Lord's Covenant Church, a Christian Identity organization, which calls Aryan whites the true children of Israel and advocates that the others who are called Jews today should be eliminated; Paul Parsons and Rick Tyler's "Voice of Liberty" radio show, close to the militia movement, which warns the public that the New World Order is about to take over the United States; Mark Koernke, has been on and off the air; Ernst Zundel was taken off the air, and moved to the Internet; the neo-Nazi National Alliance's "American Dissident Voices," a leading extremist program; the Kingdom Identity Ministry's "Herald of Truth," which concentrated on white supremacist, anti-Semitic content; Pete Peters, preaching Christian Identity ideas and calling for the execution of homosexuals.[86] These are only a few of the organizations and personalities who would not be as successful in proselytizing and recruiting if it weren't for their use of shortwave and microstation radio. So powerful are the effects of talk radio that the watchdog Radio For Peace International went beyond just monitoring right-wing waves of rancor, and in 1994 began publishing the *Far Right Radio Review* to keep the public up to date. A few years later its name was changed to the *Global Community Forum*.[87]

In a column in the *Detroit News,* Mario Morrow summed up many of the attitudes toward talk radio. "Talk radio is real. The personalities have a strong hold on our society. They are the political spin or sin doctors of the '90s. It is as rich as voodoo and as cool as the bottomless pit. . . . They [the talk show personalities] all have a strong following who hang onto every word that comes from their lips. Some consider this dangerous to the tenth degree. Others are thankful for the freedom of speech that our country has bestowed on us."[88]

Low-Power Television

The high cost of buying time on full-power commercial television stations, no less the enormous cost of buying or building such a station, has by and large ruled out traditional television as a media outlet for right-wing groups. They have had to seek alternative video outlets that are more accessible.

Low-power television stations (LPTV), authorized by the Federal Communications Commission in 1983, are run in many instances by local political, religious, or other common-interest groups. LPTV stations normally have a radius of from five to ten miles and concentrate on a local viewing audience. Setting up and operating an LPTV station is relatively inexpensive. While a full-power station would cost several million dollars (more in larger markets) to build, equip, and staff, an LPTV station can be set up in one's basement or spare room with a minimum of second-hand equipment, run by just two or three people, and cost as little as a few thousand dollars to begin basic operation. Many LPTV stations are operated by religious groups, including the religious right, by ethnic, racial, and civic groups who normally have been denied equitable access to the airwaves, and by far-right and extremist organizations and individuals. To date, however, LPTV has not been a particular target of the far right and may not be in the future if the medium is successful in gaining Class A status (as the mainstream media make the transition to digital). Above all else, LPTVs are on a quest for legitimacy and typically will avoid any form of controversy that may jeopardize the realization of this goal.

Cable Access Stations

Another major area for individual dissemination of right-wing philosophy or invective or advocacy of violence is the public-access channels of local cable systems. Many cable franchises issued by municipalities throughout the United States require the cable systems to provide public-access channels. These channels are literally for use by the public, subject to the procedures and processes established by the community boards that run the city or town's access channels. These channels provide the opportunity for anyone who resides in the community to produce and air programs. In some cases the opportunity is taken by right-wing advocates representing varying degrees of the political spectrum.

In Oakland County, Michigan, for example, viewers of the public-access channel were "getting an earful from the far right, stories of secret government arms deals, suggestions of a cover-up in the death of White House aide Vincent Foster, and tips for fighting the IRS. Justice Pro Se, a citizens group popular with members of the patriot movement and others frustrated with government, has taken its message to public access television."[89] Leaders of Justice Pro Se state, "This is just a dynamite way to get our message out to a lot of people," and "Public access is the only way we can put things on and not have them censored by the media. You can have your own show about anything you want."[90] Interviewees have included right-wing extremist leaders from throughout the country.

In the Twin Cities area of Minnesota a public access cable station began carrying a program series called "The Truth," which by June 1997 had been broadcast 217 times with such subjects as the New World Order, conspiracies, end-time prophecies, and the "truth" about the bombing of the federal building in Oklahoma City.[91]

In Guilford, Connecticut, the cable-access station has a weekly hour-long program entitled "Things That Make You Go Hmmm." The show features material prepared by members of the community that by general community standards might be considered off the beaten path. One program, aired a number of times, was "Biblical End: Times Prophecies II, Exposing the Agents of Anti-Christ." The producer of the program, local resident Michael Dimond, appears in the garb of a Catholic priest, "spewing claims that a new world order was secretly being created by a cabal made up of Jews and Freemasons who wanted to take over the world. . . . Behind this conspiracy are members of the United Nations, government representatives from many nations, members of the Jewish faith and Freemasons."[92] In upstate New York a cable-access station carried several of Ernst Zundel's "Voice of Freedom" Holocaust-denial programs, but dropped them following protests by Jewish members of the community. One resident, however, planned to take advantage of any citizen's right to produce on an access channel by putting on more "Voice of Freedom" programs.[93]

The regional director for the Connecticut Anti-Defamation League, Robert Leikind, expressed his concern "about the ease with which people who espouse bigotry can reach out to impressionable young people. 'We're in a new age with things like public access television and the Internet. . . . People with these types of views can reach many more people today than 10 years ago." Leikind made it clear that he was opposed to censoring such programs, even if he was greatly concerned about their impact. "If we start censoring things, where do we stop?"[94]

Fax and Film

While not part of the airwaves as discussed in this book, two other media used by the right-wing are worth mentioning. One is the fax. Along with the Internet, the fax has been used by many underground or rebel groups in many countries as at least a temporary alternative to media access controlled by the governments they oppose. One dramatic use of the fax was by the students in Tienanmen Square in Beijing in 1989 to send to Hong Kong the story of what was happening when other means of communication were shut off by the government. In the United States—for what are perceived by many as diametrically opposite goals and ideals—the right-wing movement has also used the fax to communicate with and organize its members. The American Patriot Fax Network (APFN) faxed an appeal on November 2, 1997, that stated: "We are in an information war. Networking is the weapon, knowledge the truth. . . . Networking and cross-networking is . . . the answer."[95]

More pervasive is the use of films and videos for spreading the right-wing gospel. Some of the films and videos are home-grown with limited circulation among members of the individual group making the film. Others are professionally made, of good technical quality with a wide circulation. All are agit-prop ("agitational propaganda," a term from the 1930s left-wing movement in the United States). Most of the films and videos are short—about thirty minutes or so—and made in documentary or semi-documentary form.

An example of the kinds of films and videos made and circulated by the right wing is "Deceiving America: Communist Influence in the Media," a ninety-minute production by filmmaker Angus Paul Sullivan, distributed exclusively by the New World Order Intelligence Report. NWO describes the video: "During the first 30 minutes, Sullivan interviews outstanding American journalists and journalism professors about the role and influence of the media in American life, thought and society. During the following sixty minutes a panel of distinguished journalists, including Reed Irvine of Accuracy in Media [a group that was reported to have called 'traitors' people who voted Democratic] intensively question . . . a Russian defector . . . revealing the extent to which Russian 'sleepers' and left-wing sympathizers had been 'planted' in journalistic and editorial positions throughout the American and Canadian media. Stories favorable to the Communist cause are given wide coverage; articles and book reviews which are unfavorable, however, are quietly 'spiked' and allowed to 'die.' "[96]

Another example is "Anguish in Oklahoma City," a thirty–minute video produced by The Truth, a right-wing cable access production organization in the Minneapolis–St. Paul, Minnesota, area. The video is promoted as being "packed with controversial information about the bombing that the mainstream press simply won't touch,"[97] presenting viewpoints tending to both absolve and justify the right wing's role in the bombing.

One of the key right-wing movement films is "Waco: The Big Lie," produced by Linda Thompson. It reportedly has been responsible for greatly increased recruitment into the militias not only after Waco, but after Oklahoma City as well. Timothy McVeigh supposedly often watched this film prior to the Oklahoma City bombing. When the film was first released, it was reviewed by a "new age" magazine, *Nexus,* which distributed the film. Its review stated: "There is a very big underground movement building up in the U.S. at the moment. Every night, someone is showing this video to a bunch of friends. Nobody remains unaffected after seeing it. It is contagious, so beware!"[98]

Many of the right-wing organizations with their own Web sites offer merchandise for sale, including videotapes and audiotapes as well as books, magazine subscriptions, T-shirts and other paraphernalia such as arms materials, clothing, and swastika caps and armbands. Catalogues for videos, films, and audiotapes can be obtained by mail or through the Internet. Some of the video and audio titles are: "Gun Control and the New World Order," "The Coming Russian-Chinese New World Order and the Planned Subjugation of America," and "Clinton Chronicles" (described as "horrifying, shocking").

The Internet

Returning to the airwaves, we find that the fastest growing medium for right-wing outreach is in itself the fastest-growing medium: the Internet. More and more political groups, from the far left to the far right, are using the Internet to reach not only their traditional constituencies, but also new constituencies who for the first time are able to have easy access to new and different ideas, information, and exhortations. The Internet is being used increasingly not only for persuasion, but also for recruitment. Fringe groups that were barely heard before are now able to make their views known nationally and internationally through the Internet.

Amy Harmon writes: "Marginalized by traditional media and short on funds, hate groups have been learning to use low-cost online communications to gain recruits and spread propaganda across state and even national boundaries, giving them access to a far wider audience than they have historically been able to reach."[99]

The Anti-Defamation League has stated that "the low cost and the relative ease of Internet publishing is . . . expanding the number of lesser known haters cranking out the extremist message." The ADL notes numerous new groups with names like "Cyber-Nazis" and "Women for Aryan Unity," with many of the racist sites consisting of only one or two people who pretend they are complete organizations.[100] Rabbi Abraham Cooper of the Simon Wiesenthal Center believes that "you can see the beginning of a kind of subculture on the Net" that is part of the far-right hate literature, Skinhead rock music, and guerrilla tactics.[101] His concerns were echoed by leaders of a number of governments, who found especially "scary" the proliferation of bomb recipes on the Internet.[102]

Cyberspace has hardly been scratched in terms of its political potentials. Will new political parties emerge solely on the Internet? Will governments themselves find that their most powerful means of reaching the largest segments of their populations is through the Internet? Will politicians turn more and more to the Internet to get across their messages, spins, sound bytes and even their entire live-action speeches? At the present time it appears that those on the cutting edge of cyberspace information, misinformation, and disinformation use are the right-wing groups, including those on the extreme radical edge. Joseph T. Roy Sr., director of the Klanwatch/Militia Task Force of the Southern Poverty Law Center (SPLC), says, "The tentacles of the hate movement are reaching places where they've never been before. Mainstream America is being targeted in a way this country hasn't seen in decades."[103]

According to Brian Youngblood, the Internet information specialist at the SPLC, there were 20 million Web pages online at the end of 1997.[104] The Internet's rapid growth is dramatically illustrated by the fact that in 1994 about 3 million people worldwide used the Internet, and in 1998 it had grown to over 150 million users.

One study stated that from 1995 through 1997, "163 Web sites have popped up on the Internet preaching hatred. . . . While the Ku Klux Klan was still the largest hate group, growing in popularity were the neo-Nazis, Skinheads, white Christian fundamentalists and black separatist organizations."[105] A study by the Simon Wiesenthal Center determined that at the end of 1997 there were more than 600 "hate-oriented" sites on the Internet, with many of them in the northeast United States.[106]

False Patriots: The Threat of Antigovernment Extremists, published by the SPLC, states, "The computer is the most vital piece of equipment in the Patriot movement's arsenal. It has given those who might never have crossed paths an opportunity to build alliances based on their common hatred of the federal government. In cyberspace, people from all walks of life and from all areas of the country can debate the effectiveness of various assault rifles and detonators without revealing their identities."[107] *False Patriots* notes that the Patriot members who use the Internet are from a wide variety of groups, including Christian fundamentalists, anti-abortion fanatics, neo-Nazis, survivalists, libertarians, neo-Nazis, white supremacists, militias, and anarchists.[108] "It's cheap. it's efficient. It gives you instant communication," Joe Roy said.[109]

A 1997 FBI report linked the use of the computer to the increased ability of terrorist groups to raise money, propagandize, collect information on weaponry, and cause havoc by spreading computer viruses.[110] Steve King of Isis/New Media, the company that created and maintains the Wiesenthal center Web site states: "What makes hate on the Net different from off-line hate is that in the past this [neo-Nazi] stuff was under rocks, now they have a distribution network of unparalleled power."[111]

One of the most important and effective uses made of the Internet by right-wing groups is convincing and recruiting through the use of so-called "white power rock-and-roll" music.[112] One 1998 newspaper story headline said: "Internet Music Aids 20% Rise in Hate Groups."[113] Brian Youngblood of SPLC stated that one example of the effectiveness of music on right-wing Internet sites is the 100 megs of power for high-quality music used by one far-right Web site. Internet users can download the music, put it on CD or tape, and listen to it in their cars. The lyrics promote the views of the given hate group. Young people are especially susceptible to this use of the Internet.[114] Teens are one of the special targets of hate groups. Troubled youth are being reached at home with "an underground culture featuring violent rock 'n' roll."[115]

Individual Web sites, of course, reflect the specific character and purposes of the organization using that site, although an examination of Web sites of different groups shows underlying common threads, such as Christian identity, white supremacy, anti-Semitism, and conspiracy beliefs. For example, anyone logging onto the Alpha organization Web site finds the following: "ALPHA HQ Website—Aryan Men and Women Welcome!" And below that: "This web site is dedicated to the countless Aryan men and women who have given their lives for our race." Reading further, one finds "the correct path of Alpha would be the teachings of National Socialism which promotes a strong and healthy race. . . . ALPHA is the racial/political/paramilitary organization of the Aryan people. . . . All avenues of activism must be traversed for our goal to be reached. . . . Our first and primary activity is the Internet web site you are currently on."[116] At another Web site you are greeted with a "Welcome to Underground Software!" This online catalogue encourages you to buy software for "Homemade Explosives," "Lockpicking Made Easy," "Check Fraud Simplified," "The World of Credit Fraud," "How to Survive and Profit in Prison," "Fake ID," and "The Militia Workshop."[117]

In late 1998 ALPHA HQ was shut down by the attorney general of Pennsylvania for allegedly threatening two members of the Reading-Berks Human Relations Council. The Web site warned that "traitors like this . . . will be hung from the nearest tree or lamp post" and included a photograph of one of the persons threatened. The Web site also showed an office building being blown up.[118]

The Web site of the Aryan Crusaders Library shows a Nazi flag on a red background that dissolves into a map of the United States with a logo over it that says "keeping America White." Another Web site, Stormfront, describes itself as a "resource for those courageous men and women fighting to preserve their White Western culture, ideals and freedom of speech and association—a forum for planning strategies and forming political and social groups to ensure victory." It includes a picture of a young couple holding a baby, with the caption, "It is simple reality that . . . to be born WHITE is an honor and a privilege." A Christian Identity Web site states: "Judaism never was and is still not the religion of the Old Testament . . . nor was Jesus a jew [sic] . . . Judaism's blasphemous and God-hating filth is 100% diametrically opposed to all that is right and good. We must have no fellowship with this satanic religion."[119] One Web site called Sniper Country has as its motto the words "Happiness is a Confirmed Kill," and offers those who log on "detailed information on sniper skills, fieldcraft, basic and advanced marksmanship, clandestine patrolling, survival, basic reloading, and ballistics."[120]

The Aryan Female Homestead Web site "lambastes marriage and preaches racial purity." The world Church of the Creator Web site advocates a "racial holy war" against its "mortal racial enemies." The Nuremberg Files Web site states that "legalized abortion is war" and provides the names, addresses and phones numbers of doctors who perform legal abortions.[121]

The World-Wide White Power Website states: "Racial discrimination and prejudism are indeed facts of life, but unfortunately White people are the main victims!"[122] The Holocaust-denial Zundelsite is owned and operated by an American citizen, Dr. Ingrid A. Rimland, although Zundel himself lives in Canada. Rimland's "Z-grams" not only reach, but inflame millions of "subscribers."[123]

Canada has had a number of crises in attempting to stop the hate on Web sites in that country and at the same time protecting everyone's freedom of speech. One of its problems was with a server called Fairview, which allegedly carried more than a dozen ultra-right organizations' hate sites, particularly that of a neo-Nazi group, the Charlemagne Hammer Skins (CHS). Some of its leaders were arrested in Britain and France for inciting to murder over the Internet. They listed the names and addresses of people to assassinate and gave the would-be CHS killers instruction on how to make the bombs.[124] While a number of groups were urging the British Columbia telephone company, BC Tel, to "pull the plug" on service providers who carry such Web sites, others echoed the statement of BC Tel vice president Dorothy Byrne that "some people are very strong on us acting quickly to terminate the service. Others— and I think it's most of them—are opposing action by BC Tel because for them the implications for free speech . . . would override the concerns that these people have regarding the content."[125] (As noted in chapter 1, Canada's government offices attempted to shut down the Zundelsite, but the Canadian Supreme Court upheld its freedom of speech rights.)

Another use of the Internet by far right groups is e-mail. United States intelligence officials expressed concern over what they called the first concerted attack by a terrorist group to disrupt a government's operations by swamping its offices with e-mail.[126] A more direct use of e-mail for spreading hate occurred on the campus of Manchester College in Indiana, where some 700 Asian students were sent racist e-mail. Asian students at the University of California received e-mail stating that the sender was going to "kill every one of you," and in New York there has been an increase in anti-Semitic e-mail sent to Jewish students on college campuses.[127]

Joe Roy, in comparing the Internet and radio use, says that common use of radio, sometimes the same networks and frequencies, has brought together a number of disparate and sometimes otherwise confrontational right-wing groups. "The enemy of my enemy is my friend syndrome" seems to apply, Roy says. He points out that the radio payoff in recruiting new members to the various right-wing groups is not as much as was expected, but that radio "has gotten sympathy for their ideas." However, while radio is more dramatic, Roy says, "the Internet's printed word seems to be more effective and believable."[128]

In 1996 the Heritage Front Lobby, a right-wing organization based in Canada, issued a booklet for use by right-wing groups which included addresses for media, government agencies, cabinet members, racialist organizations, shortwave radio broadcasts, and Web sites. Its Web site list, entitled "Resource Web Pages for Racialists and Freedom Fighters"—grown considerably since it was issued—may be found as Appendix B at the end of this chapter, providing a partial sampling of some of the most-used right-wing Web sites.

William Pierce, head of the neo-Nazi National Alliance, states, "We've seen a huge growth in the use of the Internet by our people. The major media in this country are very biased against our political point of view. They present us with ridicule or in a very distorted way. The information highway is much more free of censorship. It's possible for a dedicated individual to get his message out to thousands and thousands of people."[129]

Appendices to Chapter 3

Appendix 3A: Hate Groups on the Internet

(from the *Intelligence Report*, Winter 1998; reprinted with permission from the Southern Poverty Law Center)

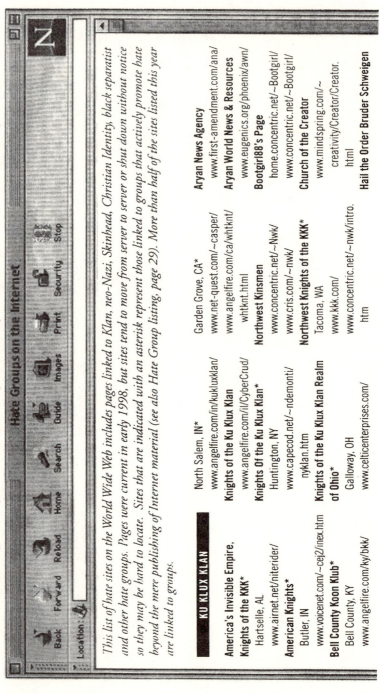

Hate Groups on the Internet

This list of hate sites on the World Wide Web includes pages linked to Klan, neo-Nazi, Skinhead, Christian Identity, black separatist and other hate groups. Pages were current in early 1998, but sites tend to move from server to server or shut down without notice so they may be hard to locate. Sites that are indicated with an asterisk represent those linked to groups that actively promote hate beyond the mere publishing of Internet material (see also Hate Group listing, page 29). More than half of the sites listed this year are linked to groups.

KU KLUX KLAN

America's Invisible Empire, Knights of the KKK*
Hartselle, AL
www.airnet.net/niterider/

American Knights*
Butler, IN
www.voicenet.com/~cej2/inex.htm

Bell County Koon Klub*
Bell County, KY
www.angelfire.com/ky/bkk/

North Salem, IN*
www.angelfire.com/in/kukluxklan/

Knights of the Ku Klux Klan
www.angelfire.com/il/CyberCrud/

Knights Of the Ku Klux Klan*
Huntington, NY
www.capecod.net/~ndemonti/nyklan.htm

Knights of the Ku Klux Klan Realm of Ohio*
Galloway, OH
www.celticenterprises.com/

Garden Grove, CA*
www.net-quest.com/~casper/
www.angelfire.com/ca/whtknt/whtknt.html

Northwest Kinsmen
www.concentric.net/~Nwk/
www.cris.com/~nwk/

Northwest Knights of the KKK*
Tacoma, WA
www.kkk.com/
www.concentric.net/~nwk/intro.htm

Aryan News Agency
www.first-amendment.com/ana/

Aryan World News & Resources
www.eugenics.org/phoenix/awn/

Bootgirl88's Page
home.concentric.net/~Bootgirl/
www.concentric.net/~Bootgirl/

Church of the Creator
www.mindspring.com/~creativity/Creator/Creator.html

Hail the Order Bruder Schweigen

(continued)

Christian White Knights of the Ku Klux Klan*
Chesterfield, VA
www.angelfire.com/ak/christianwhiteknight/index.html

Imperial Klans of America*
Powderly, KY
www.kkkk.net/index.html/

Invisible Empire, Pennsylvania Ku Klux Klan*
Punxsutawney, PA
www.nb.net/~gijoe/web.raex.com/~moezit/invisible.html

JWS Militant Knights of the Ku Klux Klan*
Valley Head, AL
www.mindspring.com/~awol/scross.html

Knights of the KKK*
Iota, LA
www.acadian.net/~shanekwk/
Grants Pass, OR*
home.cdsnet.net/~wotan/main.htm

whiteboy/
Knights of the KKK Realm of Michigan*
Caledonia, MI
members.aol.com/realmofmi/index.htm

Knights of Michigan
www.angelfire.com/ak/knightsofmichigan/

Knights of the White Kamellia*
Austin, TX
members.aol.com/realmoftex/index.html

Knights of the White Kamellia*
Chesterfield, VA
members.aol.com/realmofva/

Missouri Federation of Klans Inc.*
St. Louis, MO
www.angelfire.com/mo/MissouriFOK/

New Order Knights of the Ku Klux Klan*
Overland, MO
www.angelfire.com/va/rattler/rattler/html

Coeur d' Alene, ID*
www.nidlink.com/~idrealm/realm.html

Official Ku Klux Klan Home Page
shell.idt.net/~edoneil1/kkkhom.html

Southern Cross Militant Knights*
Cartersville, GA
www.angelfire.com/ga/SCMK/index.html

NEO-NAZI

Aryan Angel's White Links
www.aryan.com/

Aryan Nations*
Hayden Lake, ID
www.nidlink.com/~aryanvic/
204.181.176.4/stormfront/an.htm
stormfront.wat.com/stormfront/an.htm
www.stormfront.org/aryan_nations/
www.stormfront.org/an.htm

www.14words.com/theorder/
National Alliance*
Hillsboro, WV
www.natvan.com/
www.natall.com

National Socialist German Workers Party*
Lincoln, NE
www.alpha.org/nsdap/
alpha.ftcnet.com/~skinhds/neworder/

National Socialist Movement of IL
alpha.ftcnet.com/~schlis/aryan.html

National Socialist Student Union
www.nb.net/%7Enewdawn/nssu.html

National Socialist Vanguard*
The Dalles, OR
www.alpha.org/nsv/

National Socialist White People's Party*
Charleston, SC
www.nswpp.org
Toledo, OH*

Appendix 3A *(continued)*

Hate Groups on the Internet

Back Forward Reload Home Search Guide Images Print Security Stop

Location:

www.glasscity.net/users/stein/
reich.html
www.io.com/~claudius/
members.aol.com/logic88/index.
html

Nazism Now!
www.celticenterprises.com/nazi/

Rahowa
www.rahowa.com

S.S. Enterprises Home Page*
Fresno, CA
www.qnis.net/%7ewhiteboy/

The Library
alpha.ftcnet.com/~ourhero/

Unofficial Rahowa Page
www.whitepride.com/rahowa/

Volksfront*
Portland, OR
www.volksfront.org/

White Aryan Resistance*
Fallbrook, CA

Confederate White Pride
home.earthlink.net/~aryanresist

ghettostorm
www.whitepride.com/
ghettostorm

Hammerskin Nation
home.att.net/~wpsh8814/L

Hate Mongers Hangout
www.hatemonger.com/

Her Race
www.ftcnet.com/~adp/herrace.
htm

Minneapolis Skinheads
www.usinternet.com/users/
sonic88/home.html

National Party Home Page*
Los Angeles, CA
www.cyberg8t.com/natlprty/

Nationalist Skinhead Voice
www.angelfire.com/tv/
nsvpage/

Resistance Records Home Page*
Detroit, MI
www.resistance.com/

Right as Reina
user.mc.net/~reina/

Sacto Skinheads
home.earthlink.net/~odin88/sacto.
html

SiegHeil88's Homepage
www.concentric.net/
%7eseigheil/

Skin-Net
alpha.ftcnet.com/~skinhds/
index2.htm
ftcnet.com/~skinhds/main.htm

Skinheads on the Internet
www.ksu.edu/~lashout/
skns.html

SS Bootboys*
San Francisco, CA
www.angelfire.com/ca/onlywhite2/

Essays by Louis Beam
www.yosemite.net/beam/
Default.htm

**God's Order Affirmed in Love
(G.O.A.L.)**
Reference Library
www.melvig.org/
Library Web Page
www.nilenet.com/~tmw/

Gospel Broadcasting Association*
Houston, TX
www.neosoft.com/%7epreacher/

Gospel Ministries Online*
Boise, ID
www.melvig.org/gmo.html

Jim Wickstrom's Home Page*
Munising, MI
www.logoplex.com/resources/
wickstrom
www.webexpert.net/posse/
default.html

(continued)

www.resist.com/

www.free.cts.com/crash/m/metzger

World Church of the Creator for Kids
www.ariskkamp.com/kids/

World Church of the Creator Headquarters*
East Peoria, IL
www.creator.org/
flashback.net/~wcotc/
www.ariskkamp.com/imperium/
www.mindspring.com/~creativity/Creator/
www.ariskkamp.com/kfr/
Ohio*
www.blackplague.org/mindslayer/wcotc.html
Florida*
www.ariskkamp.com/wiking/

SKINHEAD

Blood and Honor*
Minneapolis, MN
www.skrewdriver.com/blood.htm

New Dawn*
Los Angeles, CA
www.nb.net/~newdawn/

New Jersey United Skinheads
members.gnn.com/misfitx/skins2.htm

New Jersey Skinheads Page
members.gnn.com/misfitx/skin2.htm

New Order
ftcnet.com/~skinhds/neworder/index.html

Northern Hammer Skins*
Hartland, WI
www.angelfire.com/wi/hammerskins/index.html

Oi! Boys*
Kenosha, WI
www.execpc.com/~odinthor/oi.html

Plunder and Pillage
www.excaliber.com/thor/home.htm

Rebel___88's White Patriot Page
www.angelfire.com/ca/onlywhite/

Tri-State Terror*
Strudsburg, PA
www2.cybernex.net/~odin/tst1.htm

Wolfpack Services*
St. Paul, MN
www.skrewdriver.com/

CHRISTIAN IDENTITY

America's Promise Ministries*
Sandpoint, ID
rand.nidlink.com/~amprom/index.htm

Bible Restoration Ministries, Inc.*
Royal Oak, MI
www.swiftsite.com/restoring/

Carl Klang's Home Page
Colton, OR
www.klang.com/

Christian Separatist Church Society*
Kodak, TN
www.webspawner.com/users/chrse/

Crusade for Christ*
Little Rock, AR
ftp.netcom.com/pub/lj/lja/JMOHR

Jubilee*
Midpines, CA
www.jubilee-newspaper.com

Kingdom Identity Ministries*
Harrison, AR
www.kingidentity.com/

Lighthouse
www.sodak.net/%7ethelighthouse/index.htm

Lord's Work, Inc.*
Austin, KY
www.thelordswork.com/

Melchizedek Vigilance*
Denver, CO
www.melvig.org/mel/MELVIG.HTM

New Beginnings Home Page*
Waynesville, NC
www.ioa.com/home/new_beginnings/

New Christian Crusade Church (CDL)*
Arabi, LA
home.inreach.com/dov/cdl/htm

Right of Israel Online
home.arkansasusa.com/dlackey

Appendix 3A (*continued*)

Scriptures for America*
LaPorte, CO
www.identity.org/
Stone Kingdom Ministries*
Asheville, NC
www.rust.net/~wkalivas/Stone_
Kingdom/
Tom Blair's home page
www.enter.net/~blair/
index.html
Virginia Publishing Company*
Lynchburg, VA
soli.inav.net/~victory/vpc/
Weisman Publications
www.seek-info.com/

BLACK SEPARATIST

Blacks and Jews Newspage
www.tiac.net/users/lhl/
House of David*
New York, NY
www.hodc.com/

www.alpha.org/
Ariskkamp
www.ariskkamp.com/
Aryan Book Center*
Decatur, IL
www.aryanbook.com/
CAUSE Foundation*
207.15.176.3:80/cause/
defaulthtm
Cyber Nationalist Group
207.105.95.101/
texts/cng
Library of Yggdrasil
www.first-amendment.
com/ygg/
Micetrap*
Oley, PA
www.whitepower.com/
Minuteman Ministries Home Page
www.oz.net/~iloveyah/
MSR Productions*
Wheat Ridge, CO
www.pipeline.com/~david/

naawpoftennessee/
Houston, TX*
www.flash.net/~guardian/signup.
html
Nationalist Movement*
Learned, MS
www.nationalist.org/
Nationalist Observer*
San Diego, CA
members.aol.com/AxCurtis/
natob.html
**Occidental Pan-Aryan
Crusader**
www.crusader.net/
atropos.c2.net/~crusader/
**Protocols of the Learned Elders of
Zion**
xxx.flashback.se/~rislam/
www.ptialaska.net/~swampy/
illuminati/zion.html
Stormfront*
West Palm Beach, FL
www.stormfront.org/stormfront/

www2.stormfront.org/
www3.stormfront.org/
StormFront Records
www.execpc.com/~strmfrnt/
stormfront.html
Sunwheel Records*
Baton Rouge, LA
www.whitepower.com/
sunwheel/
Truth at Last*
Marietta, GA
www.stormfront.org/
truth_at_last/
Voice of White America
members.aol.com/tsaukki/
groups.htm
White Power Central
lochnet.com/mindslayer/main.
html
www.blackplague.org/
mindslayer/
White Power World Wide
www.wpww.com/

TOTALS		
KU KLUX KLAN	29 WEB SITES	21 GROUPS
NEO-NAZI	39 WEB SITES	12 GROUPS
SKINHEAD	27 WEB SITES	9 GROUPS
IDENTITY	25 WEB SITES	13 GROUPS
BLACK SEPARATIST	8 WEB SITES	6 GROUPS
OTHER	35 WEB SITES	20 GROUPS
TOTALS	163 WEB SITES	81 GROUPS

Nation Of Islam*
Chicago, IL
www.noi.org/main.html
Atlanta, GA*
www.noi.org/atlanta/index.html
Boston, MA*
www.noi.org/boston/index.html
Durham, NC*
www.noi.org/durham/index.html
Los Angeles, CA*
www.noi.org/losangeles/index.html
Miami, FL
www.noi.org/miami/index.html

OTHER

14 Word Press*
St. Maries, ID
www.nidlink.com/~fourteenwords/
Alpha.org*
Philadelphia, PA

NAAWP of America*
Tampa, FL
www.angelfire.com/fl/naawp4usa/
Callahan, FL*
www.angelfire.com/fl/naawpofcallahan
Hilliard, FL*
www.angelfire.com/fl/naawpofneflorida/
Hogansville, GA*
www.angelfire.com/ga/naawpofgeorgia/
Honolulu, HI*
www.angelfire.com/hi/naawpofhawaii/
Garden City, MI*
pw2.netcom.com/~tlemire/naawpmic.html
Brookhaven, MS*
www.angelfire.com/ms/naawpofms
Nashville, TN*
www.angelfire.com/tn/

Appendix 3B: Resource Web Pages
for Racialists and Freedom Fighters

CyberHate: (Negative Articles about the Racial Awakening Movement)
http://wwwvms.utexas.edu/~axl/hate.html

Homelands: secessionist movements http://www.wavefront.com/~contra_m/homelands/

Alaskan Independence Party http://www.polarnet.fnsb.ak.us/End_of_Road/soapbox.dir/aip.dir/

Jim Kalb's Home Page: (thought provoking) http://www.panix.com/~jk/

Traditionalism Home Page: (Jim Kalb's traditionalist conservative HP) http://www.panix.com/~jk/trad.html

The Divine Conception:and crisis of the modern world http://www.panix.com/~jk/solar_temple_cr

Nation of Hawaii Home Page http://hawaii-nation.org/nation/

International Secessionist Movements http://dixienet.org/foreign/foreign.htm

Scottish Nationalist Party http://www.tardis.ed.ac.uk/~alba/snp/

Quebec secessionist home page http://www.gouv.qc.ca/anglais/premin/premin_comnat.html

Peaceful Secession page http://www.wavefront.com/~contra_m/homelands/peaceful.html

The Original WWW Banned Media Page I: (The Aryan Master file) http://www.gsu.edu/~hisjwbx/

The British Nationalist Party: http://ngwwmall.com/frontier/bnp/

WWW radio stations: http://sunsite.unc.edu/wxyc/howto.html http://www.kpig.com

The Southern League: (The south shall rise again) http://www.dixienet.org/

American Renaissance WWW page: http://www.amren.com

RESISTANCE RECORDS: (An Excellent Music Site) http://www.resistance.com

THE STORMFRONT WWW: (An Excellent and Informative resource site!) http://stormfront.org/stormfront

Underground CyberRailroad: (A Black Power WWW Page) http://www.GroupZ.net/~naturner/

The FYI Resource Page: http://www.getnet.com/azconnect/fyi.html

Anglo-Saxon/Christian Nationalism: http://www.cris.com/~Chrident/Nationalism.html

Christian Identity Online WWW Page: http://www.cris.com/~Chrident/

The Aryan Crusader's Library: (Excellent site w/ YGG files) http://www.io.com/~rlogsdon/

The California Civil Rights Initiative!: (Ending ALL Racial/Gender prefs!) http://www.cal-net.com:80/ccri/

The Spirit of Truth: (Politics & Current Events) http://www.ucc.uconn.edu/~jpa94001

The American Revolution: (The Name says it all) http://www.demon.co.uk/walden/revolt/aug95/revolt.html

The Northern Information Exchange: http://icewall.vianet.on.ca/pages/dwyerj/

Be Wise as Serpents: (Christian) http://www.pixi.com/~bewise/

The National Alliance: (An Excellent National Socialist Site) http://www.natvan.com

Militia of Montana: (Support the 2nd Amendment) http://www.shore.net/~adfx/2455.html

Irish Political Republican Movement: http://www.cs.yale.edu/homes/fodea/aprn/current/news/index.html

The Communist Party: (Another name for the Democratic Party)
http://www.tiac.net/users/brownh/cp-usa/cp-usa.html

Internet Users Consortium: http://www.indirect.com/www/molsen/IUC.html

SUBROSA Home Page: (Guns & Freedom) http://rmet.com:80/~subrosa/

Firearms & Liberty: (The Struggle for Freedom is Eternal)
http://www.cica.indiana.edu/hyplan/scotto/firearms/firearms.html

The Waco Index Page: (They need your voice) http://www.getnet.com/azconnect

The Codex Home Page (Anti-Big Brother Technologies) http://www.interaccess.com/trc/tsa.html

Anarcho-Discordia: (Anarchy) http://www.paranoia.com/~fraterk

Militias in the United States: (Join the Struggle Today!) http://www.acsys.com/~sims/revolution/militia.html

Conspiracy Materials: http://www.primenet.com/~lion/index.html

Libertarian Party Home Page: http://www.lp.org/lp.

Anarchy List: http://www.cwi.nl/cwi/people/Jack.Jansen/anarchy/anarchy.html

Young Americans for Freedom (YAF): http://www.crayola.cse.psu.edu/~humbert/Default.html

Dave Sims Militia Page: http://www.acsys.com/~sims/revolution/militia.html

RPI Objectivist Club: http://www.rpi.edu/dept/union/objectivist/public_html

The Ayn Rand Page: http://www.rpi.edu/~pier1/phil/objectivism.html

All URLs listed ! http://www.galcit.caltech.edu/~ta/revdoor/oldurls.shtml

The Right Side of The Internet: (The Republican fight for freedom) http://www.clark.net/pub/jeffd/index.html,
http://www.clark.net/pub/jeffd/mr_newt.html

The Electronic GunShop: http://www.xmission.com/~chad/egs/egs.com

Sk-Internet: (A Skinhead site) http://www1.usa1.com/~skrewdri/skinnet.htm

Patriots Web Page: (Important Patriot information) http://www.tezcat.com/patriot/

2050 Save the Earth: (environmental, save the planet) http://www.microserve.net/~heberts/

The Red Avengers: (conservative) http://sunsite.unc.edu/owl

Ernst Zundels: (Voice of Freedom) http://www.webcom.com/~ezundel/english/

The A-political SKINHEAD WWW page: http://www.ksu.edu/~lashout/skns.html

An excellent article on the Weaver incident: (Playboy) http://www.playboy.com/expose/overkill.html

War Against Racism (negros and liberals on dah Net) http://www.talink.com

Three Politically Incorrect E-Magazines: http://www.ionet.net/~ordway

Census Information: (Monitor The Third World Invasion)
http://www.tiac.net/users/ljohnson/census/census.html

The Nation of Islam: (Black Nationalism and Repatriation!) http://www.afrinet.net:80/~islam/
http://sunsite.unc.edu:80/nge/

World Wars Historical Page: http://reenactor.net

The EFFWeb Page: (Anti-Censorthought/censorshit) http://www.eff.org/pub/Alerts/

Bob's Firearms Page: (A good Second Amendment page) http://ramcad2.pica.army.mil/~rjd/guns/

Militia Watch: (A Left-Wing Liberal anti-Militia/Freedom page) http://paul.spu.edu/~sinnfein/progressive.html

The anti-facist Germany Alert!: http://www.webcom.com/~chantry/ga/

The Anti-Racist Action: (A Big Brother Organization in Canada) http://www.web.apc.org/~ara/

Arm The Spirit: (An other left-wing Big Brother Organization) http://burn.ucsd.edu/~ats

Here's a valuable one - the ACLU: gopher://aclu.org:6601/

The National Rifle Association: (The NRA needs Members) http://www.nra.org//

Milton Kleim's National Socialism Primer: (4 sites!) http://www.gl.umbc.edu/~laude/natlsocial.html, file://www.clark.net/pub/murple/local/nazi.faq - http://204.137.145.254/~tintin/ns/nsprimer.html, ftp://ftp.almanac.bc.ca/pub/people/k/kleim.milton/kleim.1294

Appendix 3C: Far Right Shortwave Program Log

(from the Web site for *VISTA*, the newsletter of Radio For Peace International; reprinted with permission)

Rarely do your Far Right Radio Review hosts listen to the worst of shortwave all day long. It is damaging enough to one's mental stability to check in on it at periodic intervals. But to demonstrate the collective strength of the multitude of radical reactionary right-wing radio programs now available on shortwave, we have compiled this log -- a sampling of what can be heard in a typical day.

FRRR Log. Monday, August 19, 1996.

9-10 am. Bo Gritz, *Freedom Calls,* WWCR.
> Freemasons are taking over. Jewish bankers attack Pat Buchanan. Life on Mars story a hoax to destroy Christianity. History of KKK. Selling land in Idaho separatist colony. Selling gold coins for survival of economic crash.

10-10:30 am. Ron Wilson, *Hour of Courage,* WWCR.
> Dixie theme. Report on stories in John Birch Society's New American. Relinquishing U.S. sovereignty with foreign troops on U.S. soil. Will be forced to bow to all demands of Japanese. Vince Foster "murder cover-up." Moral decline -- prepare for disaster -- buy gold.

11-11:30 am. Ron Wilson, *Hour of Courage,* WHRI.
> Repeat of 10am.

11am-12pm. Lynn Standewick, *Freedom Forum,* WWCR.
> Phones down. Explanation of all products in survivalist catalog -- water purifiers, Dutch oven recipes, night vision goggles. Roman Catholic Church is a tool of Satan.

11:30am-12pm. Larry Bates, *Unraveling the New World Order,* WHRI.
> Welfare reform is a big give-away to the poor. 80% tax rate coming. How to have all of your tax debt cancelled.

12-12:30 pm. Bill Lauderbach, *Domestic Shortwave Report,* WGTG.
> Analysis of other reactionary shortwave talk radio programs. Christian Identity, conspiratology, freedom of racist speech.

12:30-1 pm. Bob Spear, *Preparedness Hour,* WGTG.
> Time is running out. Tough financial times. Learn to defend yourself. Buy survivalist products.

12-3 pm. Chuck Harder, *For the People,* WHRI.
> U.S. Taxpayers Party propaganda. Cover-ups surrounding rencent spate of plane crashes. On Wall St. Journal article about gov't cover-up: "It's an interesting article. I haven't read it as yet, but the headline suggests that it might have been a bungle."

1-2 pm. Randall Terry, *Randall Terry Live,* WWCR.
> Report on U.S. Taxpayers Party convention. Bible-based legislators needed. No other issue but abortion. Aim to take over the world.

1-2 pm. Jim Ceaderstrom, *Financial Survival in the '90s,* WGTG.
> Promotion of coming survivalist convention in Indianapolis -- The Preparedness Expo. Only hope is gold, silver, platinum. Best prices.

1-3 pm. Henry Feinberg, *Henry Feinberg Show,* WWCR.
> Income tax is illegal. 1040 Form is voluntary. Right to travel freely is God-given; driving licenses are unconstitutional. Public schools are instituting hierarchy which New World Order will step into. Babies are marked at birth by governor for future roles in state service. Council on National Policy will make political representation obsolete.

2-3 pm. David Smith, *Newswatch Magazine,* WGTG.
> Why the 13th and 14th Amendments (abolishing slavery and guaranteeing freed slaves full citizenship) were undesirable and unconstitutional. Except on the larger plantations, slaves were better off than slave-owners, as they were able to enjoy a stronger sense of family and community. The Illuminati's control over the U.S. government.

3-4 pm. John Johnson, *Patriot News Hour,* WGTG.
> Report from the Republic of Texas, now an independent country once again.

3:30-4 pm. Ron Wilson, *Hour of Courage,* WHRI.
> Repeat of 10am program.

3-5 pm. Norm Resnick, *The Norm Resnick Show,* WWCR.
> Information from the Creation Research Center, "evaluating science in a biblical manner." Public schools can take your children and turn them over to Social Services whenever they care to.

4-4:30 pm. Stan Johnson, *The Prophesy Club,* WHRI, KWHR.
> The New World Order is going to come crashing through your front door.

4:30-5 pm. David Smith, *Newswatch Magazine,* WHRI.
> Repeat of half of 2pm program.

5-6 pm. Paul Parsons/Rick Tyler, *Voice of Liberty*, WWCR.
    Need for militias to stand ready. One-world socialist government is already upon us.
5-6 pm. George Douglas, *Common Sense*, WGTG.
    Off the air today.
5-6 pm. Pete Peters, *Scriptures for America*, WRNO.
    One of America's leading Christian Identity leaders, today speaking on the importance of tithes and offerings. Give generously.
5-6 pm. Steve Quayle, *Blueprint for Survival*, WWCR.
    Why citizens should build their own criminal justice system.
5-6 pm. Mark Koernke/John Stadtmiller, *The Intelligence Report*, WRMI.
    Lots of self-promotion as premier leaders of militia movement. Outcome-Based Education is training our children as soldiers for the New World Order.
6-6:15 pm. Bob Hallstrom, *Herald of Truth*, WRMI.
    Crying about his free speech rights to attack Jews as Satan's spawn and blacks as subhuman mud-people.
6-7 pm. Mark Koernke/John Stadtmiller, *The Intelligence Report*, WWCR.
    On a different station for their second hour. More on public education. Promotion of upcoming events -- protest the raising of the UN flag on UN day in Lansing, MI; attend a public hearing of the common law court of the "Republic of Texas." Federal detention centers are being built to house all objectors when the crash comes. Solicitation to rebroadcast program locally on micro-power FM stations.
6-7 pm. David Smith, *Newswatch Magazine*, WWCR.
    Repeat of 2pm program.
6-7 pm. Jeff Baker, *The Baker Report*, WGTG.
    Program from violent anti-abortion activist and Florida head of U.S. Taxpayers Party. Not on the air today.
6-7 pm. Suzanne Harris/Jack Ludlow, *The Law Loft Report*, WWCR.
    Ultra-conservative interpretation of the day's events on Capitol Hill.
7-8 pm. Viking International Trading, *Protecting Your Wealth*, WWCR.
    Land rights, gun rights, county supremacy. Total financial collapse is on the way. Buy gold; best prices.
7-8 pm. Pete Peters, *Scriptures for America*, WRMI.
    Anti-Christ forces are taking over the world. Fight for God's true chosen ones: the white race.
7-8 pm. Kurt Saxon, *The Kurt Saxon Show*, WWCR.
    Readings from 19th century letters relating to his Root Rot book. Exposing Alex Haley as a liar and explaining that blacks brought to America as slaves were better off than those left in Africa. Prepare for the end.
7-8 pm. Jack McLamb, *The Jack McLamb Show*, WHRI.
    Former Phoenix police officer recruits active duty law enforcement officers and military personnel to the militias.
8-10 pm. Tom Valentine, *Radio Free America*, WWCR.
    British Israel and Masonic lore. Challenge any civil authority. "Ethnic cleansing is not a war crime. It is a natural thing. It's a normal thing."
8-10 pm. John Bryant, *The John Bryant Show*, WWCR.
    Militia march on Washington planned for Labor Day. This is the 11th hour. Children born today will pay over 85% of earnings in taxes by the time they hit the workforce.
8:30-9 pm. Ron Wilson, *Hour of Courage*, WHRI.
    Repeat of 10am program.
9-11 pm. Chuck Harder, *For the People*, WHRI.
    Repeat of two hours of 12-3 program.
9:30-10 pm. Stan Johnson, *The Prophesy Club*, WHRI.
    Repeat of 4pm show.
10-11 pm. William Cooper, *Hour of the Time*, WWCR.
    The leader of the "Second Constitutional Army of the Republic" complains about a lack of support, about other militia leaders, and of the power of secret societies.
10-11 pm. Bob Enyart, *Bob Enyart Live*, WHRI.
    "The nation's most popular self-proclaimed right-wing religious fanatic, homophobic, anti-choice talk show host" rants about gays.
10-11 pm. Paul Parsons/Rick Tyler, *Voice of Liberty*, WWCR.
    The heads of Citizens for a Constitutional Georgia bring us more on the militia movement.

It is easy enough for most of us to pass off the wild idea that United Nations troops are going to storm out of manholes and invade the U.S. as crazed paranoia. We can hear sporadic calls for violent action and take heart that such hysteria is not rampant everywhere. We can be disgusted at overt racism, but realize that it is a small number of people who would actually hope to see a race war.

In most spaces, this is certainly the case. The racist and violent fringe does not dominate in the town square. On U.S. domestic shortwave, however, reactionary filth is the norm. People who might not otherwise fall for the scapegoating rhetoric of the far-right are being worn down by the sheer volume of it. A constant flow of programming, one feeding off the twisted logic of another, breaking down the good sense of good people hour after hour, day after day, month after month.

It is easy enough to understand why these racist and militant organizations have turned to shortwave. AM radio networks are expensive, and often a programmer will get run out of town when a community realizes that a particular show cannot be squeezed into the broadest interpretation of their standards of decency. Shortwave radio does not reach most people's daily commutes, and often they are not even aware that the medium exists. For those who seek it out by simply buying a shortwave radio and turning it on, however, it is as real as any information source.

Since the Federal Communications Commission in the United States went through a deregulatory binge and seemingly eliminated the requirement that shortwave broadcasts be directed at a foreign audience, the capacity of U.S.-based stations to carry this type of programming has grown enormously. With this, the character of the medium itself has been transformed as well. While international broadcasting was traditionally the realm of the open-minded listener who wanted to hear transmissions direct from overseas, it is now the place to go for the inspiration to build explosives and instructions for doing so. Pick up a shortwave radio next time a gun show comes to town.

Brad Heavner, October 1996

Appendix 3D: American Patriot Network Booklist

The APN offers its suggested reading list over its website on the Internet. It states that it does so because "You can never find these resources available in public libraries and these issues are never taught to our children in public schools." Amazon.com carries these titles--for which APN gratefully salutes it. Among APN's recommended titles are the following:

Federal Mafia: How it illegally Imposes and Unlawfully Collects Income Taxes by Irwin Schiff

The Social Security Swindle: How Anyone Can Drop Out by Irwin Schiff

The Rape of the American Constitution by Chuck Shiver

Why Government Doesn't Work by Harry Browne

Lost Rights: The Destruction of American Liberty by James Bovard

From Freedom to Slavery: The Rebirth of Tyranny in America by Gerry Spence

With Justice for None: Destroying an American Myth by Gerry Spence

Tax Protestors [sic] Handbook by Max

101 Uses for a Dead IRS Agent by Jim Waltz, et al

Ambush at Ruby Ridge: How Government Agents Set Randy Weaver Up and Took His Family Down by Alan W. Bock

The South Was Right! by Milton William Cooper

Chapter 4

But Carry a Big Stick

He rather hated the ruling few than love the suffering many.
—Jeremy Bentham

Rush Limbaugh

Without question the best-known and probably the most influential political talk show host on the air in the last decade of the twentieth century has been Rush Limbaugh. Although Howard Stern and Larry King may have more viewers and, to many people, are as great as or greater than Rush Limbaugh, Stern's forte has been essentially adolescent bathroom humor, mixed with an appropriately outrageous blend of right-wing libertarian political attitudes (he once ran for governor of New York on the Libertarian ticket), and King is essentially oriented to personality entertainment, with an occasional mixture of liberal politics.

Limbaugh came into national radio at the right time, in 1988, with the right format. William B. Falk wrote in *Newsday* in 1996 that "he struck several chords simultaneously, tapping middle-class resentment of Washington, welfare recipients, feminists and environmentalists, with humor and bombast that listeners found entertaining. By 1990 he was on 200 stations. Today, he's on 600."[1] With talk radio continuing to grow throughout the 1990s—one estimate determined that some twenty stations were converting to talk formats every month—Limbaugh's audience continues to grow. He does not hesitate to use name-calling, innuendoes, and falsehoods to attack people and ideas he disagrees with or who disagree with him. He will attack Bill Clinton with impunity as a draft dodger, yet he himself sought and received a draft deferment. He rails against most accepted government responsibilities toward the public and against humane social values. He capitalizes and appeals to his listeners' fears, prejudices, and anger. But he does so with panache and humor and has amassed a huge reputation and a huge following.

Limbaugh says:

> Liberals fear me because I threaten their control of the debate. . . . I have not attracted my audience by being a blowhard, a racist, a sexist, a hate-

131

monger. . . . If I were truly what my critics claim, I would long ago de-
servedly have gone into oblivion.[2]

Limbaugh encourages the belief, held by many, that he is not an extremist,
and that people who tried to link the Oklahoma City bombing to right-wing
extremists were wrong. He states

> as a member of the New Media, I have many responsibilities that the Old
> Media—the networks and big national newspapers—no longer seem to
> shoulder. . . . Since the beginning of our nation, citizens have been debat-
> ing the size, scope and role of federal government. Now, suddenly, in
> 1995, it is claimed that this two-century old argument caused the Okla-
> homa tragedy. . . . My audiences are mainstream Americans, and they
> lay blame solely on the criminals who committed this crime. And that's
> as far as the blame will go."[3]

Writing in the *Sacramento Bee* (this newspaper actually helped launch
Limbaugh with the aid of staff writer Dick Tracy—cousin of one of this book's
authors), William Endicott suggested that Limbaugh did feed right-wing extremist frenzy. "If he had been around in the 1960s," Endicott wrote, "Rush
Limbaugh would have been among the first to label the anti-Vietnam War
maniacs who were bombing in the name of peace as left-wing extremists. . . .
But it took him only about a millisecond [to blast] the mainstream media and
others for labeling as right-wing extremists the maniacs who bombed the federal building in Oklahoma City." Endicott noted that TV producer Stephen
Talbot, who did a PBS documentary on Limbaugh, said that Limbaugh "was
never a pure hatemonger, never anti-Semitic, never like the worst of these
people out there on radio." But, said Endicott, "at the same time, he
[Limbaugh] is stirring up this angry white guy, anti-government feeling, and
for him to deny that is totally disingenuous."[4]

Talk radio has made Limbaugh an icon for many Americans who believe he
gave them a public voice. As one newspaper story began, "The silent majority
is mute no more."[5] One argument for Limbaugh's popularity is that he is an
entertainer. Some sources say there are fewer liberals on the air because they
are boring. "Liberals are for things," William B. Falk wrote, "conservatives are
against them, and it's a lot more fun to be in the opposition, the argument goes.
If you don't kick around Hillary Clinton, tree-huggers and feminists, how can
you be entertaining?"[6] Limbaugh appears to be the sophisticated exemplar of
Falk's assertion that "on 1,300 stations across the country pumping out all talk,
all the time, you can hear raw, undigested material you don't find anywhere
else. Naked racial animus. Vicious political partisanship. Unsubstantiated

rumor. Bawdy irreverence about subjects your mother taught you not to discuss."[7] After Limbaugh used most of the three hours of one of his shows in 1998 to denigrate Hillary Clinton, critic Norma Greenaway wrote: "It was tacky and crude. . . . He mixed his vitriol for the Clintons with angry rants about such other favorite targets as 'Ivy League lesbians,' feminists, liberals and the wimpy mainstream media. . . . Die-hard fans cheered him on."[8]

Limbaugh's rhetoric reaches far. Larry King once estimated that "if you do the full swing of radio and TV, you are going to reach 80% of the public in a week."[9] Limbaugh has become not only an outlet, but a safety valve for many Americans who resent the power of those who control America, especially the federal government leaders who believe that the government has an important role to play in the progress of American society. The power to influence is not with the content of the talk show, it's with the moderator. Journalist Donella H. Meadow wrote: "He or she establishes the rules, decides who to call on, changes the subject, cuts people off. . . . Some call-in moderators are neutral. Then there's Rush Limbaugh, who is funny and pompous and a scapegoater and hatemonger. . . . Limbaugh's show is pure put-down humor."[10] Former Republican cabinet member William J. Bennett, however, praises Limbaugh as a survivor of a Clinton White House effort to "jump" on him, and states that his popularity is due, in part, to the fact that "he makes effective use of the time-honored American practices of satire and humor."[11]

Despite many brickbats, Limbaugh became, as Ronald Reagan said in 1992, "the number one voice for conservatism in our country."[12] William Buckley's *National Review* has declared him to be "the leader of the opposition."[13] And Mary Matalin, political director of the failed 1992 presidential campaign of George Bush, recalled "those dreary, dark, depressing, despondent days after that defeat in 1992. All we had to hold us together was Rush Limbaugh."[14] Even the senior analyst, Steven Randall, of the liberal watchdog group Foundation for Accuracy in Reporting, which has caught Limbaugh in a number of false statements on the air, noted that "Limbaugh and other talk hosts take credit for the 1994 Republican takeover of Congress . . . they admit their words can lead to actions."[15]

Limbaugh's opponents are just as passionate. An article by journalist Stephen Talbot, "Wizard of Ooze," begins:

> As we approach the millennium, this is the astonishing reality of American political life: A radio talk show host occupies center stage. Rush Limbaugh is an unlikely man for the role: a college dropout, fired from four radio jobs, twice divorced, obese, and insecure. Yet he has become one of the most influential forces in the country.[16]

While acknowledging his impact on the American public, many attack what they feel is Limbaugh's deliberate insensitivity on the air. Molly Ivins criticized Limbaugh for several vulgar cruelties, including one TV program where he noted there was a White house cat and showed a picture of Socks, and then noted there was a White House dog and showed a picture of Chelsea Clinton, then only a child of 13. On another show Limbaugh presented a picture of Labor Secretary Robert Reich that showed him only from the forehead up, making fun of Reich's short height that was due to a childhood bone disease. At the same time Ivins noted that the reason she takes Limbaugh "seriously is not because he's offensive or right-wing, but because he is one of the few people addressing a large group of disaffected people in this country" and that he does have a cultlike effect on them.[17] Some of Limbaugh's major targets have been women and racial minorities. He frequently uses the terms "feminazis" and "environmental whackos." Some of his comments: "The NAACP should have riot rehearsal. They should get a liquor store and practice robberies." "If you want a successful marriage, let your husband do what he wants to do. . . . You women don't realize how fortunate you are to be watching this show. I have just spelled out for you the key ingredient to a successful marriage [advising women to give up their careers to make their marriages work]." "I think the reason why girls don't do well on multiple choice tests goes all the way back to the Bible, all the way back to Genesis, Adam and Eve. God said, 'All right, Eve, multiple choice or multiple orgasms, what's it going to be?' We all know what was chosen." "I don't give a hoot that [Columbus] gave some Indians a disease that they didn't have immunity against." "If we are going to start rewarding no skills and stupid people . . . [let them take] the unskilled jobs . . . the kinds of jobs that take absolutely no knowledge whatsoever to do . . . let stupid and unskilled Mexicans do that work."[18]

A few audience statistics indicate some of the reasons for Limbaugh's popularity. A 1996 study by Shane Media showed that 48.5 percent of the listeners to talk shows consider themselves to be conservative, 40.3 percent moderate, and only 11.2 percent liberal. Forty percent of all listeners had tuned in to Rush Limbaugh's program in the month preceding the study, 59 percent within the two months before the study, and 45 percent had been listening to Limbaugh for three years or more. Ninety percent liked his aggressive political edge, the same number found the show entertaining, and 53 percent said they would consider any ideas endorsed by Limbaugh.[19] In another study, 35 percent of radio talk show hosts described themselves as conservative or very conservative, 45 percent said they were moderate, and 13 percent said they were liberal.[20] At the National Association of Radio Talk Show Hosts conference in 1995, a survey was quoted stating that 70 percent of the talk show hosts considered themselves conservative.[21]

While Limbaugh supporters swear by his "revelations," reveling in information he presents that they cannot find in the mainstream media, Limbaugh's critics point out that much of this so-called information—designed to influence the minds and hearts of his listeners and successfully doing so—are simply lies or half-truths. Foundation for Accuracy in Reporting (FAIR)—which Limbaugh has described as a left-wing propaganda organization—made a study of Limbaugh's shows and published a long list of misstatements—and corrections. Among them were the following:[22]

Limbaugh: "Don't let the liberals deceive you into believing that a decade of sustained growth without inflation in America [in the 1980s] resulted in a bigger gap between the haves and the have-nots. Figures compiled by the Congressional Budget Office [CBO] dispel that myth."

Fact: The CBO figures showed that after-tax incomes in 1980 for the richest 20 percent of our country was eight times the income of the poorest 20 percent; by the end of the 1980s that figure had jumped from eight times to twenty times.

Limbaugh: "The poorest people in America are better off than the mainstream families of Europe" [1993].

Fact: [from the World Bank Development Report of 1994]: The poorest one-fifth of the United States has a purchasing power of $5,433 worth of goods; mainstream or average persons in Germany have a purchasing power of $20,610; in France, $19,200; in the UK $16,730.

Limbaugh: "All these rich guys—like the Kennedy family and Perot— pretending to live just like we do and pretending to understand our trials and tribulations and pretending to represent us, and they get away with this. [1993]

Fact: [*Forbes* magazine, 1994]: Limbaugh's income over the past two years was estimated to be $25 million.

Limbaugh: "I have yet to encourage you people or urge you to call anybody. I don't do it. They think I'm the one doing it. That's fine. You don't need to be told when to call. They think you're a bunch of lemmings out there."

Fact: Later, on the same radio show, discussing President Clinton's tax proposals, Limbaugh said: "The people of these states

> where these Democratic senators are up for re-election . . .
> have to let their feelings be known. . . . Let's say Herb Kohl
> is up . . . you people in Wisconsin who don't like this bill,
> who don't like the tax increase, you let Herb Kohl know
> somehow."

Limbaugh has frequently replied to such charges, sometimes quoting conservative sources as the basis for his conclusions, and dismissing FAIR's reality checks by charging that it is a left-wing group bent on discrediting the right with disinformation. Limbaugh supporters say that catching Limbaugh in allegedly false statements constitutes "desperate attempts by some liberal members of the media to marginalize Rush Limbaugh."[23]

G. Gordon Liddy

For most Americans G. Gordon Liddy—convicted Watergate conspirator and advocate of assassinating journalist Jack Anderson, a severe critic of Liddy's boss, Richard Nixon—would appear to be an extremist in his talk-show rhetoric. His program is nationally syndicated on hundreds of stations. They point to his instructions on how to kill federal agents (using his knowledge as an ex-FBI agent). They would be surprised to learn that compared to most of the true extremists on the far right, Liddy is considered by many to lean more toward the center of conservatism, although perhaps frequently tending toward the fringe. Liddy epitomizes California Governor Pete Wilson's description of talk radio as an "outlet for the disenfranchised [that] galvanizes and expresses public opinion to produce change in a forceful way."[24] It is safe to say that the disenfranchised racial and ethnic minorities and poor people who rely on the government for protection and survival would not designate right-wing talk radio as a support and comfort. Accused of stoking the flames of intolerance, Liddy has strongly denied such allegations. "If you have ever listened to my program," Liddy has said, "you will know that there are people who from time to time have been so foolish as to send me a fax or to get on the air and to attack black people because they're black or Jews because they're Jews or something like that, and I will make mincemeat out of them promptly. . . . It is perfectly within the job description of a talk show host to use persuasive speech to try to get something corrected."[25] Liddy is very popular among militia groups and refers to himself as "the voice of hope and freedom" and his talk show as "Radio Free DC."[26]

Perhaps Liddy's most outrageous—certainly his most publicized—talk show advocacy was his description of how to shoot a federal agent who one might believe was threatening one's life. Liddy recommended that the shooter aim for the head or the groin because federal agents usually wear bullet-proof vests. Invoking a fear of agents of the Bureau of Alcohol, Tobacco and Firearms, and referring to the destruction of the Branch Davidian compound in Waco, Texas, he said to shoot at the groin area because "they cannot move their hips fast enough and you'll probably get a femoral artery and you'll knock them down at any rate."[27]

He also suggested that his audience prepare themselves with target practice, using cardboard figures of Bill and Hillary Rodham Clinton as targets.[28] For some, even conservatives, Liddy's remarks went too far. Shortly after his "federal agent" recommendation, he was disinvited from a National Republican Senatorial Committee dinner he was about to attend.[29] For others, however, his talk show comments were regarded with favor, not disdain, and not only by the right-wing extremists who routinely advocate the murder of the president and first lady and federal agents. At its 1995 convention the National Association of Radio Talk Show Hosts (NARTSH) gave Liddy its annual "Freedom of Speech" award. Some NARTSH members objected, with comments such as: "If he uses speech that inflames and that may encourage some extremists to rationalize confronting or harming law enforcement, that is not speech that should receive an award." Other comments were stronger, objecting to "honoring explicit calls to violence and bloodshed," and saying "we have awesome power on the air and we need to use that for good, not for smut or evil." Most NARTSH members supported Liddy, with comments like those of convention chairman Michael Harrison, publisher of *Talkers* magazine: "The spirit of the award was not for honoring G. Gordon Liddy's ideology. Our point is, we don't think Liddy is such a monster as the mainstream press has made him out to be."[30] Harrison has described Liddy as "a benign entertainer."[31] Harrison further explained NARTSH's motivation for the award to Liddy: "We saw it as our role to protect the image of talk radio and the right of its people to free speech."[32]

Bob Grant

As viciously racist as Bob Grant may seem to many, in comparison to the rhetoric and rantings of extremist right-wing talk radio he does not seem so inflammatory. His rhetoric can probably be best described as usually on the edge of extremism, but not too often over it. For years Grant was a talk-host centerpiece for the American Broadcasting Company's flagship station, WABC, in New York. With more than an estimated million listeners a day, he pulled in big bucks from advertisers such as Sears, Amtrak, and Lincoln-Mercury—and big kudos and raspberries from the public. His unabashedly racist programming—"Grant runs a program that often resembles a Ku Klux Klan rally of the airwaves—cruel, racist, with hints of violence,"[33] as it was once described—

led to his eventual firing by ABC. He was quickly picked up by another key New York station, WOR.

Grant's style is not sophisticated and satirical, like Limbaugh's, nor does it have cold, matter-of-fact purported logic, like Liddy's, but is overtly crude and insulting. For example, Grant generally describes African-Americans as "savages" and "subhumanoids." On one program, referring to a gathering of African-American students at Belmar Beach in New Jersey, Grant talked about their "savage mind, the primitive, primordial mentality. . . . As far as that stretch of beach there at Belmar, it's being written off by, shall we say, civilized people."[34] African-Americans who have called in to his show to protest his remarks have been dismissed with epithets such as "swine" and "shoeshine boys."[35]

Some quotes from Grant's programs: [to a Black male] "Get off my phone, you creep, we don't need the toilets cleaned right now"; [to a Black woman] "I don't need the windows washed today"; [to another Black caller] "On the evolutionary scale, you're about 25 generations behind me"; "I'd like to get every environmentalist, put 'em up against a wall, and shoot 'em." Commenting on a Gay Pride parade in New York City, he expressed his wish that the police had machine-gunned the marchers. He has also expressed his hope for the death of people he disliked, including President Clinton, basketball athlete Magic Johnson, and Haitian refugees.[36] When the plane carrying Secretary of Commerce Ron Brown went down, Grant expressed his hope on the air that Brown had died—before anyone knew whether Brown had been killed or not.[37] This was apparently the final straw for ABC, which was deluged by protests from the public, and resulted in Grant's being fired.

While most of his rhetoric is negative, he has at times advocated positive action—for violence. When a caller complained about his frustration with the state of society and the federal government, Grant said, "Well, get a gun and go do something, then." And his solution when callers complained about the welfare system was to recommend a mandatory sterilization plan for women on welfare.[38]

Grant has been accused of directly promoting the causes of white supremacist and neo-Nazi groups on the air, those that overtly and passionately call for violence. He has denied this. However, tapes of his programs show that he has from time to time allowed callers from extremist groups to give out not only information about their philosophies and goals, but their addresses and telephone numbers as well, for recruiting purposes. Among the organizations he has promoted in this way are the neo-Nazi National Alliance (whose head, William Pierce, authored *The Turner Diaries* novel, which served as a blueprint for The Order, the group that assassinated liberal talk-show host Alan Berg in 1984); the National Association for the Advancement of White People (founded by David Duke); and White Aryan Resistance.[39] Grant's rhetoric became so harsh that many of his supporters ultimately turned away. George

Bush, for example, had sought his endorsement, and Christine Todd Whitman, after winning the New Jersey governorship, appeared on Grant's show to thank him for "all that you did to help the campaign," and went on his show again to invite him to her inauguration. They no longer cozy up to Grant.[40]

Grant has had his defenders other than the right-wingers who agree with his rhetoric. Journalist Marc Fisher of the *Washington Post*, for example, believes that Grant's kind of "hate radio" is a positive "venting mechanism" for people who otherwise might resort to violent action. "By giving extremists an outlet," Fisher wrote, "radio has spared the rest of us from whatever other tricks they might have dreamed up had society not given them a voice." Others have countered this defense by pointing out that, in effect, this logic gives right-wingers the right to blackmail society by saying, "Listen to me, or I'll kill you."[41] Other defenders stand by America's First Amendment rights, free speech for anybody and everybody as a cornerstone of democratic freedoms. Some insist that the best way to deal with "hate" speech is not by suppression but by expanding opportunities for varied points of view to access the airwaves. Parenthetically, such opportunity virtually disappeared when President Ronald Reagan vetoed a Fairness Law in 1987, effectively abolishing the long-standing Fairness Doctrine which authorized the FCC to require stations to offer reasonable time for opposing views when only one side of a controversial issue was presented by a radio or television station. Since 1987 neither Congress nor the White House has made any attempt to reinstate a Fairness Doctrine, despite (or because of?) the increasing dominance of the airwaves by one-sided right-wing rhetoric.

Tom Gresham

Taking to the air in 1996, Gresham exemplifies the single-issue right-wing talk show host. While including some of the rhetoric of far-right and extremist-right groups, Gresham's show, "Gun Talk," is essentially that—"high power intellectual ammunition on guns, crime, politics, the 2nd amendment, hunting, competitive and recreational shooting."[42] Gresham offers technical and political information. In the latter category, for example, "the *L.A. Times* twists, distorts, and just plain lies to further its effort to confiscate firearms"; [concerning assault weapons] "In Switzerland many civilians are required to keep fully-automatic weapons at home, yet they have a very low crime rate"; "latest study entitled *Guns in America: National Survey on Private Ownership and Use of Firearms,* validates the usefulness of firearms for self-defense." As might be expected, his sponsors have included the Remington Arms Company, Browning, Smith & Wesson, Pentax Corporation, and the National Rifle Association. His program is heard on the Talk America Radio Network, encompassing some 100 stations coast-to-coast.[43]

Hometown Demagogues?

Jerry Williams is typical of the local talk show host who not only garners a large following but exercises strong impact on the community. Operating out of Boston, Williams essentially falls into the libertarian category, not spouting hate or prejudice but taking a right-wing approach to government. In 1986 Williams was a leader in a campaign to repeal a Massachusetts law requiring drivers to wear seat belts; he urged his listeners to vote for a referendum overturning the law. Many critics feel that Williams bears a major responsibility for the death of hundreds of drivers in Massachusetts who would not have been killed had the seat belt law been in effect. He was also a key factor in a national campaign in 1989 in which he enlisted talk show hosts throughout the country to urge citizens to lobby Congress to kill a proposed pay raise for legislators. In 1989 he played another national leadership role, convening the first conference of what became the National Association of Radio Talk Show Hosts. While local talk-show personalities (many of whom reach beyond their communities through regional and sometimes national syndication) do not have the power of the Limbaughs and of the Liddys, they can, as Williams has done, affect the political and social fabric of their communities and even the nation. A former Federal Communications Commissioner once called Williams-type local talk show hosts "a bunch of hometown demagogues."[44]

Spencer Hughes, based in San Francisco, is one of the local talk show hosts who defended Timothy McVeigh after the latter was accused of bombing the Oklahoma City federal building. On one of his three-hour call-in shows, devoted to a discussion of what role talk radio might have played in inciting McVeigh, Hughes sardonically remarked: "Three people saw him in front of the building, he didn't react to pictures of dead babies, and he's not talking or cooperating. . . . Is he supposed to break down on his hands and knees and 'Boo-hoo-hoo, it's so horrible what happened'?"[45] Shortly afterward Hughes supported G. Gordon Liddy's attack on President Clinton for saying that "we must stand up and speak against reckless speech that can push fragile people over the edge, beyond the boundaries of civilized conduct." Referring to the federal destruction of the Branch Davidian compound in Waco, Hughes said: "They knew they were taking out kids, they knew they were crushing innocent people. As far as I'm concerned, if you go into my house, and try to gas my wife and my kids and my neighbors to death . . . you better damn well believe I'm going to fire back."[46]

Sounds violent? But even some of Liddy's and Hughes's critics have said "they are the voice of reason compared to some of the extremist ranting on . . . radio."[47]

Bob Mohan, a Phoenix talk-show host, not considered far right or extremist, typifies the local host who from time to time goes into or over the fringe area of conservative content. Reflecting the anti-gun-control attitudes of his constituency, Mohan criticized the gun-control efforts of Sarah Brady, the wife of President Reagan's press secretary, Jim Brady, who was seriously wounded and left with a permanent disability in the attempted assassination of Reagan. Mohan, on Sarah Brady: "You know, she should be put down. A humane shot at a veterinarian's would be an easy way to do it. Because of all her barking and complaining, she really needs to be put down." With the insensitivity that marks many other right-wing hosts who lamely attempt to be satirical, he continued: "I wish she would keep wheeling her husband around to go to speaking engagements—wiping the saliva off his mouth once in a while—and leave the rest of us damn well alone."[48]

Tom Donahue gained adherents as a libertarian talk-show host in Dallas. Donahue's rhetoric was essentially the same anti-government commentary that marks most right-wing radio shows: he called for the impeachment of President Clinton, referred to Attorney-General Janet Reno as "Butcher Reno," and attacked Hillary Clinton ("Hillary's Hellish Health Care"). Although a member of a "Freeman" group, he generally stopped short of the extremist advocacy of many Freeman organizations, and concentrated on protesting the economic role of the government in people's lives, principally that of the Internal Revenue Service and the Federal Reserve Bank. Donahue's show, "America's Town Forum," was being carried by some sixty stations nationally on the Talk America Radio Network and he seemed on his way to becoming one of the top right-wing national radio personalities. However, he was arrested and convicted in 1994 of conspiracy and money laundering, operating a pyramid scheme that bilked millions of dollars out of hundreds of people—a sideline to his radio show. Ironically, he continued to appear on his radio show from prison and even ran for Congress—from prison—on the Libertarian ticket, getting a surprising 9 percent of the votes. Donahue insists that he was innocent and was made a political prisoner because of his right-wing beliefs. "A prisoner of war," he said, echoing the far right's rhetoric.[49]

Sean Hannity in Atlanta is another example of the power of a local right-wing radio host. Hannity grew up on Long Island, New York, where one of his favorite radio personalities was Bob Grant. The influence is clear, as Hannity made his initial reputation on radio, according to his critics, by "race-baiting and gay-bashing." His air portfolio includes the usual attacks on the Clintons and a description of homosexuality as "unnatural . . . weird." While principally oriented to negative anti-liberal commentary, Hannity has one subject he takes a strong positive stand on: He describes Newt Gingrich as "an absolute genius." Although his local status does not give him the power of national talk radio personalities, he has clout in his own state. In 1994, after the Republicans won control of Congress, President Clinton called Newt Gingrich to offer his congratulations. Gingrich reportedly put off taking the call because he did not want to interrupt his conversation with Hannity.[50]

One of the most popular so-called moderates is Chuck Harder. He is considered by many to have perhaps the most loyal and consistent audience of any right-wing radio talk-show host. As noted in chapter 1, his words appears reasoned rather than inflammatory. But Harder has also been called the "King of the Conspiracy Theorists," and although his rhetoric is not as extreme as other leading conspiracy theorists, he is profiled with them in chapter 7, along with a statement of his principles and approach he prepared exclusively for this book.

Individual right-wing personalities make an impact even when they don't have their own shows. For example, "The McLaughlin Group" is seen regularly on television on more than 300 public television stations nationwide and on a number of commercial TV outlets, as well. In a sense, the program is public broadcasting's answer to the oft-repeated right-wing accusation that the non-commercial network is too liberal. John McLaughlin himself is an acknowledged conservative and as host he decides on the topics, the direction of the discussion, and the participants. Avoiding the inflammatory rhetoric of most talk shows, "The McLaughlin Group" is able to reach many decision-makers with moderate to strongly conservative ideas.[51] Under the guise of being mainstream conservative, shows like "The McLaughlin Group" are able to deliver to unwary listeners ideas that are associated more with the far right. It is no accident that one of the regular panelists is Pat Buchanan, an advocate of the Christian Right and considered by many to be closer to the far right than to the center he frequently claims to represent. In fact, when he ran for president, one of Buchanan's strongest supporters was the far-right-wing Liberty Lobby. In its publication, *Spotlight,* Liberty Lobby wrote: "A quick run through the 112 issues or legislative positions that Liberty Lobby has taken over the past 40 years . . . shows that Pat Buchanan stands with us. Liberty Lobby is proud to have laid the groundwork for Buchanan's candidacy. . . . He supports prayer in the schools, the right to keep and bear arms, the right to life, reconfirmation of federal judges by the electorate, an honest welfare system, protective tariffs and a strong dollar. . . . The victory of Buchanan would be the best thing for America since Andrew Jackson. . . . This is the moment Liberty Lobby has long awaited."[52] Conservatism, especially on the airwaves, frequently wears several faces.

While many have decried the preponderance of right-wing rhetoric filling the airwaves and the ears, eyes, and minds of the American public, most of those most opposed to the right-wing philosophy have strongly defended the conservatives' right to be heard. Even when the rhetoric advocates and even results in violence, the First Amendment is strongly defended. Columnist Carl T. Rowan summed it up when he wrote:

And, please, no laws designed to gag even the worst of the talk show fanatics or the politicians who turn verbal fertilizer and snake oil into an explosive concoction. In a free society, no one is permitted to say by fiat where the line is between incitement to violence and courageous political commentary.[53]

Ed Shane, president of Shane Media in Houston, Texas, is one of the country's experts on talk radio. He has analyzed the success of conservative talk radio from Rush Limbaugh's impetus, giving both right-wing talk shows and Limbaugh himself prominence. Essentially, Shane believes that Limbaugh and his followers "paralleled a rise in conservative political thinking" and offered what their "listeners felt needed to be said."[54] (See Appendix A, following.)

Appendices to Chapter 4

Appendix 4A: Talk Radio

"I don't have time for a newspaper. I listen to radio for the news and to Rush Limbaugh to find out what's going on." The comment came from a man in his mid-thirties on a cramped commuter flight into Atlanta. It's the same comment heard everywhere since Rush Limbaugh began his reign over talk radio.

Of himself, Limbaugh said, "I validate what people hold dear." He was responding to questions from *USA Today* about his book, *See, I Told You So*, his second to reach the newspaper's best-seller list.

Limbaugh didn't invent talk radio, but he was the first talk-show host many of his white, baby boom-aged, male audience encountered. His rise to prominence in the late 1980s paralleled a rise in conservative political thinking and public discourse. If Limbaugh didn't "validate" what his listeners said, he could be characterized accurately as articulating what his listeners felt needed to be said.

The Talk Radio Phenomenon

From two full-time talk stations in 1960, the number grew to 858 stations by the close of 1993. This number included a dramatic increase of 68 percent from the 583 stations broadcasting talk in April 1992.

Growth was fueled by Limbaugh. however, other big-name talk talents laid the groundwork for his emergence. Larry King, long-time dean of late night talk radio kept insomniacs informed with live interviews from Washington, D.C., and public response by phone from across the United States.

Bruce Williams, on NBC Radio's "Talknet," answered financial and legal questions in an understanding, fatherly manner long before Limbaugh came to the nation's attention. In addition, most major cities had a prominent talk-show hot who personified talk radio in each market.

On Limbaugh's coattails came other talk hosts and upstart networks that fed local stations hungry for talk radio. In May 1993, *Radio Business Report* listed fifteen networks supplying talk programing. Some supply enough programming for twenty-four-hour broadcast. Others, like Limbaugh's network, provide only a few shows.

Paralleling Limbaugh's rise was that of shock-jock Howard Stern, who is not a talk host per se, but whose program abandoned music in favor of free-wheeling conversation often centered on Stern and his private parts. A *Time* magazine article profiling both Stern and Limbaugh in 1993 compared and contrasted the two men. The similarity is that both discuss in public ideas audiences seemed unable to articulate on their own.

Stern's program was seldom heard on talk stations; his affiliates were primarily rock music outlets. As one station manager described it, "Stern says what The Who used to sing." That reinforces the rock context of Stern's unpredictable broadcasts.

Evolution of Talk Formats

Early radio seemed unpredictable, but it was fully scripted. In the 1930s, the spoken word was, in reality, the read word. It was not until the 1950s and 1960s that improvisation and informal discussion helped radio develop its own character.

Talk shows became familiar to listeners in the 1950s as music stations devoted time to discussion of local issues. The motivation behind most early talk programming was to satisfy public affairs requirements as specified in licenses granted by the Federal Communications Commission.

"Arthur Godfrey Time," a program on CBS Radio, was considered by some an early talk show. Godfrey would chat, sing, and play the ukulele in a relaxed, conversational style. Even though Godfrey's program has since been classified "variety" by radio historians, the host traded on public response: "Did you hear what Godfrey said this morning?" That same word-of-mouth "advertising" helped to drive the 1990s version of talk.

The term "talk station" came into being when KABC in Los Angeles discarded its records in 1960 and filled its twenty-four-hour day with talk shows. The station was originally promoted as "The Conversation Station."

Not long afterward, KABC's sister station, KGO in San Francisco, used the designation "News-Talk" because it carried news blocks in morning and afternoon drive-time periods with talk shows between. "News-talk" has become the generic radio industry term for all stations that carry both news and talk programming.

One of the first stars of the new talk radio medium was Joe Pyne, who appeared on KLAC in Los Angeles in the mid-1960s. Pyne's reputation was built on his style of verbal bombast against almost everyone, guest and caller alike. Pyne had no philosophical leaning except to the contrary. He established the habit of hanging up the phone on callers he disagreed with, a habit later adopted by talk hosts seeking to create the reputation of firebrand.

Pyne achieved some national notoriety, primarily through a short-lived television show. His radio work was not syndicated because technology of that time was too expensive to link stations not already affiliated with the three major networks.

Satellite technology in the 1980s gave syndicators the type of access to local stations that the networks had previously had. That gave rise to ABC Talkradio, featuring hosts from various ABC-owned talk stations. Technology also fueled NBC's Talknet, Business Radio Network (later known as American Forum Radio), Sun Radio Network, and others who distributed talk shows on a regional or national basis.

New York's WOR Radio, long a leader in talk programming in its own city, used satellite technology to deliver its talk shows to a national audience. Former libertarian candidate Gene Burns, money advisers Ken and Daria Dolan, psychologist Dr. Joy Browne, and others talked about issued that transcended local New York concerns.

The Influence of Talk

If technology was one parent of talk radio's availability, deregulation was the other. For forty-two years radio and television were ruled by the "fairness doctrine," which required stations to broadcast opposing views on public issues. Deregulation abolished the rule in 1987, leaving talk hosts unrestrained.

The power of talk radio had been felt on a local level since the format's inception. Local stations traditionally staged debates and allowed unprecedented access to politicians. Deregulation merged journalism and populism. The public asked questions that had been previously the domain of reporters and gossip columnists.

Boston's Jerry Williams and listeners who heard his show on WRKO were credited with overturning Massachusetts's seat belt law in 1988.

At an organizational meeting of the National Association of Radio Talk Hosts (NARTH) in 1989, Williams called talk radio "the greatest forum in history . . . the last bastion of freedom of speech for plain ordinary folks." The organization attempted to set a political agenda: "It's our government and we're going to take it back from those aristocrats," said Mike Siegel of KING Radio in Seattle.

Talk radio created a new dynamic during the 1992 Presidential campaign. Most candidates, prompted by exposure given independent Ross Perot, appeared on both radio and television talk shows to disseminate their views and corral support. The notable exception was then President George Bush, who lost to a talk show regular, Bill Clinton.

Aides in the Clinton campaign believed their candidate turned around his chances in New York with an early morning appearance with Don Imus, morning man on Sports-talk WFAN.

California's Jerry Brown surprised political pundits by winning Connecticut's Democratic primary. Some observers felt his key move was an appearance on Michael Harrison's program then heard on WTIC in Hartford. Brown later hosted his own talk show.

Brown was not the only talk personality to join the talk host ranks from outside radio. G. Gordon Liddy, of Watergate infamy, had the highest profile because of his national network program. On the local level, former Los Angeles police chief Daryl Gates, former New York Mayor Ed Koch, and former San Diego Mayor Roger Hedgecock started new careers as talk hosts in their hometowns.

Radio industry observers expect talk radio to continue its growth well into the 2000s. The number of stations broadcasting the format is predicted to rise, probably adding FM stations to the predominantly AM base talk radio has now. Specialized types of talk radio, like sports-talk, will add to the growth in numbers of stations.

Ed Shane
Shane Media Services
Houston, Texas

Bibliography

Asker, Jim. "Talk radio popularity rise crackles with controversy." *Houston Chronicle,* June 11, 1989.

Broadcasting. "Medium is message at talk radio conference." July 19, 1989.

Bulkeley, William M. "Talkshow Hosts Agree on One Point: They're the Tops." *Wall Street Journal,* June 15, 1989.

Buxton, Frank, and Owen, Bill. *The Big Broadcast 1920–1950.* New York: Viking, 1972.

Green, Lee. "All Talk, All the Time." *Spirit.* March 1994.

Henabery, Bog. "Talk Radio: from Caterpillar to butterfly." *Radio Business Report,* January 17, 1994.

James, Rollye. "The RUSH to Talk Continues . . ." *Radio Ink.* January 17–30, 1994.

Keith, Michael C. *The Radio Station.* Stoneham, MA: Focal Press, 1989.

King, Larry, with Yoffe, Emily. *Larry king by Larry King.* New York: Simon and Schuster, 1982.

Marr, Bruce. "Talk Radio Programming," in Eastman, Susan, Head, Sydney, and Klein, Lewis, eds. *Broadcast Programming.* Belmont, CA: Wadsworth, 1981.

Postman, Neil. *Amusing Ourselves to Death: Public Discourse in the Age of Show business.* New York: Viking, 1985.

Postrel, Virginia I. "Revived fairness doctrine only a scheme to muzzle talk radio." *Houston Chronicle,* August 22, 1993.

Priest, Patricia Joyner. *Self Disclosure on Television: The Counter-Hegemonic Struggle of Marginalized Groups on "Donahue."* Unpublished doctoral dissertation, University of Georgia, Athens, GA, 1992.

Radio Business Report: "Programming for Profit with Satellite Talk." May 17, 1993.

Ibid. "Talk Radio Today: Pulling it all together." May 24, 1993.

Rosentiel, Thomas B. "The talk-show phenomenon." *Houston Chronicle,* May 31, 1992.

Schwartz, Tony. *Media the Second God.* New York: Random House, 1981.

Appendix 4B: Reactionary Forces
Link Up in Militias

(from the "Stop the Hate" Web Site; http:\\www.stop-the-hate.org)

The currents that coalesced into the militia movement arose from three principal sources, the openly racist, anti-Semitic Christian Identity movement, the conspiratorialist, paranoid Christian Patriot movement, which incorporates a tacitly white supremacist ideology of "Constitutionalism", and the theocratic, repressive anti-gay and anti-woman Christian Reconstructionist and Christian Right forces. To these fascist elements were added a more mass base drawn from "wise use" anti-environmental forces and Second Amendment groups opposed to gun control. Shortly after the Ruby Ridge stand-off between the FBI and white supremacist Randy Weaver, a meeting convened in Estes Park Colorado by Christian Identity "pastor" Pete Peters drew more than 150 participants, mostly from the racist right. At this gathering, Christian Reconstructionist Larry Pratt proposed the formation of militias as a direct action armed formation to defend gun rights, based on the model of armed Christian evangelical forces that had fought insurgencies in the Philippines and Guatemala. Pratt enjoyed solid connections and credentials with the mainstream Reagan right, and heads up both Gun Owners of America (to the right of the NRA) and English First (an anti-immigrant group to the right of US English). His militia proposal carried the day, and shortly thereafter, in the wake of the Clinton election, the Brady Bill and the Waco tragedy, the militias took off as a national phenomenon.

- Movements and groups:
  - CHRISTIAN IDENTITY
  - ARYAN NATIONS
  - SCRIPTURES FOR AMERICA
  - JUBILEE
  - THE ORDER
  - KU KLUX KLAN
  - CHRISTIAN PATRIOTS
  - POLICE AGAINST THE NEW WORLD ORDER
  - S.P.I.K.E.
  - STATE CITIZENSHIP SOVEREIGNTY
  - CHRISTIAN RIGHT
  - FREE MILITIA OF WISCONSIN
  - U.S. TAXPAYERS PARTY
  - GUN OWNERS OF AMERICA
  - ENGLISH FIRST
  - CHRISTIAN RE-CONSTRUCTIONISTS
  - OPERATION RESCUE
  - RESCUE AMERICA
- KEY INDIVIDUALS:
  - John Trochmann
  - Pete Peters
  - "Bo" Gritz
  - Larry Pratt
  - Ron Arnold
  - Joe Fields
  - Gen. John Singlaub

CHRISTIAN IDENTITY

This racist theology preaches that whites are the true Israel, America is their promised land; that non-whites are "pre-Adamic, sub-human, and that Jews are the spawn of Satan.

ARYAN NATIONS

Headquartered in an Idaho para-military compound this racist group has spread nation-wide as the militia movement has grown. More and then 30 militias now use a surveillance system promoted by the Aryan Nations to spy on their "enemies".

SCRIPTURES FOR AMERICA

Pete Peters' "Bible Study" group hosts annual retreats for leader of the racist Christian Identity movement, and was a recruiting ground for the bloody "Order conspiracy, along with the Aryan Nations.

JUBILEE

The leading Christian Identity group in California has brought together Louis Beam of the KKK and Aryan Nations, neo-nazi Joe Fields. State Senator Don Rogers and Christian Reconstructionist John Quade to promote "state sovereignty".

THE ORDER

A white supremacy underground the robbed banks and Brinks' trucks, distributing the loot to public racist leaders. They killed Jewish radio host Allen Berg.

KU KLUX KLAN

The oldest racist political group in the world has gained a new lease on life with the adoption of its slogans by mainstream politicians. On the offensive again in the midwest and southeast.

CHRISTIAN PATRIOTS

This movement often overlaps with Christian Identity. Christian Patriot Defense League founder Jack Mohr is a close ally of Pete Peters. These tax protesters also call themselves Constitutionalist and provide a big base of support for the militias.

POLICE AGAINST THE NEW WORLD ORDER

This group, initiated by an ex-Phoenix cop, promotes the racist and anti-Semitic views of Eustace Mullins, and seeks to recruit active duty law enforcement officers to support the militia movement.

S.P.I.K.E.

"Specially Prepared Individuals for Key Events" is Bo Gritz's attempt to provide Green Beret training and national para-military organization into "A-teams" for the Christian patriots.

STATE CITIZENSHIP SOVEREIGNTY

They believe that the only true citizens are those whose citizenship predates the 14th amendment (essentially, white male property owners). The militias have popularized this view through support for the Organic Constitution (original articles plus the the Bill of Rights only).

CHRISTIAN RIGHT

Ranging from Pat Robertson's Christian Coalition, which is committed to whatever cosmetic changes are necessary to play in the big leagues of the political mainstream, through other big national organizations like Focus on the Family, to Operation rescue, to "fringe" groups involved in gay bashings and clinic violence, this movement has provided a conduit for anti-semitic and clerical fascist views into the dominant political agenda. Many local, smaller groups, particularly devoted to anti-gay and a anti-abortion causes, have developed close ties with militias and with racist groups.

FREE MILITIA OF WISCONSIN

Led by Matt Trewhella, this state militia is one that got organized principally as an anti-abortion force. Militia forces in Wisconsin have also been in the forefront of opposition to native sovereignty and treaty rights.

US TAXPAYERS PARTY

Promoting a third party convention in San Diego after the Republicans meet there, this pro-militia group is virulently anti-abortion. Used the CA ballot line of the racist American Independent Party initiated by George Wallace.

GUN OWNERS OF AMERICA

Pratt's group is a national fund-raising organization and lobby to the right of the NRA. A supporter and originator of the militias. GOA provided funds to help elect several pro-militia Congress-members in 1994.

ENGLISH FIRST

Another of Pratt's operations, again to the right even of US English, has ties to some of the most reactionary forces in the anti-immigrant movement and to the former World Anti-Communist League, an amalgam of Hitler collaborators, neo-nazis, Asian dictatorships and Latin American death squads. It considers bilingual education a threat to national security.

CHRISTIAN RE-CONSTRUCTIONISTS

A movement, founded by R. J. Rushdoony, which preaches that America must be reconstituted as a theocratic state under Biblical law. A chief theoretician, John Quade, is a practitioner of state citizenship and has appeared at Christian Identity gatherings along with open white supremacists.

OPERATION RESCUE

A training ground for anti-abortion fanatics, the group has associated itself closely with the US Taxpayers Party. Leader Randall Terry would be a possible USTP nominee.

RESCUE AMERICA

More openly supportive of violence than OR. The Pensacola leader, John Burt, is a former Klansman who has been closely linked to clinic bombers and murderers.

KEY INDIVIDUALS

John Trochmann

This leader of the Militia of Montana and his family have connections to the Aryan Nations.

Pete Peters

Principal "theologian" of Christian Identity helped finance Bo Gritz' autobiography and initiate the national militia movement.

"Bo" Gritz

Ex-Green Beret, one-time running mate for David Duke and former Populist Party presidential candidate is conducting para-military training at 10 locations across the country.

Larry Pratt

Former adviser to the Reagan and Bush administrations on Latin America, Pratt is a bridge between the old right, the Christian reconstructionist, and racist, neo-nazi forces. His book, "Armed People Victorious" details the use of reactionary militias in Guatemala and the Philippines to enhance the repressive reach of the army and the state.

Ron Arnold

Like Pratt, he has many irons in the fire. A leader of both the anti-gun control movement and the anti-environmental wise use movement, he has served as a bridge to the Reagan right, the pro-militia forces and even the Moonies.

Joe Fields

A neo-nazi now active in the militia movement in southern CA, Fields has been associated with Tom Metzger, David Duke, Richard Barrett and Willis Carto. He was once a swastika-wearing member of the nazi party and has run as the AIP candidate in two recent LA elections.

Gen. John Singlaub

This Iran-Contra figure, head of the former World Anti-Communist League, supplied weapons and training to Philippine counter-subversives in a model for Pratt's militia proposal.

Chapter 5

Gott Mit Uns

We have just enough religion to make us hate.

—Jonathan Swift

The title of this chapter is not meant to be either flip or satirical. The influence of the religious right in America, in particular the Christian Coalition, has been so strong, in great part through the airwaves, that their doctrines of exclusion and prejudice have affected many religious groups, including individual churches that have traditionally been conservative but have not necessarily preached hatred. Many churches have been racist or, at the least, segregationist in the makeup of their congregations. Although many other churches and ministers took leadership roles during the civil rights revolution of the 1960s, some churches still are intolerant of other races and religions. Some Christian groups are even hostile to other Christian groups that follow only slightly different paths to reach their common beliefs. Of course, non-Christian religious groups frequently are considered completely beyond the pale and therefore considered open to attack. Intolerance among religious conservatives appeared to be growing in the last decades of the twentieth century, in part fueled by the political control over the Republican Party by the Christian Coalition (which boasted in 1997 that it controlled the Republican party apparatus in at least thirty states.

Some of the religious right principles match—if they do not stem from—those of Hitler's Third Reich: white, de facto racist practices and beliefs, inherent if not blatant anti-Semitism, homophobia. Another hallmark is intolerance of any disagreement with their religious principles and practices, including those that have been translated into political terms, as illustrated by their attacks on the constitutional principles of separation of church and state. They would impose their religious beliefs on everyone else in their society, similar to the Orthodox Jews in Israel and the Muslim fundamentalists in Islamic countries. In the United States the attempts of the far right to effect a religious society include advocating prayers in schools and the use of general tax moneys to support education in religious institutions. It is no accident that the religious right takes leadership roles in the right-to-life movement, seeking to have the federal government control an individual woman's choice concerning abortion. Contrary to the right's efforts to limit or eliminate virtually all other federal government participation in its citizens' lives). In Hitler's Germany the government could tell a woman she must have an abortion or that she must not. To a greater extent the United States has retained the individual woman's democratic freedom of choice. The religious right has used the airwaves to try and change that. It is no accident that there is strong crossover of membership and leadership between the religious right and the other far-right and extremist groups such as the neo-Nazis, white supremacists, Skinheads, and others who would impose Nazi-style government edicts on the United States. More and more the religious right has been reflecting the hate principles of the Third Reich, which used the "Gott Mit Uns" slogan as justification for the horrors it perpetrated upon all of Europe and much of the rest of the world. Like the Nazis, many of the religious right groups tend to label as "communist" or, almost as denigrating in their minds, "liberal," any attitudes of individuals who disagree with their right-wing beliefs. Like the Nazis, much of the religious right believes that their particular religion and its practice by white Americans makes them superior to other human beings, especially "foreigners." The religious right has been active in restricting immigration and the right of other people—especially those from Africa, Asia, Latin America, and other non-white areas—to avail themselves of democratic opportunities in the United States. Some religious right groups, especially those on the extremist end, believe they have a God-given right to denigrate, subjugate, and even kill those whom they deem inferior, blasphemers, or the spawn of Satan.

Many people are fooled by religious groups that claim they simply practice "old-fashioned conservatism" when in fact they border on hate-advocacy. One of the twentieth century's leading conservatives, former Senator Barry Goldwater, once a Republican nominee for president, put it into perspective. In a 1981 speech Goldwater said, "Religious factions will go on imposing their will on others unless the decent people connected to them recognize that religion has no place in public policy. They must learn to make their views known without trying to make their views the only alternative." More specifically, he said of Rev. Jerry Falwell's "Moral Majority" attempts to impose its will on public policy: "Every good Christian ought to kick Jerry Falwell right in the ass."

Religious-right broadcasting is not new. Fundamentalist and evangelistic broadcasts began on radio from its very beginning, even before the first regularly scheduled station went on the air in 1920. One radio evangelist, Dr. John H. Brinkley, used a mixture of evangelistic religion and snake oil in 1923 to promote his own patent medicines and other dangerous or false nostrums, including a goat gland operation for male sex rejuvenation. Another evangelist,

Aimee Semple McPherson, achieved great popularity on the radio in the early 1940s. Unlike her contemporary, Father Coughlin, she did not overtly attempt to influence American politics or to attack other religions, but simply promoted her own brand of fundamentalist belief. These early evangelists paved the way in the media for later fundamentalists whose religious orientation was sometimes based on right-wing political policies. Jerry Falwell's "Moral Majority," established in part to promote Ronald Reagan's presidential candidacy, became expert at using the media to forward its policies and had a big impact on American life. Pat Robertson founded the Christian Broadcasting Network in 1959 and established television's "700 Club," which became a fixture on Falwell's cable TV Family Channel, attracting viewers with popular entertainment and proselytizing them with right-wing religious viewpoints. In 1962 fundamentalist preacher Rex Hubbard established a church ministry totally oriented to television, the Cathedral of Tomorrow. The Trinity Broadcasting System created Jim and Tammy Bakker's "Praise the Lord" (PTL) TV show, which took take advantage of the religious needs of millions of gullible Americans, bilking them of millions of dollars that were used for the televangelists' personal lifestyles. In the 1980s Rev. Ron Haus established another Christian-right TV network, the Family Christian Broadcasting Network.

One of the more infamous religious-right radio stations was WGCB in Red Lion, Pennsylvania, where Rev. Billy James Hargis personally attacked a journalist, labeling him a communist for negatively covering Barry Goldwater's presidential campaign. The "Red Lion" case—as noted in chapter 1—strengthened the Fairness Doctrine, to an extent reducing the power of far-right radio by requiring stations to provide time for a response to personal attacks. It was not surprising, then, that when the Fairness Doctrine was on the verge of becoming a law in 1987, President Reagan vetoed it, responding to the urging of some of the far-right leaders who had strong influence over his administration.

More recently, in 1993, the right-wing Free Congress Foundation (FCF) established a satellite TV network, National Empowerment Television (NET), to add to its on-air subscription TV signal, C-NET. NET and C-NET have reflected the views of the Heritage Foundation, which has provided programming and staff and featured both religious and lay right-wing advocates such as Oliver North and Jesse Helms. It carries "Capital Watch," a daily program in which then House Speaker Newt Gingrich reported on the state of the government. It has maintained close relationships with Christian-right leaders Jerry Falwell and Pat Robertson. Its head, Paul Weyrich, has described NET as "an unfettered link between the American electorate and their representatives in Washington" and C-NET's purpose as "not for ordinary people. It's for people . . . who want to make a difference in the political process."[1]

As noted in chapter 3, many of the shortwave stations used by the far and extremist right are basically Christian religion stations. One of the most effective forces in right-wing radio has been the National Religious Broadcasters Association, established in 1944 by the National Association of Evangelists. While much of its membership of some 1,700 religious broadcasters does not have a political agenda, its lobbying strength has provided umbrella protection and support for far-right Christian fundamentalist religious broadcasters who use the airwaves for messages of hate.

Professor William Martin, who wrote the companion book to PBS's 1996 documentary series on the rise of the religious right, has said "The religious right is the most important special interest group in American politics. It is certainly more important than organized labor is now and plausibly more important than labor ever was."[2]

The nature of right-wing religious radio programming is clarified in a memo by Burns Media Consultants to Christian-right radio station WORD in Greenville-Spartanburg, South Carolina. Burns Media polled WORD's audience as part of a study of the station's programming, and it concluded that listeners prefer "Southern Style Christian Fundamentalism. As with many fundamental faiths, religion tends to take all aspects of life under its wing. As a result, politics is often mixed with religion. In reality, it is religion that is conditioning politics."[3] The report also noted that "the expression of views in disagreement with a fundamental Christian approach is always disturbing to most of [the listeners]. In many cases it is downright insulting." The report goes on to suggest, "We need to reflect the values of James Dobson . . . a remarkable phenomenon in this country . . . articulated the essential consciousness of this fundamental approach to Christianity."[4] As noted later in this chapter, Dobson is considered even further to the right than the leaders of the Christian Coalition.

Another example of the use of media to disseminate a Christian-right message is the work of the Aggressive Christianity Missions Training Corps (ACMTC), based in Berino, New Mexico. Its "Battle Cry" radio program is carried on international shortwave by WWCR (World Wide Christian Radio) and by WRMI (Radio Miami International). It has an Internet Web site and also promotes its fundamentalist beliefs through numerous booklets, pamphlets, and flyers. In addition to extremely strict interpretation of the Bible, ATMCT promotes its principal tenets, which are anti-abortion ("Abortion—the Silent Holocaust"), anti-Islam, and anti-gay/lesbian, and the belief that the government is anti-Christian and "Satanism is practiced in the Vatican."[5]

ATMCT is concerned that "governments permit, even fund abortions and the protection of AIDS carrying homosexuals (two forms of murder), they are infested with corruption of every type and work hand in hand with organized crime, yet at the same time continue to use God's name as though they still serve Him. . . . The enemy's greatest concern is to get God's people confined, neutralized, and then totally eliminated if possible. This is why the call for REVOLUTION is being sounded."[6]

ACTMC, while a passionate advocate of its fundamental Christian beliefs, does not advocate physical violence in its call to revolution, as some Christian-right groups do. In warning its adherents to "Arm Yourself" it adds the following:

> Strategy, Tactics And Techniques: Revolutionary warfare is the logical, inevitable answer to the political, economic and social situation in history today. We do not have the luxury of an alternative. We are faced with a necessity. Join The Army That Sheds No Blood.
>
> Our war is not a war of conquest, it is a war of revolutionary liberation. We fight not only in self-defense but to free, unite and reconstruct. Truth must always be told. It is a means of liberation, an instrument of clarification, information, education and mobilization.[7]

The ACMTC was established and is headed by James and Deborah Green, who have assigned themselves the title of "major general" at the organization's "Royal Headquarters" in New Mexico. A second address, Divisional Headquarters with "brigadier generals," is in Nigeria. In an exclusive interview for this book with co-author Michael C. Keith, James Green answered several specific questions, his comments illustrating the tendency of many Christian-right practitioners to believe that what they are doing is right, without caring or being aware that they are hurting other people in the process:

Keith:	What is the primary goal of your broadcast service and/or programming?
Green:	To teach the Word of God.
Keith:	How do you respond to claims that you are broadcasting messages of hate?
Green:	Every group in the world will be branded as hate messengers by someone!
Keith:	What is the greatest threat to your broadcast mission?
Green:	We have no threat. When the Lord is done with us, we are done on the radio.
Keith:	Do you think the current administration's pledge to cur-

tail broadcasts of "malicious and hateful intent" will affect you?

Green: We [ACMTC] try to keep strictly to biblical teaching. To do this we *will* step on toes!

There are many groups that use religion as a rationale for what is, in fact, racist and anti-Semitic advocacy. The Kingdom Identity Ministries in Arkansas has a Bible correspondence school which it calls the American Institute of Theology, and sells books, charts, and other materials representing its goals. Its purpose, as stated in a flyer, is to "establish God's heavenly Kingdom upon this earth [and] to identify the true children of Israel, God's chosen people." Its "Herald of Truth" radio broadcasts are heard internationally over three short-wave stations, IRRS (originating in Milan, Italy), WRMI (Florida), and WRNO (New Orleans). One "Herald of Truth" fifteen-part series on "Judeo-Christianity," available on tape as well, "irrefutably shows the total incompatibility of Christianity and Judaism. The absurd oxymorons of 'our Judeo-Christian heritage' and 'our Judeo-Christian religion' are exposed and completely demolished through impeccable Biblical scholarship." A corollary teaching is that "fundamentally, Judaism is anti-Christian." Reflecting the supremacy tenets of similar organizations, Kingdom Identity Ministries asserts that the true Hebrews are the white Christians. It also reflects other aspects of far-right religious hate, including the belief that homosexuals should be put to death.[8]

Another group that has come into prominence principally because of the charismatic success of its leader is the LaPorte Church of Christ, with headquarters in LaPorte, Colorado. Although it appears to have had not more than a few dozen regular members at a given time, its head, pastor Peter J. Peters, has become nationally known through his use of radio and other media. Peters was one of the early organizers of the Patriot movement, capitalizing on the siege at Ruby Ridge in 1992. He had been "a prominent fixture in the far right for years, forming a bridge between those who just like to go to conferences and talk and [those] who are more interested in direct action."[9] His consistent, unrelenting extremist views and his persuasive speech have made him a favorite of militias throughout the country. Peters falls into the Christian Identity fold, as do the other groups already mentioned that foment not only hate but violence. Peters describes himself on the Internet as the "evangelistic head of 'Scriptures for America Ministries Worldwide,' a national outreach ministry dedicated to preaching of the Kingdom of Jesus Christ and revealing to the Anglo-Saxon, Germanic and kindred (white) Americans their true Biblical *Identity*." Peters combines the conspiracy theory with survivalism in much of his rhetoric, believing that Armageddon—a war between the races—is inevitable and near at hand and that the only survivors will be those adherents of Christian Identity who are properly trained in militia encampments and who will stockpile adequate weapons and supplies. He quotes the Bible to justify his racist and anti-Semitic preaching and his warnings against the New World Order.[10] He proclaims that "Jews pose a Satanic threat to America, that blacks and other people of color are genetically inferior to whites, and that homosexuals should be executed."[11] So vitriolic and violence-engendering have Peters' radio talks been that from time to time even the far-right radio stations, such as WHRI in Indiana, have dropped his show.[12] He advocates armed vigilance against the government and its accompanying New World Order forces.

Peters is a fixture on Jubilee Radio's "Newslight" program, joining other personalities such as Willis Carto, tax protester Red Beckman, founder of the Montana militia, John Trochmann, Louis Beam, and Christian Identity preacher Bob Hallstrom.[13] Some of Peters' on-air remarks reveal his agenda and the beliefs of his followers:

- "Who has had the talent to stir up and deceive people so as to . . . persecute the Christians? The Jews."
- "Do not think you're all that smug and secure here . . . 'cause the truth of the matter is those UN helicopters fly just as well over this county as they do over any other county in this nation."
- "What most American citizens haven't stopped to think about is that if the UN can come into one country and disarm the citizens of that country, what is to stop 'em to come into our country and disarm us? . . . We're not giving up our guns! We might give up our ammo . . . yeah, one bullet at a time."
- "The United Nations is in rebellion to God Almighty, the God of the Christian bible. . . . It's very obvious the United Nations is endorsing every type of heathen religion that is coming along and that is in opposition to the Christian religion. . . . We need to say: we are Christians and we do not unite with a bunch of people-starving, cockroach-protecting Hindus or a spear-chucking, big, sun-worshipping heathen."[14]

On Peters' house in Wyoming is a picture of a gun, with the unequivocal warning, "We don't dial 911 here." He has been quoted as saying: "These are perilous times. Good and evil will fight it out, and this is where I'm taking my stand."[15]

Some organizations don't use the media to make their points. Their objective is to censor, to stifle other people's points, to ban any content they do not agree with. Right-wing groups have been remarkably successful in doing so, thus removing from the airwaves ideas they dislike and leaving on the airwaves those programs that promote their own right-wing viewpoints. Jerry Falwell's Moral Majority was quite successful in organizing instant letter-writing and phone campaigns to networks and stations and sponsors, threatening product and service boycotts if a given program or segment of a psogram was not removed from the air. Media executives, fearing the loss of advertising revenue, usually complied. In the 1990s one of the leading organizations attempting to affect what the U.S. public sees and hears is Rev. Donald Wildmon's American Family Association (AFA), which Wildmon formed in 1988. It describes itself as "a Christian organization promoting the biblical ethic of decency in American society with primary emphasis on TV and other media."[16] Wildmon has been able to generate boycott campaigns and threats of boycotts through mail, phone, the Internet, fax, and full-page newspaper ads, and has also been able to frighten many media executives into doing his bidding. The *American Family Association Journal* periodically lists a " 'dirty dozen' sponsors of TV sex, profanity, and violence,"[17] noting products and the programs they sponsor.

Two of the American Family Association's key concerns for opposition are "the promotion of the homosexual agenda (through [corporate] liberal human resources policies)" and "the perpetuation of the welfare state (through foundation support of liberal charities)."[18] AFA takes after companies, including media companies, that it believes are promoting homosexuality and welfare. Two of its major targets in the mid- and late 1990s were the Disney Corporation and AT&T, both of whom had established "partner" benefits. Rev. Wildmon has said, "It's unconscionable how these corporations help glamorize homosexuality when it is the leading cause of AIDS." Bauer of the Family Research Council has said, "A lot of the leftist effort to redefine what a family is by extending benefits to same-sex partners, and to advance the multi-cultural agenda with its insistence on quotas of all sorts is actively being embraced by large companies."[19]

Even religious organizations not usually identified with the radical right frequently have been influenced by and have tended to adopt the beliefs of the hate groups. For example, in 1996 the Southern Baptist Convention, most of whose members would vigorously deny any connection with or support of the agendas of the hate groups, nevertheless voted to give serious consideration to a boycott of the Disney corporation unless the latter reversed its "anti-family, anti-Christian trend." The Convention objected principally to the Disney theme parks' providing insurance for gay couples, for hosting gays and lesbians at the parks, and for producing a film that dealt with homosexuality in the church. The Southern Baptist Convention's homophobia clearly paralleled that of some of the far-right and extremist hate groups.[20]

While there is a range of Christian right organizations, almost all—including the Christian Coalition—adhere, to greater or lesser degrees, to most of the far-right religious-based beliefs. Many individual members do not subscribe to the hate principles and some are not even aware of the degree to which their leaders and those who have influence over their organizations do. Chip Berlet has said, "[We] underestimate how many people involved in the Christian Right actually believe that they're doing the right thing, no matter how destructive it is to other people . . . [including] the use of the electronic media in a demagogic manner."[21]

Ironically, one of the religious groups practicing misogyny and homophobia has itself been a centuries-old victim of intolerance against minorities. Reverend Irene Monroe, herself African-American, has criticized Black churches and the Nation of Islam for their biases. "There is a hierarchy of oppression," Monroe has stated. "Being black is at the top of the hierarchy and everyone else, women, queers, Latinos, Asians are below. We need to realize that we don't have a patent on oppression. . . . People who are secure in themselves and in their faith don't go around preaching hate, they preach love and acceptance."[22] Also ironically, still another religious grouping that has been the ages-old target of prejudice, Orthodox Judaism sects, joins the Nation of Islam in patriarchal discrimination against women and intolerance of homosexuals. The religious groups that attack homosexuality fuel the actions of the many far-right and extremist groups that include "gay bashing" as part of their agendas.

While the Christian Coalition has not been considered an extremist group, insofar as it does not advocate overt violence, its political power makes it easier for farther-right religious organizations to exercise political influence, reach the public with their ideas, recruit members, and move toward their goals. Pat Robertson, the founder of the Christian Coalition, stated in 1995 that his organization had strong and sometimes deciding influence over the Republican Party in thirty-one states. Robertson said that in eighteen states the Christian Coalition is the dominant force in the Republican Party. Robertson has been quoted as saying, "We are only a portion of the way there. We must complete the job in all fifty states."[23] By the election campaign of 1998, they were almost all the way there. Robertson has also been quoted as predicting that by the beginning of the next century the Christian Coalition will be more powerful than any other political organization in the United States. The Coalition's former executive director, Ralph Reed, was expert at getting his followers elected to majority positions on school boards, organizing congressional support for bills to use tax moneys to pay for education in religious schools, allowing and even mandating prayer in secular schools, and censoring textbooks, among other activities. Its use of the airwaves to spread its messages has helped the Christian Coalition recruit an estimated 2 million members in about 2,000 local chapters in all fifty states.[24]

As the year 2000 presidential election neared, it appeared that most Republicans either were supportive of the increasingly far-right views and practices of the Christian Coalition and welcomed its control of the Republican Party, or were too afraid to challenge the Coalition because of its increasing political power and influence on voters. Some Republicans were becoming more and more concerned, making their misgivings known publicly. One of these was former President Gerald R. Ford, who criticized House Speaker Newt Gingrich for partisan remarks and expressed his concern that unless the Republican Party is free from far-right control, it will lose the next presidential election. Ford said, "We should not permit an element in the Republican Party to dictate policies ... and if we do, if they're the extreme right, we'll be doomed to defeat in the elections ahead."[25] Aside from partisan political fears, the question has been raised as to what effect such control, plus a Republican victory at the polls, will have on the democratic structure of the United States and rights of most Americans. Some critics contend that the 1998 impeachment of President Bill Clinton by a Republican-controlled House of Representatives, despite warnings against such an action by Republicans Ford and former presidential nominee Bob Dole, was a reflection of the influence of the religious far-right and the Christian Coalition of the Republican party.

The Christian Coalition is influenced by even farther-right groups. One of these is Focus on the Family. Its founder, James Dobson, has a weekly radio program broadcast worldwide by more than 2,500 stations to more than 5 million listeners. Among his key issues are abortion and prayer in the schools. As reported by Associated Press writer Jennifer Mears, "Dobson has met with every major Republican presidential candidate. He has warned party leaders— and the Christian Coalition's Ralph Reed—that if they stray from strict moral values such as opposition to abortion, they stray at their peril."[26] Barry W. Lynn, executive director of Americans United for Separation of Church and State, has described Dobson's image as friendly, paternal, and nonthreatening, which, in Lynn's opinion, makes Dobson "a more powerful religious figure than ... even Pat Robertson."[27]

The extent of Dobson's influence was manifest in the 1998 annual meeting of the Southern Baptist Convention. While the Southern Baptist Convention, the denomination to which President and Mrs. Clinton belong, would not likely be labeled by most citizens as part of the political far right, its pronouncements and actions reflect the extent to which the far right has infiltrated and, perhaps taken the leadership of that religious group, and similar ones. One of the 1998 changes in the Convention's core declaration of beliefs was to adopt a Faith and Message amendment reflecting the far right's stance on women: it declared that wives must be submissive to their husbands. The keynote speaker at the conference was James Dobson. The Reverend C. Welton Geddy, executive director of the Interfaith Alliance in Washington, D.C., and a former leader of the Southern Baptist Convention, stated that it was not a coincidence that James

Dobson and the ultraconservative policy adoptions were part of the same conference. He said: "All of this may be more about politics than religion."[28] Dr. Bill C. Leonard, dean of the Wake Forest University Divinity School, said, "They're using the same method to talk about the submission of women that they used to promote slavery in 1845."[29] The significance of this action goes beyond narrow church doctrine. While there are no statistics available on crossover membership between the Southern Baptist Convention and extremist hate groups, the adoption and endorsement of some key far-right beliefs—principally on homosexuality and women—underlines the extent to which the far right has infiltrated and taken over generally mainstream organizations.

As indicated earlier, the Christian Identity groups are probably the most militant, with their spokespersons unrelenting on the airwaves. In his book, *Dragons of God,* Vincent Coppola writes:

> Among Identity Christians, meekness is not virtue. Turning the other cheek is pure cowardice. In this religion, blacks and minorities are "pre-Adamic" mud races. Over the last decade, far-right groups like The Order, Posse Comitatus, Ku Klux Klan, skinheads, and an increasing number of militias have woven Identity "truths" into their nightmare scenarios for America. Racial identity is the thread that ties disparate crazies together, that turns isolated hatemongers into crusading zealots. "Identity breaks the power Jewry has over America" [a Klansman explained].[30]

The Christian Identity movement describes itself in one of its Internet disseminations. "Reconstructing a National Identity for Christian Whites" includes the following statements:

> Christianity has historically been a religion of the white race . . . . We desire an aggressive optimistic Christian agenda . . . motivate Christian-Whites to provide an alternative agenda by and for Christian-Whites to reform or constrain the Criminal Left. . . . We need a preservationist ethic to replace the "Racial Nihilistic" Judeo-liberal, "tolerant" egalitarianism that is destroying the races as God created them. . . . Working to put God first in all things and fighting to secure the existence of our people and the future for white children, we are calling for "Christian Activism" in defense of all that is holy, pure and sacred.[31]

As emphasis for Christian Identity white supremacist and anti-Semitic policy and practice, among the list of books recommended by Christian Identity for reading are these titles: *The Rising Tide of Color, The Passing of the Great Race, White America, Separation of Mongrelization, The International Jew*

(Henry Ford), *The Jews and Their Lies, Race War of Black Against White, The Jewish Communist Holocaust Against Christians, Jewish Ritual Murder, The Martyrdom of Julius Streicher.*[32]

In 1997, *Newsweek* magazine published an overview of the extremist religious groups, and some examples of "the thousands of cult-like sects headquartered throughout the country."[33] It describes the International Churches of Christ (California based) as actively recruiting on many college campuses, and blackmailing any members who might try to resign; The Way International (based in Ohio), which combines military training and the deprivation of food as a means of controlling its members; the Church Universalist and Triumphant (out of Montana), prepasing for the end of the world with weapons and bomb shelters; the Nation of Yahweh (with a Florida base), which insists that the Blacks are the true Jews. Many of the survival skills learned and practiced by many of the far right religious groups, as they prepare for Armageddon, are learned from militia organizations and from the even more militant Posse Comitatus.[34]

Michael Barkun, writing in *The Christian Century,* points out that the radical right is a conglomerate of many groups and beliefs, including Christian Identity adherents. "A person may be a survivalist Christian Identity believer who likes skinhead music, has a fondness for Nazi symbols, and is sympathetic to Christian constitutional arguments. Another participant in the movement might accept some parts of this world but not others."[35] Barkun further sees the use of fundamentalist religious beliefs as the hallmark of most of the radical right groups, which rely on "higher law" arguments to justify their existence and role, including confrontation and armed struggle to defend God against the Satan-inspired forces that are trying to destroy America, the white race, and Christian culture through international conspiracies to establish a New World Order. Christian Identity adherents believe, Barkun says, that "most other Christians have been duped or co-opted by the conspiracy." Racism and anti-Semitism are an essential part of their beliefs and motivations.[36]

While the majority of conservative religious groups use the airwaves to teach, proselytize, and recruit in terms of their individual Christian beliefs (much of which is exclusionary but not necessarily actively racist or anti-Semitic), much of the religious right uses the same fundamental concepts to advocate racism and anti-Semitism. In addition, as reflected in a Kingdom Identity Ministries decal, "Conquer We Must For Our Cause It Is Just," the religious right frequently suborns and, in many cases, justifies and practices violence to achieve its goals. On the extremist end are groups like the Army of God, which has claimed responsibility for a number of bombings resulting in deaths including the Atlantic Olympic Park and family planning and abortion clinics.

(Some of the more extreme Christian Identity media personalities are discussed in chapters 7 and 8.)

Chapter 6

High-Stepping for Hitler

The worst of the present day is that men hate one another so damnably.

—Lord Melbourne

There is such a crossover of membership, beliefs, and sometimes cooperative projects among conservative, far-right, and extremist-right groups that it is difficult to find clear dividing lines. Some groups concentrate on propaganda; others concentrate on threats; and still others are committed to actual violence. In this chapter we propose to deal with some of those groups that may foment violence through their rhetoric but are not, in themselves, organized for actual violence or do not include such actions in their agendas.

The National Alliance

"American Dissident Voices" (ADV) is a key radio program that preaches hate and engenders violence, as does its sponsor, the National Alliance. The National Alliance not only directly influences the public through its effective use of the airwaves, but indirectly as well, through its strong impact on other right-wing practitioners.

The National Alliance is arguably the most effective racist, anti-Semitic, and homophobic right-wing organization in the United States, especially because of its professional use of radio and the Internet for the dissemination of its ideas. It has also been successful in finding persuasive writers and speakers to present its views.

In September 1998, a report by the Anti-Defamation League labeled the National Alliance "the single most dangerous organized hate group in the United States." One example cited, to some extent typical throughout the country, is the conspiracy of some National Alliance members in Florida to set off fourteen bombs, including one near Disney World in 1997, and to rob banks while the police were occupied with the bombings. The Florida Department of

165

Law Enforcement's domestic terrorism office has been involved in monitoring the state's chapters of the National Alliance, which, according to the ADL, has active cells in sixteen states. Florida ADL director Arthur Teitelbaum said of the National Alliance: "A small number of sociopaths who care nothing about human life can cause traumas not only for a local community, but for a nation." Former Ku Klux Klan leader David Duke appeared at several 1998 meetings organized by Florida National Alliance members.[1]

The National Alliance uses a variety of media to bring its message to the public, sometimes combining several media as part of an issue campaign and frequently cross-promoting its various communication arms. It reaches into all parts of the country, including areas generally considered unfriendly to the right. For example, in December 1998, National Alliance propaganda encouraging violence was distributed in several cities in Massachusetts, including Cambridge, Somerville, Arlington, and Medford, part of liberal districts that elected Kennedys, Tip O'Neill and, currently, Mike Capuano and Ed Markey to Congress. Leaflets left in doorways and on car windows and pasted to utility poles included "racist cartoons, encouraged whites to join the National Alliance and work to eliminate immigration, homosexuality, and interracial marriages." It also "encourages violence toward non-whites, and advertises 'American Dissident Voices' . . . where 'white men and women worldwide are represented.' "[2]

William Pierce

Perhaps ADV's most prolific and dedicated performer is Dr. William Pierce, chairman of the National Alliance and director of National Vanguard Books. In 1996 the Klanwatch *Intelligence Report* of the Southern Poverty Law Center described Pierce as "the white supremacist movement's undisputed master of propaganda."[3] Known for his neo-Nazi, anti-Semitic views, Pierce, along with Ernst Zundel, has become perhaps the world's leading Holocaust denier. ADV describes him as having "retired from an academic career in physics nearly thirty years ago to devote his life to patriotic renewal of his nation and people. . . . [He] covers a wide range of topics ranging from President Clinton's connections to the insidious 'New World Order' scheme to submerge our country into a world government, to the teaching of twisted history in our classrooms, to the alien control of our mass media, and to the efforts we are now making to restore our nation." Pierce appears almost weekly on ADV, sharing programs principally with Kevin Alfred Strom and another National Alliance favorite, Scott Spencer. In 1997 and 1998 Pierce dealt with a number of topics that not only illustrate the mind-set of the National Alliance, but are representative of other far-right and extremist-right radio presentations.

Some of ADV's promotional descriptions of Pierce's programs are:[4]

December 21, 1996: "Clinton's new security team consists entirely of Jews." Dr. Pierce believes "the United States may be led into a war in the next four years."

December 28, 1996: Dr. Pierce calls the twentieth century "a disastrous century for Whites." "In the nineteenth century, Whites were firmly in control. What mistakes did we make?"

January 18, 1997: "There is real hope for the future. More and more Whites feel that something is wrong, and are realizing what it is."

February 1, 1997: "American universities are phasing out Shakespeare and the other creators of our European culture and replacing them with non-Whites of various stripes. . . . Our universities have been subverted."

February 28, 1997: "The controlled media constantly covers 'Holocaust' related stories. And in many countries it is illegal to question the official, Politically Correct version of what happened during World War II. Those who ask questions—virtually any questions—are labeled 'Holocaust deniers.' "

February 22, 1997: "People no longer feel a sense of kinship with other Americans. The main reason for this is the increase in what liberals and media fondly call 'diversity,' that is, the great increase in the number of people with different roots, people who look different, think differently, behave differently, and have different values."

March 1, 1997: ". . . the extortion campaign being waged by Jews against Switzerland using the 'Holocaust' as a pretext. This is a good example of how Jewish behavior engenders a dislike of Jews."

March 8, 1997: Dr. Pierce explains he is not "anti-Christian. . . . However, it is undeniable that virtually all of the major Christian churches today are detrimental to White survival."

March 22, 1997: "Bill Cosby's son was apparently killed by a so-called 'Russian' (and so-called 'refugee') who was allowed into the United States under a program that allows Jews from the former Soviet Union to meet refugee status under less stringent rules than other would-be refugees from around the world."

March 29, 1997: "South Africa and the rape of White women in the U.S. Army. What do they have in common? The reality of both situations has been distorted by the controlled media."

April 4, 1997: "Having a small number of terrorists running around bombing buildings is one thing. But having the Federal government committing massacres is quite another thing. A criminal government is much more a threat to its citizens than are a few individual criminals not connected to the government. We know how to deal with individual terrorists, but how do you deal with a terrorist government?"

January 24, 1998: "Jews have a long history of involvement in organized crime both in the United States and abroad. An old standard organized crime has been prostitution. In recent years, the involvement of organized crime in prostitution has skyrocketed. And prostitution is becoming forced prostitution more and more commonly. Many of these virtual slaves are White European women. And one of the centers for this activity is Israel."

January 31, 1998: "The Jews cannot help but to make the world more and more Jewish. And this increasingly causes Whites to be more and more troubled and disaffected. Many average people can sense that the world is becoming sicker and more brutal, but they do not know why. . . . Those who understand have the obligation to spread their understanding and to offer alternatives."

March 7, 1998: Bill Clinton is a "constitutional psychotic. Will the massive corruption of his administration, and the disgust it engenders, bring a second American revolution closer?"

Pierce is probably best known in the right-wing for a novel entitled *The Turner Diaries*. The book deals with the inescapable war between the white and non-white races, and is considered by many a blueprint of how the whites will win such a war. The novel is graphic, including descriptions of mutilated white corpses hanging on street corners with signs reading "I defiled my race." Published in 1978, the book has become a bible among far-right and extremist groups on how to prepare for Armageddon. It includes a detailed segment on a truck-bombing of FBI headquarters. *The Turner Diaries* is one of Timothy McVeigh's favorite works, one he reportedly read repeatedly before the Oklahoma City bombing. Southern Poverty Law Center director Morris Dees said: "We've come across *The Turner Diaries* in almost every single case we've had against white supremacy, neo-Nazi, Ku Klux Klan–type activity that resulted in violence, that caused deaths and injuries to many innocent people."[5]

Pierce himself says "I am a peaceful man. All I can do is get people to think." At the same time, he vows, "We will do whatever is necessary to achieve this white living space and keep it white." On one hand he denounces violence and attempts to portray the National Alliance as within the mainstream, and on the other states: "All the homosexuals, race mixers and hard case collaborators in the country who are gone too far to be re-educated can be rounded up, packed into 10,000 or so railroad cattle cars, and eventually double-timed into an abandoned coal mine in a few days time."[6] He does not claim that plan to be original, as anyone looking at the practices of Nazi Germany might surmise.

Kevin Alfred Strom

One of ADV's key hosts and commentators is Kevin Alfred Strom. An example of Strom's rhetoric, featured on the National Alliance Internet "main page" as well as radio's American Dissident Voices, includes a condemnation of "the Jewish leadership and their anti-American agenda . . . the Jewish kingpins of international finance who control the major news media in the United States . . . telling us we must bring unlimited numbers of non-White immigrants into our country . . . telling us that any speech or action which tends to preserve our unique genetic and cultural heritage is 'racism' and must be outlawed . . . telling us that interracial sex and homosexuality, perversions which our ancestors have condemned and punished as crimes for millennia, are just 'personal lifestyle choices' and must be tolerated and even promoted . . . telling us that we must give up our hard-won national independence and freedom and become part of a global tyranny which they call the New World Order . . . telling us that we must give up our right to own effective firearms, and leave their BATF, their FBI, their UN armies, and their poets in the ghettoes as the only ones with guns." Strom then seeks historical and Biblical justification for denigrating Jews as dictators and parasites with "undeserved sympathy" for having been the target of "persecution, pogroms, and expulsions." He paints the Jews as non-whites, whose race and religion are as destructive "as an arrow aimed at America's heart." He concludes that "this overwhelming preponderance of Jews in anti-American and anti-White activities is a biological rather than a political phenomenon."[7]

On another program, Strom called the B'nai B'rith's Anti-Defamation League (ADL) "America's greatest enemy," categorically stating that the ADL is an agent of Israel, has stolen thousands of police intelligence documents and confidential government files on thousands of Americans, and has "been working for decades to disarm law-abiding Americans, to control our sources of news and other information, and enslave us under a totalitarian world government . . . the New World Order."[8]

As might be expected, much of ADV programming is devoted to denying that the Nazi Holocaust against the Jews ever happened. Commenting on the opening of the "Holocaust Memorial Museum" in Washington, D.C., Strom called it a "huge monument to bigotry and falsehood," that "the loss of millions upon millions of innocent lives" in World War II is "being twisted and distorted for political purposes and monetary gain. . . . because of the single-minded agenda of one particular group." He denies that 6 million Jews were killed (he quotes one study as proving that in Auschwitz only 70,000 died, not all of them Jews), that "there were gas chambers for killing Jews on German soil," and that there were concentration camps in Germany. He repeats the frequent revisionist claim that "after the war, a simulated 'gas chamber' was constructed.

(This myth was invented by the Nazis shortly after the end of World War II, in an attempt to escape retribution for the horrors they had committed. Like many thousands of American soldiers in Europe in World War II who were committed to stopping the Nazis in their goal to destroy the United States and dominate the rest of the world, one of this book's authors himself saw the gas chambers in camps liberated prior to the end of the war, and the nearby furnaces still full of human ashes and bones.)

ADV programs not only perpetuate anti-Jewish myths, but sometimes even make them up. "A REAL Holocaust museum," Strom opined, "would also have the intellectual honesty to mention the intentional starvation of millions of Ukrainians by the largely Jewish Communists there during the 1920s." Strom concludes that the Holocaust is a fiction and that its perpetuation in the Washington museum is attributable only to the "power and money" of the Jews.[9]

The National Alliance and American Dissident Voices do not restrict their attacks to the Jews. In the publication *Stormfront*, the Alliance states that "National Socialism represents the most sound means of assuring the biological and cultural rejuvenation and progression of the White, or Aryan, race. National Socialism is the product of over a century of political and social thought cultivated in Germanic Nations, popularized and first put into action by its foremost proponent, German Fuhrer and Chancellor Adolf Hitler." As in most right-wing rhetoric, the "Creator's Will" and the "Divine Master of the Universe" are used to justify the necessity for National Socialism, Aryanism and, indeed, for the Nazi swastika and the Aryan salute, "the right arm extended forward with an open hand." The Alliance states that National Socialists "do not 'worship' Adolf Hitler, [but] do offer Hitler deserving veneration for his role in bringing our Race a message of hope through his leadership of the German people, and as a visionary of a new Europe and a new world." To be part of the master race, one must be Aryan. The National Socialists, states the Alliance, "recognize individuals as biologically Aryan if they are wholly of non-Jewish, non-Asiatic European ancestry." The Alliance goes on to insist that National Socialists don't hate non-whites; they simply love their own race above all and "support and often work with racialists of other Races, such as Black Muslims." (As noted earlier in this book, the current Nation of Islam in the United States is the other side of the coin representing neo-Nazi principles.) The National Socialism primer goes on to explain the phenomenon of the "Skinheads" as "young Aryan men and women who having been bluntly exposed to the tragic realities of today's 'New America' consequently become disillusioned with the Establishment's 'multicultural' deathstyle and turn to racial Idealism as a sounder means of individual and community development. . . . National socialism

Skinheads possess virtuous character and have realistic yet positive attitudes about life in today's corrupt society." The primer defines ZOG, "an acronym for *Zionist Occupation Government* . . . a popular euphemism for the alien anti-Americans, the Washington Criminals, and their willing collaborators within Federal, State, and local government agencies that dictate directives to the American people and force our compliance." The primer urges active membership in the National Socialist movement in order to save the Aryan race: "Your efforts, no matter how small or great, in concert with those of your racial brothers and sisters across this Nation and around the world shall result in The Triumph of the Aryan Will."[10]

It should come as no surprise that Kevin Alfred Strom, on another American Dissident Voices radio program, asserted that the government has allowed AIDS to run loose in America as one means of achieving a "multicultural New World Order." The reasoning goes that homosexuals, with the aid of the Jewish-controlled media, hold "most of our craven and criminal politicians in thrall . . . the power of organized perversion is a factor in the suppression of the truth about AIDS . . . the darling deviants are a part of the media's push to destroy America. . . . the uncensored truth about AIDS . . . would have the potential of waking up the sleeping American people—and our masters in Washington, New York and Tel Aviv cannot allow that to happen."[11]

Racism is an essential part of National Alliance broadcasting, reflecting that of Hitler Nazism. Another radio speech by Strom:

> When the Communists took over a country . . . revered national heroes were excised from the history books, or their real deeds were distorted for Communist ideology, and Communist killers and criminals were converted into official 'saints.' Holidays were declared in honor of the beasts who murdered countless nations. Did you know that much the same process has occurred right here in America? Every January, the media go into a kind of almost spastic frenzy of adulation for the so-called 'Reverend Doctor Martin Luther King, Jr.'. . . he is not a legitimate reverend, he is not a bona fide PhD, and his name isn't really 'Martin Luther King, Jr.' What's left? Just a sexual degenerate, an American hating Communist, and a criminal betrayer of even the interests of his own people."[12]

That radio show concluded with an appeal to the American people to "wake up," to see how the controlled media have "suppressed the truth" and painted a picture of King that is a "colossal lie."[13]

On one program, Strom devoted his entire time to telling about himself—the situations, events, and people led him to his present commitments and beliefs.

Strom's early exposure to shortwave radio had a significant influence on his later life. He says that he grew up in "the old America. . . . I loved my country and I loved my race, I was a born patriot." Strom sees the 1950s and 1960s as a time when American were "carefree . . . innocent . . . foolish . . . they allowed . . . mind-molders and subversives" to take America away from them. "They didn't listen when patriots tried to warn them of the conspiracy against their freedom and their very race itself." In the 1960s, as a student he was "disgusted" with so many of his classmates who supported the anti-Vietnam marches on Washington, which "the largely Jewish New Left leaders had organized." He not only believed that the demonstrators were communists, but that the government, in only "making a pretense of fighting communism," was a "corrupt, criminal, and pro-communist establishment." From his point of view as a youngster, "decent Americans were being squeezed from both above and below; from below came the Black and Communist rioters in the street and on the campus—and from above came news media, mainline churches, Liberal think-tanks, foundations, and other powerful institutions promoting a 'social change' agenda." Strom states that he began to look for answers and found help from a junior high school history teacher who "brought into his classroom a number of books, newspapers and magazines with a pro-American, Rightist, or pro-White point of view, for his students to read . . . . Inspired by my courageous teacher, I began to seek out the truth on my own." At first he joined the John Birch society, was inspired by it, but eventually felt that it was not going anywhere. He moved onward to other organizations, coming to believe in what he considered evidence of the conspiracy of the New World Order and the control of the United States and much of the rest of the world by the Jews.[14]

Like many others, Strom moved deeper and deeper into the more and more extreme reaches of the right wing. One can understand from his experiences alone why the right wing has placed such an emphasis on impacting on American education and why those oriented to political action, such as the Christian Coalition, have been so intense—and successful—in directing much of their political clout at winning seats on local school boards. They have done so frequently through the apathy of others in the community who do not understand the right wing's motives and methods and therefore do not perceive any threat.

ADV: A Reflection of the Far-Right Media

Another ADV program dealt with the alleged differences between Black and White intelligence and media presence. "Blacks can be trained to read news scripts with competence, to get to work on time and sober, and to dress and talk almost exactly like the best types of Whites," ADV intoned. "But the differences between Black and Whites nevertheless run far more than skin deep. Those concerned with the survival of America and of Western Civilization need to understand these differences fully." ADV continued: "The difference which has been most widely discussed is the quantitative difference in the average Intelligence Quotient ... between Blacks and Whites. ... there is also a qualitative difference in the intelligence of Blacks and Whites. ... Blacks ... are not just on average slower to learn than Whites, but their mental processes differ in their essential nature from those of Whites. ... The Black inability to reason inferentially and to deal with abstract concepts is reflected in the almost total absence of Blacks, despite decades of 'affirmative action,' in those professions requiring abstract reasoning ability of high order. ... you may see Black nuclear physicists in the movies, but in real life the only Blacks you will find in physics labs are janitors and technicians—and not many have qualified as technicians. This qualitative difference in racial intelligence is overlooked by many."[15]

ADV moved from racist assumptions, ignoring logic, into conclusions: "We have been taught by TV that our former classification of Blacks as a race of village idiots was in error. So now we make the opposite error of assuming that, since many of them have a quick tongue and a neat appearance, they are approximately as 'bright' as White people. ... It is in precisely those portions of the brain which in Blacks are less developed than in Whites that abstract reasoning takes place."[16]

ADV also advocates, as do many other right-wing hate groups, the expulsion of African-Americans from the United States and relocation to other countries. It gleans comments from speeches and writings of Thomas Jefferson and Abraham Lincoln to maintain that this is what both of these "liberal" presidents wanted. ADV praises Louis Farrakhan, "the most widely known of the nationalists, who want a separate nation, preferably in Africa. ... It is the leftist and communist-associated integrationists, the followers of Martin Luther King," who are opposed to this separatism.[17] Hate beliefs and practices make strange bedfellows!

American Dissident Voices also presents what it considers definitive information on the "Intentions of the Founding Fathers" of the United States. For example:

On immigration: "Our Founding Fathers, if they would have been able to look into the future and see the America of today, would have a word for the millions of non-Americans now flowing virtually unchecked across our borders from Haiti, from Central America, from Asia, and elsewhere: That word is invaders. And they would also have a word for those who encourage this invasion through lax laws and nearly non-existent enforcement: That word is traitor."

On civil rights and the Founding Fathers: "They intended that interracial marriage be forbidden ... in most States of the Union, from the early years of this country and even up until the 1960's, interracial marriage was a punishable crime. Our founders saw such unnatural sexual connection as a crime against Nature." But a Supreme Court, "led by a well-known Communist-fronter named Earl Warren," struck down these laws.

On civil liberties: "They intended sodomy to be a punishable crime . . . laws against the disgusting, immoral, and disease-spreading crime of homosexual sodomy."

On conspiracy: "They intended America to be free and independent . . . the decision by the internationalist manipulators who control both political parties to shut down the overtly Communist part of their operation in Russia in no way altered their drive for world government . . . a New World Order."[18]

The National Alliance and ADV stress the importance of the media as a principal means of controlling people's hearts and minds: "There is no greater power in the world today than that wielded by the manipulators of public opinion in America." With that as a base, the Alliance heavily promotes its own media outlets: "America's only uncensored patriotic radio program, American Dissident Voices"; ADV Internet Radio, whose broadcasts can be downloaded and played in real time; *National Vanguard* magazine, with "the information and insights that White America's future leaders will need to guide our nation through the dangerous, revolutionary times ahead"; and National Vanguard Books.[19]

One National Alliance flyer declares that "ADV Needs Your Support" because "it is now quite obvious from the activities of several Jewish and allied groups, which have acted on numerous occasions to have us taken off the air, that there is a determined conspiracy to deny us our freedom of speech on the public airwaves."[20] ADV is not alone in its conspiracy paranoia; other rightwing media also tend to pick out a hate target to blame for the concern and rejection by the overwhelming majority of Americans of their antidemocratic divisive broadcasts. Their rhetoric is also mutually marked by accusing—in general without even offering what they believe is proof—liberal and/or Jewish groups of attempting to censor them.

The American Dissident Voices programs are carried principally by shortwave station WRNO and touted as "the only radio program for White men and women worldwide." ADV is also carried by a number of AM and FM stations in various parts of the country, including Wichita Falls, Texas; Huntsville/Decatur, Alabama; Tampa, Florida; Little Rock, Arkansas; and Providence, Rhode Island. Texts of the broadcasts are made available through the Internet as well as through print publications. Some of the broadcast titles promoted are: "The NEA's Anti-American Agenda Threatens Our Nation," "The Fallacy of 'Equality,' " "The Racial Double Standard," "The ADL: America's Greatest Enemy," "The Wisdom of Henry Ford," "Destructive Immigration," "America Awake!"[21]

One of the darlings of ADV is Henry Ford, who was responsible for distributing one of the most effective anti-Semitic tracts of the century, the fictional

Protocols of Zion, which Ford passed off as a true account, and for bankrolling of other anti-Jewish ventures. That the neo-Nazi National Alliance sees Ford as a hero is not surprising. One Pierce broadcast, devoted to Ford and the Jews, stated, "Henry Ford devoted years of his life and a substantial part of his fortune to awakening the American people to the enemies of our nation. You see, the movement to free America from international domination did not begin with the Chuck Harders and Tom Valentines. . . . It certainly didn't begin with me, either, though I think it is becoming clearer with every passing day that American Dissident Voices alone dares to tell our listeners the whole truth about our nation's plight." Centering on Ford's efforts to moderate World War I, and his backing of a Peace Ship project, the broadcast alleges that Ford became convinced, through Jews he had met, that the "German-Jewish bankers" started the war and that only the Jews could end it, but didn't in order to make money from it. "Ford had become convinced that there was an organized, dangerous, largely secret, and incredibly powerful menace to America, almost completely Jewish at its highest levels. . . . Ford believed that if the kept press would not tell the truth on what he termed the Jewish Question, then it was his duty to his God and his country to do it himself." The program then states that Ford bought a newspaper, the *Dearborn Independent,* and "gathered around him some of the most talented writers and researchers in the business." Each week the paper "carried a major story exposing an aspect of Jewish power and influence." The articles were eventually reprinted in book form, in four volumes, entitled *The International Jew.* The broadcast states that 10 million copies of the book were sold in the United States alone.[22]

In addition to praising Henry Ford's vicious anti-Semitism, the program inadvertently reveals a dichotomy between the right wing's allegations about the mainstream media and the media's actual practices. Instead of reporting the extent of Ford's anti-Jewish paranoia, the mainstream media and book publishers have generally ignored it, with most of the American public thinking of Ford as an entrepreneurial hero, with little or no inkling of his personal anti-democratic attitudes and practices. Yet, the National alliance, ADV, and other right-wing groups continue to insist that the media and the publishing houses are controlled by Jews.

Israel is a frequent target of ADV radio. A typical attack will focus on "the power of the Israel lobby." "They take our money, we fight and die in their wars, and, since both political parties are in their pocket, the American people don't have any choice in the matter. How do they do it? They can do it because they are rich, they are organized, and they have the power to suppress criticism through their control of the American media." This broadcast concludes that "this effective control of our government by a foreign power is the greatest peril that our people have ever faced."[23]

One of the hallmarks of the ADV's anti-Semitic propagandizing is the stating of a falsehood or half-truth as an accepted fact and the basis for further conclusions. Removing the lie lets the house of cards tumble of its own weight. Jewish control of the media is a basic tenet of right-wing groups, in part as a base for anti-Jewish rhetoric and in part as an element of fear to be injected into the consciousness of American thinking. Many Americans, having heard this often enough from right-wing media, parrot it as an accepted fact. How many times have you heard an otherwise rational person state with conviction, "Oh, everybody knows that television is controlled by the Jews." So ingrained is such propaganda that even when it is pointed out that NBC is owned by General Electric, ABC by the Disney Corporation, CBS by Westinghouse, and the FOX network by Rupert Murdoch—none of them Jewish—the allegation continues, much like the canards of Henry Ford's publications about the Jews, even long after they were proven to be hoaxes.

Immigration is another key issue for ADV. An example from one program: "With rare exceptions, the immigrant, legal or illegal, from a third world area is fleeing, not political persecution, but economic deprivation as a direct result of indiscriminate breeding and its consequence, over-population, in quasi-feudalistic societies steeped in ignorance and authoritarian religious dogma. Decades of experience has shown that these immigrants and their numerous offspring end up as drains on one or more of the myriad Liberal-sponsored country, state, and federal give-away programs. Not satisfied with our bounty, they have leisure to turn to violence and jam our law enforcement, judicial, and prison system. All of this is paid for by confiscatory taxing of a diminishing number of mostly White, legitimate U.S. citizens productively employed in the private sector."[24]

One of this book's authors was involved in a discussion of "immigration welfare" with a middle-class, educated couple in Alaska. They reiterated many of the arguments made by ADV and other far-right programs, insisting that giving any moneys from the state of Alaska to people on welfare or not holding jobs or not being citizens or otherwise receiving such funds for doing nothing was unconscionable. They did not consider it an offensive handout, however, when it was pointed out that each citizen of Alaska (this couple's family members included) received (at that time) $1,000 from the state each year as a share of the state's oil income, while doing nothing to earn that stipend.

Other ADV programs are concerned with international politics, lamenting what ADV considers a lack of freedom of speech in Germany because of the German government's restrictive attitude toward neo-Nazis;[25] praising Russian political fascist Vladimir Zhirinovsky for "exposing the role of Jewish international financiers" [like the Morgans, Mellons, and Rockefellers?] in founding Communism and fomenting both world wars;[26] attacking the South African "lying and traitorous politicians of the misnamed National Party [who are] now in the final stages of handing power over to the U.S.-supported Communist African National Congress . . . to out-and-out Communist terrorists like Nelson Mandela;"[27] emphasizing that "the New World Order conspiracy had its origins in a series of international Zionist conferences held around the beginning of this century"[28] as part of an attack on free trade.

ADV serves as the voice of a number of right-wing groups, not only neo-Nazis but also militias, survivalists, and others. For example, in promoting survivalism and unlimited gun ownership and use, ADV concludes that if the American people "want to be safe in their homes, they're going to have to ensure their own safety." The rationale is that our federal government is "out of control," and that self-protection is a key element that bound together those "victims of government terrorism, the 'Branch Davidians' and Randy Weaver."[29] A corollary and frequent type of program on ADW deals with gun control. One broadcast, by William Pierce, used the example of a Black person opening fire on a crowded subway train in New York City, killing five whites. "People . . . rush to gun stores, determined they will be prepared to defend themselves if any White-hating Black ever threatens them or their families. Now, this divide certainly didn't exist a century ago. Then every White man was armed, and every woman expected him to be." Pierce goes on to say that giving the vote to women in 1920 "shifted the burden of personal protection from the individual to the government," and the Jewish control of media and legislators led the drive to "restrict or abolish the private ownership of firearms." A further reason, Pierce claimed, was the Anti-Defamation League's "program to subvert police departments" or disarm America so there could be no citizen defense against the imposition of the New World Order. Under the New World Order "Blacks and whites must be integrated, without regard for the consequences." Pierce concludes that "before too many steps have been taken there will be compulsory registration of all firearms and firearm owners, in order to facilitate confiscation later. This bleak prospect has a silver lining, and it's this: a very substantial portion of gun owners will defy the government and become outlaws rather than give up their weapons . . . many will be ready to fight it when the time comes for fighting." And in a final plea for what appears to be a subornation of violence, Pierce says: "They [the gun-owning dissenters] have passed the first test of manhood in the new world of repression and revolution we are entering now. The more such armed, angry outlaws the government makes, the better it will be for all of us in the long run."[30]

Multiculturalism is a continuing key issue, too. Strom offered the solution to what the far right considers a serious problem. "Civilizations decline and fall," Strom said, largely because civilization itself, through its shielding of the less fit, puts an end to the natural selection that caused us to evolve in the first place. "The less intelligent and the less fit half of any population nearly always have more offspring than the other half. . . . Eugenics, or racial hygiene, says that we can so arrange our society so as to reverse this degenerative process so that the best elements of our population will have the most children; and so that each succeeding generation will be stronger, healthier, more intelligent, more creative, and better able to solve problems than the one before. . . . Only through eugenics can we achieve the world of beauty, order, knowledge and freedom that we long for."[31] Sound familiar? Almost word for word Adolf Hitler's justification for the ethnic cleansing of Europe and, had he won the war, of the rest of the world as well. The National Alliance—and other neo-Nazi organizations—have already made it clear that only Whites of European descent, excluding Jews, homosexuals, and all people of color may be considered Aryans, their own designation of "God's chosen people." They have not overtly advocated the establishment of death camps in order to eugenically eliminate those they consider unfit—that is, non-Aryans—as Hitler's Germany did. Their goals, however, have been clearly stated. Those who do not take the extreme right seriously may find themselves someday the victims of a new master race.

American Dissident Voices alternates its pleas to listeners in terms of triumph and tragedy. It continues to draw millions of listeners—or so it claims—through continuing expansion of its shortwave outlets, including increases in power, and carriage on AM and FM domestic stations. It boasts of adding new 50,000–watt clear channel transmitters to carry its programs farther around the globe. Part of its fund-raising pitch stresses the need to continue ADV outreach, saying "America cannot wait—our people need to hear the truth about their peril NOW, not later. We urgently need every person who hears this program and understands our nation's plight to give sacrificially to keep American Dissident Voices on the air. To every one of you who gives $12 or more this week we will send a copy of one of the finest patriotic speeches ever committed to audio tape."[32] At other times ADV has lamented the cancellation of its programs by some of its independent radio outlets. It appears to have a consistent paranoia. "Another form of intimidation of stations into canceling ADV shows practiced by America's enemies is economic intimidation. . . . Here's how it usually works: agents of the criminal foreign spy agency, the Anti-Defamation League of B'nai B'rith . . . approach the radio station or some of its major advertisers threatening advertising [withdrawals] or cancellation of lucrative contracts or unfavorable publicity."[33] Another concern of ADV is what it considers a government conspiracy to get it off the air. The Federal Communications Commission licenses shortwave stations for international broadcasting only. Domestic broadcasting is available on regular wave AM and FM stations. However, right-wing groups using shortwave do so as the easiest and cheapest way of reaching their actual principal and potential—constituents: Americans living in the United States. The FCC has become concerned that shortwave stations are being used illegally in a manner not provided for in their authorization, and from time to time cracks down on such operations. Right-wing broadcasters, such as ADV, see it as a plot directed specifically against them, orchestrated by the usual scapegoat: international Jews who they believe unquestionably control the U.S. government and its agencies.

Neo-Nazi/Anti-Semitic Groups

Neo-Nazism and anti-Semitism go hand-in-hand in radical-right groups. Using the ingrained anti-Semitic beliefs as motivation, many of these groups also fall into the revisionist category—that is, rewriting history to claim that the Holocaust did not take place and that Hitler and Nazi Germany were not the evil perpetrators they have been shown to be by eyewitnesses and history scholars. The Holocaust-denial/revisionist movement will be discussed in detail in chapter 8. Almost all of the neo-Nazi/anti-Semitic groups have Internet Web sites that literally can reach millions of people in the United States and globally. Some have particular axes to grind; others attack in more general stereotypes. Some of the more prominent groups and Web sites were summarized by the HateWatch project of the Southern Poverty Law Center, citing the description that each organization gave about itself over the Internet. Here are a few typical examples. Keep in mind that although some organizations' aims may appear to be solely white supremacist and do not mention Jews, the radical right does not consider Jews to be "white."

Al-Moharer Al-Australi. "Hassidic Jews are top money launderers" . . . Jewish religious institutions launder money for Colombia's drug traders . . . the synagogue or yeshiva gets a percentage of the drug money that they launder.[34]

Alpha. "Alpha struggles to promote truth about racial differences and works in local communities to establish a strong sense of White Aryan unity and pride. . . . We at Alpha seek radical change in the present system and the ultimate establishment of a racial homeland.[35]

American Times Today: U.S. "goyim" citizens "were treated like rats by Jewish doctors and scientists" in government-supervised nuclear radiation experiments . . . this shows "another dark side of Jewish physics."[36]

First Amendment Exercise Machine. "The Jews will remain the unquestioned leaders of the trade union movement so long as a campaign is not undertaken . . . for the enlightenment of the masses, so they . . . understand the causes of their misery . . . the same end might be achieved if the government authorities would get rid of the Jew and his work . . . The masses will follow whatever leader makes them the most extravagant promises in regard to economic matters. The Jew is a past master at this art . . . not hampered by moral considerations of any kind."[37]

Fur Das Vaterland. "It is simply fact that the White race faces certain extinction in the near future, unless we identify and destroy our executioners. Any white person who refuses to make a stand" is a traitor.[38]

Heritage Front. "Pity the poor white man, blamed for everything . . . past and present." Many have succumbed to the propaganda and "have chosen partners from outside their race." White women must not succumb to the "notion of sisterhood," but must support the white male, who is your ultimate defense.[39]

Independent White Racialists. "An all-out war exists on our People, our culture, our heritage, and our very existence. . . . All three major TV news stations, ABC, NBC, and CBS are owned and controlled by jews [sic]. . . . The head of the private Federal Reserve is the jew [sic] Alan Greenspan. The Secretary of the Treasury is the jew [sic] Robert Rubin. There is not one Straight White male on Clinton's cabinet!"[40]

The Library. "On Jewish character . . . the jew [sic] revels in cowardice, expounds backstabbing, loves to look like a downtrodden worm, so that his enemy (i.e., all gentiles) can turn their backs on him or lay down to sleep while hymie slits their throats in the dark."[41]

Nation of Europa. "The canard of gas chambers is propaganda fiction. It has no basis in fact, whatsoever. The 'gas chamber' propaganda is a disgusting smear on Germans as a people, and an indirect smear on the 'Nation of Europa.' "[42]

National Alliance. "We must have White schools, White residential neighborhoods and recreation areas, White workplaces, White farms and countryside. We must have no non-Whites in our living space and we must have open space around to use for expansion. We will do whatever is necessary to achieve this White living space and to keep it White."[43]

The National Party. "The National Party advocates a White nation which is a complete society. . . . a complete national socialist viewpoint . . . can become the culture of our nation."[44]

National Socialist Movement. "It has been proven that the races cannot live peaceably together. We demand racial separation."[45]

National Socialist Vanguard. "Early in this century there was a young man named Adolf Hitler who dreamed of building a great civilization. Through intelligence, leadership ability and sheer willpower, he got the opportunity to build that great civilization in Germany, even though he was Austrian. The international Jewish power structure hated Hitler's new and vastly superior civilization because it did not include Jews. The Jews made up myths about gas chambers designed to gas their holy highnesses. The ignorant, gullible Gentiles banded together to destroy the protector and the greatest civilization ever known. As the Jews and their non-White hoards fry in the fires of their own making, the most intelligent of them will wish that Hitler had prevailed."[46]

National Socialist White People's Party. [We] will replace the "neo-Marxist dogma of political correctness . . . and return this country to the structure of the

Authoritarian Republic it was meant to be." [We] advocate "complete White Power" against "the vast swarms of sub-human scum who have been gathered up under the banners of Jewish Marxism."[47]

New Dawn. [We] will "bring to light the Jewish factors involved in the revolution, corruption, degeneracy and eventual destruction of the Western World and its creator, the White Man."[48]

NSADP/AO. "Our government is so influenced and controlled by Jews . . . They are destroying our very way of life from within."[49]

Reichsfreudigkeit (Joy in the Reich). "The movement continues with increasing strength and loyalty to our Fuhrer, Adolf Hitler."[50]

Schutz Staffell/Computer Abteilung. [We are] "a National Socialistic computer group who's foremost purpose is to put together, produce and spread serious material, which every Aryan users of a computer can have joy and advantage of. . . . We are here to save our White race!!"[51]

Appendix to Chapter 6

Appendix 6A: Hate Crime Legislation in the United States

(from the *New York Times*)

What follows are lists of those states that have legislation that make it a crime to perpetrate acts of hatred. As of January 1999, despite the alarming average yearly total of such crimes in the country (8,800 in 1998), ten states still did not have laws making it illegal to commit crimes of hate.

States with laws that include crimes based on sexual orientation:

Washington, Oregon, California, Nevada, Arizona, Nebraska, Minnesota, Iowa, Wisconsin, Illinois, Kentucky, Louisiana, Florida, New Jersey, Delaware, Connecticut, Rhode Island, Massachusetts, Vermont, New Hampshire, Maine.

States with hate crime laws that do not include sexual orientation:

Idaho, Utah, Colorado, Montana, North Dakota, South Dakota, Oklahoma, Missouri, Mississippi, Alabama, Michigan, Ohio, West Virginia, North Carolina, Virginia, Maryland, Pennsylvania, New York, Alaska.

States with no hate crime laws:

Wyoming, Kansas, New Mexico, Texas, Arkansas, Indiana, Georgia, South Carolina, Tennessee, Hawaii.

Source: The *New York Times*

Chapter 7

In No One Do We Trust

Extremism in defense of liberty is no vice.

—Barry Goldwater

All government is evil and the parent of evil.

—John L. O'Sullivan

While using Barry Goldwater's words quoted above to justify their existence and behavior, many of the far right and extremist organizations are not so quick to acknowledge Goldwater's other statements, such as his defense of homosexuals in the military and his admonition to the Christian right to stay out of politics.

Patriots

The "Patriot Movement" is the generic term under which most of the far right and extremist groups fall. There have always been self-designated "patriots," some stemming from the colonial revolution against what were considered to be oppressive (perhaps equated with "dictatorial" today) policies of the English crown, others periodically rising and falling as individual state governments or the federal government was threatened by outside forces, and still others simply the result of jingoistic or nationalistic fervor engendered by headline- and power-seeking politicians (as during the McCarthy era). Some individual "patriots" adopt that designation as a means of aggrandizing or, perhaps, finding a substitute for, a weak, unsuccessful, useless, frustrating, or impotent personal life. Many in today's Patriot Movement have joined for those very reasons. But the movement has grown beyond simply a handful of emotionally ill or societally sad men and boys. The federal government's use of excessive force on the Branch Davidian compound in Waco and against the Weaver family in Ruby Ridge, Idaho, provided the flashpoint of political justification for the Patriot Movement and spurred the development of a key part of that movement, the armed militias. The militias have used Waco and Ruby Ridge as proof of long-standing conspiracy theories: that the government will disarm all true patriots as a prelude to the United Nations taking over the United States as part of a New World Order orchestrated by international Jewish bankers. That belief goes back to the hoax text perpetrated on the world by Henry Ford, *The Protocols of the Secret Elders of Zion*. Although long ago proven to be totally false, contemporarily written as part of an anti-Jewish campaign, it is still held by the Patriot Movement as valid proof of its concerns. Another key belief is that the New World Order is dedicated to destroying the white race and forcing integration and multiculturalism upon everyone. Thus, white supremacy, with its neo-Nazi master race concepts, is also an important part of the Patriot Movement. Believing that all mainstream media are part of the New World Order conspiracy and controlled by Jews, the Patriot Movement has, as frequently noted in this book, aggressively used alternative electronic media, including radio talk shows, shortwave and microradio stations, fax networks, and, increasingly in the 1990s, the Internet.

One example of such use occurred during the 1996 siege of the Freemen farm in Jordan, Utah. The Freemen, who decided that they were immune from all federal laws, even those relating to fraud, robbery, and other criminal activity, held out for sixty days against federal marshals sent to arrest them. The Freemen claimed that during the siege they were unable to telephone or otherwise communicate with the outside world without being jammed. When they did get a call out, a priority was to the John Bryant call-in show on the American Freedom Network, which links a number of radio stations by satellite. The call lasted about a half-hour, providing the Freemen with their first direct opportunity to let their views on the siege be known. The show's host and his guest, discussing the call, indicated the importance of getting on the Internet, with the expectation that none of the mainstream news media would carry the story.[1]

Host John Bryant said: "My friends up there . . . Freeman on the outside with their families who I've been in contact with, they seem to be wonderful people. They've been on the show. I just want people to see both sides of this thing because the media is just reeking with mind control. . . . It's totally controlled and slanted. The coverage on this story is pathetic."[2]

Militias

As noted in the chapter on shortwave radio, broadcasting "has become one of the most vital tools of far right extremists, both a medium for organizing and a forum for their anti-government views."[3] But the Patriot Movement and its offspring, the militias, have gone far beyond radio. "Today, high-powered short-wave radio broadcasts, Internet bulletin boards, fax machines, phones and videos spread the militia word, uniting isolated bands from Idaho to Michigan to Potter County, PA, into one big virtual community. . . . the militia movement is also speeding down the ingormation highway, using the Internet to exchange information, engage in debate or find each other."[4] Shortwave radio stations send out militia messages all over the world, although their principal targets are Americans living in the United States. For example, "WWCR's 100,000 watt signal [the most powerful domestic AM stations are 50,000 watts]—heard all over the world—carries programs Monday through Friday nights that target the hearts and minds of America's militia movement and its sympathizers."[5] Using radio is cheaper and easier than the now old-fashioned mailing of pamphlets and distribution of flyers. A militia group or representative can buy a half-hour of air time for between $100 and $200, depending on the reach of the station, and doesn't even have to appear in person. An audiotape does the job.[6]

In 1995 the Crime Subcommittee of the House Judiciary Committee of Congress held a hearing on militias. Rick Eaton, senior researcher of the Simon Wiesenthal Center, commented on the militias' use of communication technology in his testimony:

> For more than a decade, racist, neo-Nazis, and other American-based hate groups have been attempting to build a constituency utilizing the cutting edge of technology. Throughout the 1980s and 1990s, extremists have used cable access, television, short-wave radio broadcasts, satellite television to inject their venom into the mainstream. But whereas Mark Koernke of the Michigan militia has been using short-wave radio to broadcast his vehemently anti-government and sometimes anti-Semitic messages to the public, he and other extremists are now turning more and more to the technology of choice, the superhighway of information. Cyberspace has suddenly empowered marginal local groups militias, and outright hate groups. with the sense that they are part of an increasingly powerful nationwide movement.[7]

Eaton noted for the congressional subcommittee some of the postings on the Internet:[8]

- One posting stated: "We need revolution now, without delay—revolution to cleanse our grand nation of undesirables—niggers, beans, Jews, and the like—and return the white man to his rightful place atop America."
- Another message encouraged the disruption of universities through the use of homemade button and pipe bombs. Complete instructions for these devices were included.

- A number of postings gave directions for making weapons of destruction, including ammonium nitrate bombs [the kind used in the Oklahoma City bombing], hand grenades, C4 plastic explosives, chlorine bombs, and Sarin gas.

In an investigative report in the *Tennesseean,* Sheila Wissner detailed some of the general uses of the Internet by militias, including the following:[9]

- Send e-mail to each other, post documents, and engage in debates.
- List files of Patriot and militia material on Web pages, including "state-by-state lists of militia contacts and underground militia newsletters."
- Send messages that provide "evidence" of the New World Order plot and how to avoid paying taxes.
- Exchange information with and for other hate groups, such as the Ku Klux Klan.
- Carry lists of videos, books, tapes and other materials for sale to militias, their members, and the public.

In addition to Web sites and e-mail, the militias attract members and potential recruits to Internet chat rooms. The American Patriot Chat Room has been one of the most popular.[10]

The militias have been vigorously denounced and vigorously defended. Some militias are considered by expert observers to be groups interested in getting together on weekends to learn military maneuvers and practice shooting their guns. Others have been described as paramilitary organizations that meet in secret to plan and practice for the overthrow of the U.S. government. One Web site, gives the following definition of militias:

Self-styled defensive paramilitary groups that coalesced in the early 1990s around far-right hatred of 'big government.' Though diverse, militias tend to agree that the U.S. is on the verge of a military takeover by United Nations forces bent on creating a global government—called the New World Order—controlled by nefarious banking and industrial interests; that all such plots to curtail citizen rights are marked by attempts to limit gun sales and gun ownership . . . and that the bombing of an Oklahoma City federal building . . . was a Clinton administration stunt to discredit the miliuias. Rallying causes include the 1992 shootout at supremacist Randy Weaver's Idaho farm and the 1993 siege of David Koresh's Branch Davidian compound in Waco, Texas (the Oklahoma bombing took place on Waco's two-year anniversary, April 19, 1995). Militias and related 'patriot' groups rally their members to arms through a home-grown network of computer bulletin boards, fax linkups, public access cable shows, and short-wave radio broadcasts.[11]

Militia members are not full-time professional terrorists, as are some of the dissident groups in other countries. "They consider themselves 'minutemen,' ordinary citizens and patriots ready to take up arms at a moment's notice to defend their inalienable rights.... The Michigan Militia, the 12,000 strong paramilitary survivalist organization that [convicted Oklahoma City bomber] Timothy McVeigh has been linked to, for example, believes that the U.S. government has already initiated a programme to control the lives of every American. Accordingly, through training in guerrilla warfare and survival techniques, the militia prepares to resist what it maintains are plans by the Clinton administration to crush any opposition."[12]

A simple explanation for joining militias is one suggested by Jack McLamb, one of the more effective militia radio spokesperson. "The people that make up the majority of the militias and the patriot movement," McLamb said, "are those that have been victimized, they believe, by the government. And that number is growing every day."[13]

Despite a history of violence, death threats, and plans to kill or destroy—for which a number of militia members have been arrested, tried, and convicted—the militias themselves deny that they are practicing or preparing for violence, except in self-defense. Their goals, however, are clear. Simply put by the head of the Michigan militia, Norm Olson, "the federal government needs a good spanking to make it behave." He wants all federal law enforcement officials to relinquish all jurisdiction in local matters. "We will defer to the lawful historic authority which is the county sheriff."[14]

The basic militia motivational concern—a conspiracy by the New World Order, controlled by an elite few, to take over the United States—is frequently added to by issues that relate to their preparations for defense. Freedom to own guns, including automatic weapons and even weapons of mass destruction, is important. Environmental and land-use issues are critical, especially in the western part of the United States. For example, at a public hearing in the State of Washington, militia members threatened an Audubon Society activist, Ellen Gray, by placing a hangman's noose on a nearby chair and saying, "This is a message for you." She was also told, "If we can't get you at the ballot box, we'll get you with a bullet."[15]

Those representing the militias present a different view. One article in a right-wing journal dealt directly with negative descriptions of the militias, attempting to ameliorate them in moderate tones:

> Although our investigation leads us to believe that the vast majority of individuals involved in militia organizations do not remotely resemble either the menacing villains or the pathetic misfits portrayed by the media and the militia critics, those elements do indeed exist. In fact, we found

that it is often the militia leaders themselves who are most acutely aware of this problem, and who are working conscientiously to weed out the extremists, racists, and hatemongers.[16]

Another militia leader, Colonel Jim Wade of the Indiana Militia, also defended the militias' purpose and membership. "The controlled media, liberals, and the enemies of freedom have been trying desperately to paint the militia as criminal, as a private army, or outside the law books." He stated that militia members are law-abiding, that millions of militia members in the United States have taken oaths to support the Constitution and defend the United States. "These militia men and women are good, hard working individuals [who] have seen our nation going down the drain for years. . . . The only course left for us is to stand firm."[17]

Some of the militia Web sites state their purposes in more strident tones: "Fed up with Communist indoctrination in our public schools, the traitorous Communist Clintons and comrades-in-arms, the complete failure of our leaders to lead in a pro-America direction?" "The dictatorial Communist One World threat is real. Cadres of stealth-Communists fill all areas of government, the unions and our schools. A loathsome danger has crept into our nation's highest offices of government." "Remove your children from the slaughter-house public schools." "If our nation shall beat back those who would murder three-quarters of her to end with one-quarter brainwashed Communist robots, the battle must begin today and on our shores."[18]

The rhetoric and behavior of the militias are sometimes contradictory, sometimes creating differences of opinion and commitment among the militia members themselves. The 1998 murder of a Cortez, Colorado, policeman split militia members' reactions. While the three suspects, who were clad in camouflage and had stolen a water tanker truck, were not directly linked to any militia, the suspects, who were survivalists, did reflect the same concerns and frustrations with society as do most militia members, and the killing itself became a topic of debate. Using the Internet to exchange ideas, militia members and members of other Patriot organizations had differing views. One major viewpoint was posted from a militia site in Michigan: "The truth is, those men in Colorado acted exactly the way all true militia should act when confronted by enemy troops." Another major viewpoint was the statement, "I believe the three men were in the wrong in what they did. Just like I believe the ATF and other federal agencies were wrong in their actions at Waco, Ruby Ridge and other places where lives were lost needlessly."[19]

A leader of the Arizona Patriots, one of the militia groups in that state, put it this way: "We are the good guys. . . . We are here to protect you."[20] The Arizona militias, like those in other states, have stockpiled food, water, and weapons. Many moderate members of the militias, disturbed and disenchanted by the Oklahoma City bombing that killed 168 people, left the Patriot Movement. But their places were more than filled by extremists who saw the Oklahoma City bombing as justifiable, a logical step in their plan to take over the federal government, and some militias have estimated thau their overall ranks grew by 500 percent after Oklahoma City.[21] In his book, *Dragons of God: A Journey Through Far Right America*, Vincent Coppola states that neo-Nazis have joined militia groups and have spread among them their "virulent anti-Semitic and racist beliefs and paranoid fantasies."[22]

It is important to reemphasize that in most cases the militias developed out of other reactionary forces, principally, as one watchdog organization put it, "the openly racist anti-Semitic Christian Identity movement, the conspiratorialist, paranoid Christian Patriot movement, which incorporates a tacitly white supremacist ideology of 'Constitutionalism,' and the theocratic, repressive anti-gay and anti-woman Christian Reconstructionist and Christian Right forces." To these groups were added anti-environmentalist and anti-gun control groups. "In the wake of the Clinton election [1992], the Brady Bill and the Waco tragedy, the militias took off as a national phenomenon."[23]

Perhaps the best way to understand the structure and goals of the militias is to look at some of the rhetoric their leaders and spokespersons have used in reaching out to the public through the media.

Mark Koernke

As stated previously, one of the most infamous and successful representatives of and recruiters for the armed militias is Mark Koernke, known for his highly effective radio broadcasts as "Mark from Michigan." So inflammatory has Koernke been that from time to time he has been thrown off the air even by the far right radio stations that have carried him. Koernke has also used videotapes to recruit militia members. A typical story is that of Morris Wilson, who reportedly was frustrated, economically debilitated, and psychologically depressed by federal "taxes and regulations." Then he heard Mark Koernke. "I saw one of his videotapes and heard his radio show," Wilson said, and arranged for him to speak to a group in Wilson's home town of Topeka. "He just seemed to have answers to people's questions." Wilson was so impressed that some months later he became commander of the Topeka Brigade of the Kansas Unorganized Citizens Militia.[24]

Koernke's day job was as a janitor at a University of Michigan dormitory in Ann Arbor. But when not at work he became the "Mark from Michigan" whose "The Intelligence Report" is heard throughout the country on shortwave stations and on many microstations. He concentrates on what he believes are government conspiracies, coverups, and cabals, and an imminent invasion by the forces of the New World Order. As proof, he has stated that 15,000 troops from India were hiding in the hills of Michigan, ready to join with National Guard units from Michigan, Ohio, and Indiana, ready to follow secret markings on the backs of roads signs that will guide the United Nations takeover of Michigan.[25]

Koernke has described himself as a former U.S. Army intelligence officer. He has urged "militia members to go underground, to form small cells, to secretly stockpile weapons, and avoid the public displays of paramilitary uniforms and weekend outings in the woods."[26] Koernke was one of the first to charge the government with bombing the Oklahoma City federal building itself. It was Koernke who sent a fax to a Republican congressman in Texas, describing the bombing in Oklahoma City one hour before it actually took place. (A Koernke assistant later said that the fax clock had not been set correctly and that the fax was sent after the bombing.) It is believed that two of the perpetrators of the bombing, McVeigh and Nichols, were part of the splinter militia cells that Koernke had formed in Michigan.[27]

Koernke has warned his listeners that the government has set up concentration camps in various states where it will put "patriots." He urges citizens to arm themselves. "How many of you out there have firearms? How many of you are home-schoolers? How many of you like your Constitution? Well, we can make you all criminals real quick."[28]

Koernke has also warned about urban warfare training centers, where he says government troops are preparing for what he calls "sewer warfare," the way they will invade the country's cities and arrest patriotic citizens. "One nice thing about that," Koernke said, "is that a five-gallon can of gasoline and a match kind of cleans out sewers real quick."[29]

Another of his statements: "I did some basic math the other day. I found that using the old-style math, you can get about four politicians for about 120 feet of rope. Remember, when using this stuff, always try and find a willow tree. The entertainment will last longer."[30]

Koernke has emphasized the need to be ready to fight the New World Order. "At some point you're going to confront the federal agencies and the UN." He has claimed that Belgian and Russian troops are already in training on U.S. soil. "At any given point in time, we're going to have to pick up arms. And I'm going to fall. And you'll go back to Washington and liberate our country. God bless the Republic! Death to the New World Order! We shall prevail!"[31]

WWCR (World Wide Christian Radio), which provides an outlet for a number of far right and extremist programs and personalities, finally felt that Koernke had gone beyond even its philosophy and was hurting the station's image, and in 1995 "temporarily pulled" "The Intelligence Report"—according to its station manager "in the best interests of the country." Koernke's sponsor, the head of the Viking International Trading Company, Michael Callahan, claimed that the FCC ordered the program off the air. In fact, the FCC has no such authority and made no contact with WWCR regarding the program. However, Koernke remained on the air on a number of smaller stations throughout the country, the air time paid for by Callahan's company.[32]

Of great importance to right-wing talk shows is what they perceive as a government plot to shut them down. They remain convinced that the FCC had a hand in Koernke's being dropped, which fit well into their conspiracy-theory beliefs that the government was arranging to force others off the air, too. When any given station finds a particular right-wing show too extreme and alienating of much of their audience, and either suspends it, cancels it, or asks for a format change, the affected program usually blames it on the government and what they believe are left-wing Jewish-controlled media, as part of the New World Order plot.

Norm Resnick

One of the most avid Patriot supporters is Dr. Norm Resnick, whose radio talk shows on the USA Patriot Network, carried principally by station KHNC in Colorado, not only emphasize a need to build armed militias to protect the public against the government, but have special appeal for another reason: Resnick is an Orthodox Jew. A former university professor of educational psychology, he appears not to be aware of the real attitudes of his militia, survivalist, and conspiracy-theory colleagues toward him. While encouraging him in his media dissemination of extremist views, they disparage him behind his back, using him but not accepting him, given the basic Christian-right anti-Semitic beliefs that are incorporated into most far-right and extremist thinking. Resnick nevertheless talks and behaves much like those who denigrate him. It was reported that Resnick was carrying a gun. His response: "We're in for some very hard times. The government and the media—I mean, it's a feeding frenzy out there. I'm carrying two guns now."[33] Resnick's demeanor sometimes appears paranoid; sometimes calm and seemingly logical, at other times flagrantly emotional. On one show he admitted: "I am out of control." But he is a staunch apologist for the far right: "They're calling us white supremacists, neo-Nazis. The media paint us as racist, anti-Semites, nameless, faceless bombers. Those allegation are bizarre."[34] Resnick, however, also felt that Koernke had gone too far. "I told him he was full of shit," Resnick said.[35]

Nevertheless, Resnick's show continues as one of those strongly justifying the militia movement. Some of his avowed beliefs broadcast in the 1990s: Chinese troops are conducting maneuvers in Montana; the Federal Emergency Management Agency (FEMA) has established concentration camps throughout the United States; microchips have been implanted in the heads and buttocks of a number of unaware Americans; the country will be taken over momentarily by the New World Order and the United Nations—George Bush will conduct a ceremony celebrating the takeover in the year 2000 (the millennium syndrome) while a secretly launched U.S. nuclear missile sets fire to the planet Jupiter.[36]

Linda Thompson

Linda Thompson has been a key militia supporter in the 1990s. Thompson moved from Army enlistee to housewife to lawyer, overcoming the discriminatory difficulties women face when trying to climb the professional, economic, or political ladder. At one time an ardent defender of freedom of choice, when she became a militia supporter she abruptly reversed herself and adopted the anti-abortion stance of the right wing. Before her militia "conversion," she was, one former colleague said, "a very feminist, pro-woman civil rights lawyer."[37] But even then she appeared to subscribe to the conspiracy theorists' fear of a New World Order. The major reason for her apparently complete conversion into the extreme right is similar to that of many others in the militia movement: the events at Ruby Ridge and Waco. "I vowed then," she said, "I would make it my personal responsibility to expose the truth to America . . . [about] the New World Order."[38]

One key to Thompson's success, one reporter wrote, "comes from deft manipulation of the movement's favored media: specialty magazines, short-wave radio, computer bulletin boards, local access cable stations and videotapes."[39] Her influence among militias came principally through a videotape series she made titled "Waco: the Big Lie," which asserted that the Waco attack was orchestrated by the New World Order. A reporter wrote: "Her Waco videotapes are almost coin of the realm to the militia masses."[40] As noted earlier, Timothy McVeigh and Terry Nichols supposedly watched these tapes a number of times before going to Oklahoma City to blow up the Murrah building.

Thompson's rhetoric probably reached a peak a year before the Oklahoma City bombing when, on radio and the Internet, she called for an armed march by militias on Washington. She had given herself the title of Acting Adjutant General of the Unorganized Militia of the USA and sent a certified letter to every member of Congress, telling them they would be put on trial for treason if they didn't eliminate a number of laws and functions she believed were unconstitutional, such as the Brady Bill, the Internal Revenue Service, and the Federal Reserve Bank. In calling for an armed march on Washington, she reportedly said such things as "Let's take guns to Washington, D.C., take U.S. senators and congressmen into custody, hold them for trial, and, if necessary, execute them. We've got to hang those bastards in Washington."[41]

While many individual militia members cheered her with "Let's hang Reno and the Clintons," this particularly volatile rhetoric was too much even for such far-right groups as the John Birch Society, the Liberty Lobby, and a number of militia leaders. Gary Hunt of the American Patriot Fax Network, who called the Oklahoma City bombing far less tragic than the Branch Davidian deaths, said, "She's caused more divisiveness and disruption in the Patriot movement than anyone else."[42] Even her Waco videotapes were criticized by some rightist publications, including *Soldier of Fortune* and the Liberty's Lobby's *Spotlight*, as having a number of inaccuracies. Her responses generally have been counter-accusations that her critics were, in reality, either traitors or government agents. The strongly negative reaction of the militias to her call for an armed march on Washington caused her to withdraw her plan. She said, "We got word that if we did the march, the CIA was going to use bombs [around Washington] and blame it on the militia."[43]

While denounced as "crazy" or "emotionally disturbed" by some militia members for some of her specific statements and behavior, her goals are strongly supported and "she really is contributing fuel to the flames of those who seem to feel that the government's their enemy," according to ADL researcher Irwin Suall.[44] Her Internet Web site bears that out. To access her bulletin board, it is necessary to give a "correct" answer to such questions as "Are you ready, willing and able to provide at least one of the following for Patriots defending the Constitution: a safe house; a training area; equipment or supplies such as food, medicines, ammunition, clothing, or money?"[45]

Credos On-Line

The militias have individual leaders who are media personalities and use radio, cable access, and video to disseminate their messages. While each militia is basically a separate organization, the use of the Internet and fax to link up has given them common practices as well as goals. Those who do not conform to the beliefs of militias in general are quickly declared persona non grata. For example, Norm Olson was Commander in the Michigan militia, and was highly effective with rhetoric such as the following from one of his videos: "I say to you fainthearted, if you love wealth more than liberty, if you love the quiet tranquillity of servitude more than the animating contest of freedom, then go home in peace, we ask neither your counsel nor your arms."[46] But shortly after the Oklahoma City bombing he was forced to resign when other militia leaders were unhappy with his blaming the bombing on the Japanese government—a scenario inconsistent with the militias' allegations that the federal government, under control of the New World Order, was itself responsible.

Some militia supporters use the media to paint an entirely different picture of the Patriot groups. One such Internet publication is *Reason,* produced by

Mack Tanner, whose Web site states that he spent twenty-five years in the U.S. diplomatic service. He says that the messages he saw on the Internet "explaining and defending the militia movement didn't read like the ravings of white racist paranoids looking for an excuse to go to war with the government. They [the messages] described the militia movement as a reasonable extension of the philosophy of armed self-defense." He further stated that the groups advocating violence are relatively small in number and do not pose a threat. He says that the "peaceful survivalists, racial separatists, and religious cult groups [include] Mormon polygamists, the Universal Church Triumphant, Bo Gritz, the Branch Davidians and similar survivalist groups . . . may evade taxes, stockpile illegal arms . . . but seldom threaten harm or commit crimes against their neighbors." He further says that "the armed, but legitimate, political activists . . . are socially successful people who respect and obey the law, but who are organizing and arming themselves because they fear they may be attacked by agencies of their own government . . . they believe that maintaining freedom depends, ultimately, on the deterrent of an armed populace." He quotes a Michigan militia training officer: "We really are a bunch of Boy Scouts."[47] This benign view of armed militias and other extremist groups, many of whose members have been convicted of armed robbery, bombings, and other crimes against their neighbors and their governments, is effectively misleading. Many otherwise peaceful citizens believe, in fact, that they are joining essentially law-abiding groups whose purpose is neither paranoid nor conspiratorial, but legitimate preparation for possible self-defense. After their indoctrinations, most either adopt the proactive beliefs and practices of the militia or are psychologically or physically afraid to leave.

The performance of the militias, including actual violence as well as threats, and the constant stream of hate disseminated through the media have caused concern in a number of private and public areas. A number of states have enacted anti-militia laws. These statutes do not generally prevent militias from organizing and meeting, but do generally restrict their right to function as paramilitary organizations in ways that threaten public safety. While the militias believe that the Second Amendment guarantees them the right to operate armed military units, the states with anti-militia laws point out that the Second Amendment refers to state-regulated militias.

The Southern Poverty Law Center established a Militia Task Force in 1994 when its Klanwatch Task Force discovered strong links between the white supremacist organizations and the more recent armed Patriot groups. Other organizations, such as Political Research Associates, maintain files on militias and other right-wing groups. A number of Internet sites, such as Militia Watchdog, monitor militia activities and the content of their media outreach. Chapter 9 of this book presents information on various watchdog groups.

Freemen

Freemen are sometimes erroneously confused with militias, although there is much overlap of beliefs, actions, and membership. However, while militias are open about changing society in a proactive way, Freemen simply withdraw from society. They set up their own legal structures, rejecting any legal responsibility to the federal, state, or local government. Freemen are armed and resist any attempt to arrest them for breaking civil or criminal laws that they refuse to recognize. One of the most dramatic incidents was the 1996 eighty-one day standoff of Freemen against the authorities at an eastern Montana Freemen ranch. This Freemen group, believing they had the right to do so, issued false bank notes in order to obtain money for ammunition, issued judgments and threats against officials on the grounds that "under Christian common law" their courts are superior to state courts, attempted to kill police and federal officers, and accused arresting officers of violating their constitutional rights. Put on trial for bank fraud, armed robbery, weapons and tax violations, and death threats against a judge, the Freemen refused to recognize the jurisdiction of the United States to try them, recognizing only their own "common-law" courts.[48] (In 1998 most of the defendants were found guilty.) One report stated that "Freemen . . . generally are reclusive bookworms who shun organizations and wage paper warfare against public officials. They are so isolated that they speak in a sort of code, referring to states as countries and themselves as states. They refuse to be identified as 'persons.'"[49] A prosecutor in a county attorney's office in Arizona, where Freemen have congregated, said: "You never know what they're going to do. . . . Any violation of what they deem as their rights is treason. And what's the penalty for treason? It's death."[50]

Another example of Freemen philosophy and practice: In 1993 a number of Freemen farms in Montana failed and faced foreclosure by the Farmers Home Administration (FHA). The Freemen believed this was part of a government plot to destroy them. They asked County Attorney Nickolas Murnion to prosecute the FHA. He didn't and the Freemen declared the area a Freemen Republic. Murnion charged them with a number of felonies, and they responded with a $1 million dollar bounty on Murnion, saying they would hang him from a bridge. For five years Murnion continually received death threats from the Freemen. He refused to be intimidated, and he did not acquiesce in the Freemen's breaking of established law. In 1998 he was awarded the Kennedy "Profile in Courage" award.[51]

Survivalists: Kurt Saxon

Kurt Saxon's shortwave radio program has been not only the strongest advocate for the survivalist movement, but also a key show for conspiracy theorists, for militia groups seeking more and easier ways of obtaining weapons, and for other Patriot groups in general. Saxon also has an Internet Web site. He describes himself as a MENSA member and the father of survivalism. He is the owner of Atlan Formularies, which makes and sells various chemical, herbal, and mechanical substances and how-to books on radio and the Internet. His Internet declaration reads, in part: "For years he has collected knowledge on trades, crafts, cottage industries and survival skills from a past when our immediate ancestors had to do for themselves on a day to day basis. His work is in anticipation of a time when our overcrowded and down-bred system goes the way of Rome." The Web site further states that "his program is in no way political, racist or religious," although some of his publications appear to contradict this claim. Saxon states that "the only inalienable right is to die for one's beliefs. Those who choose beliefs over knowledge, as well as those who don't know the difference, will not survive the collapse. In most cases, they will have done the only good thing they have ever done, which is to take their defective genes out of our species. Atlan Formularies supplies the knowledge to survive. Those who reject such knowledge are welcome to share the fate of the rest of the doomed herd."[52]

In an interview for this book,[53] Saxon summarized for co-author Michael C. Keith some of the key beliefs that he has disseminated for years over the airwaves. Keith asked about conspiracy theorists and militias, as well as about survivalists. Saxon said:

- He founded survivalism in 1976, coining the term at that time.
- Survivalism has no connection with race, religion, or politics.
- Conspiracists blame everyone for the state of the world, hate the FBI, are essentially either business people or "nuts," and the Conspiracy Patriots, who have formed organizations, are the "new anarchists." Conspiracists are member of the "lie-of-the-week" club.
- Conspiracists keep their radio listeners so agitated that they can't think about anything else.
- Militias have no concept of real power. They operate like franchises or businesses. Mark Koernke, for example, is "clinically nuts." People are "afraid of these idiots."
- Survivalism's principle is self-reliance.

Let's look at some of what Saxon's listeners and viewers hear on radio and see on the Internet.

The survivalist philosophy is perhaps most succinctly explained in Saxon's paper, "Dictatorship of the Intelligensia." Here are excerpts, chronologically chosen to present the essence of the article:

Power, wealth and reverence are all basic survival mechanisms. . . . If only hardy and intelligent people were allowed to reproduce, a civilization would never die. . . . Unfortunately, there has always been an underclass to prevent real progress. . . . The underclass outbreeds their betters, swamps the system and the civilization collapses. . . . The Power Elite has always had a vested interest in more citizens. . . . The rulers wanted subjects, taxpayers and soldiers, the merchant class wanted customers and laborers and the clergy wanted worshipers and contributors. As the quality of the Power Elite degenerated, so did the quality of the underclass. . . . So, in time, the civilization was headed by self-serving incompetents and not only overpopulated, but swamped by the simple-minded. . . . The collapse of world civilization is a mathematical certainty. . . . The Third World systems are hopelessly dependent on [the United States], doomed after our fall. Many who have a vested interest in our system deny the consequences of overpopulation and down-breeding. . . . The main theme of Rush Limbaugh, for instance, is that our system is sound, it just needs reprogramming to bring it back to the health of the "Leave It to Beaver," "Father Knows Best" era of the 1950s. . . . When the U.S. goes the rest of the world will follow. Riots, wars, starvation, plagues, will take up to 80% of the world's population. . . . A system's collapse is usually followed by a takeover by political or religious fanatics who feel most secure in an atmosphere of ignorance. So the collapse of our system will be a real danger to the surviving intellectuals. . . . Intelligent people have three basic reasons for preparing to survive [survival, to prevent domination by the fanatics, and] . . . most important, is to rebuild on the ruins and to establish the Dictatorship of the Intelligensia. . . . The idea is to upgrade our species by eliminating the parasites and predators. Without them, with only well-motivated, intelligent citizens, a system of order and liberty will evolve naturally . . . [T]he great majority of the underclass will die in the chaos. Then it will only be a matter of sterilizing those parasites and killing those predators left, as they show themselves for what they are, thereby eventually ridding our species of its underclass. . . . This is the first time in history the machinery has been in place for intelligent people worldwide to be in contact. With the Internet . . . the people of intellect can organize, prepare and consolidate.[54]

While Saxon denies a political base for his program, and he does not use the terms "master race" or "Aryan" as many overtly neo-Nazi groups do, his philosophy appears to be reminiscent of the rationale of the Third Reich and of the Nazis' final solution for "inferior" peoples.

Saxon does not shy away from other far-right or extremist philosophies. Some of his presentations reflect a belief in conspiracies to destroy the United

States. His paper, "The Ugly Truth About the CFR [Council on Foreign Relations]" alleges that "the writing and speeches of CFR members reveal that the failures of the West [regarding post–World War II Communism] have not been accidents." He implies that Senator Joseph R. McCarthy "met his doom" at the hands of conspirators when he tried to uncover subversive plotting in the Army. Yet, in a presentation entitled "Conspiracy Patriots—The New Anarchists," Saxon attacks those who attempt to destroy the government, the FBI, and the police. "From early childhood," he says, "I was taught that the police, whether civil or Federal, were protectors of society. . . . People who want to bring our government down do not know the difference between patriotism and treason. They are plainly and simply anarchists."

Confusing? Perhaps the dichotomy becomes more so when looking at the differences between some of Saxon's rhetoric and the products he promotes through Atlan Formularies. Some of the products appear to be benign survival materials: *The Gardener's Bug Book; The Herbal Body Book; Secrets of Plant Propagation; The Canning, Freezing, Curing & Smoking of Meat, Fish & Game; The Bread Book; Making and Using Dried Foods;* and similar titles. Some of Atlan's products, conversely, seem to relate directly to violence and destruction and are sought after by armed militia memcers who wish to destroy the government, the FBI, and the police. Saxon's four-volume *The Poor Man's James Bond* includes the following sections: "Fireworks and Explosives Like Granddad Used to Make," "Full Auto Conversion of the AR-15, Mark 1, Mini-14, and Sten Gun," "Arson by Electronics," "Silencers from the Home Workshop," "Chemicals in War," and "Viet Cong Mines & Booby Traps." A Saxon videotape, "The Poor Man's James Bond Greets the Russians," is described in the Atlan catalogue as "chillingly matter-of-fact about such subjects as gas tank bombs, poisons, the hoped-for slaughter of our Russian friends. Saxon puts the gun in your hand." Another videotape, "The Poor Man's James Bond Strikes Again," advises: "Extract your own highly poisonous nicotine. Make fangs and super fangs so you can reach out and touch someone with no fear of apprehension. And would you believe? A fireball fifty feet high and thirty-six feet across, from two quarts of gasoline, initiated by 160 book match heads."[55]

Seemingly contrary to some of his comments about militias, Saxon publishes *U.S. Militia* magazine, with articles and instructions that include diagrams similar to a combination of shooting range targets and anatomy charts of " 'Knock-Out' Spots on the Human Body," and detailed drawings of the US Rifle M-1 and a "simplest Pipe Shotgun." Saxon also states that the "U.S. Militia trains people to protect themselves and their neighbors . . . for community defense."[56]

Saxon verbally disavows race as well as politics as factors in his program.

Another dichotomy: *In Root-Rot: Kurt Saxon's Answer to Alex Haley,* Saxon states that *Roots* by Alex Haley is a slander against all white Southerners in the days of slavery and has caused humiliation to all their descendants. . . . *Roots* is a fabrication of lies and half-truths. . . . Most American slaves lived a better life than free Americans of their day and even now."[57]

Perhaps Saxon's approach is best summed up in a bit of sloganistic doggerel he wrote:

> A pistol for the bedroom
> A shotgun over the door
> A 30.06 for reaching out
> You don't need any more.[58]

Anti-Environmentalists

Although they have not received as much publicity as have other Patriot-type groups, there are citizen organizations whose principal goals are to fight the environmentalists. Some are in bed with the companies that despoil our natural resources for profit. Others see environmentalists as pawns or agents of the New World Order conspiracy, out to take U.S. land for use by the invading UN. Many otherwise-oriented right-wing groups include anti-environmentalism as one of their purposes. The anti-environmental movement has generally been a loose confederation of a wide spectrum of the right, from some congressional supporters of then-Speaker Newt Gingrich to the armed militias. Although some of the people who are anti-environmentalist "genuinely believe American life is over-regulated, many of them are fronts for industrial polluters or have ties to radical right organizations, including the John Birch Society and anti-government militias."[59] The anti-environmentalists, although principally ideologues, tend to be financed by land developers and industry trade groups in the east and by mining, timber, and cattle interests in the west that use public lands at low cost. Some of the armed groups threaten to kill forest rangers and other federal officials who are trying to enforce environmental laws. These groups sometimes even deliberately kill endangered species, such as owls and seals, that the environmental laws are designed to protect.[60]

Some of their strongest efforts have been directed through and at the media. A key anti-environmental organization is ironically named Wise Use, and has served as a coordinating organization for opponents of environmental laws. Many individual anti-environmental groups, particularly in the West, fall under the Wise Use banner. Another group dedicated to anti-environmentalism is People for the West, a Wise Use organization, which has principal backing from the mining industry. It tried to stop the airing of a PBS documentary,

"Public Lands, Private Profits," through a nationwide "fax alert." Similar groups have put pressure on journalists and media covering environmental issues, with the result that between 1989, when the Exxon Valdez oil spill alerted the nation to the need for environmental protection legislation, and just a few years later, coverage of environmental problems by the media dropped by about 60 percent.[61]

Conspiracy Theorists and Scapegoating

As noted earlier, conspiracy beliefs run through most right-wing organizations. Some are motivated principally by their fear of a worldwide conspiracy threatening their key issues. Some are mainly concerned that a New World Order is about to impose upon them a multicultural society and destroy the white race. Others are mainly concerned that the New World Order conspiracy will create a communist society and destroy the country's monetary system and confiscate all private property. Others see conspiracies in almost every event, not necessarily part of a worldwide plan. The blowing up of TWA flight 800 in New York? The sabotage of Pan Am flight 103 over Scotland? The Vincent Foster suicide? The real perpetrator of the Oklahoma City bombing? The spreading of AIDS and the distribution of crack in urban minority areas? Were these all conspiracies involving the UN or the federal government or Bill and Hillary Clinton? Was there a cover-up by Jewish bankers of what really happened in all these instances? By Bill Clinton's Democratic cronies? Was Janet Reno behind any or all of these? Talk to various right-wing groups and you'll get, over and over again, affirmative answers. And in almost every instance, it will be the government that is to blame. "While conspiracy theories are ancient phenomenon," a *Newsweek* article stated, "the U.S. government has replaced Masons, Catholics, Jews and communists as the scapegoat of choice."[62] Unable to obtain logical explanations for an event as it happens, the far right frequently seizes a scapegoat on which to heap blame, a scapegoat that conveniently happens to be one that is among their hate targets to begin with.

In their book, *Too Close for Comfort,* Chip Berlet and Matthew N. Lyons write, "The fear that a conspiracy of secret elites is poised to install a tyrannical New World Order is common in modern right-wing populist movements." They note that many people who join right-wing organizations are desperately seeking some answers to what they feel is an earless government and an uncaring world, who find mutual comfort with others who are in the same predicament, and who "sometimes direct their anger at demonized scapegoats." These dissidents see the scapegoat not only as evil, but as part of a larger conspiracy of destruction and control. "Scapegoating," Berlet and Lyons say, "provides a simple explanation for complex problems, and promises a simple and quick solution." Conspiracy theories evolve naturally from the scapegoating syndrome. Berlet and Lyons again: "One effective way to mobilize mass support against a named enemy is to allege the enemy is part of a vast insidious conspiracy against the common good." The leaders against the perceived conspiracies must be by nature, or at least act like, demagogues, Berlet and Lyons say, infusing their followers with the same kinds of hatred against specific target groups or individuals. These leaders "create for themselves a special status as gatekeepers of secret knowledge," according to Berlet and Lyons.[63]

In listening to the conspiracy theory leaders, one is struck again and again with what they present as secret, inside information, no matter how bizarre, that appears not to be available to anyone else, or, if common myth, subject to meaningful interpretation and explanation only by the demagogic leader. As discussed earlier in this book, conspiracy theorists usually have a fundamental religious base to support their righteousness. These religious bases usually have racist or white supremacy principles attached to them and an intolerance of other religions as spawns of Satan. As noted in chapter 5, the "Gott Mit Uns" syndrome pervades the conspiracy-scapegoating approach. The most effective demagogue-leaders of the conspiracy theorists are, like the leaders of other far-right and extremist groups, effective users of the media. Those leaders who do not have the ability to perform in the media usually have media surrogates who can use the airways to persuade, incite, and recruit. The Koernkes, the Thompsons, the Resnicks, and many of the others already discussed under other organizational banners are all conspiracy theorists, within the context of their principal beliefs and allegiances. Some conspiracy theorists have been highly effective outside of a given affiliation, in a sense providing a broad base of conspiracy theory to a broader cross-section of the right.

Chuck Harder

One of these is Chuck Harder who, according to editor Michael Harrison of *Talkers* magazine (the magazine of talk show hosts) is the "King of Conspiracy Theorists" and who "pound for pound engenders more listener loyalty than any talk show host in America."[64] As noted earlier in this book, Harder uses what appear to be reasoned, logical arguments to get across his messages to his listeners, as differentiated from some of the frenetic rhetoric used by other hosts with the same messages and political agenda. Compared to most of the far right media personalities, Harder must be considered a moderate, akin to Limbaugh. Yet, on occasion, his words are far from moderate. For example, when the United Nations International Conference on Women was held in China, Harder's anger exploded into "They eat human fetuses in China, ladies and gentlemen. They make soups and stews out of them." One critic wrote that

Harder's point was that by holding a conference in China, the UN would try to force such a diet on us.[65]

Harder founded the People's Radio Network in 1991 and his promotional literature describes him as a "true icon in broadcasting," covering "consumer issues to the state of the union." One press release calls him "a walking encyclopedia of information." Couched in moderate language, his programs nevertheless frequently espouse far-right beliefs. Harder's daily three-hour show is broadcast on the Talk America 2 Radio Network, with principal dissemination through right-wing short-wave station WWCR.

In a statement prepared for this book, Harder says that "our broadcasts are for the sake of advancing the welfare of the American people and their standard of living. We take the logical position that no matter if you are white, black, brown, or any color in between, and no matter if you go to church, temple, synagogue or mosque, or don't go at all, we're still all American people . . . hatred has no place in our organization. Thus, we examine public policies, not rhetoric." He goes on to say, on one hand, what liberal consumer groups have been saying, that the Telecommunications Act of 1996 has allowed huge conglomerates to monopolize the radio and television stations in the country, denying the opportunity for any dissident voices to be heard. On the other hand, he strongly disagrees with liberal beliefs when he notes that Bill Cosby's son was killed, it appears, by a Russian immigrant, implying that it was the direct result of a too liberal immigration policy. He further notes that Time-Warner Chairman Gerald Levin's son was killed by a rapper, implying that this was a direct result of Levin's own promotion and distribution of rap music. He believes that "America's leaders have broken the promise of 'the American dream' to the American people," a basic premise of right-wing radio expressed in many different formats. While not considered to be engendering violence, one of Harder's comments appeared to be a prophetic warning. In reference to the belief of many conspiracy theorists that the year 2000 heralds the beginning of a God-ordained showdown with the New World Order and between the races, Harder stated on his "For the People" radio show in June 1998: "I must tell you that the millennium bug is going to bite."[66]

Harder's programs (see Appendix A at the end of this chapter for Harder's complete statement) are illustrative of one of the more effective right-wing approaches on the airwaves.

Jack McLamb

Another key conspiracy theory radio personality is Jack McLamb. A former police officer in the early 1990s, he established in the early 1990s the Police Against the New World Order. He describes his organization's mission as "the outreach, education, and recruiting of all police and soldiers that will stand with the free people of the world against the well-entrenched globalist in each of our governments . . . stopping the plan of these enemies of God and Liberty . . . to enslave the people of free nations under the anti-God, anti-Freedom, United Nations lead [sic], World Government."[67] McLamb's Internet biography states that he was "the most decorated police officer in Phoenix's history" and that, because of his stand on constitutional issues, he was the target of a vendetta by the police department. He was "forced to take an early medical retirement" due to an injury "during the arrest of a violent drug pusher." He founded the American Citizens & Lawmen Association and "is committed to 'protecting the people from the System and putting an end to Weaver Mountain and government planned holocausts by reminding those in uniform of their Oath of Office to uphold the constitution.'" One of his publications is entitled "Vampire Killer 2000: A Police Action Plan for Stopping World Government Rule."[68]

McLamb early recognized the importance of the airwaves for getting his message across, and has been very successful at doing so. A press release to radio stations in 1995 headlined that McLamb "takes to the airwaves." It goes on to say that "his dedication to his country and its constitution goes beyond the unusual—and now he's broadcasting his message on nationwide radio."[69] McLamb's allegations are at the cutting edge of the conspiracy theorists New World Order syndrome. He has called the Los Angeles riots "an orchestrated rehearsal for martial law." He sees the police as part of the conspiracy, and refers to his own presence at Waco and at the Randy Weaver siege. "You have to be there to understand that we police officers are the terrorists. We've drawn first blood, we've killed women and children."[70]

McLamb has become "a national figurehead among patriots" with his short-wave programs. He is convinced and has convinced other patriots that a civil war in the United States is imminent.[71] McLamb's goals will be reached if he can successfully "educate our lawman/soldier to the truth so if the order to confiscate weapons, books, property or arrest law abiding citizens who have been declared the enemy of the state is ever given—they will stand firm, knowing the support of the community is behind them, and refuse to carry out those unlawful orders."[72]

As with other right-wing groups, religion plays an important role in McLamb's conspiracy theory organization. In a statement prepared for this book, McLamb answered co-author Michael C. Keith's question concerning the future of radio in light of the government's concern with "broadcasts of malicious and hateful intent." McLamb stated: "With both the Republican Socialists/Globalists and Democratic Socialists/Globalists in power any pro-God (of the Bible) pro-nationalism/freedom programming will be curtailed."[73]

James "Bo" Gritz

One of the most charismatic extreme right media personalities is Colonel James "Bo" Gritz, who describes himself as "the living role model for Rambo." The most decorated Green Beret commander in Vietnam and the subject of numerous books and periodical articles, Gritz states that he has studied law, hypnotherapy, locksmithing, education, journalism, communications, Chinese, and Swahili, and, in addition, is an ordained Christian pastor. The *Atlanta Constitution* has dubbed him the "Renaissance Green Beret." In 1989 Gritz and his wife, Claudia, founded the Center for Action (CFA),[74] a quasi-survivalist, quasi-militia organization. Gritz is one of the most vocal and persuasive declaimers of antigovernment rhetoric, and is considered by many the leader of the armed faction of the Patriot Movement. He has called for the execution of those in government he considers "tyrants" and responsible for the Randy Weaver siege and the Branch Davidian raid. To prepare his followers for action against government forces, Gritz has conducted a training course, SPIKE (Specially Prepared Individuals for Key Events) in the use of weapons.[75] He claims 5,000 people either were trained in person or through purchase of his video training tape in the first three years after SPIKE's establishment in 1993.[76]

Gritz's popularity has been enhanced not only by videos he has made, but by his daily radio program, carried nationally by a combination of shortwave, AM, FM, and micro-stations. His standing with the Patriot, and especially the survivalist, movement has been so strong that he served as a negotiator between the BATF government forces and the Randy Weaver compound in Idaho and, later, the Freemen in Jordan, Montana. In fact, his popularity was such that in 1992 he ran for president on a "Constitutional" ticket and was on the ballot in a number of states. He built a survivalist community in Idaho and in the past few years appears to have become more militant, reinforcing in his own practices not only the beliefs but the actions of the armed militias. Like many other extremist leaders, he has publicly denounced the Oklahoma City bombing. But he has praised its technique, calling it a "Rembrandt ... a masterpiece of science and art put together."[77]

William Cooper

Another key far-right radio personality is William Cooper, who—like many others in the overlapping segments of the Patriot Movement—combines conspiracy theory with paramilitary militia advocacy with white supremacy. His nightly shortwave radio show, "Hour of the Time," on WWCR, promotes the arming of militias as a necessary defense against the coming attempted takeover by the New World Order. His anti-government statements include the allegation, as noted earlier in this book, that only the federal government "has the expertise and power to pull off such a precision bombing" as that of the Murrah federal building in Oklahoma City, and that the government continues to cover it up.[78] Yet, in the months preceding the bombing, Cooper more and more strongly urged his listeners to take violent action, with such exhortations as "go there bodily and rip down the UN building," "kick those bastards off our soil," and "we are at war."[79]

On his radio shows he has called for the militias to "be ready in all respects . . . to fight the war to reinstate the Constitution . . . within six months," noting that militias would be receiving legal justification and battle plans and to "use these materials as they become available."[80] On one program Cooper became so upset at the Far Right Radio Review's comments on the Oklahoma City bombing and on Timothy McVeigh's listening to far-right radio programs that he publicly warned, over the air, "Remember what happened at Dealey Plaza at high noon."[81] His influence is great. His "Hour of the Time" is reported to have been Timothy McVeigh's favorite radio program.

Bob Hallstrom

Pastor Bob Hallstrom uses the name "Jacob Israel" in his radio broadcasts. He operates, like most far-right "pastors," out of a church, his Kingdom/Gospel Ministries in Arkansas. Principally a Christian Identity adherent, Hallstrom's airwave sermons are predominantly racist and anti-Semitic. Some quotes from several of his radio programs indicate his approach:[82]

> Why do we continue to bear it, my white Aryan Jacob Israel, brothers and sisters? You continue to bear it because the satanic cainite . . . Jews and their ill-witted followers lie to you, cheat you, and cloud your racial vision so that you fail to see the enemy that walks among you and who afflicts you with all of your grief and woes. . . .
>
> Do not attempt to tell me that you love Yashua when you are unwilling to fight against the class rule of this cainite, satanic . . . and democratic system of darkness. . . .

The Patriots, survivalists, conspiracy theorists do not, for the most part, fall neatly into one category or another, but usually combine a number of right-wing orientations. Neo-Nazis, white supremacists, racialists, revisionists, and others frequently seem interchangeable in their adherence to crossover principles and missions. What holds most of them together, however, is their far-right to extremist attitudes, in most cases based on conspiracy beliefs, and their intolerance of those who do not agree with them, even those on the right who espouse many of the same goals but do not necessarily base them on the same motivations and methods. For example, Rush Limbaugh, considered right wing and anathema to many moderates as well as liberals, is reviled by the far right. As Professor James Abo of Idaho State University has said, "Rush Limbaugh up here is just a moderate who is considered naive about the conspiracy."[83]

Appendix to Chapter 7

Appendix 7A: Letter from Chuck Harder

From: **Chuck Harder**
Voice: **(941) 483–4195**
Fax: (941) 488–9536
Main Office: (941) 480–0038

Peoples Network, Inc.
Direct New Address
Post Office Box 67
Venice, Florida 34284–0067

Dear Mr. Keith: June 27, 1997

I do not know the situation regarding "right wing" radio as I pay no attention to other broadcasts. I just don't have time to comment on "commentary." Yes, I have heard both "Right" and "Left" talk shows in the past and such nonsense is heard everywhere across the dial and other than "infotainment value" they leave me cold.

I am however having a problem in that several false stories have been written about me and are in various databases. My attorney is preparing a Federal defamation suit to be filed against those who have smeared me and cast me in a false light.

Our broadcasts are for the sake of advancing the welfare of the American people and their standard-of-living. We take the logical position that no matter if you are white, black, brown, or any color in-between, and no matter if you go to church, temple, synagogue or mosque, or don't go at all, we're still all American people. As none of us plan to leave the country we are therefore "all in this together" and need to work for the common good. Hatred has no place in our organization. Thus, we examine public **policies** not rhetoric.

The policy that becomes law in the USA is not decided by a cab-driver in Brooklyn or a housewife in Peoria. We have traced the birth of policies such as NAFTA to the Wall Street bankers. Using computer searches of databases we found an old article in *Financial World* that clearly shows that NAFTA began as a method to pay back the New York banks for their uncollectable loans to Mexico. The people of the USA had no input as it was a "done deal." Today, under NAFTA and according to US Government trade sources Mexico now exports more motor vehicles than the USA! Mexico is now "Detroit South." Is this good for the people of the USA who lost jobs when the factories closed? Hardly.

Congressman Robert Mitsui of California recently admitted we were "transferring jobs." He said the trade deficit didn't matter. Oh, then where did Japan get all the money to buy 1/3 of our US debt? And what happened a few days ago when Wall Street shuddered because Japan threatened to sell them off? How did we get into this mess?

Gerald Levin the Chairman of Time-Warner (TW) recently lost his son when he was murdered by a "rapper" with a long criminal history. Chairman Levin had defended TW's advancement of rap music by the TW record labels as "good business and harmless," at a recent TW stockholders meeting. TW has also advanced globalistic agendas such as free trade. Now, he has been directly affected by the result of such failed policies by the tragic loss of his own son.

During the last 30 years such public policies have resulted in breakdown of the core family. There are no jobs to pay the unskilled a decent paycheck so that Mom can stay home. The "elite" have totally had their way and made the policies. Now factories close everyday putting Americans out of work and their shoes (and consumer goods), are now made by frightened Asian people who work in sweat shops for pennies an hour to make NIKE shoes that sell for $100.00. America loses and Mr. Phil Knight of NIKE gets richer by the minute. Is this fair?

The US government agencies such as the Overseas Private Investment Corporation (OPEC) and Aid for International Development (AID) use US taxpayer's funds to move their factories offshore and put them out of work. The New York Times recently disclosed that the average welfare family costs the public $50,000.00 yearly when all the costs are added-up. So, tell me how this policy helps the USA?

Bill Cosby recently lost his son and the suspect is a Russian immigrant who may have been the murderer. Now it turns out that the suspect has had an association with another Russian immigrant who has also been involved in criminality. Had it not been for the failed policy of "loose immigration" and "open borders" I wonder if Bill's son would be dead today? There are many more cases in California where a Mexican illegal has murdered Americans or committed rape and other horrible crimes. So I ask, is "open borders" good policy?

Check out what it takes to LEAVE the USA and emigrate elsewhere. Mexico won't let you in unless you have big bucks. Nor will any other country for that matter. Most Caribbean islands require work permits or residency permits and you stay on good behavior or go back home in chains. Their policies work for them. Ours have failed.

Recently a fine black man called my show. He used to drive a garbage truck for the City of Tampa. As a city employee he had benefits and good pay. Several years ago Tampa's new Mayor fired the garbagemen and hired one of the big corporate waste haulers. Cost of refuse-hauling to the citizens didn't go down. Instead the pay to the truck drivers plummeted, they have no benefits and the difference goes to the corporate managers as big paychecks and profit. So, is this good policy?

I even had a man on my show that used to be an independent refuse hauler in rural Tampa. Once the big corporations moved in they found a way to put him out of business. I had him in the studio and he cried on the air as he was losing everything he had built over the years. Welcome to predatory corporate America, you're fired and out-of-a-job.

Those who say it's the fault of the unions need to look to Jasper and Lake Butler, Florida. At Jasper a one-mile square industrial park now sits empty with all factories gone. Buildings the size of football-fields sit empty. Most of the jobs were minimum-wage of slightly above. No unions operated here and people worked hard and lived cheap. No matter, they cannot compete with 23 cent hourly workers in Guatemala, El Salvador, or Haiti where the pay is 8 cents an hour.

Were some or all of the empty buildings built with industrial bonds having no-recourse provisions? Check this out across the USA. In many cases the cost of paying off the buildings will go to the taxpayers when the companies desert. Now out of a job, the local folks pay higher taxes. Is this good policy?

Why are these topics ignored by major media? Could it be that they are owned by giant conglomerates who benefit by moving factories offshore? Try to buy a GE radio or TV that is made in the USA. Well, GE owns NBC. The same situation is true in other media or their stock is owned and held by Wall Street. We took the trouble to pull the 10–Ks of all the big media and found the top 200 stockholders of same were New York banks or Wall Street investment houses. Check it out and get your eyes opened.

Rupert Murdoch was in USA TODAY this last week and admitted that the cable-TV industry is all cross-owned and is an octopus.

The predatory new Telecommunications Bill allows giants like CBS who is Westinghouse, Jacor, Clear Channel and other media giants to own hundreds of radio stations. They in turn rely on the big agencies for income to run ads for Delta, Campell Soup, and so forth. Those companies have informed their agencies NOT TO BUY ADS IN TALK RADIO SHOWS. We have the memos.

DirecTV and the new small-dish satellite companies refuse to allow us to put our channels up in the sky. Big corporate media won't run our shows as they don't want to offend advertisers. Corporate media has shut us off and we are only carried by "Mom and Pop" stations as a general rule. Sadly, those are vanishing as they are being snapped-up by giant corporations who want to own it all.

This means that we must rely on using short-wave, the internet, and satellite to distribute our shows plus whatever remaining stations that will carry us. Thus we get labeled as "kooks."

Our shows have been on the "cutting-edge." We get boxes of clippings from local papers across the USA and follow up on the stories. We get letters and first hand accounts and investigate.

We spent over $35,000.00 to send a team to Oklahoma City after the bombing. We learned that it was a sting operation gone sour. This was told to us by local media and the families of the victims and local officials. We broke the story thereafter. Now, two years later ABC-TV ran a similar story. Up until then we were wackos.

Gulf War Syndrome was first heard on our show when the Pentagon said we were nuts. Randy Weaver's story was told long before he was vindicated. The New York Times even admitted the government had prior knowledge of the Trade Center bombing and knew the date and time. Why didn't they stop it? Has our government used innocent citizens as bait?

The optical and watch industries were lost during the Eisenhower, Kennedy and Johnson administration. Johnson started the policy of Maquilladoras along the US-Mexican border. Nixon gave-away the electronics industry and Reagan, Bush and Clinton have given away the rest. Clinton is now giving high-tech to China. What then is left for America as a future?

Now here's the answer to your questions:

1. I don't know as I have never studied the issue. I will say however that the policies enacted by the US Government have been mostly a "left wing" agenda. These agendas are promulgated in the mainstream press, on PBS, and commercial TV. No other country has open borders, gives welfare to illegal immigrants and uses taxpayer funds to move their factories and jobs offshore. Why us?

2. Mainstream media (newspapers, radio, TV), is left-wing and globalist which far outpaces the reach of all other media.

3. People who lose their jobs and homes have "nothing to left to lose." Historically such people take the law into their own hands. They see shows like McGyver and others on TV that show them how to do it. I doubt if the rapper who is charged with killing Gerald Levin's son, or the Russian who killed Bill Cosby's son ever listened to any talk radio. Neither of them understands "standard English." I also doubt that the people who beat Reginald Denny nearly to death at a California intersection were tuned into a talk show.

If your logic says that Talk Radio fuels "extremists" then it must be true that country and western music is the root cause of all alcoholism, divorce, and suicide. What the recent columns critical of Bill Clinton and his antics in the *New York Times* by William Safire, Abe Rosenthal, and Maureen Dowd have done to incite action across the USA is also anyone's guess.

4. I don't know. I do however object to the word "Patriot" being demonized. I can remember only a few years ago when "Mother" was a wonderful word and "Gay" meant you were happy.

5. Until Pearl Harbor, those who warned about the threat from Japan were demonized. Those like me who confront reality will be demonized and marginalized until things decline further. After which we will be called "Statesmen."

LSD was tolerated until rich kids started walking into trains and jumping out of windows. Crack cocaine is a Mexican industry that is winked at as long as the problems stay in the ghetto. Now, these demons are emerging into the mainstream and confronting the super-rich also. Now, watch for reactions.

I don't know what the future is for ultra right-wing radio because I'm not sure what it really is. Should you be talking about my show that deals in cold hard facts, failed policies, and the declining standard of living—and if you call such reality "right wing" then you are "shooting the honest messenger." Be careful when pinning labels on radio.

Ten years ago my show focused on lemon cars and consumer scams. While we still expose scams and recalls, most of the concern now is "How do I continue on after I have lost my job and there are no others that pay a living wage."

The fix is easy. Put a tariff on all incoming goods that protects USA citizens. Have it so that NO COMPETITOR can move offshore and cut the throat of a US-based factory-produced item. The big boys can still make their profits in a level playing field. Costs won't go up much or if they do the taxes and welfare will go down in time. Items will be made better and consumer stuff won't clog our dumps. Radios, TVs and other consumer goods can be made better so that they can be repaired instead of going to the dump. A repair industry will then prosper again and that's better for planet Earth and our people.

Right now we're losing tool and die makers, industrial engineers, draftsmen, and all other support staff that industry requires. Instead we only need people to put stuff on the shelf at Wal-Mart. Well Sir, those jobs would still be there if the product was made in the USA instead of China. Countries like ours that sell raw materials abroad and then import finished goods are known as, "colonies."

Now to the subject of violence. Those who listen to me hear me constantly say, "Work within the system." While that is an admirable policy, the facts are changing. Everyday people realize that the system has broken down. The *New York Times* revealed that Red China has bought the White House and we see trade policies by the Clinton administration that should be called economic treason. Result: Our armed forces cannot purchase LCD screens or certain needed microchips from USA sources. We have to go to Japan to get parts for our Patriot missiles and tanks. Worse, Japan recently told us they did not want to sell us parts to be used in warfare. Yet, while this goes on China is selling high-tech cruise missiles to Iran and other countries that worry us. What will we do to protect ourselves? We also have no defense against incoming missiles?

The young "rapper" that killed Gerald Levin's son is the perfect example of the "post-industrial society" that we have entered. This failed ideology was enacted by those social engineers who were so sure that their untested policies would work just fine. These are the same people that bulldozed neighborhoods and built hi-rise welfare slums that recently have been dynamited across the USA. America is awash in failed policies from wrongheaded social engineers.

The sad reality is that nobody but the very elite have a future other than mid-level technocrats. Other than those service jobs, the industrial paycheck is about gone and all the support industries and services are going also. You don't need foundries if you don't make metal items. Nor do you need the services of engineers, designers, chemists, and so forth. We're also seeing colleges downsize and unhappy graduates flipping hamburgers.

What has really happened is that America's leaders have broken the promise of "the American dream" to the American people. The deal used to be simple: obey the laws, finish school, go into the service when called, be a moving target to defend the nation when at war, come home, go to work, then retire in a decent degree of dignity. In short, the American people didn't own the factories or banks, but they owned the jobs and had a future. Take that away from them and they won't behave. It doesn't take a rocket scientist to realize that there is no future in America for rocket scientists. If you don't believe me check the real estate prices at Cape Canaveral. They are depressed.

Put America back to work and you'll be able to go on to other topics.

You have my permission to reprint this *only* if you print the entire letter here. Good luck in your endeavors. All the best,

Chuck Harder

Chapter 8

Up Close and Right

Opinions founded on prejudices are always sustained with the greatest violence.

— Old Proverb

There is a code-word, a Hitler-oriented phrase, that permeates the far right and extremist groups: "fourteen words." Anyone in the movement hearing those words knows that it means "to secure the existence of the white race and a future for our children."[1]

At one time the dominating white supremacist organization in the United States was the Ku Klux Klan. But, coincidental with the increasing use of radio, television, and video, and the emergence of the Internet as a means of spreading the word and recruiting new members into narrower affinity groups, the KKK has become just one, albeit still a leading one, of a number of racist groups. For example, the Aryan Nation goes beyond the original KKK in unabashedly adapting the Hitler Third Reich concept of racial identity and the Nazi solution to what it considers a world problem. Unlike the KKK, which initially wanted to keep African-Americans in a position of total economic and political servitude, separate from any possibility of social or professional contact with whites, the Aryan Nation's Louis Beam has stated: "We do not advocate segregation. That was a temporary measure that was long past. . . . We intend to purge this entire land area of every non-White person."[2]

Even more militant and activist white supremacy groups, such as the neo-Nazi Skinheads, have emerged from the KKK legacy. The Knights of the White Kamellia (spelled with a "k" instead of a "c") is an offshoot. Another is the Knights of the KKK, founded by David Duke in the 1970s, which has become prominent in KKK-type activities. Most Christian Identity groups have white supremacy as a primary goal. Many religious groups, such as the Church of the Creator, established in 1973, are founded on white supremacist principles. Adherents of the Christian right, led by Pat Robertson, support in large

218

measure the belief in white supremacy, as do the followers of the politically oriented conservative movement led by Pat Buchanan.[3] Smaller groups, such as the White Nurses, which prepares its members for what they believe will be a holy war between the "white" and "colored" races, have a white-supremacy foundation. Even movements principally based on anti-Semitism, such as the Holocaust-denial movement, include white supremacy as a key tenet. The white supremacists also tend to be homophobic, many members calling for the death of homosexuals, and to be against women's rights, seeking to control women by attacking feminists, lesbians, white females in interracial relationships, and abortion choice.[4] In fact, the extremist positions have proliferated to such a degree that what were once considered dangerous advocacies are now frequently taken in stride as almost expected everyday rhetoric. Even veiled threats of violence seem to be ignored by the authorities and by the media. In mid-1998, after Disney World announced it was opening up the theme park to "gay days" and allowing gay organizations to put up rainbow flags for those specified days, Pat Robertson warned "the city of Orlando that it risks hurricanes, earthquakes, and terrorist bombs"[5] if it does so. There was hardly more than a passing mention in the media and no official condemnation of or action against Robertson.

The growth of more extreme organizations does not mean that the KKK itself has abandoned violence. Loretta Ross writes in *Eyes Right!* that "it is typical for the 1990s Klan, reeling from criminal convictions, to publicly disavow violence while secretly encouraging its followers to commit hate crimes under the cover of darkness."[6] In mid-1998, for example, the men who kidnapped an African-American man in Jasper, Texas, beat him, chained his ankles to the back of their truck and dragged him to his death, were linked to white supremacist, KKK, and neo-Nazi organizations. Although some "white supremacists are following less violent strategy: exchanging bullets for ballots and running for political office," the "fanatics are terrorists who use bombs, murder, arson, and assaults in their genocidal war."[7]

One important approach all these groups have in common is their use of the media to persuade and recruit. "When they wish," Loretta Ross writes, "hate groups get lots of free publicity from tabloid talk shows eager to boost ratings with the winning combination of race, guns, and violence. Such hosts may hypocritically hold their noses while racists, particularly Skinheads, advertise their toughness and their addresses on national TV."[8] The Knights of the White Kamellia, for example, boast that they "have defended White rights on the following National Television Shows: 'The Jerry Springer Show,' 'The Phil Donohue Show,' 'Day & Date,' 'CNBC,' 'CNN News,' and 'CBS Evening News.' "[9] A group called the Nationalist Movement, which stresses "white pride," distributes a TV show called "Airlink" and has an active Internet Web page. A former grand dragon of the KKK, Don Black, operates "Stormfront," an Internet site dedicated to "those courageous men and women fighting to preserve their white western culture, ideals, and freedom of speech and association." Black has said that he sees the Internet as having "the potential here to reach millions. I think it's a major breakthrough. I don't know if it's the ultimate solution to developing a viable white rights movement in this country, but it's certainly a significant advance."[10]

Music has been an important part of white supremacist persuasion and recruitment. Many hate groups, reported the *Christian Science Monitor* in 1998, are now using the Internet and rock music to promote their messages, selling professionally packaged CDs and establishing sophisticated Web sites that advocate violence and racial separation to a new market—the American mainstream. At a Web site for Skinheads, originating in Minneapolis, one "clicks" on a swastika icon to join discussions on white pride, read about Skinhead "victims" of the U.S. government, or discover new neo-Nazi rock bands."[11] The Church of the Creator, a white supremacist organization, formed a band with the name of RaHoWa. The name stands for RAcial HOly WAr. Ironically, the Church claims it worships "no gods," and that the "most outstanding feature of the White race is creativity." The band's lyrics stress the distinction between the Aryan "white" race and the other "mud" races. They not only proclaim a holy war to destroy non-white races, but encourage followers to actively pursue such a course. One of RaHoWa's recorded albums is entitled "Cult of the Holy War" and one of their most popular songs is "Declaration of War." The band plays at special occasions, such as celebrations of Adolf Hitler's birthday. It's called "white power music," and attracts young people, including teenagers, who might not otherwise have an interest in white supremacy ideology, but listen to its messages through the music.[12]

Probably the leading distributor of white power music is Resistance Records in Detroit, which not only handles RaHoWa recordings (George Hawthorne—his legal last name is Burdi—is lead singer of RaHoWa and leader of the Church of the Creator in Canada, and is a founder of Resistance Records), but those of other white supremacist bands as well, such as The Voice, New Minority, Aggravated Assault, Centurion, Bound For Glory, Berserkr, Aryan, and Nordic Thunder.[13] The names are self-descriptive. Hawthorne bases his musical composition and distribution on the premise that the "White Race" is dying. He stresses a number of themes that he feels must be made known to the public through white power music. He decries "race-mixing, especially amongst White girls with black males. Without the wombs of our women, we cannot reproduce our own dwindling numbers. Race-mixing spells death." He is against immigration: "non-Whites are swarming into our countries." He is concerned that the media are portraying "pro-White individuals like myself" as "evil." Resistance Records reaches out through a Web page, e-mail, flyers, and other promotion and advertising means to many people—young and old—who are attracted to the music and then hear the messages. Resistance Records' slogan: "Forging a new destiny for White Power music!"[14]

White power music is not subtle. It is designed to inflame and recruit. "During the 1980s something fundamental happened to rock music," William Shaw wrote in *Details*, a music periodical. "It used to be how young people communicated with each other. . . . These days . . . it's selling fascism . . . and fueling the hatred that nazism thrives on."[15] At one concert featuring Bound For Glory (considered by many to be America's leading neo-Nazi band), for example, "two forty-foot swastikas draped down. . . . Brownshirts in perfect 1933 uniforms . . . swagger around and 'Sieg-Heil' showily to anyone ready to lift an arm."[16] The music, too, is explicit. Some white power bands begin and end their concerts with special homage to Adolf Hitler, playing the Nazi anthem of the German Third Reich, the Horst Wessel song. (It reminds one of this book's authors of an incident in Germany two decades after the end of World War II. He went into a bar where there were several men whose age indicated they had been young adults in the Nazi era. When they saw he was an American, they put some money in the jukebox and abruptly left. Two songs were played for the American's ears: a tune then popular in the United States, "Memories," followed by the "Horst Wessel" song. The meaning was explicit and chilling.) A Bound For Glory song played by the band shortly after the Oklahoma City bombing was "Time Bomb," with lyrics that promise revenge against the federal government.[17] Appropriately, white power music has also become known as "skinhead rock."

While most of the hate groups proclaim individual identities, common beliefs and goals bind them together, as often noted in this book, so that "in recent years there has been an informal alliance of white supremacist groups, sometimes in conjunction with private militias." Klanwatch director Danny Welch has stated that "by exploiting the broader issues of immigration, gun control, states rights, abortion, and homosexuality, these militant racists and anti-Semites are tapping into a larger audience than they've been able to reach in years past."[18] The rapid rise of the Internet is an example. In 1995 there were only a few "hate" Web sites in the United States; in 1998 there were literally hundreds. Not too long ago promotion of hate violence was found principally in print, notably in books such as the novel by former Nazi Party leader and current National Alliance head William Pierce, *The Turner Diaries,* which, as noted earlier, reportedly served Timothy McVeigh and Terry Nichols as motivation, justification, and a model for the Oklahoma City bombing. While *The Turner Diaries* and similar literature remain mainstays of right-wing persuasion, you can now find such material much more easily through radio, television, fax, cyberspace, cable, videos, and music.

"When you just had a printing press," Chip Berlet has said, "or someone in a public square starting to emote this stuff, there would be somebody right there to stand up and say this is nonsense. But with development of the new electronic media—the fax networks, talk radio, the Internet, and new use of shortwave—there is a lag between use of this media by demagogues and development of a 'normative behavior' of checks and balances." Berlet suggested that the new media have made it possible to organize and develop virtually instant movements; as an example, the armed militias may be "the first U.S. social movement to be organized primarily through nontraditional media such as the Internet."[19] Even far-right classic books are now found on the Internet. Another work of fiction, *Report from Iron Mountain*, was published in 1967 as a political satire and republished in 1996. It was written in the form of a real government document, as a satire on the government's conspiracy to lie to the American public during the Vietnam War, and deals with the government's conspiring to delude the people into believing that for society to continue, war is necessary. Patriot groups have put it on the Internet (illegally, and in defiance of copyright suits by the publisher and author) as if it were a legitimate government document, providing to their followers this purported further validity of their anti-government conspiracy theories. Through the Internet they've reached many more adherents than they would otherwise, almost all of whom believe that it really is a factual document.[20]

Some critics have suggested that the mainstream media have made far right and extremist hate in the media acceptable by pretending that more moderate hatemongers essentially reflect mainstream America, and the media not only carry them but promote them. For example, although Rush Limbaugh insists that there is a difference between "dissent" and "hate," his rhetoric nevertheless encourages many listeners to move from passive dissidence to active hate. Moreover, some critics make a direct correlation between the sometimes violence-fomenting of G. Gordon Liddy's radio show and far-right violence, but despite the fact that Oliver North admittedly subverted the Constitution and was a traitor to his military allegiance to his country, the media saw fit to reward North with a radio talk show, giving him acceptable societal status and even enabling him to obtain strong support in a race for governor of Virginia. By pandering to such hatemongers, some critics say, the mainstream media are acting as enablers for the violence-producing rhetoric.

More than one presumably mainstream radio station has attempted to legitimate hate radio. In 1995, for example, San Francisco's KSFO-AM, which described itself as "hot talk radio," gave "the people what they want, chucking its formerly liberal talk format in favor of an all-right-wing lineup."[21] The importance to the right wing of accommodating talk show hosts espousing their ideas was emphasized by the head of the Southern Illinois Patriot League, Glad

Hall: "There's no doubt that the talk show hosts are really the ones who are responsible for educating as many people as to what's going on . . . and are really the fuel that is feeding the whole thing. We're indebted to them an awful lot."[22] Even in the shadow of Washington, D.C., in Falls Church, Virginia, hate radio operates. "WFAX broadcasts . . . the continuing message that America is 'poisoned by Jewish money.' Dale Crowley Jr. holds forth with a regular monologue."[23]

Some of the far-right and extreme right groups that continue to make full and effective use of the media include the Identity Church Movement, the National Alliance, the Liberty Lobby, the Aryan Nations, the Ku Klux Klan, the Institute for Historical Review, and the Skinheads.

A discussion of some of the key personalities who represent these—and other organizations—may shed additional light on the purposes, goals, and impact of hate on the airwaves.

David Duke

David Duke is perhaps the best known of the far-right/extremist personalities. Over the years Duke has used the media very effectively: for disseminating his ideas, for recruiting, for persuading, and even for changing his image. A former leader of the Ku Klux Klan, in the 1970s Duke formed what appears to be the largest Klan organization today, the Knights of the KKK. Although Duke has since left the organization, his successor, Thom Robb, appears to have effectively followed Duke's example and transformed the Knights of the KKK into national leadership of the two-to-three dozen Klan organizations said to be in operation throughout the United States.[24] Duke's leadership ability and literate charisma was such that Willis Carto, who established the Liberty Lobby, became one of his leading backers. In 1984 Carto founded the Populist Party, which ran Duke for president in 1988.[25] Duke's popularity probably reached its height when he ran for governor of Louisiana and almost won the Democratic primary, which would have likely made him governor of the state. To be so successful in the polls, he changed his public persona from a militant advocate to a more reasoned, moderate-appearing candidate. He has since metamorphosed into an even more moderate image, moving away from the political arena to find solitude and God in nature. His newfound approach has also moved him from the lecture platform and writing into "The David Duke International Internet Radio Show." The David Duke Report, on the Internet, added AM-quality sound, which could be downloaded as an audio program. Some of the topic titles of his program during the latter part of 1997: "A Black Leader's Welfare Admission"; "The Immigration Disaster"; "Black Crime Spurred on by Hate Movies" ("the real purveyors of racial hatred, the makers of anti-white, hate movies and documentaries that ultimately instigate black criminals to rob, rape, and murder White people"); "Standing Up for Our Heritage"; "Not a Dime's Worth of Difference" (Democratic and Republicans both "ignore the most vital, compelling issue of our time—RACE").[26]

For this book, co-author Michael C. Keith asked David Duke some questions about his use of the airwaves.

Keith: What is the primary goal of your broadcast programming?

Duke: To awaken the people of European heritage to the crisis affecting their genotype. To instill a racial consciousness that will encourage them to preserve both their gene pool and the culture it erected.

Keith: How do you respond to claims that you are broadcasting messages of hate?

Duke: It is the mainstream media that constantly broadcasts hate messages against our founding European heritage. We are assigned a collective guilt for slavery, while blacks are never called into account—as a race—for the vicious crime and social problems that have emanated from the black community.

Keith: What do you perceive as the greatest threat to your broadcast mission?

Duke: The greatest is the mass media masters who want to shut down free speech on the air. To talk about white slavery or Jim Crow laws of the past is called justice. To object to the massive black robbery, rape, and murder of whites in America is called "hate."

Keith: Given the administration's pledge to crack down on "broadcasts of malicious and hateful intent," what do you see as the future of right-wing radio?

Duke: Its future is doubtful.[27]

Tom Valentine

Tom Valentine is another highly popular and effective far right talk show host. Valentine's success in reaching a broad spectrum of Patriot followers is to follow the attempt of his organization, the Liberty Lobby, "to put as populist or as friendly a face on neo-Nazism as they can."[28] Like Chuck Harder, he appears to be using facts and logic to prove his points, conveying in a more palatable fashion the ideas of far-right and extremist-right groups, including ultra-patriotism, white supremacy, and anti-Semitism. Valentine's daily talk show, "Radio Free America" (RFA), is sponsored by the neo-Nazi Liberty Lobby, whose publication, *Spotlight,* sells audiotapes of RFA programs. Valentine is persuasive, echoing the far right's condemnation of Waco and Ruby Ridge and calling for a stop to what the rightwing increasingly refers to as an out-of-control federal government. At one point he responded to President Clinton's post-Oklahoma attack on "these little shortwave programs that plainly are encouraging violence" by saying, mockingly, "I don't think Tim McVeigh listened to me."[29]

Valentine promotes the usual far-right anti-Jewish conspiracy theory and is a strong Holocaust-denier, claiming that the 1938 Nazi pogrom against the Jews, "Kristallnacht," was actually perpetrated by the Jews themselves.[30] He has blamed many of the attacks on programs such as his on the Jewish Anti-Defamation League (ADL) and on alleged Jewish control of the mainstream media. "The ADL has the ear of the government," Valentine has said. "Look at the power of Israel. The media does what the ADL tells them to do." And, despite his blasting of Bureau of Alcohol, Tobacco and Firearms agents for their actions in Waco, at a later law enforcement conference where an all-white group of ATF agents bought T-shirts emblazoned with racist legends, Valentine defended them. "It looks like the ADL is doing it again, trying to stir up racism where it doesn't exist, to keep themselves in business."[31]

Valentine's "Radio Free America" (RFA) is considered to be the longest-running short-wave program of its kind. An RFA promotional flyer says, "Tom Valentine fearlessly probes the dark corners of every important aspect of life in these United States. He not only covers corruption as no other talk host dares to do, but he has the intelligence and the experience to challenge the establishment in realms of technology and science, health and energy, as well as politics and big and intrusive government."[32] A newspaper story put Valentine and his program into the category of "Radio Paranoia, where suspicious minds meet every day to churn current events through various conspiracy theories and arrive at the real truth, the one that the government and mainstream media would hide from you . . . short-wave . . . has become the place to tap into the dark and embattled mood that has settled over the country."[33] Another of Valentine's charges, for example, is that the federal government is deliberately holding back a number of inventions that, if released, would make Americans' lives much easier.[34]

In an interview for this book with co-author Michael C. Keith, Tom Valentine offered his views and goals, answers to criticism that shows like his are dangerous to the country, and what he perceives as the greatest threat to his mission.

> *Valentine:* I was the first one on shortwave. We kicked off with RFA on satellite radio in 1987 on North America One. The Liberty Lobby, founded by Willis Carto, funded our efforts from the beginning.
>
> The ADL is always working overtime to stop the Liberty Lobby.
>
> The establishment media wrongly exploit the airwaves. The vast majority of the media are controlled by corporate institutions which are governed by Plutocrats and they fail in their duty as watchdogs of the Fourth

Estate. There are people with lots of animosities out there, but I'm not one of them. I don't possess ethnic animosity.

I'm very pro-America First. I'm a little Libertarian, a little Populist and a lot Patriot, who wants a strong and intelligent middle-class. We (RFA) are part of the Patriot Movement, which is anti-government for numerous valid reasons. I'm seldom singled out for criticism, but the Liberty Lobby is always criticized as being right-wing, anti-Jew, and Nazi, all of which is false. RFA's purpose is to get people to become aware of the problems created by an ever encroaching government. Radio is the best medium for the propagation of ideas, because Americans don't read anymore. This sad fact gives radio its tremendous power. Limbaugh and others tell their listeners what to think and they think it. Chuck Harder is an outstanding radio guy. It hurt our effort when Sun Radio management forced him out. It's certainly no secret that the pro-Zionist Jews have the greatest and most powerful influence on American media. I believe that everyone has the right to employ the public airwaves to communicate their ideas, regardless of the nature of those ideas. It is up to the listener to use the on/off switch or the tuning dial.

The biggest threat to this country is the American people themselves. It is their ignorance and their mindless willingness to go along with the dictates of the Plutocrats that constitutes this country's greatest threat. RFA currently can be heard on satellite, the Internet, shortwave, and on six or seven broadcast stations. A while back RFA was aired by 44 broadcast stations.[35]

Dale Crowley Jr.

Dale Crowley Jr. is director of "The King's Business" and "Focus on Israel" radio programs, which are heard over a combination of shortwave, microradio and AM stations. He began broadcasting in the 1940s on his father's radio show. "Father [Dale Crowley Sr.] began Christian, patriotic broadcasting in 1925," Crowley stated for this book. "I was guest on his programs in the 1940s, 1950s, and 1960s. I began my own Christian, patriotic (right-wing extremist) [Crowley's words] in 1979."[36] Crowley is also the editor of a bimonthly pamphlet, *Capitol Hill Voice*. He disseminates views generally reflective of the far right, with an emphasis on anti-government, anti-Semitic/anti-Israel, and pro-Christian fundamentalist rhetoric. For example, his pamphlet has condemned lawmakers for supposedly creating legislation as a means of oppressing the people and to gain personal advantage for them and their supporters, and has alleged that more laws merely put new limits on our personal liberties.[37] He has presented the view that Israelites strayed from God by not putting strong limits on their children to make them acceptable to God, thus turning God against the Jews.[38] He states that the government supports the abandonment of Christians for Jews. "Israel-first dispensationalism," Crowley has stated, "has adversely affected the preaching of the Gospel to the Jews, and adversely influenced the foreign policy of the United States toward Israel, hurting our nation and Israel as well, and unconscionably laying the foreign aid debt on our children and grandchildren. Repayment of this debt will be required of our children and grandchildren, while the futures of the little Jewish boys and girls of Israel are guaranteed to be debt-free. But that's the way dispensationalists like to think—that doesn't bother them—the cult of Israel."[39]

In his interview for this book, Crowley describes himself as a "Right Wing Extremist, Big Time." Asked how he responds to claims that he is broadcasting messages of hate, Crowley says, "I expose the hatred of those who make such charges." He believes that the greatest threat to his broadcast mission is the "Don't care' apathy on the part of listeners, and demands by such as the ADL that I be put off the air." His response to the pledge from the White House to curtail "broadcasts of malicious and hateful intent" is that "We will continue to expose the president's hypocrisy, disdain, and hatred for all that is right."[40]

Bob Enyart

Bob Enyart has been one of the most incitive right-wing extremist personalities on the air. His forte has principally been television, and in the mid-1990s his syndicated call-in TV show originating at station KWHD in Denver was distributed by satellite to more than 750 cable systems across the country and into Canada. His potential audience has been well into the millions. Enyart describes himself as a "right-wing religious fanatic." It does not appear to be a tongue-in-cheek description. He strongly advocates declaring homosexuality and abortion to be crimes punishable by death. He believes children should be spanked to make them learn proper behavior. He declares that only evil leaders would support gun controls. On one show, in a segment titled "A Holiday Abortionist Home Visit," he showed a map with the location of the house of a local doctor who performed legal abortions. A representative of Planned Parenthood has alleged that "Bob Enyart and other leaders of the anti-choice movement have very much created the atmosphere of violence that has made it acceptable for the John Salvis and other lunatics who have murdered abortion providers."[41] One of Enyart's most graphic recommendations was a list of what a government that was doing the right thing would do in its first 100 days in office. After the takeover of the American government by Enyart's people— presumably armed militias aided by white supremacists, Christian Identity groups, Skinheads, and neo-Nazis, among others—here is what should and would happen, according to Enyart:

- Abortion will be criminalized. Anyone who performs abortions will be executed.
- People caught with sexually stimulating materials will be flogged the first time and thereafter executed.
- All recreational drug users and sellers will be executed.
- Bureau of Alcohol, Tobacco and Firearms employees will be "terminated."[42]

Like many ideologues, Enyart does not practice the so-called family values that he espouses. He is a convicted child abuser, having beaten one child with a belt, his behavior with children resulting in the courts' denying him custody of two natural children and two stepchildren.[43]

Chuck Baker

Chuck Baker, whose radio show originates in Colorado Springs, is a master of extremist rhetoric regarding gun control. On a number of occasions he has encouraged his listeners to get their own guns and go to Washington to protest a ban on assault weapons. It was Baker's broadcasts that allegedly inspired Francisco M. Duran to do just that: take a gun and ammunition, go to Washington, and shoot at the White House, presumably in an attempt to kill the president. Baker denied that talk radio was to blame.[44] "So what if the jerk, the wacko, the creep, this piece of crap shot up the White House," Baker said. "If he thinks I or Rush Limbaugh are the reason he went out there, the man needs psychiatric counseling."[45]

Baker often is not only on the fringe, but goes over it, especially in the encouragement he gives his guests. In his advocacy of the "cleansing" of the government, Baker hosted Linda Thompson when she promoted (but later stopped) an armed march on Washington to rid the Congress of "traitors." When she made the proposal, Baker assured her the U.S. military would not defend Congress, but "will come over to our side." When Baker asked her what to do about the cameras used in that part of town to monitor and control traffic flow, she said "shoot 'em out." A few days later snipers, avid followers of Baker's program, did just that. Liddy and Baker are sometimes considered in the same breath as super-patriots by the far right, including the militias, which both support and promote.[46]

But Baker goes much further than Liddy with accusations that appear to be more threatening and bizarre. Baker has openly advised his listeners to stockpile arms and ammunition, to join armed militias, form guerrilla cells, march on Washington, and shoot members of Congress. He accompanies these exhortations with "ping-ping" sounds of a gun's firing pin. Baker talks about the need for an armed revolution to "take out the slimeballs in Congress" and to eliminate the "bureaucrats" who are "too stupid to get a job."[47] He embraces many extremist-right beliefs, such as that there is a secret national police force commanded by Janet Reno, that microchips are being implanted in babies, and that driver's licenses are fingerprinted.[48]

Baker can be general in his attacks: "Am I advocating the overthrow of this government? . . . I'm advocating the cleansing. If you combined everybody in the United States of America that you would even estimate to be on the other side, you would only have a drop in the bucket compared to the masses in rebellion. . . . Why are we sitting here?" And he can be specific: "creeps like Metzenbaum and Kennedy are going to think that we're sitting back thinking [and not taking action] . . . you know how these slime balls operate. The only way you're ever going to get rid of Metzenbaum is when you're finally at a point that you can stand over there, put the dirt on top of the box and say, 'I'm pretty sure he's in there.' "[49]

Louis Beam

Louis Beam is a long-time leader of the racist right. He has been head of the Texas Knights of the Ku Klux Klan, a key representative of the Aryan Nation, and an accomplished writer and speaker for white supremacist groups in general. His rhetoric is activist. He has called for the overthrow of the U.S. government, "by blood" if necessary, and the establishment of an all-white America in the northwest part of the country. He even developed a priority system for identifying which government officials should be executed first. At one point in his career he was indicted, along with other extremist leaders, for plotting to overthrow the government by force and violence. He left the country, was captured, and was tried and acquitted of seditious conspiracy. After Ruby Ridge, Beam joined the United Citizens for Justice organization and urged Patriot members nationally to prepare to go to war against the government.[50]

Beam has used the media well. He is credited with developing the first white supremacist Internet bulletin board network. He is a principal personality on the Jubilee radio program, "Newslight," which is carried on short-wave and also on a number of AM and FM stations throughout the country. Jubilee Radio, discussed in an earlier chapter, is a function of the *Jubilee,* a newspaper that serves as a "national, umbrella publication for neo-Nazis, Identity followers, racist skinheads and some militia factions."[51] Both the newspaper and the radio show are credited with forging strong links among a variety of extremist groups. Two other important right-wing media names, Tom Blair and Paul Hall Jr. are regulars with Beam on Jubilee radio, the latter as host of the show.[52] Hall is the publisher/producer of *Jubilee* and is known for his virulent racist and anti-Semitic rhetoric and attacks on the federal government.[53] Hall, as well as Beam, makes extensive use of the Internet. Beam has urged *Jubilee* readers to join him on America Online, where there is "no one between you and me . . . to filter the exchange."[54]

Sharp Rhetoric

Hate groups may not necessarily sponsor regular programming of personalities on the airwaves, but may use the media when and where they can place spokespersons. Neither are hate groups always Christian white supremacist anti-Semites; they are sometimes Christian Black anti-Semites. One of the most notorious is the Reverend Al Sharpton, known for both his anti-white and anti-Semitic radio rhetoric. He has been a fixture on radio station WWRL in New York and has also appeared on WLIB, with his programs reportedly picked up by other area stations. His approach is similar to that of other right-wing extremists, vitriolically attacking designated groups in ways that might engender violence against that group by fanatical listeners and supporters. One such incident occurred after Sharpton and some others had "broadcast a series of rallies attacking non-Black Harlem store owners in the vilest of terms." The fervor succeeded in generating an attack in 1995 on a clothing store owned by a Jew, killing eight people.[55] Like his counterparts in Ku Klux Klan, survivalist, militia, white supremacist, and similar organizations with radio shows, Sharpton could not be legally held responsible for the deaths. Ironically, also like his anti-Black counterparts, he was more lionized than vilified by a large number of New Yorkers, resulting in his almost winning the race for Democratic nominee for mayor of New York in 1998.

Another representative of a hate group not as well known as some but growing in influence is Arthur Jones of the America First Committee. In its neo-Nazi orientation, it is not too unlike the pro-Nazi America First Committee that was active in the United States prior to and even for a time after the United States entered World War II. Appearing on Knowledge TV, Jones's presentation included the following: "Everything was the creation of white genius." "Each kind should mate with their own—it says so in the Bible." "It is a sin to mingle races." "The anti-war movement [during the Vietnam era] was financed by Jews." "Seven out of ten blacks are born feeble, with IQs below 70." "The Jews are behind the rot." "The two-party, Jew-party, queer-party system."[56]

A Publisher's Perspective

Eric Rhoads is publisher of *RADIO INK*, a leading industry periodical. In an exclusive interview for this book with co-author Michael C. Keith, Rhoads commented on several key issues relating to right-wing media use. Rhoads states that he makes sure his magazine expresses all viewpoints. It is interesting to note, however, how effectively right-wing rhetoric has infiltrated mainstream publishing as well as electronic media, as one reads his answers.

Keith: How have right-wing extremists exploited the various audio media?

Rhoads: Mike, I'm concerned that your book has an automatic bias toward "right-wing" extremists. It seems to me that all sides of the political spectrum have the ability and often exercise the ability to exploit a media [sic] like radio. True, I hear a lot of right-wingers on shortwave, but I also hear a lot of lefties. It strikes me that the whole movement toward people believing this misperception is a direct result of a spin created by the Clinton White House, who [sic] was reacting to the impact of Rush Limbaugh. The Clintons hired a talk radio consultant/network executive because they were so concerned that Limbaugh was hurting them. They also started raising the issue of right-wing control and exposure of radio when it just isn't true. What is true is that Limbaugh rose to the top because he had listeners in droves who agreed with his philosophy and supported him like no talent in radio history. It was Limbaugh's act which saved AM radio.

Keith: Talk radio has been accused of giving too much air time to ultraconservative views. What do you think?

Rhoads: It's all spin. People listen and react to what they want. An advertiser cannot force a person to buy a product. They can only expose the product and hope the product strikes a chord and people buy it. Radio is no different. Hundreds of radio talents bomb every year. Those that succeed do so because people keep listening and coming back. Radio is a reflective medium. I've always believed that a program director's title should be changed to program 'reflector' because reflecting people's tastes and desires is what sells.

Keith: What's your response to critics who contend that right-leaning talk show hosts fuel extremist hatred and behavior and are often the inspiration for radical right actions?

Rhoads: There are people who make foolish decisions in their lives as reactions to something someone has said. The problem is not in what is said, it is in the level of responsibility of the individual. We each have individual discernment to make choices. If you believe the hosts have that level of influence, then one must also believe that the lyrics of rap songs will drive everyone to rape or murder. True, some will rape and murder, usually because they would anyway. The driving force (host or music) is merely an excuse. If I hear a host tell me to go out and shoot everyone who is not like me, do I do it? Of course not. I may listen to hear their viewpoint, possibly for education, entertainment, or out of boredom. Though I think radio is a compelling medium, I don't think anyone can convince someone to do something they don't want (or plan) to do. Supposedly a hypnotist can't get you to do something you don't want to do.

Keith: How would you contrast the text of conservative mainstream talkers with that of the radical-right talkers (Patriots, Identity movement, separatists, conspiracy theorists, survivalists, etc.)?

Rhoads: Credibility vs. no credibility. Wild claims vs. logical arguments. However, I've heard some very radical arguments that made me think twice. They made me aware, watch things carefully, and pay attention to see if what they said would come true. We walk a fine line. Imagine if radio had existed at the time of the Revolutionary War. Would those telling the truth about the British government been categorized as right-wing extremists? Would the war have occurred if the government could have controlled the spin and written the militia off as radicals? Would people have been willing to fight? My guess is that some of these people do have some factual information which could be considered by some as crackpot. Unfortunately, most are crackpots. How does one discern?

Keith: What do you see as the future for ultra-right-wing radio?

Rhoads: I hope it has a future. If it does not, we're all in trouble. We must FIGHT to preserve the right of these people to make their claims and speak their mind. We must never allow anyone to control what is said on the air. As a listener, I want the choice of making up my own mind. If I want to send my money for a tape on the Clinton Chronicles, I should be able to do it without worrying that someone is putting my name on a list of subversives. As a broadcaster I should be able to broadcast my views at any time. I should not be required to air opposing views. The reality is that more radio properties are owned by people who might have a tendency to lean to the left rather than those who lean to the right. Yet, even those people see this for what it really is—good business. Give the people what they want.[57]

Revisionists/Holocaust Deniers

"The Holocaust is a Jewish Invention—It Never Happened"

Tell this radical-right assertion to the thousands of survivors still alive who saw their families led into the gas chambers, massacred in the ghettos, machine-gunned in the fields of Lublin and in a hundred other cities, shot in the blood ditches of the concentration camps, starved to death in urine- and feces-filled barracks, beaten to death in work gangs, and systematically exterminated in a dozen other ways as part of a planned and meticulously carried-out final solution. Tell that to the American soldiers who stumbled upon the concentration camps at the end of World War II and saw the skeletal bodies of the few still living and the skeletal remains of the many who were not, buried by the thousands in human garbage pits and fertilizing the soil as ashes dumped from the death furnaces.

Yet, the prejudicial hatred of Jews has so permeated so much of society, especially the right-wing hate groups, that Holocaust-deniers have become a key part of the extreme right—as well as a profitable business. As pointed out frequently in this book, most far-right and extremist organizations combine patented anti-Semitism with a denial that the Holocaust happened or, if it did, that it was not responsible for the extermination of more than a fraction of the seven million Jews, Gypsies, homosexuals, anti-Nazi priests and ministers, and others who disappeared from the face of the earth.

The Revisionists—those who arbitrarily rewrite history in order to claim that there was no Holocaust and that Hitler and Nazi Germany were not the evil perpetrators that eyewitnesses and historians have made them out to be—do not expound their beliefs in a vacuum. They stem out of the more pervasive and deeper anti-Semitism that marks virtually all right-wing groups. And almost all of these have Web sites that can literally reach millions of people in the United States and globally. Some have particular axes to grind; others attack in more general stereotypes.

Aside from Holocaust-denial as part of the broader philosophy and rhetoric of right-wing groups, there are organizations almost totally devoted to disseminating this belief. Some have become world-famous (or infamous). Some are small and not as well known. A few of the more prominent revisionist organizations and individuals who reach out through their Web sites are the Adelaide Institute, Air Photo Evidence, Prof. Arthur R. Butz, Student Revisionists' Resource Site, Institute for Historical Review, the Committee for Open Debate on the Holocaust (CODOH), and, probably the most potent and influential of all, the Zundelsite. The Internet has become a special province of the Revisionists. An Anti-Defamation League report stated that anti-Semitic and Holocaust-denial groups and individuals, who often pretend to be scholars and historians, are the fastest-growing Web sites on the Internet.[58]

The Institute for Historical Review (IHR) was founded in 1978 and describes itself as "an educational and publishing center devoted to truth and accuracy in history . . . in the tradition of historical revisionism." It notes that the "best-known and most controversial aspect of [its] work has been its treatment of the Holocaust issue. . . . The Institute does not 'deny the Holocaust'. . . . At the same time, though, a growing body of documentary, forensic and other evidence shows that much of what we're told about the 'Holocaust' is exaggerated or simply not true." The Institute believes it has been the target of "bigoted attacks." It states, "Well-financed special-interest groups, seeking to curtail open discussion of vital historical issues, have for years targeted the Institute, grossly misrepresenting its work and purpose. Prominent among these are the Simon Wiesenthal Center (Los Angeles) and the Anti-Defamation League of B'nai B'rith (New York)—stridently partisan organizations with well documented records as staunch apologists for narrow Zionist-Jewish interests."[59]

The Institute has made good use of the media for dissemination of its ideas and purported historical findings. Its Media Project not only distributes material, but places its representatives on the air. For example, it notes that its Media Project director has appeared on literally hundreds of radio talk shows, reaching audiences literally in the millions. In addition, it was the subject of a "60 Minutes" feature in 1994.[60]

Like IHR, the Committee for Open Debate on the Holocaust (CODOH) attempts to gain credence as an objective, unprejudiced research body in order to entice interest in its work. Rather than denying the Holocaust outright, as most revisionist groups do, CODOH states that "it is not [our] purpose to prove 'the holocaust never happened.'" It adds, further, that it does not intend to prove either that "gassing chambers 'never existed' or that European Jews did not suffer a catastrophe during the Hitlerian regime." CODOH then adds that "while we no longer believe the gas chamber stories (we used to very much believe them) or the 'genocide' theory, we remain open to being convinced we are wrong." Many otherwise knowledgeable and rational people, especially youngsters, are thereby hooked. The contents of CODOH transmissions are not ambiguous. Its Web page has stated that the "Holocaust-story fraud" was a false creation and was being disseminated by the "Holocaust lobby . . . owned and run by Jews."[61] Some of the titles of its Internet presentations clarify the CODOH's bottom line: "Gas Chambers and Gas Vans—Technical and historical non sequiturs are discussed"; "The Tangled Web: Zionism, Stalinism and the Holocaust Story." CODOH founder and director of CODOH Bradley R. Smith has stated that one day a problem that will have to be addressed by anthropologists is "how a crude taboo protecting gas chamber stories from criticism could have operated so successfully in Western culture through the last half of the 20th century."[62]

Ernst Zundel and the Zundelsite

Thus far the most powerful and effective Holocaust-denial/revisionist operation is the Internet's Zundelsite. In the early 1990s Ernst Zundel was already earning praise from the radical right for his media programs. On one of the neo-Nazi National Alliance's American Dissident Voices show, William Pierce told his audience, "I'd like to remind you again that there is a new and highly recommended patriotic radio program on the short-wave dial. It is called the 'Voice of Freedom,' and it's hosted by a man who has devoted his life to the

cause of free speech, justice, and the survival of our people, Mr. Ernst Zundel. . . .
We at American Dissident Voices salute you, Ernst Zundel!"[63]

Who is Ernst Zundel? What is the Zundelsite? Excerpts from Zundel's "Mission Statement" say it all:

> The Zundelsite has as its mission the rehabilitation of the honor and reputation of the German nation and people. Specifically, the Zundelsite challenges the traditional version of the "Holocaust"—an Allied propaganda tool concocted during World War II—that is not based on historical fact but is a cleverly used ploy to keep the German war time generation and their descendants in perpetual political, emotional, spiritual and financial bondage.

> The Zundelsite challenges three specific, commonly accepted, monstrous lies pertaining to the "Holocaust": that there ever was a Führer order for the genocidal killings of Jews, Gypsies and others, that the chief murder weapon or instrument for the alleged mass killing, called a "gas chamber," was designed for the express purpose of targeting groups of human beings and that the numbers of victims claimed to have been killed are anywhere near the number of people who actually died in concentration camps of whatever cause—including lack of food, shelter, medicines, epidemics and old age.

> Jews were a small vocal minority in a global struggle involving many nationalities. It is deceptive to portray them as prime "victims" of a non-existent German genocidal policy. To claim that World War II was fought by the Germans, as the Holocaust Lobby incessantly claims, to kill off the Jews as a group, is a deliberately planned, systematic deception amounting to financial, political, emotional and spiritual extortion. The "Holocaust," first sold as a tragedy, has over time deteriorated into a racket cloaked in the tenets of a new State religion. It is high time to subject the "Holocaust" to public scrutiny—like any other historical issue. The Zundelsite will do just that. The Zundelsite documents will chip away at this World War II propaganda monstrosity. The Zundelsite web pages will prove in many different ways—statistically, forensically, and logically—that it is historically inaccurate, emotionally misleading and cruelly unfair to claim the "Holocaust" took place in the form portrayed by conventional media.[64]

Ernst Zundel migrated to Canada from Germany and lives in Toronto. Because of tighter restrictions on hate speech in Canada, he uses a Canadian Internet server to send materials to a colleague, Dr. Ingrid A. Rimland, in the United States. The message goes out over a U.S. Web site in the form of "ZGrams," which sometimes include the following notation: "The Zundelsite, located in the USA, is owned and operated by Dr. Ingrid A. Rimland, an American citizen." Each transmission begins, "Good Morning from the Zundelsite." Rimland, like Zundel, came from Europe, from the Ukraine. Both suffered from the defeat of Germany, and blamed Stalin and the Jews for the Nazi loss of the war. Rimland has stated:

> We do admire Hitler more than Stalin while speculating that, in all likelihood, the opposite is true for members of the tribe [a euphemism for Jew]. . . . we grieve for some 50 million people (and possibly many, many more!) who lost their lives as a direct or indirect result of too many Aryans having chosen Stalin over Hitler, thanks to a lot of tribal coaching, which is why the entire world now fears the 'New World Order' and shivers at what it might mean."[65]

A sampling of some of the materials on the Zundelsite includes the following titles: "The Natural Sciences and Technology under National Socialism," "Nuremberg: The Crime that Will Not Die" "Inside the Auschwitz 'Gas Chambers,'" The "Liberation of the Camps: Facts vs. Lies," "A Revisionist Challenge to the U.S. Holocaust Museum," "What Is Holocaust Denial?," "The Big Lie," "Keystone of the New World Order: The Holocaust Dogma of Judaism," "Did Six Million Really Die?"[66]

A look at some quotes from a number of Zundelsite transmissions provides a clear indication of Zundel's philosophy, beliefs, approach, and goals. While the Zundelsite is principally devoted to Holocaust denial, it includes continuing anti-Semitic commentary not necessarily tied to the Holocaust, plus the usual far-right conspiracy fear.

> July 1, 1997: It is important to show the Holocaust did not take place because: "Without the 'six million,' Nazism loses it image of diabolism. . . . The Zionists routinely use the 'gas chamber' hoax to attack white racial solidarity . . . Money has always been a prime purpose of the Holocaust hoax . . . covering up Zionist crimes is another purpose of Holocaust propaganda."
>
> July 11, 1997: "It is a huge jump from being in a concentration camp to a 'Holocaust survivor'—and to expect someone to pay reparations for confinement in a camp during a war is to open the door to reparations to

everyone in the world who was confined during WWII. But, not so. It seems that one must be a member of a certain race to qualify for reparations."

July 28, 1997: "Unless we wake up, we will find someday the political situation will not be to the liking of the international elitists, and we may find foreign troops in blue UN helmets on OUR shores, to 'correct' the situation. . . . Their bombs and bullets, I assure you, will kill your family quite as dead as any others."

September 3, 1997: "The story about the so-called 'Nazi Gold' is still making news. I assume it will be thus until Switzerland really pays the Zionist blackmailers the billions of dollars they are demanding. . . . The 'Nazi gold' matter might just be another method of keeping the 'Holocaust' myth alive."

September 23, 1997: [A review of *The World Conquerors* by Louis Marschalko, first published in 1958.] ". . . the real reasons for the war [World War II]. Hitler's Germany had to be destroyed if the program of the "Protocols" [the hoax book, *The Protocols of Zion*, promoted by Henry Ford, fabricating documents to prove the existence of a Jewish world conspiracy] were to be fulfilled. . . . The Jewish staffing and orchestration of the Nuremberg Trial, the east-west collaboration in the hounding of 'war criminals,' the real fate of the fabled Six Million, the setting up of Jewish persecution as the moral standard of the post war era, all are devastatingly analyzed to show the vested interests at work."

September 28, 1997: From a correspondent. "I know I owe Ernst Zundel a lot. . . . Among the truths learned: Adolph Hitler was not a comical, craven lunatic, but rather the great and gentle leader who served his people so selflessly and earned their undying love in return."

The Zundelsite has more than once been accused not only of incitement to hate but of fomenting violence. Many of its ZGrams deal defensively with court cases, investigations, and legal maneuvers, all revolving on Zundel's right to the kind of freedom of speech that Zundel's goals would effectively deny to others. Indeed, some of his severest critics have also been the staunchest defenders of his right to disseminate his views on the Internet. On a number of occasions the Canadian government and provincial government of Toronto have attempted to find grounds for deportation. Canada's Human Rights Act follows the provisions of the Universal Declaration of Human Rights that "everyone has the right of freedom of opinion and expression; this right includes freedom to hold opinions without interference and to seek, receive and import information and ideas through any media and regardless of frontiers." However, it also provides that "nothing in the Declaration may be interpreted as implying for any State, group or person any right to engage in any activity or to perform any act aimed at the destruction of any of the rights and freedoms set forth herein."

On the latter ground Canada took legal action against Zundel. On the Zundelsite, Zundel claimed that the actions against him suggest that "it is quite all right to harass, stalk, beset and administratively target perfectly law-abiding citizens, writers, broadcasters and publishers because these self-appointed censors don't like someone else's political viewpoint."[67] In 1992 the Canada Supreme Court decided that Zundel was protected under Canada's constitution to express his political beliefs without censorship or prosecution. However, his problems were not over.

Zundel didn't fare so well in Germany, where in 1996 a number of Internet sites, including the Zundelsite, were barred from access by Internet users in Germany. The government stated that the Internet should not be allowed to freely dispense any and all material because some of the information transmitted on Web sites, is clearly harmful to certain segments of society, and especially to minors.[68] In early 1996, Deutsche Telekom in Germany blocked access to a California-based supplier of Internet-accessible space, Webcom, because one of its 1,500 Web pages was the Zundelsite.[69] (Germany prohibits the dissemination of neo-Nazi and Holocaust revisionist materials, so the Zundelsite must be received from the U.S. by the growing Skinhead and neo-Nazi German population.) The action had an unintended effect. Zundel was pleased to have the additional notoriety and increased attention to his Web site. "It is every dissident's dream come true,"[70] he said. The banning drew assistance from sources otherwise opposed to his rhetoric, including universities such as Carnegie-Mellon University and the Massachusetts Institute of Technology, which provided "mirror" sites for transmission of the ZGrams as a statement of the principle of free speech.[71]

Germany is not the only country to be concerned about Internet hate home pages. In the United Kingdom, Parliament has also wrestled with the matter, and "new laws to stop neo-Nazi organizations and other racist factions from using the Internet to spread their propaganda are being considered by the Government."[72]

Hundreds of individuals, as well as organizations such as the Anti-Defamation League, the Southern Poverty Law Center, FAIR, and Radio For Peace International, operate Web sites to counter Zundel and similar Holocaust deniers. For example, in the United States one individual, Ken McVay, quit his job to apply his knowledge of history full-time on an Internet bulletin board to refute the Zundels (see chapter 9). He is opposed to government censorship as a solution. "Government cannot, and will not, short of fascist means . . . deal with it effectively."[73]

Zundel continues to be the subject of investigations by the government of

Canada for his alleged violations of human rights and for allegedly being a national security threat.[74] Zundel's ZGrams blame communists and Jews, among others, for his plight.[75] In addition, Canada's Human Rights Commission held hearings on whether Zundel was in violation of a section of Canada's Human Rights Act that prohibits use of telephone lines in a way that likely would expose people to hatred or contempt because of their race, religion, or ethnic origin.[76] In May 1998, Zundel's hearing before the human rights tribunal was still going on.[77] (Neither Ernst Zundel nor Ingrid Rimland accepted invitations to provide their own unedited statements for this book, although they were invited to do so on numerous occasions.)

It is important to understand that the so-called paranoid fringe radical right organizations do not see their rhetoric and exhortations in a negative light. They do not see their law-breaking, robberies, bombings, and other violence as immoral or unjust. What most Americans may see as evil, they see as good. John Trochmann, a founder of the Montana Militia, sees the militia actions, for example, as those of messenger, not instigator. He put it this way: "We're not the ones who are setting up to kill millions of people here in America. We're the ones who are exposing what the evil forces are doing in this country. Why should we feel that we're responsible?"[78]

We have discussed only a few of the right-wing media users who disseminate hate. Some readers will think of the names of other personalities they've heard on radio, seen on television or logged onto in cyberspace—names such as Tom Donohue, John Stadtmiller, and Don Weideman, among others.

We believe that those we have discussed represent a reasonable cross-section of examples of how the airwaves have been used for rancor, and to those who are disappointed that we seem not to have recognized their roles and have not included them here, we offer our regrets.

Chapter 9

Armed for the Right

Every man has a right to utter what he thinks truth, and every other man has a right to knock him down for it.

—Samuel Johnson

Although the world is full of suffering, it is full also of the overcoming of it.

—Helen Keller

Opposition to "hate" media takes many forms, including individuals who set up counterpoints on radio or the Internet; citizen groups spontaneously forming in communities where hate messages are prevalent over the air; radio, TV, and cable owners acting out of personal concern or pressure from their audiences; formal organizations established for the express purpose of fighting hate media. In some cases the opponents of hate media advocate censorship; in most cases they strongly support the freedom-of-speech rights of those who would, conversely, deny them their freedom of speech and, in many cases, even kill them if their airwaves missions are successful.

As evident throughout this book, the strongest pro and con attitudes toward the radical-right occurred right after the Oklahoma City bombing, as did pro and con censorship demands regarding right-wing media. Perhaps the greatest furor was generated by President Clinton's denunciation of right-wing media as progenitors of attitudes and behavior that led to the federal building bombing, and his call to curb such hate speech. On May 3, 1995, the president submitted to Congress the Antiterrorism Amendments Act of 1995. The Act proposed to give federal law enforcement authorities the legal tools and resources to examine financial reports in antiterrorism cases, obtain transportation and lodging records, deepen electronic surveillance, include greater analysis of bombing materials, and raise penalties for transferring firearms or explosives, among other things. However, the bill did not touch on any aspect of censorship, or in any way gag the free-speech entitlements of even the most rabid right-winger. As angry as the nation and the government were, First Amendment freedoms were not abrogated. Subsequently, however, Clinton continued to warn right-wing broadcasters that he would not tolerate their hate messages and would try to shut them down, and some began looking for transmitter sites in South America in order to be sure there would be no interruption in getting their views aired throughout the United States and globally.[1]

Ironically, it was the Antiterrorism Amendments Act of 1995 and the threat of government sanctions against any illegal use of the airwaves that contributed significantly to the right-wing's most successful use of media. Fearful of losing its foothold in radio, the radical right explored a new unregulated medium, cyberspace. The Internet soon became its principal propaganda and recruiting communication tool.

An example of the pro-censorship thinking that cut across the country right after Oklahoma City was expressed by the *Hartford Courant*. In an article headlined, "Hate Radio Deserves Criticism," the newspaper stated: "Too much of talk radio is a sewer of invective. The public dialogue is becoming polluted—and respect for institutions and for one another is a casualty. . . . Extremist talkmasters and others on the fanatical fringe almost certainly have helped to create a hateful climate in which acts of violence might seem to the deranged mind to be a legitimate response to provocation. . . . The president has summoned us all to stand up to the 'purveyors' of hatred and division."[2] At about the same time the *Denver Post* reported a protest movement seeking to "Boycott Hate Radio." The newspaper stated that such action would be treading on dangerous ground, moving toward censorship. It suggested, instead, that "with the definition of 'hate talk' nearly impossible to pin down, it's more important for concerned citizens to be aware of the idiocy on the air and figure out who's sullying the airwaves . . . [and] decide for themselves about the extremists."[3] Attorney Alan Dershowitz warned against limiting free and open debate. To do so, he said, might "be playing right into the hands of the terrorists. . . . The goal of the terrorist is to provoke overreaction, to generate suppression of civil liberties, to foment repression . . . designed to destabilize democracies and create a frightened citizenry, receptive to the warped messages of hate, fear and paranoia."[4]

Mainstream Media

As important as the role of those opposing hate media is the role of the mainstream media that carry and report hate speech. The mainstream media have been seriously remiss in reporting the extent of far right and extremist right activities, as well as the right's use of the airwaves and Internet to achieve their goals. It might be surprising to find the radical right so pervasive, so large, so outrageously full of hate, and so adept and effective in their use of the media to disseminate their messages and recruit Americans to their points of view and activities.

The reasons? In part because the media are owned, by and large, by rich and powerful interests who believe, by their status in society, that the status quo represents the best of all possible worlds, and that conservatism, per se, is the ideal political, social, and economic philosophy. In part because of the apathy of most media owners to the reality of the world, in order to concentrate on the escapist entertainment factors that will bring in the most advertising dollars and the largest bottom line. In part because even in media news and features, journalists are either unprepared by training or unwilling to cover any stories that do not "bleed." Thus, although there was extensive coverage of Oklahoma City, of Waco and Ruby Ridge, and of the Jasper, Texas, lynching, there has been little coverage of the hundreds of pipe bomb attacks, bank robberies, gay-bashing incidents, armed threats, political blackmailing, and other events that together would provide the public a more legitimate view of America's right-wing activities and goals. And there has been little revelation of the far right's media use. In fact, ask almost anyone to name some far-right-wing media personalities and you'll likely hear only names such as Limbaugh or Liddy or North—all of whom are moderate compared to the Pierces, Peters, and Stroms, whose names and positions the mainstream media have largely hidden from the public.

Some mainstream media have taken action—unfortunately, in the view of most groups dealing with hate media, through censorship rather than revelation and education. One controversial case occurred in late 1997, when a National Public Radio station rejected the bid of the Knights of the Ku Klux Klan, Realm of Missouri, to underwrite some segments of "All Things Considered." The president of NPR, Del Lewis, didn't see why any station should accept support from any group that opposes the station's mission. "Otherwise," Lewis stated, "public radio risks being taken over by extremists."

The KKK attorney, Bob Herman, who said that as a Jew he rejects what the KKK stands for, stated that "if you don't apply the First Amendment to protect everyone's views, especially the views you don't like, then you don't have a First Amendment. . . . The government shouldn't have the right to decide whose ideas are correct."[5] An example with a slightly different approach was a 1996 statement issued by a national conference of religious leaders in relation to "hate talk" on radio. The statement said, "Our American public square is being systematically poisoned by the language of assault," and urged media owners and performers and the listening public to reject such material in favor of more responsible programming.[6]

Right after Oklahoma City a number of stations pulled the programs of some of the more outrageous radical right talk show hosts. A shortwave station in Nashville suspended Mark Koernke's show, a station in Michigan suspended the program of Bo Gritz, and the Oklahoma Senate voted unanimously to ask stations to stop broadcasting G. Gordon Liddy's program.[7] One example of a citizen group formed to counter "hate radio" is the Buffalo (New York) Coalition to Halt Hate Talk Radio, established in 1995 with a membership representing ethnic and religious organizations, labor groups, racial groups, churches, gay-lesbian associations, women's groups, and others. The Coalition's approach was to convince stations to halt racist and bigoted programming, and to use the boycott as a persuasion device, if necessary.[8] Some corporations have taken stands on hate speech. One, for example, is Bell Atlantic, which donated $100,000 to develop, with the Leadership Conference on Civil Rights, a Web site to fight hate speech in cyberspace. The Web site is designed to "give data on hate crimes around the country, strategies to address those crimes, diversity education materials, and other information, including Congressional voting records on civil rights issues."[9] The conundrum of censor–no censor, of First Amendment freedoms–incipient violence, was succinctly expressed by James Latham, station manager of Radio For Peace International and its right-wing-radio watchdog, Global Community Forum. "We don't want them with their mouths taped, so to speak," Latham said, concerned not only with freedom of speech, but also that censorship would reinforce the right wing's conspiracy theories about government and media owners. On the other hand, he is also concerned that although many people might simply turn off hate radio programs "my neighbor may not. The radio may be telling him to go kill the liberal next door."[10] Latham believes that the U.S. government should monitor hate radio to determine whether the United States, like Germany and the united Kingdom, should pass laws banning programs advocating racial hatred and violence.[11]

Radio For Peace International

RFPI is a key global monitor of right-wing media. It was founded in 1987 by Debra Latham, general manager, and James Latham, station manager, as a radio station with one transmitter, broadcasting from Costa Rica. In 1998 RFPI, as stated in its brochure, "beams its signal around the world utilizing five transmitters. Thousands of letters have been received from listeners in more than 100 countries on all continents. RFPI's studios and transmitters are on the campus of the University for Peace (created by the United Nations) in Costa Rica. RFPI is a joint project of the University of Global Education (formerly World Peace University), Earth Communications, and the University for Peace. Short-wave signals can be heard worldwide. RFPI's own short-wave radio provides the most cost effective and accessible medium of alternative global news and views."

RFPI broadcasts in several languages, including English, Spanish, German, and French Creole. It originates programs and receives programs from a large number of individuals and organizations for broadcast. Some of its topics include conflict resolution, peace education, personal growth and development, environmental issues, world hunger, social justice, human rights, and cross-cultural understanding. It also broadcasts a program entitled "FIRE, Feminist International Radio Endeavor," covering such topics as women's human rights, racism, militarism, sexuality, and culture from a gender perspective.[12] RFPI also publishes a quarterly newsletter, *VISTA*.

In 1994 RFPI established a watchdog arm, the Far Right Radio Review, as a response to the growing use of radio by far-right organizations and personalities. The Far Right Radio Review became the Global Community Forum a few years later as the far right began shifting from radio and rapidly increased its use of the Internet, including the dissemination of radio shows over cyberspace. "The program features details on the backgrounds of far right-wing radio producers, analyses of the history of organized racism, and commentary on the activities of people within the 'Patriot' movement. The program also examines the reasons that people are so receptive to the message of this movement and recommends alternative solutions."[13]

In explaining the origins of the Far Right Radio Review, RFPI stated:

> In 1990, Willis Carto's Liberty Lobby put a talk show called "Radio Free America" on short-wave, with Tom Valentine as the host. They found that they were able to spread their holocaust revisionism, conspiracy theorizing, and subtle racism quite effectively in this medium. Since then, a radical right-wing movement with roots in white supremacy, tax protest, and county power organizations has resurfaced in the form of the "Patriot" movement, which includes militias, "Christian Identity" groups, and 'Wise Use' anti-environmentalism. A major factor in the growth of this movement has been its use of short-wave for organizing and recruitment. Leaders learned from Willis Carto's experience that with one program on one station which broadcasts nationwide, they can reach all of their potential supporters without arousing the attention of the community in a local station's broadcast area. One can now hear programs about "racialism," militancy, and/or "conspiratology" nearly 24 hours a day. In response, the Far Right Radio Review has been taking a crucial look at this phenomenon since February, 1994.[14]

In addition to "Global Community Forum/Far Right Radio Review," RFPI's radio schedule in June 1998 included several other programs that dealt with radical right rhetoric and activity, including "Counterspin" (media analysis), "Alternative Radio," "Rebel Radio," "RadioNation," and "World of Radio."[15]

The Anti-Defamation League of B'nai B'rith

ADL is probably the organization cited most often by right-wing media as their worst nemesis and is the subject of much of the right wing's strongest vilification. The ADL's mission has been to fight racist and ethnic bias, particularly anti-Semitism, in whatever form, and the organization has used exposure, pressure, and legal means to do so. Right-wing media is only one area and is essentially an outgrowth of the ADL's concern with the right-wing groups that use and sponsor hate programs on radio, television, cable, and the Internet. It monitors right-wing media through a project entitled HateWatch. "We as citizens must exercise our own free speech rights by denouncing bigotry and appeals to violence," the ADL says.[16] ADL has also expressed special concern over the right's use of the Internet: "Haters have seized on the Internet to establish new vehicles for global recruitment, marketing and dissemination of propaganda."[17]

The ADL has variously been described by the right-wing as a tool of the UN, a part of the New World Order, a spy group for international Jewish bankers, an arm of the Jewish-owned media, a hate group, a money-launderer for drug lords, and similar appellations. The Zundelsite, when its revisionist views were challenged by the ADL, replied that "the ADL is a spy group, among other nefarious activities, who routinely advocates hostility toward individuals they unilaterally label as anti-Semites."[18] The Zundelsite had it strongest words for ADL's HateWatch, which includes the Zundelsite in its monitoring of right-wing media. "Hate Watch and its ilk are doublespeak promoters of hostility. . . . They are disingenuous, slippery-talking, self-righteous-appointed and anointed, biased if not bigoted . . . they sow the toxic seeds of eventual mob justice."[19]

On the radio side, the National Alliance's American Dissident Voices has similarly attacked the ADL. On a program entitled "The ADL: America's Greatest Enemy," host Kevin Alfred Strom also labeled the ADL a "spy" organization that has accumulated an "enemies list." Strom said: "Many groups on the Left—and make no mistake about it, the Left is very influential in academic and media circles in this country—had regarded the ADL as an ally in their quest to change America and turn her away from her Western, European roots toward a Third World future. . . ."[20]

The ADL not only monitors hate media, but represents its views to stations carrying such programs, seeking to have such programming stopped. One example was when a Houston television station aired a video version of "Witch's

Invitation," a musical film showing a Jewish God as the source of "AIDS, murders, and other evils throughout the centuries" and "linking Satanism to Judaism." ADL pressured the station to discontinue airing the program.[21] In 1996 the ADL published a research report entitled "Poisoning the Airwaves: The Extremist Message of Hate on Shortwave Radio," which describes the key stations and personalities broadcasting racist and anti-Semitic rancor.

In late 1998, as part of its effort to counter cyberspace hate, the ADL introduced a noncommercial software package called HateFilter, which "blocks specific hate sites and redirects browers to the ADL's education site." Its Internet front page lists the following hate subjects to click on: Internet Hate, Anti-Semitism, Racism, Holocaust Denial, Neo-Nazi Skinheads, Identity Church Movement, Nation of Islam, and Homophobia, against a background logo of "STOP HATE."[22]

The Southern Poverty Law Center

The SPLC in Montgomery, Alabama, headed by Morris Dees has been referred to frequently in this book, particularly in regard to its Klanwatch and Militia Task Force activities in monitoring right-wing media use. Joseph T. Roy Sr., director of these projects, has cited radio and the Internet as special fields of Patriot activity and, as noted earlier, SPLC published *False Patriots: The Threat of Antigovernment Extremists*, with special material on "Patriot" leaders and the movement's use of the airwaves. It also issues a quarterly journal edited by Mark Potok, entitled *Intelligence Report*, which provides up-to-date information about the activities of the far right, including articles and features on the right's media use and lists of Internet sites and radio stations. For example, its summer 1998 issue includes an article by Carla Brooks Johnston on far-right and extremist radio, "Radical Radio Redux." The SPLC pays special attention, in its monitoring of far-right Internet sites, to the use of cyberspace to transmit radio programs that can be downloaded for playback on tape or CD. One of its techniques in fighting hate in cyberspace is to lure hate browers away from their intended sites. In searching for a Ku Klux Klan Web site, for example, a browser will find directions to a site that offers a Ku Klux Klan robe and its blood-drop shoulder patch for only $85. However, in following through with that search, the browser will find himself or herself on Klanwatch, the site operated by the SPLC. *Boston Globe* reporter Patti Hartigan observed that "the same technology that provides a forum for extremists enables civil rights groups and individuals to mobilize a response in unprecedented ways."[23]

So effective has the SPLC's work been that not only has the Center been described by some right-wing organizations and spokespersons as part of a Jewish communist World Wide Order plot to take over America in order to destroy the white (i.e., non-Jewish Aryan European) race, it has been the target of numerous bomb and assassination threats. The Center has publicized what it considers to be terrorist-type activities by Patriot groups, and has the legal system to prosecute hate activity and to defend citizen targets from such activity. It has also lobbied for legislation to curb certain Patriot activities. For example, its Militia Task Force has made the following recommendations:

1. States should prosecute those who violate anti-militia and anti-paramilitary training statutes. States without such laws should enact them.
2. A federal statute should be enacted that prohibits private militias not specifically authorized by the states.
3. The current federal anti-paramilitary statute should be broadened.
4. Federal legislation should be passed regulating the dissemination of dangerous substances used to make weapons of mass destruction, like ammonium nitrate.
5. The Department of Defense should prohibit military personnel from involvement in unauthorized militia activity.
6. Law enforcement agencies at all levels should prohibit their personnel from involvement in unauthorized militia activity or groups that promote violence against the government.
7. Federal authorities should be allowed to collect data from public sources about people who call for violence against the government.
8. Law enforcement officials nationwide should develop systems for monitoring and sharing information on antigovernment terrorists.
9. Each state should establish a special law enforcement task force to respond to militia activity.
10. Government employees should be trained in identifying extremist threats and drilled in emergency procedures.
11. Journalists should be careful not to present Patriot views of the Constitution without balancing them with prevailing legal interpretations.
12. Local clergy should build interfaith allegiances to challenge [Christian] Identity teaching in their communities.
13. Schools should promote civic ideals.
14. Charges of governmental misconduct must be investigated promptly and thoroughly.[24]

Fairness and Accuracy in Reporting

FAIR is another of the organizations monitoring and countering right-wing media. It concentrates entirely on the media, including the electronic media and cyberspace, as well as print. It describes itself as:

the national media watch group offering well-documented criticism in an effort to correct media bias and imbalance. FAIR focuses public awareness on the narrow corporate ownership of the press, the media's allegiance to official agendas, and their insensitivity to women, labor, minorities, and other public interest constituencies. FAIR seeks to invigorate the First Amendment by advocating for greater media pluralism and the inclusion of public interest voices in national debates.[25]

FAIR was established in 1986 and states that it is an "anti-censorship organization." While FAIR's main purpose is to promote the airing of views of groups traditionally excluded from mainstream media, it also focuses on so-called hate radio and its personalities.

FAIR publishes a journal, *EXTRA!*, and a newsletter, *EXTRA! Update*; reports to students on Channel One, the in-school cable news service; operates a Internet Web site; has a weekly radio program, "Counterspin," which can be heard on about ninety AM and FM radio stations in thirty states and several Canadian provinces and also can be downloaded in RealAudio from FAIR's Web site. FAIR also issues periodic reports in *EXTRA!* over the Internet, and on "Counterspin," such as the 1994 analysis of more than 100 "inaccuracies" from Rush Limbaugh on the air; the 1996 quotes from Pat Buchanan that appear to support far-right views on race, Jews, women, immigrants, and government; a 1996 statement on WABC and Bob Grant's talk show's extremist views; and a 1995 report on Chuck Baker's extremist views over the airwaves.[26] (These reports have been referred to in discussions on the respective personalities earlier in this book.)

Political Research Associates

Political Research Associates (PRA) and its senior analyst, Chip Berlet, have provided some of the most significant research on the right wing. Founded in 1991, PRA describes itself as "an independent source of opposition research and analysis on the political right wing." PRA studies the relationship between the right wing and the established political and social processes and institutions. It does so first-hand, where possible, attending right-wing meetings and conferences. It believes that currently "we find ourselves in a moment when tolerance, pluralism and fairness are under severe attack. . . . If we hope to respond effectively to the scapegoating, reactionary attacks, economic redistribution, and encoded bigotry of the right, these practices must be exposed for what they are." PRA also functions as a clearinghouse, a library (one of the largest in the country on the right wing), and a source of information on right-wing funding and activities, to help people "understand the right wing threat to democracy and diversity." It publishes a quarterly newsletter, the *Public Eye*, and operates a Web site, both providing information on right-wing philosophies and specific anti-democratic campaigns.[27]

A number of other well-known and not-so-well-known groups and individuals have also taken stands against right-wing hate speech on the airwaves. See Appendix A at the end of this chapter for PRA's list of some of the organizations. A number of groups present counter-views, to greater-or-lesser degrees, through the media. One such organization is the Keeping Watch Coalition, established in 1996, along with a Web site, "to monitor and counter the agenda of the right-wing in America." Its stated purposes are

1.   To monitor the political, social, and religious right wing and develop effective responses to their activities, statements, and agendas.
2.   To raise awareness and educate citizens on the nature, history, beliefs, and activities of the various right-wing reactionary movements.
3.   To train a network of Watchers to monitor and gather information on the right-wing.
4.   To organize a network of activists to respond to the far right through writing, phoning, or e-mailing Congress; calling talk shows on radio and television; and writing 'letters to the editor' at newspapers, magazines, and other media outlets.[28]

In 1995 the Center for Campus Organizing was formed from the University Conversion Project, a national student peace group. While it covers a broad range of services and goals, it includes the dissemination of information about and counterviews concerning right-wing activities on campuses, particularly those that attack "equality and social justice." One of its goals is to help campus activists create alternative media and link up with other groups through the country. It sponsors projects such as an e-mail network, an electronic article exchange, and an alternative journalism. It has a Web site.[29] Some former peace/anti-nuclear war organizations moved into other areas that they considered critical to society after the end of the Cold War. One of these is the Center for Defense Information, which had been spearheaded by retired Admiral Gene R. LaRoque, and which still deals principally with what it considers problems in the military, such as gender bias, the reliance on nuclear weapons, military spending, unneeded expensive weapons, nuclear power, policy toward Cuba, and similar issues. It includes, however, a concern with the role of America's far- and extremist right within a safe and sane defense policy for the United States. Two of its means of dissemination are a radio program, "The Question of the Week," which is carried on some 50 public radio stations throughout the country, and a television program, "America's Defense Monitor," distributed via the PBS network.[30]

Individuals using the Internet to combat the rhetoric of the far right run into the hundreds, perhaps thousands. Some have extensive backup, such as that of Ken McVay, mentioned earlier. McVay has some 200 assistants around the world providing him with first-hand accounts of the Nazi death camps, to counter the Holocaust-denial/revisionist organizations and Web sites. McVay himself spends about sixteen hours every day copying history books about World War II onto his computer. His Nizkor Project (which means "we will remember"), has compiled the largest collection of Holocaust-related materials that can be found on the Internet—literally thousands of documents. Its purpose is to offer point-by-point refutation of materials on Holocaust-denial/revisionist and anti-Semitic Web sites.[31]

An example of individuals doing the same thing without extensive support is Ohio State University history professor Mark Pitcavage. "The Web offers the same advantages to us that it does to the extremists," Pitcavage said. He operates a "Militia Watchdog" home page. "With a post-office box, moderate long-distance phone expenses, and Internet connection and Web site provider," Pitcavage added, "I am able to provide a fair amount of current information on the militia movement to people interested in knowing more."[32]

If you tune in your radio these days, as the century turns into a new millennium, you will hear fewer far right voices than you heard several years ago. This is true even as many of the extremist groups prepare for the Armageddon that they believe will come with the millennium. Shortwave broadcasts have been cutting back and microstations are not proliferating as they did in the mid-1990s. On television you see far-right productions and personalities only rarely, principally on cable channels such as the Family Channel, controlled by right wing religious groups, and on community cable-access programs. The right wing has been moving principally to cyberspace. Because the broadcast media are regulated, right-wing broadcasters have come under more and more scrutiny by the Federal Communications Commission. One reason is their use of shortwave stations, which are licensed solely for overseas broadcasting, for domestic distribution. Another is the unauthorized use of frequencies to set up the "pirate" microstations, creating potential interference problems with other stations. But the right is not giving up the traditional airwaves. One expert estimated that in mid-1998, in addition to five shortwave stations and countless dozens of pirate microstations, far-right and extremist "hate" programming was still being carried by about 400 AM stations, about 50 FM stations, and about 20 television stations nationwide.[33]

On the Internet the hate purveyors are subject to no regulation whatsoever. The Internet is now a province of the radical right. They have greater exposure through cyberspace than they ever had with radio and television. And the cost is considerably less—there are no time-access fees on the Internet. The Internet gives the right wing potential access to every home in the world that has an Internet connection, and the number is growing exponentially. For different reasons, frequently economic, but justified with the allegation that Jews control all the other media and prevent them from gaining access, many radical right groups in the United States and abroad have turned to the Internet. It is safe to say that the biggest single boon ever to the radical right in disseminating their message, persuading, recruiting, and organizing, is the Internet. As one example of how the Internet has rapidly been replacing traditional media as the medium of choice by right-wing groups, note the following statement on the Web site of the German National Socialist and Hammerskin Page: "This is the first German NS page on the Internet . . . the Jew's laws in the Fatherland do not allow freedom to express [our] beliefs, so we must go through an American server . . . you must no longer believe the lies from the Jewish media. We shall make our own media here on the Internet!!!!"[34] Another example is the action of Steven Krom, who, as a student at Albion College, had difficulty persuading his classmates to follow his "white power" philosophy. But then he established a Web site and "found support, adulation and a common understanding from the growing cadre of white supremacists, neo-Nazi and other hate groups that have taken to the world wide web to spread their word."[35] Krom said: "It's one of the good things about the Internet."[36]

There has been special concern that children might not be able to distinguish the difference between a legitimate history site and one that, for example, describes the Holocaust as a hoax.[37] David Waren of the Anti-Defamation League expressed concern that "children and students, the biggest users of the Internet, are especially vulnerable to the subtle messages of hate and half-truths, which are presented without any context or background and liable to be taken at face value by the unsuspecting and uninformed."[38] Some parents have even expressed concern that their children, logging on to these Web sites, were becoming Nazis through the Internet.[39]

The authors of this book believe that exposure and countereducation, not censorship, are the best solutions to the increasing right-wing rancor on the airwaves. As one individual operator of a Web site, Philip Winn, put it, "A recent survey showed that barely a majority of Americans believe that groups such as the Ku Klux Klan deserve unlimited freedom of speech. Less than 70%! Don't people understand that unless everybody has the same freedom, nobody has any freedom? . . . If you don't like it, don't listen!"[40]

However, in February 1999, the Southern Poverty Law Center reported that the incidence of hate sites on the Internet had grown by 60 percent between 1997 and 1998. It also declared that nearly half of the nation's 500 identified hate groups are employing the Internet to promote their agendas.

Said SPLC spokesman Mark Potok, "It has become the propaganda venue of choice." Potok also noted that the number of hate groups rose almost 20 percent in the one-year period from 1997 to 1998 and that KKK and neo-Nazi organizations have grown the most.

Appendices to Chapter 9

253

Appendix 9A: Resources for Studying
Patriot and Militia Movements

Alternet
77 Federal Street, San Francisco, CA 94107
(415) 284-1420
Contact: Christine Triano
Bibliography of resources dealing with the militia movement

American Jewish Committee
165 East 56th Street, New York, NY 10022-2746
(212) 751-4000
Contact: Ken Stern
Race Hate/White Supremacy connection to militias

Anti-Defamation League
National Office
823 United Nations Plaza, New York, NY 10017
(212) 490-2525
Published report includes a state by state look at militias

CLEAR (Clearinghouse on Environmental Advocacy and Research)
1718 Connecticut Avenue, NW Suite 600,
Washington, DC 20009
(202) 667-6982
Wise Use/militia links

Center for Democratic Renewal
PO Box 50469, Atlanta, GA 30302
(404) 221-0025
Helps communities combat hate

Center on Violence and Human Survival
John J. College of Criminal Justice
City University of New York
899 Tenth Avenue, Suite 434, New York, NY 10019
Contacts: Robert J. Lifton, Charles B. Strozier, Michael Flynn
Studies Fundamentalism, Apocalyptic Thinking, and Totalitarian Groups (cults)

Coalition for Human Dignity
PO Box 40344, Portland, OR 97240
(503) 281-5823
Race Hate/White Supremacy connection to militias

Institute for First Amendment Studies
PO Box 589, Great Barrington, MA 02130
(413) 528-3800
Militia connection to Religious Right

Montana Human Rights Network
PO Box 9184, Helena, MT 59604
(406) 442-5506
Information about organizing responses militias in Montana

NW Coalition Against Malicious Harassment
PO Box 16776, Seattle, WA 98116
(206) 233-9136
Community organizing against intolerance

People For The American Way
200 M St., NW, Ste. 400, Washington, DC 20036
(202) 467-4999
General information on the Right

Planned Parenthood Federation of America
National Office
810 7th Avenue, 14th floor, New York, NY 10019
(212) 541-7800
Contact: Claire McCurdy
Specifically looks at militia/anti-abortion connection

Political Research Associates
120 Beacon Street, Suite 202, Somerville, MA 02143
(617) 661-9313
Think-tank monitoring full spectrum of the right

Southern Poverty Law Center
PO Box 548, Montgomery, AL 36195-5101
(205) 264-0286
Race Hate/White Supremacy connection to militias

Western States Center
522 SW 5th Avenue, #1390, Portland, OR 97204
(503) 228-8866
Wise Use/militia links

Radio For Peace International
PO Box 20728, Portland OR 97220
(506) 249-1821
Contact: James Latham
Study rise of far-right/hate programming on short-wave bands

Simon Wiesenthal Center
9760 West Pico, Los Angeles CA 90035
(310) 553-9036 ext. 220
Contact: Avra Shapiro
Has information on Far right and the Internet

Appendix 9B: Reading List on the History and Politics of the American Right

(reprinted with permission of Political Research Associates)

Chip Berlet
Political Research Associates.

Revised October 17, 1994

Table of Contents

256

Appendix 9B: Reading List on the History and Politics
of the American Right

Fast Study Section

The Religious Right

Most Concise Introductory Pamphlet

"The Political Activity of the Religious Right in the 1990's: A Critical Analysis," by Rabbi Lori Forman. (New York: American Jewish Committee, 1994).

Key Readings on the Religious Right

Rabbi Forman, author of the above pamphlet, suggests consulting the following works by critics, advocates, and observers of the religious right:

The Coors Connection: How Coors Family Philanthropy Undermines Democratic Pluralism. Bellant, Russ (Boston, MA.: South End Press/Political Research Associates Series, 1991).

The Culture of Disbelief: How American Law and Politics Trivialize Religious Devotion. Carter, Stephen L. (New York: Basic Books, 1993).

Culture Wars: The Struggle to Define America. Hunter, James Davison (New York: Basic Books, 1991).

Fundamentalisms and Society: Vol. 1. Marty, Martin E., and R. Scott Appleby, eds. (Chicago: University of Chicago press, 1993).

Fundamentalisms Observed: Vol. 2. Marty, Martin E., and R. Scott Appleby, eds. (Chicago: University of Chicago press, 1993).

Natural Adversaries or Possible Allies? American Jews and the

The Old Christian Right. Ribuffo, Leo P. (Philadelphia: Temple University Press, 1983).

The Religious Right: The Assault on Tolerance & Pluralism In America. Anti-Defamation League (New York, ADL, 1994).

To the Right: The Transformation of American Conservatism. Himmelstein, Jerome L. (Berkeley, California: University of California Press, 1990).

Broad Background On Democracy & Pluralism

Key General Newsletters Critiquing The Right:

Culture Watch. The Data Center.

Freedom Writer. Institute for First Amendment Studies.

Group Research Report. Group Research.

The Public Eye. Political Research Associates.

Right Wing Watch. People for the American Way.

Books & Reports:

A Scapegoat in the New Wilderness: The Origins and Rise of Anti-Semitism in America. Jaher, Frederick Cople. (Cambridge, MA: Harvard University Press, 1994).

America's Original Sin: A Study Guide on White Racism. (Booklet) Sojourners. (Washington, D.C.: Sojourners Resource Center, 1993).

New Christian Right. Cohen, Naomi. (New York: American Jewish Committee, 1993).

The New Millennium. Robertson, Pat (Irving, Texas: Word Publishing, 1990).

Old Nazis, the New Right and the Reagan Administration: The Role of Domestic Fascist Networks in the Republican Party and Their Effect on U.S. Cold War Policies. Bellant, Russ. (Boston, MA: South End Press/Political Research Associates Series, 1991).

Redeeming America: Piety and Politics in the New Christian Right. Liensch, Michael. (Chapel Hill: The University of North Carolina Press, 1993).

Spiritual Warfare: The Politics of the Christian Right. Diamond, Sara (Boston, MA: South End Press, 1989).

Understanding Fundamentalism and Evangelicalism. Marsden, George M. (Grand Rapids, MI: William B. Eerdmans Pub. Co., 1991.)

Other Useful Critiques of the Religious Right

Books:

Fundamentalisms and the State: Vol. 3. Marty, Martin E. and R. Scott Appleby. (Chicago: University of Chicago Press, 1993).

Heaven on Earth? The Social and Political Agendas of Dominion Theology. Barron, Bruce (Grand Rapids, MI: Zondervan, 1992).

Jesus Doesn't Live Here Anymore: From Fundamentalist to Freedom Writer. Porteous, Skipp (Buffalo: Prometheus Books, 1991).

The New Religious Right: Piety, Patriotism and Politics. Capps, Walter H. (Columbia: U. of South Carolina Press, 1990).

Architects of Fear: Conspiracy Theories and Paranoia in American Politics. Johnson, George (Boston: Houghton Mifflin, 1983).

Debating PC: The Controversy over Political Correctness on College Campuses, Berman, Paul, ed. (New York: Laurel/Dell, 1992).

The Emergence of David Duke and the Politics of Race. Rose, Douglas D., ed. (Chapel Hill: U. of North Carolina Press, 1992.)

Race in North America: Origin and Evolution of a Worldview. Smedley, Audrey. (Boulder, CO: Westview Press, 1993).

To Reclaim a Legacy of Diversity: Analyzing the "Political Correctness" Debates in Higher Education. (New York: National Council for Research on Women, 1993). (212) 274-0730.

Watch on the Right: Conservative Intellectuals in the Reagan Era, Hoeveler, J. David (Madison: U. of Wisconsin Press, 1991.)

Articles:

"The American Neo-Nazi Movement Today," a special report by Elinor Langer in The Nation, July 16/23 1990.

"Backlash?" by Henry Louis Gates, Jr., in The New Yorker, May 17, 1993, pp. 42-44.

"Black Conservatives" (Parts One and Two), by Deborah Toler, in The Public Eye, September 1993 and December 1993.

"Black Demagogues and Pseudo-Scholars," by Henry Louis Gates, Jr. in The New York Times, (Op-Ed) July 20, 1992.

"Burgeoning Conservative Think Tanks," a special issue of Responsive Philanthropy newsletter, Spring 1991, National Committee for Responsive Philanthropy. (202) 387-9177.

"The Politics of Frustration," by Kevin Phillips, in The New York Times Magazine, April 12, 1992, pp. 38-42.

(continued)

Appendix 9B (continued)

"Rightwing Attacks on Corporate Giving," a special issue of Responsive Philanthropy newsletter, Winter 1990, National Committee for Responsive Philanthropy. (202) 387-9177.

"Watch on the Right: Change in Strategy" (column), by Sara Diamond, in *The Humanist*, January/February 1994, pp. 34-36.

"What is Anti-Semitism Now?: An Open Letter to William F. Buckley," by Norman Podhoretz, in Commentary, January 1992.

Reference Shelf

A New Rite: Conservative Catholic Organizations and Their Allies. Askin, Steve. (Washington, D.C.: Catholics for Free Choice, 1994) (202) 986-6093.

The Activists Almanac: The Concerned Citizen's Guide to the Leading Advocacy Organizations in America. Walls, David (New York: Fireside/Simon & Schuster 1993).

Challenging the Christian Right: The Activists Handbook. Clarkson, Frederick, and Skipp Porteous. (Great Barrington, MA.: Institute for First Amendment Studies, 1993). (413) 274-3786.

Extremism on the Right: A Handbook. Anti Defamation League of B'nai B'rith (New York: Anti-Defamation League of B'nai B'rith, 1988).

Fight the Right. Gregory, Sarah Crary, and Scot Nakagawa, eds. (Washington, DC: National Gay and Lesbian Task Force, 1993).

Guide to Public Policy Experts: 1993-1994. Atwood, Thomas C., ed. (Washington, DC: Heritage Foundation, 1993).

How to Win: A Practical Guide to Defeating the Radical Right in Your Community. Radical Right Task Force (Washington, D.C.: Radical Right Task Force, 1994). (202) 544-7636.

The Right Guide. Wilcox, Derk, Joshua Schackman & Penelope Naas. (Ann Arbor: Economics America, 1993).

UCP's Guide to Uncovering the Right on Campus. Cowan, Rich and Dalya Massachi. (Boston: University Conversion Project, 1994) (617) 354-9363.

When Hate Groups Come to Town: A Handbook of Effective Community Responses. Center for Democratic Renewal. (Atlanta, GA: Center for Democratic Renewal, 1992). (404) 221-0025.

Topical Section

The Religious Right

Critiquing the Religious Right:

"The Christian Coalition: On the Road to Victory?" by Fred Clarkson, in Church & State, Jan. 1992.

"Christian Coalition Steps Boldly into Politics," by Michael Isikoff, in Washington Post, Sept. 10, 1992.

Christian Reconstructionism: Religious Right Extremism Gains

Newsletters:

Church and State. Americans United for Separation of Church and State.

Freedom Writer. Institute for First Amendment Studies.

The Fundamentalism Project Newsletter. The Fundamentalism Project

The Public Eye. Political Research Associates.

Right Wing Watch. People for the American Way.

Voice of Reason. Americans for Religious Liberty.

Books & Reports:

The Covert Crusade: The Christian Right and Politics in the West. (Report). (Portland, OR: Western States Center/Coalition for Human Dignity, 1993) Available from the Western States Center. (503) 228-8866.

Religious Liberty and the Secular State, by John M. Swomley. Available from Americans for Religious Liberty.

Rolling Back Civil Rights: The Oregon Citizens' Alliance at Religious War. Gardiner, S.L. (Portland, OR: Coalition for Human Dignity, 1992.) Available from the Coalition for Human Dignity. (503) 227-5033.

Visions of Reality: What Fundamentalist Schools Teach, by Albert J. Menendez. Available from Americans for Religious Liberty.

Articles:

"Bible Belt Blowhard," by Bill Dedman, in Mother Jones, Nov. Dec. 1992.

"Cardinal Mindszenty: Heroic anti-Communist or anti-Semite or Both?" by Chip Berlet in The St. Louis Journalism Review, April 1988.

Influence. (Parts One and Two), by Fred Clarkson, in The Public Eye, March 1994 and June 1994.

"Christian Right's New Political Push," by Don Lattin, in San Francisco Chronicle, May 12, 1992.

"Confessions of a Religious Defender," a book review by Jean Hardisty of Stephen L. Carter's The Culture of Disbelief: How American Law and Politics Trivialize Religious Devotion, in The Public Eye, December 1993.

"Covering the Culture War," a special section with articles by James Davison Hunter, Laurence I. Barrett, and Joe Conason, in Columbia Journalism Review, July/August 1993.

"Credulity, Superstition, and Fanaticism," special issue with articles by Chip Berlet, Allen Lesser, Albert J. Menendez, Fred Pelka, & Jeffrey Victor, in The Humanist, September/October 1992.

"Crusade for Public Office in 2nd Stage," by Barry Horstman, in Los Angeles Times, March 22, 1992.

"Faith and Election: The Christian Right in Congressional Campaigns 1978-1988," by John C. Green, James L. Guth, and Kevin Hill, in The Journal of Politics (University of Texas Press), Vol. 55, No. 1, February 1993, pp. 80-91.

"Four Articles on the Religious Right," by Suzanne Pharr, from Transformation (1992-1993). Women's Project (501) 372-5113.

"HardCOR," by Fred Clarkson, in Church and State, Jan. 1991.

"Inside the Covert Coalition," by Fred Clarkson, in Church & State, Nov. 1992.

"The Making of a Christian Police State," by Fred Clarkson, in The Freedom Writer, Sept./Oct 1991.

"Opposition Research," A collection of recent columns on the religious and secular right by Sara Diamond, author of Spiritual Warfare. Available as a set from Political Research Associates. (617) 661-9313.

(continued)

"Reel Hate: A new video tries to drive a wedge between blacks and gays," by Liz Galst, in The Boston Phoenix, Supplement, October 1993.

"Religious Right Rediscovered " by Russ Bellant in Christian Social Action, Dec. 1992.

"The Religious Right's Quiet Revival," by Joe Conason, in The Nation, April 27, 1992.

"SWAT Teams for Jesus," by Skipp Porteus, in Penthouse, Sept. 1991.

"Traditional Values, Racism and Christian Theocracy: The Right-wing Revolt Against the Modern Age," by Margaret Quigley and Chip Berlet in The Public Eye, December 1992.

"When Right Goes Wrong: Word of God network wants to 'save the world'" by Russ Bellant in National Catholic Reporter, Nov. 18, 1988.

"The World According to Pat Robertson," by Skipp Porteous, in Reform Judaism, Spring 1993.

Promoting the Religious Right

A Christian Manifesto. Schaeffer, Francis A. (Westchester, IL: Crossway Books, 1981).

The ACLU and America's Freedoms: The ACLU is Defending or Destroying Our Freedoms? Rowe, Dr. Ed (Washington D.C.: Church League of America, 1984).

Against the Tide: How to Raise Sexually Pure Kids in an "Anything-Goes" World. LaHaye, Tim and Beverly LaHaye. (Sisters, Oregon: Multnomah Books, 1993).

A Time for Candor: Mainline Churches and Radical Social Witness. Institute on Religion and Democracy (Washington, D.C.: Institute of Religion and Democracy, 1983).

Modern Education

Defending Modern Education

Attacks on the Freedom to Learn. Available from People for the American Way.

Hate in the Ivory Tower: A Survey of Intolerance on College Campuses and Academia's Response. Available from People for the American Way.

Religion, Education and the First Amendment: The Appeal to History, by R. Freeman Butts. Available from People for the American Way.

Values, Pluralism, and Public Education: A National Conference. Available from People for the American Way.

The Witch Hunt Against 'Secular Humanism,' by David Bollier. Available from People for the American Way.

Attacking Modern Education

Back to Basics: The Traditionalist Movement that is Sweeping Grassroots America. Pines, Burton Yale (New York: William Morrow and Company, 1982).

Blackboard Power: NEA Threat to America. Drake, Dr. Gordon V. (Box 977, Tulsa, OK 74102: Christian Crusade Publications, 1968).

Change Agents in the Schools: Destroy Your Children, Betray Your Country. Morris, Barbara M. (Upland, California: The Barbara M. Morris Report, 1979).

Child Abuse in the Classroom. Schlafly, Phyllis, Editor (Alton, IL: Pere Marquette Press, 1984).

The Closing of the American Mind: How Higher Education Has

(continued)

Book Burning. Thomas, Cal (Westchester, IL: Good News Publishers/Crossway Books, 1983).

Children at Risk: The Battle for the Hearts and Minds of Our Kids. Dobson, Dr. James, and Gary L. Bauer. (Dallas: Word Publishing, 1990).

Communism, Hypnotism and the Beatles: Noebel, David A. (Tulsa, Oklahoma: Christian Crusade Publications, 1965).

Cultural Conservatism: Theory and Practice. Lind, William S. and Marshner, William H., eds. (Washington: Free Congress Foundation, 1991).

Cultural Conservatism: Toward a New National Agenda. The Institute for Cultural Conservatism. (Washington: Free Congress Research and Education Foundation, 1987).

Dare to Discipline. Dobson, Dr. James. (Wheaton, IL: Living Books/Tyndale House Publishers, 1987).

Forewarned. A Christian Primer to the Political Arena. The War on God, Family, and Country. Who's Waging it? Why? What Can, You Do About It? Lacy, Dr. Sterling (Texarkana, Texas: Dayspring Productions, 1988).

The New World Order: It Will Change the Way You Live. Robertson, Pat (Dallas: Word Publishing, 1991).

The Stealing of America. Whitehead, John W. (Westchester, IL: Crossway Books, 1983).

The Turning Tide: The Fall of Liberalism and the Rise of Common Sense. Robertson, Pat (Dallas: Word Publishing, 1993).

Understanding the Times: The Story of the Biblical Christian, Marxist/Leninist and Secular Humanist Worldviews. Noebel, David A. (Manitou Springs, CO: Summit Ministries Press, 1992).

Valley of Decision: A Christian Primer to the Political Arena. The War on God, Family, and Country. Who's Waging it? Why? What Can You Do About It? Lacy, Dr. Sterling (Texarkana, Texas: Dayspring Productions, 1988).

Failed Democracy and Impoverished the Souls, of Today's Students. Bloom, Allan (New York: Simon and Schuster, 1987).

Illiberal Education: The Politics of Race and Sex on Campus. D'Souza, Dinesh (NY: Free Press, 1991).

NEA: Propaganda Front of the Radical Left. Reed, Sally D. (Washington, D.C.: National Council for Better Education, 1984).

N.E.A. Trojan Horse in American Education. Blumenfeld, Samuel L. (Boise, Idaho: The Paradigm Company, 1984).

Poisoned Ivy. Hart, Benjamin (New York: Stein and Day, 1984).

School Based Clinics: And Other Critical Issues in Public Education. Mosbacker, Barrett L., Editor (Westchester, IL: Crossway Books, 1987).

Secular Humanism and the Schools: The Issue Whose Time has Come. McGraw, Onalee (Washington, DC: Heritage Foundation, 1976).

Why Are You Losing Your Children?. Morris, Barbara M. (Upland, California: The Barbara Morris Report, 1976; Revised).

Why Johnny Can't Tell Right from Wrong: Moral Illiteracy and the Case for Character Education. Kilpatrick, William. (New York: Simon & Schuster, 1992).

Withstanding Humanism's Challenge to Families: Anatomy of a White House Conference. Thomson, Rosemary (Morton, IL: Traditional Publications, 1981).

Nativist & Populist Right

Critiques of the Nativist & Populist Right

American Nativism 1830-1860. Leonard, Ira M. and Parmet, Robert D. (New York: Van Nostrand Reinhold Company, 1971).

Appendix 9B *(continued)*

Anti-Intellectualism in American Life. Hofstadter, Richard (New York: Alfred A. Knopf, 1963).

Cross-currents. Forster, Arnold and Epstein, Benjamin R. (Garden City, NY: Doubleday, 1956).

Danger on the Right. Forster, Arnold and Epstein, Benjamin R. (New York: Random House, 1964).

Hold Your Tongue: Bilingualism and the Politics of "English Only." Crawford, James. (Reading, MA: Addison-Wesley Publishing Company, 1992)

The Paranoid Style in American Politics and Other Essays. Hofstadter, Richard (New York, Toronto: Random House, 1952, 1967).

The Party of Fear: From Nativist Movements to the New Right in American History. Bennett, David H. (New York, NY: Vintage Books [Random House], 1990).

The Politics of Unreason: Right-Wing Extremism in America, 1790-1977. Lipset, Seymour Martin and Raab, Earl (Chicago and London: University of Chicago Press, 1978).

The Radical Right: Report on the John Birch Society and Its Allies. Epstein, Benjamin R. and Forester, Arnold (New York: Vintage Books/Random House, 1967).

The Radical Right: The New American Right Expanded and Updated. Bell, Daniel (New York: Books for Libraries/Arno Press, 1979). Originally published in 1963 as The Radical Right.

Strangers in the Land: Patterns of American Nativism 1860-1925. Higham, John (New York, New Jersey: Atheneum, 1963, 1975).

Voices of Protest: Huey Long, Father Coughlin & the Great De-

Totalist Networks & Cults

Amway: The Cult of Free Enterprise. Butterfield, Steve. (Boston: South End Press, 1985).

Clouds Blur the Rainbow: The Other Side of the New Alliance Party. Berlet, Chip. (Cambridge, MA: Political Research Associates, 1987).

Combating Cult Mind Control. Hassan, Steven. (Rochester, VT: Park Street Press, 1988)

Gifts of Deceit: Sun Myung Moon, Tongsun Park and the Korean Scandal. Boettcher, Robert. (New York: Holt, Rinehart and Winston, 1980).

Lyndon LaRouche and the New American Fascism. King, Dennis. (New York, New York: Doubleday, 1989).

Not For Sale: The Rev. Sun Myung Moon And One American's Freedom. Racer, David G. (St. Paul, MN: Tiny Press, 1989).

The Origins of Totalitarianism. Arendt, Hannah. (New York: Harvest Books, 1951).

Gender, Sexuality & Sexual Preference

Newsletters:

Activist Alert. National Gay and Lesbian Task Force.
The Body Politic. [(607) 648-2760].
GLAAD Bulletin. Gay & Lesbian Alliance Against Discrimination.

(continued)

pression. Brinkley, Alan (New York: Alfred A. Knopf, 1982).

You Can't Do That: A survey of the forces attempting, in the name of patriotism, to make a desert of the Bill of Rights. Seldes, George (New York: Modern Age Books, 1938 [available as a De Capo reprint, ISBN 0-306-70201-0]).

By the Nativist & Populist Right

A Choice Not an Echo: The Inside Story of How American Presidents Are Chosen. Schlafly, Phyllis (Alton, IL: Pere Marquette Press, 1964).

The Coercive Utopians: Their Hidden Agenda: (and) Government-Funded Activism: Hiding Behind the Public, Interest. Metzger, H. Peter, Ph.D. (Colorado Springs, CO: Public Service Company of Colorado, 1979 and 198). Pamphlet

The Death of a Nation. Stormer, John A. (Florissant, MO: Liberty Bell Press, 1968).

The Gravediggers. Schlafly, Phyllis and Ward, Chester (Alton, IL: Pere Marquette Press, 1964).

Growing Up God's Way: A guide for getting children ready for school and life. Stormer, John A. (Florissant, Missouri: Liberty Bell Press, 1984).

The Insiders. McManus, John F. (Belmont, MA: The John Birch Society, 1983).

The Invisible Government. Smoot, Dan (Boston and Los Angeles: Western Islands, 1962).

None Dare Call It Treason. Stormer, John A. (Florissant, Missouri: Liberty Bell Press, 1964).

The Shadows of Power: The Council on Foreign Relations and the American Decline. Perloff, James (Boston and Los Angeles: Western Islands, 1988).

NARAL News. National Abortion & Reproductive Rights Action League.

The Pro Choice Report. National Center for the Pro-Choice Majority.

Right Wing Watch. People for the American Way.

Siecus Report. SIECUS.

The Public Eye. Political Research Associates.

Sexuality Education

For Comprehensive Sexuality Education

Community Action Kit: An information pack to support comprehensive sexuality education. Available from SIECUS.

SIECUS Fact Sheets: "Siecus Fact Sheet #1: Condom Availability Programs." 1992. 4pp. "Siecus Fact Sheet #2: The National Coalition to Support Sexuality Education." 1992. 2pp. "Siecus Fact Sheet #3: Sexuality Education and the Schools: Issues and Answers." 1992. 2pp. "Siecus Fact Sheet #4: The Far-Right and Fear-Based Abstinence-Only Programs." 1992. 3pp. Available from SIECUS.

Against Comprehensive Sexuality Education

Grand Illusions: The Legacy of Planned Parenthood. Grant, George. (Brentwood, TN: Wolgemuth & Hyatt, 1988).

Sex Versus Civilization. Pendell, Dr. Elmer (Los Angeles, CA: Noontide Press, 1967).

Appendix 9B *(continued)*

Abortion Rights

General & Pro-Choice

Books:

Abortion and the Politics of Motherhood. Luker, Kristin (Berkeley, CA and London: University of California Press, 1984).

The Enemies of Choice: The Right to Life Movement and Its Threat to Abortion. Merton, Andrew H. (Boston: Beacon Press, 1981).

The Right to Lifers: Who They Are, How They Operate and How They Get Their Money. Paige, Connie (New York: Summit Books, 1983).

Other Resources:

R.E.A.L. Life (flyer series). Reality-based Education & Learning for Life. Available from Planned Parenthood Federation of America.

Who Decides? A Reproductive Rights Issues Manual. Who Decides? A State By State Review of Abortion Rights. Available from NARAL.

Conservative & Anti-Abortion

Aborting America. Nathanson, Dr. Bernard N. and Ostling, Richard N. (New York: Pinnacle Books, 1979).

The Abortion Holocaust: Today's Final Solution. Brennan, William (St. Louis: Landmark Press, 1983).

Closed: 99 Ways to Stop Abortion. Scheidler, Joseph M. (Westchester, IL: Crossway Books, 1985).

The Family, Feminism and the Therapuetic State. McGraw, Onalee (Washington, DC: Heritage Foundation, 1980).

The Inevitability of Patriarchy. Goldberg, Steven (New York: William Morrow & Company, Inc., 1974).

The New Traditional Woman. Marshner, Connaught (Washington, D.C.: Free Congress Research and Education Foundation, 1982).

The Power of the Positive Woman. Schlafly, Phyllis (New Rochelle, NY: Arlington House, 1977).

Sweetheart of the Silent Majority: The Biography of Phyllis Schlafly. Felsenthal, Carol (Garden City, NY: Doubleday and Company, 1981).

Gay Rights & Aids

(The issues are inextricably linked in much right-wing literature, and are listed together here for that reason alone.)

General & Supportive of Gay Rights

Books:

AIDS in the Mind of America: The Social, Political and Psychological Impact of a New Epidemic. Altman, Dennis (New York: Anchor Press, Doubleday, 1986).

And the Band Played On: Politics, People and the AIDS Epidemic. Shilts, Randy (New York: St Martin's Press, 1987).

Hostile Climate: A State by State Report on Anti-Gay Activity. People for the American Way (Booklet). (Washington, D.C.: People for the American Way, November 1993).

Quarantines and Death: The Far Right's Homophobic Agenda. Segrest, Mab & Zeskind, Leonard (Atlanta, GA: Center for

Women's Rights

General & Pro-Feminist

A Lesser Life: The Myth of Women's Liberation in America. Hewlett, Sylvia Ann (New York: William Morrow and Company, 1986).

Backlash: The Undeclared War Against American Women. Faludi, Susan (New York: Crown, 1991).

Feminism and the New Right: Conflict Over the American Family. Conover, Pamela Johnston and Gray, Virginia (New York: Praeger Special Studies, 1983).

Nostalgia on the Right: Historical Roots of the Idealized Family. Revised edition Theriot, Nancy. (Cambridge, MA: Political Research Associates, 1990 [originally Chicago, IL: Midwest Research, 1983]).

Talking Back: Thinking Feminist; Thinking Black. Hooks, Bell (Boston: South End Press, 1989).

The Way We Never Were: American Families and the Nostalgia Trap. Coontz, Stephanie (New York: Basic Books, 1992)

Women and Children First: Poverty in the American Dream. Stallard, Karin; Ehrenreich, Barbara; and Sklar, Holly (Boston: South End Press, 1983).

Women of the New Right. Klatch, Rebecca E. (Philadelphia, PA: Temple University Press, 1987).

Conservative & Anti-Feminist

The Failure of Feminism. Davidson, Nicholas (Buffalo, NY: Prometheus Books, 1988).

Democratic Renewal, 1989).

Rights of Lesbians and Gay Men. Hunter, Nan D., Sherryl E. Michaelson, & Thomas B. Stoddard (Carbondale, IL: Southern Illinois Univ. Press, 1992).

Sex and Germs: The Politics of AIDS. Patton, Cindy (Boston,MA: South End Press, 1985).

Articles:

"Constructing Homophobia: Colorado's Right-Wing Attack on Homosexuals," by Jean Hardisty in The Public Eve. March 1993.

"Marketing the Religious Right's Anti-Gay Agenda," by Chip Berlet, in CovertAction Quarterly, Spring 1993.

"Reel Hate: A new video tries to drive a wedge between blacks and gays," by Liz Galst, in The Boston Phoenix, Supplement, October 1993.

Against Gay Rights

Gay is Not Good. DuMas, Frank (Nashville, TN: Thomas Nelson Publishers, 1979).

Gays, AIDS and You. Rueda, Enrique T. and Schwartz, Michael (Old Greenwich, CT: Devin Adair Company, 1987).

The Homosexual Network: Private Lives and Public Policy. Rueda, Enrique (Old Greenwich, CT: Devin Adair Company, 1982).

Homosexual Politics: Road to Ruin for America. Rowe, Dr. Edward (Washington, D.C.: Church League of America, 1984).

The Unhappy Gays. LaHaye, Timothy (Wheaton, Il: Tyndale House Publishers, 1978).

What Everyone Should Know About Homosexuality. LaHaye, Timothy (Wheaton, IL: Tyndale House Publishers, 1978).

(continued)

Censorship & Intellectual Freedom

Newsletters:

ACP Newsletter. American Civil Liberties Union: Arts Censorship Project.

Censorship News. National Coalition Against Censorship.

Culture Watch. The Data Center.

Index on Censorship. [London: (071) 329-6434]

Newsletter on Intellectual Freedom. American Library Association: Intellectual Freedom Committee

Books:

Culture Wars: Documents from the Recent Controversies in the Arts. Bolton, Richard, ed. (New York: New Press, 1992).

The Sex Panic: Women, Censorship and "Pornography." (A conference report). (New York: National Coalition Against Censorship, 1993).

Sex, Sin and Blasphemy: A Guide to America's Censorship Wars. Heins, Marjorie. (New York, NY: The New Press, 1993).

The Environment

About The Anti-Environmentalist Right

By The Anti-Environmentalist Right

Ecology Wars: Environmentalism As If People Mattered. Arnold, Ron. (Bellevue, WA: The Free Enterprise Press, 1987).

Trashing the Economy: How Runaway Environmentalism is Wrecking America. Arnold, Ron and Alan Gottlieb. (Bellevue, WA: Free Enterprise Press-Dist. Merril Press, 1993)

The Wise Use Agenda: The Citizen's Policy Guide to Environmental Resource Issues. A Task Force Report to Bush Administration by the Wise Use Movement. Gottlieb, Alan M., ed. (Bellevue, WA: Merril Press, 1989).

Race And Ethnicity

Newsletters:

ADC Times. American-Arab Anti-Discrimination Committee.

ADL On The Frontline. Anti-Defamation League of B'Nai B'Rith.

CAAAV Voice. Committee Against Anti-Asian Violence.

Crisis. National Association for the Advancement of Colored People.

The Forum. Center for the Applied Study of Ethnoviolence.

Monitor. Center for Democratic Renewal.

Outlook. Asian American Legal Defense & Education Fund.

The Public Eye. Political Research Associates.

Race File. Applied Research Center.

Right Wing Watch. People for the American Way.

Books:

God, Land, and Politics: The Wise Use and Christian Right Connection in 1992 Oregon Politics. (Report). Available from the Western States Center. (503) 228-8866

The Scent of Opportunity: A Survey of the Wise Use/Property Rights Movement in New England. (Report). Burke, William K. (Cambridge, MA: Political Research Associates, 1992).

Articles:

Anti-Environmental Propaganda: Special Theme Issue. With articles by Johan Carlisle, William Kevin Burke, Stephen Leiper, Dean Kuipers, Joe Lyford, Jr., Bill Walker, Mark Dowie, and Michael Miley. Includes resource list. Propaganda Review, Spring 1994. (415) 386-4902.

"Corporate Fronts: Inside the Anti-Environmental Movement," by Chip Berlet and William K. Burke in Greenpeace, Jan./Feb./Mar. 1992.

"Greenscam," by Ted Williams, in Harrowsmith Country Life, May/June 1992.

"Hunting the 'Green Menace,'" by Chip Berlet in The Humanist, July/August 1991, pp. 24-31.

"Land-Use Advocates Make Gains," by Daniel B. Wood in Christian Science Monitor, October 3, 1991.

"Meet the Anti-Greens," by Margaret L. Knox in the Progressive, October 1991.

"Under Green Guise, Multi-use Groups Work Against Environment," by Fred Baumgarten in Audubon Activist, November 1991.

"Wise Guise," by Dan Baum in Sierra, May/June 1991.

"The 'Wise Use' Movement: Lying About the Land," in Western States Center Newsletter, Summer 1992, (No. 7), p. 7.

Liberal & Progressive Discussions of Racial and Ethnic Bias

America in the Era of Limits: Migrants, Nativists, and the Future of U.S.-Mexican Relations. Cornelius, Wayne A. (La Jolla, Calif.: Center for U.S.-Mexican Studies, University of California, San Diego, 1982).

Anti-Filipino Movements in California: A History, Bibliography, and Study Guide. DeWitt, Howard A. (San Francisco, Calif.: R & E Research Associates, 1976).

Bakke and the Politics of Equality: Friends and Foes in the Classroom of Litigation. O'Neill, Timothy J. (Middletown, CT: Wesleyan University Press, 1985).

Black Lives, White Lives: Three Decades of Race Relations in America. Blauner, Bob. (Berkeley, Calif.: University of California Press, 1989).

Bridges and Boundaries: African Americans and American Jews. Salzman, Jack, with Adina Back and Gretchen Sullivan Sorin (Eds.). (New York: Geroge Braziller/The Jewish Museum, 1992).

The Chinese Exclusion: Racism Toward Asians in California and the West, 1850-1949. Wong, Brian, ed. (Los Angeles, Calif.: Glendale Press, 1991.

Class, Race, and the Civil Rights Movement. Bloom, Jack M. (Bloomington, Ind.: Indiana University Press, 1987).

Communicating Racism: Ethnic Prejudice in Thought and Talk. van Dijk, T. Adrianus. (Newbury Park, Calif.: Sage Publications, 1987).

Death at an Early Age: The Destruction of the Hearts and Minds of Negro Children in the, Boston Public Schools. Kozol, Jonathan. (Boston: Houghton Mifflin, 1967).

Dumping in Dixie: Race, Class, and Environmental Quality. Bullard, Robert D. (Boulder, Colorado: Westview Press, 1990).

(continued)

Appendix 9B *(continued)*

Eliminating Racism: Profiles in Controversy. Katz, Phyllis A., and Dalmas A. Taylor, eds. (NY: Plenum Press, 1988).

Entry Denied: Exclusion and the Chinese Community in America, 1882-1943. Asian American History and Culture Series. (Philadelphia, PA: Temple University Press, 1991).

Fathers and Children: Andrew Jackson and the Subjugation of the American Indian. Rogin, Michael Paul. (NY: Random House, 1976).

The Fiery Cross: The Ku Klux Klan in America. Wade, Wyn Craig. (NY: Simon & Schuster, 1987).

Indians Are Us? Culture and Genocide in Native North America. Churchill, Ward. (Monroe, Maine: Common Courage Press, 1994).

Iron Cages: Race and Culture in 19th Century America. Takaki, Ronald. (NY: Oxford University Press, 1990).

Keeper of the Concentration Camps: Dillon S. Myer and [anti-Japanese] American Racism. Drinnon, Richard. (Berkeley, Calif.: University of California Press, 1987).

The Measure of Our Success: A Letter to My Children and Yours. Edelman, Marian Wright. (Boston, Mass.: Beacon Press, 1992).

The Political Economy of Race and Class. Dymski, Gray. (NY: Union for Radical Political Economics, 1986.

Power and Prejudice: The Politics and Diplomacy of Racial Discrimination. Lauren, Paul G. (Boulder, Colorado: Westview, 1988).

Prophetic Thought in Postmodern Times. (Volume One: Beyond Eurocentrism and Multiculturalism). West, Cornel. (Monroe, Maine: Common Courage Press, 1993).

Prophetic Reflections: Notes on Race and Power in America. (Volume Two: Beyond Eurocentrism and Multiculturalism).

Conservative Discussions of Racial and Ethnic Bias

The Balancing Act: Quota Hiring in Higher Education. Roche, George Charles. (LaSalle, IL.: Open Court Publishing Co., 1974).

Black Education: Myths and Tragedies. Sowell, Thomas. (New York: David McKay Co., 1972).

The Content of Our Character: A New Vision of Race in America. Steele, Shelby. (New York: St. Martins, 1990).

Counting By Race: Equality from the Founding Fathers to Bakke and Weber. Eastland, Terry and Bennett, William. (New York: Basic Books, 1979).

Ethnic America: A History. Sowell, Thomas. (New York: Basic Books, 1981).

Losing Ground: American Social Policy 1950-1980. Murray, Charles. (New York: Basic Books, 1984).

Reflections of an Affirmative Action Baby. Carter, Stephen Lisle (NY: Basic Books, 1991).

Scapegoating of Jews & Holocaust Denial

The Holocaust

The Abandonment of the Jews. Wyman, David S. (New York: Pantheon, 1984).

The Destruction of the European Jews. Hilberg, Raoul. (New York: Holmes and Meier, 1985).

(continued)

West, Cornel. (Monroe, Maine: Common Courage Press, 1993).

Race. Terkel, Studs. (NY: Pantheon, 1992).

Race and the Decline of Class in American Politics. Huckfeldt, Robert, and Carol W. Kohfeld. (Urbana, IL: University of Illinois Press, 1989).

Race and Media: The Enduring Life of the Moynihan Report. Ginsburg, Carl. (New York, NY: Institute for Media Analysis, 1989).

Racial and Cultural Minorities: An Analysis of Prejudice and Discrimination. Simpson, George E., and J. M. Yinger. (NY: Plenum Press, 1985).

Racism and Sexism: An Integrated Study. Rothenburg, Paul S. (NY: St. Martin's Press, 1988).

Settlers: The Mythology of the White Proletariat. Sakai, J. (Chicago: Morningstar Press, 1983).

Striking Back at Bigotry: Remedies Under Federal and State Law for Violence Motivated by Racial, Religious and Ethnic Prejudice. (Baltimore, MD: Center for the Applied Study of Ethnoviolence [formerly the National Institute Against Prejudice and Violence], 1986/Supplement 1988). (410) 706-5170.

Tree of Hate: Propaganda and Prejudices Affecting United States Relations With the Hispanic World. Powell, Philip W. (NY: Basic Books, 1971).

Yours in Struggle: Three Feminist Perspectives on Anti-Semitism and Racism. Bulkin, Elly, Minnie Pratt, and Barbara Smith. (NY: Long Haul Press, 1984).

Eichmann in Jerusalem: A Report on the Banality of Evil. Arendt, Hannah. (New York: Penguin Books, 1963).

From Weimar to Auschwitz. Mommsen, Hans. (Princeton, NJ: Princeton U. Press, 1991).

The Holocaust: The Destruction of European Jewry 1933-1945. Levin, Nora. (New York: Schocken Books, 1973).

Quiet Heroes: True Stories of the Rescue of Jews by Christians in Nazi-occupied Holland. Stein, Andre. (Toronto: Lester & Orpen Dennys, 1988).

When Six Million Died: A Chronicle of American Apathy. Morse, Arthur D. (Woodstock, NY: Overlook Press, 1983).

Fighting Scapegoating of Jews & Holocaust Denial

Antisemitism in the Contemporary World. Curtis, Michael. (Boulder, Colorado: Westview Press, 1986).

Assassins of Memory: Essays on the Denial of the Holocaust. Vidal-Naquet, Peirre. (New York: Columbia University Press, 1992).

A Trust Betrayed: The Keegstra Affair. Bercuson, David and Wertheimer, Douglas. (Toronto & New York: Doubleday & Co., 1985).

Antisemitic Propaganda: An Annotated Bibliography and Research Guide. Singerman, Robert. (New York & London: Garland Publishing, Inc., 1982).

Denying the Holocaust: The Growing Assault on Truth and Memory. Lipstadt, Deborah. (New York: Free Press, 1993).

Essential Papers on Jewish-Christian Relations in the United States: Imagery and Reality. by Naomi W. Cohen, editor. (NY: New York University Press, 1990).

Appendix 9B *(continued)*

Facing History and Ourselves: Holocaust and Human Behavior. Stern Strom, Margot and Parsons, William S. (Watertown, MA: Intentional Educations, Inc., 1982).

Farrakhan and Jews in the 1990's. (Booklet). Kenneth S. Stern. (New York: American Jewish Committee. 1994).

Farrakhan's Reign of Historical Error: The Truth Behind the Secret Relationship Between Blacks and Jews. Brackman, Harold. (Los Angeles: Simon Wiesenthal Center, 1992).

Hitler's Apologists: The Anti-Semitic Propaganda of Holocaust "Revisionism." Anti-Defamation League. (New York: Anti-Defamation League of B'nai B'rith, 1993).

Holocaust and Human Behavior: Annotated Bibliography. Drew, Margaret (ed.). (New York: Walker & Company, 1988).

Holocaust: Reinventing the Big Lie. Anti-Defamation League. (New York: Anti-Defamation League of B'nai B'rith, 1989).

Human Relations Materials for the Schools. Anti-Defamation League. (New York: Anti-Defamation League of B'nai B'rith, 1989).

Simon Wiesenthal Center Catalog. (Los Angeles: Simon Wiesenthal Center, 1994). (213) 553-9036.

The Tenacity of Prejudice: Anti-Semitism in Contemporary America. Selznick, Gertrude & Steinberg, Stephen. (New York/London: Harper & Rowe, 1969).

Holocaust Denial & "Historical Revisionism"

The Hoax of the Twentieth Century. Butz, Arthur. (Torrance, CA: Institute for Historical Review, 1977).

Authoritarianism, Xenophobia, Fascism & Nazism

Newsletters:

ADL On The Frontline. Anti-Defamation League of B'Nai B'Rith.

Monitor. Center for Democratic Renewal.

The Public Eye. Political Research Associates.

Searchlight. [London: (071) 284-4040].

Authoritarianism, Fascism & Nazism Through WWII

The Splendid Blond Beast: Money, Law, and Genocide in the 20th Century. Simpson, Christopher. (New York: Grove Press, 1993)

The Politics of the Body in Weimar Germany: Women's Reproductive Rights and Duties. Usborne, Cornelie. (Ann Arbor: U. of Michigan Press, 1992)

Readings on Fascism and National Socialism. Department of Philosophy, University of Colorado, ed. (Chicago, IL: Swallow Press, Inc., 1952).

Rehearsals for Fascism: Populism and Political Mobilization in Weimar Germany. Fritzsche, Peter. New York: Oxford University Press, 1990.

Sawdust Caesar: The Untold History of Mussolini and Fascism.

(continued)

No Time for Silence: Pleas for a Just Peace Over Four Decades. App, Austin J. (Costa Mesa, CA: Institute for Historical Review, 1987).

The Six Million Reconsidered: Is the 'Nazi Holocaust' Story a Zionist Propaganda Plot? Grimstad, William N., ed. (United Kingdom: Historical Review Press/Noontide Press, 1977).

Scapegoating of Jews

For Fear of the Jews. Rittenhouse, Stan. (Vienna, VA: The Exhorters, 1982).

Hear O Israel. Brooks, Pat. (Fletcher, NC: New Puritan Library, 1981).

Protocols of the Elders of Zion. No Author Listed [historic forgery]. (Los Angeles, CA: Christian Nationalist Crusade: n.d.).

The Secret Relationship Between Blacks and Jews: Volume One. Nation of Islam, Historical Research Department (Chicago, IL: Nation of Islam, 1991).

The Score: An Autobiography Exposing the Forces that Remain Studiously, Concealed and Masked. Stanko, Rudy (Butch). (Gering, NE: League of Rights, 1986).

The Ugly Truth About ADL. Editors of Executive Intelligence Review. (Washington, D.C.: Executive Intelligence Review, 1992).

Seldes, George. (New York and London: Harper and Brothers Publishers, 1935).

Sexual Politics in the Third Reich: The Persecution of the Homosexuals During the Holocaust: A Bibliography and Introductory Essay. Porter, Jack Nusan. (Montreal, Quebec: Concordia University, 1991).

Shattering the German Night: The Story of the White Rose. Dumbach, Annette E. and Newborn, Judd. (Boston and Toronto: Little, Brown and Company, 1986)

Three Faces of Fascism: Action Francaise, Italian Fascism, National Socialism. Nolte, Ernst (Originally published Munich: R. Piper & Co., 1963: New York: Signet, New American Library, 1969: Canada: Holt, Rinehart and Winston, 1969).

Weimar and the Rise of Hitler. Nichols, A. J. (New York: St. Martin's Press, 1979),

Authoritarianism, Fascism, & Nazism After WWII

The Belarus Secret: The Nazi Connection in America. Loftus, John. (New York: Paragon Press, 1982).

Blowback: America's Recruitment of Nazis and Its Effect on the Cold War. Simpson, Christopher. (New York: Weidenfeld and Nicholson, 1988).

Fascism in the Contemporary World: Ideology, Evolution, Resurgence. Joes, James (Boulder: Westview, 1978).

Inside the League: The Shocking Expose of How Terrorists, Nazis and Latin American, Death Squads Have Infiltrated the World Anti- Communist League. Anderson, Scott and Anderson, Jon Lee. (New York: Dodd, Mead and Company, 1986).

The Paperclip Conspiracy: The Hunt for the Nazi Scientists. Bower, Tom. (Boston and Toronto: Little, Brown and Company, 1987).

Secret Agenda: The United States Government, Nazi Scientists, and Project Paperclip, 1945 to 1990. Hunt, Linda. (NY: St. Martins, 1991).

Wanted: The Search for Nazis in America. Bloom, Howard. (New York: Fawcett Crest Books, 1977).

Critiques of Modern Racialist Nationalism

Bitter Harvest: Gordon Kahl and the Posse Comitatus, Murder in the Heartland. Corcoran, James. (New York: Penguin Books, 1990).

Blood in the Face: The Ku Klux Klan, Aryan Nations, Nazi Skinheads, and the Rise of a New White Culture. Ridgeway, James. (New York, NY: Thunder's Mouth Press, 1990).

God, Guts and Guns. Finch, Phillip (New York: Seaview/Putnam, 1983).

Hooded Americanism: The History of the Ku Klux Klan. Chalmers, David M. (New York and London: New Viewpoints, 1976).

The Liberty Lobby and the American Right: Race, Conspiracy and Culture. Mintz, Frank P. (Westport, Connecticut: Greenwood Press, 1985).

Right Woos Left: Populist Party, LaRouchian, and Other Neofascist Overtures to Progressives and Why They Must Be Rejected. Berlet, Chip. (Revised). (Cambridge, MA: Political Research Associates, 1994).

Terror in the Night: The Klan's Campaign Against the Jews. Nelson, Jack. (New York: Simon & Schuster, 1993)

United They Hate: White Supremacist Groups in America. Kronenwetter, Michael. (New York: Walker and Company, 1992). (Youth oriented).

Classics of Racialism, Xenophobia, & Fascism

The Dispossessed Majority. Robertson, Wilmot (Cape Canaveral, FL: Howard Allen Publisher, 1972).

Imperium: The Philosophy of History and Politics. Yockey, Francis Parker (Ulick Varange). (Costa Mesa, CA: Noontide Press, 1962).

Mein Kampf. Hitler, Adolf. (Boston: Houghton Mifflin Company, 1971; first published Verlag Frz. Eher Nachf, G.M.B.H., 1927).

Race and Reason: A Yankee View. Putnam, Carleton. (Washington, D.C.: Public Affairs Press, 1961).

The Rising Tide of Color (Against White World-Supremacy). Stoddard, Lothrop. (Orig. pub. 1920) (Brighton, England: Historical Rev. Press 1981).

===

Extracted from a series of more extensive bibliographies available from Political Research Associates. Call for a free list of resources. (617) 661-9313. Computer users with modems can download this and other PRA bibliographies by calling The Public Eye BBS, (617) 221-5815, settings (8,N,1).

Appendix 9C: From the "Militia Watchdog" Web Site (reprinted with permission)

The "Militia Watchdog" is "devoted to monitoring far-right extremism in the United States." The following document was one of many available on the group's Web Site in late 1998.

A Militia Watchdog Special Report

INTRODUCTION

The following is a chronology of some of the events surrounding anti-government criminal activity in the United States during the first quarter of the year 1998. It illustrates both the scope of such activity—from large-scale acts of terrorism to local acts of harassment and intimidation—and its geographic extent—from major cities like Minneapolis to remote rural areas in Texas and Washington. The chronology is not comprehensive. Although all major events are included, no systemized reporting system exists for smaller scale events. As a result, arrests or convictions for charges such as placing bogus liens, impersonating public officials or committing similar offenses are considerably underrepresented in this report. Such activities occur with a very high level of frequency across the nation. Some examples are included in this chronology to give some indication of the type of activities of this sort that take place. This report includes events from twenty-five states, but activity occurs in every state in the country.

JANUARY

January 5, 1998, Idaho: Professional skater Gary Beacom receives a 21-month sentence for failure to pay close to $200,000 in income taxes. Beacom, a Canadian who may be deported as a result, is a "constitutionalist" and tax protester who believes the Constitution does not require him to pay income tax.

January 5, 1998, Massachusetts: A deadline passes for John and Rhetta Sweeney of Hamilton, Massachusetts, to surrender their home. The couple lost their home to the FDIC for not paying back a $1.6 million loan, but refuses to leave. The Sweeneys instead sought support from local militia groups, who begin patrolling their property. Now U.S. marshals must decide how to evict them peacefully.

January 6, 1998, Texas: German native and Republic of Texas group member Christina Swann is ordered deported back to Germany because of two aggravated felony convictions on charges of burglary and theft. Swann had previously been in trouble with the INS for a previous arrest for numerous unpaid traffic citations. Swann refused to put state tags on her vehicles.

January 8, 1998, Wisconsin: Three Wisconsin tax protesters are sentenced to jail for leading an organization whose members filed more than 200 fraudulent income tax returns. Frank Wysocki, Sr., and Alan Cooper are sentenced to three years and ten months, while Robert Iacoe is sentenced to three years and five months. The three headed a group called "Sovereign Citizens for Liberty" which sold "untax packages" to would-be tax protesters.

January 8, 1998, California: Jeffrey Allen Campbell and Justin Bertone, two alleged members of the white supremacist White Criminals on Dope are arrested on suspicion of having been behind the planting of 10 fake bombs in Hollywood and the San Fernando Valley, targeting minority business owners. They are reportedly linked with "Peckerwood" skinhead gangs in southern California.

January 8, 1998, Nevada: Robert Storms, a Virginia City bartender and militia member, is convicted of selling illegal guns but acquitted of six counts of making and selling pipe bombs. Robert, his brother Kevin (a reserve deputy in Storey County), and former sheriff's deputy Griffith Evan Rausch, Jr., had been arrested on various weapons and bomb-making charges. Kevin Storms had previously pleaded guilty to machine guns and pipe bomb charges.

January 12, 1998, Florida, Tennessee: Florida resident Jay Maggi, a Federal Aviation Administration air traffic controller, is found guilty on two counts of tax evasion in Tennessee. Maggi, a tax protester, claimed to be exempt from taxes because he did not fit the definition of a "person."

January 13, 1998, Ohio: White supremacist and anti-government extremist Cheyne Kehoe is found guilty by an Ohio jury of attempted murder and three other counts for his part in a shootout with Ohio law enforcement officers in February 1997. His brother Chevie, also involved in the shootout, has yet to stand trial. The Kehoes reportedly were involved in various illegal activities designed to create an "Aryan People's Republic," and Chevie Kehoe and several other participants face racketeering charges for those activities.

January 14, 1998, Idaho: "Constitutionalist" Grant Walton is sentenced to six months in the Idaho County jail for refusing to buy a driver's license and register his car. There are so many spectators at his trial that many have to stand in the hall outside the courtroom. Walton receives the maximum sentence possible because prosecutors contended that he provoked a confrontation with the arresting officer during a traffic stop for speeding (later in January he will comply with a judge's order to buy a driver's license).

January 14, 1998, Texas: Five members of the Republic of Texas are indicted for failing to appear for court hearings in December 1997 in a conspiracy and mail fraud case. Indicted are Richard McLaren, Joe Louis Reece, Linh Ngoc Vu, Jasper Edward Baccus, Erwin Leo Brown and Steven Craig Crear. All had been previously incarcerated on other charges.

January 15, 1998, New Hampshire: Constitutionalist Edward James Loh is arrested for driving a truck without license plates, drivers license or registration. He is charged with operating without a valid license, having an unregistered vehicle and disobeying a police officer. Loh refuses to pay his $25 bail, which lands him in jail for months until his trial date is set. He could face up to a year in jail.

January 20, 1998, Ohio: White supremacist Cheyne Kehoe is sentenced to 24 years in prison for his conviction on attempted murder and other charges stemming from a February 1997 gunfight with Ohio police (see above entry).

January 20, 1998, Nevada: Tax protester Larry Greatwood of Henderson, Nevada, is sentenced to forty months in prison for a tax scheme in which he encouraged people to file false income tax returns. He was convicted of one count of bankruptcy fraud, one count of corruptly impeding federal officers and seven counts of presenting false claims. Greatwood also filed bogus liens of $1 million against IRS employees.

January 21, 1998, Colorado: Militia member Kevin Terry pleads guilty to illegally possessing a machine-gun in exchange for the dismissal of conspiracy and other charges. Kevin Terry was one of three members of the Colorado First Light Infantry militia group arrested on various conspiracy and weapons charges.

January 22, 1998, South Carolina: Federal Judge dismisses a lawsuit filed by tax protesters Nolan and Marcia Hoopingarner against the Rock Hill Herald (a South Carolina newspaper) and some 36 public officials. Hoopingarner had previously been acquitted by a jury trial in 1995 on charges of threatening a public official, after a county treasurer alleged that he had threatened her and her family at her office. In the lawsuit, Hoopingarner argued that sheriff's deputies trespassed on his property to arrest him and then beat him. Hoopingarner had refused to pay local taxes. The Herald had merely reported on the story.

January 23, 1998, Texas: Three Ku Klux Klan members receive lengthy sentences for their role in a 1997 conspiracy to bomb a natural gas processing plant in north Texas to act as a diversion for an armored car robbery. Edward Taylor, Jr., receives 21 years and 10 months in prison and Shawn Dee Adams receives 14 years in prison. Carl Waskom, who pled guilty to conspiracy, receives a sentence of nine years and two months. A fourth defendant, Catherine Adams, awaits sentencing.

January 26, 1998, Colorado: Militia leader Ron Cole, head of the Colorado First Light Infantry, pleads guilty on four illegal weapons charges in federal court in exchange for the dismissal of additional charges. He faces a sentence of up to 27 months in prison.

January 27, 1998, Texas: Republic of Texas member Carol Davis Walker is sentenced to ten years in prison for having burned down her home in 1996 in order to collect insurance money. The judge in the case also revokes her probation on charges of criminal conspiracy to commit capital murder and solicitation of capital murder relating to an attack a decade earlier on her sister's husband.

January 29, 1998, Utah: Dental technician and tax protester Fred Miller receives a guilty verdict for not paying state taxes for five years in the mid-1990s. Miller claimed that he was not required to pay taxes because he was not a "person." He faces up to 30 years in prison. His is one in a continuing series of prosecutions against tax protesters in Utah after the state decided to crack down; Utah reportedly has the highest per capita number of tax protesters in the nation.

January 29, 1998, Texas: Ku Klux Klan member Catherine Dee Adams receives a sentence of 15 years for her role in a plot to bomb a natural gas processing plant (see above) in 1997.

January 29, 1998, Alabama: The New Woman All Women Clinic in Birmingham, Alabama, which performs abortions, is bombed, resulting in the death of a police officer and the severe wounding of a clinic worker. The prime suspect, Eric Rudolph, becomes a much sought-after fugitive. Rudolph is alleged to be a white supremacist with connections to the militia group Northpoint Tactical Teams. Despite a massive search, law enforcement authorities cannot locate Rudolph.

FEBRUARY

February 2, 1998, West Virginia: West Virginia "Mountaineer Militia" member James Rogers is sentenced to a year in prison for his role in a plot to bomb an FBI fingerprinting facility in Clarksburg, West Virginia. The former firefighter who provided copies of facility blueprints to other militia members is the first person sentenced under the 1994 anti-terrorism law. Prosecutors had recommended he serve the full ten years possible, but the judge said Rogers had had an exemplary record as a public servant before his arrest.

February 5, 1998, Montana: Montana Freeman supporter Lavon Hanson is sentenced to a year and a day in prison for his conviction of bank fraud. Hanson had earlier pled guilty in a plea bargain, admitting to sending out bogus money orders.

February 10, 1998, Colorado: Colorado First Light Infantry member Wallace Stanley Kennett pleads guilty to possessing an illegal machine gun in a plea bargain reached between the militia member and the federal government.

February 10, 1998, Wisconsin: White supremacist and militia member Merlon Lingenfelter is sentenced to two years and three months for possessing two machine guns. As part of a plea bargain, federal authorities agreed to dismiss a pipe bomb possession count. Lingenfelter was part of an unnamed militia group led by Bradley Glover which plotted to attack U.S. military bases suspected of training UN troops.

February 10, 1998, Texas: The "secretary of state" for the extremist group known as the Republic of Texas pleads guilty to income tax evasion in Dallas. Robert Kesterson, also responsible for the group's Internet site, avoided paying nearly $13,000 in income taxes for 1995. Kesterson agreed to cooperate with federal authorities in return for their not seeking charges against his wife.

February 10, 1998, Utah: Tax protesting truck driver Brown Kaplar receives convictions on five felony counts for tax evasion and failure to file. Kaplar had claimed dthat his wages were not "income" according to the IRS code. He faces up to 30 years in prison.

February 11, 1998, Florida: Jacksonville pastor Joseph Welburn Evans is arrested for driving without a license. Evans instead had a license, license plate, registration and insurance card from the British West Indies, a non-existent country made up by anti-government extremists for the purposes of creating counterfeit documents. Evans is part of the Embassy of Heaven Church, an extremist organization whose members acknowledge no earthly laws and claim "diplomatic immunity" as "ambassadors" of the "Kingdom of Heaven."

February 17, 1998, Illinois: Militia sympathizer and gun dealer Shawn M. Cole is arrested on a charge of illegally selling a firearm to an undercover officer. State police seize more than a hundred guns from his home. The arrest is the first arrest in a probe by state police of illegal gun sales. Cole had been prohibited from selling firearms by state authorities earlier, pending an investigation of his sales activities. However, he continued to deal guns out of his home.

February 19, 1998, Nevada: Two men, William Leavitt and white supremacist Larry Wayne Harris, are jailed on charges of possessing anthrax in a much-publicized arrest. The substance turns out to be a harmless anthrax vaccine (although Harris will be found guilty of minor probation violations).

February 20, 1998, Ohio: White supremacist Chevie Kehoe pleads guilty to felonious assault, attempted murder and carrying a concealed weapon for his role in a February 1997 shootout with Ohio police. Eight other charges are dropped. Kehoe faces federal charges of murder, racketeering and conspiracy in Arkansas.

February 24, 1998, Illinois: Former Ku Klux Klan leader Dennis Michael McGiffen is one of three men charged with conspiracy to receive and possess machine guns and destructive devices as part of a wide-ranging plot to bomb public buildings across the country, rob banks, poison water supplies, and even to kill a federal judge and other people. Also charged are Wallace Scott Weicherding, a former prison guard, and Ralph P. Bock. McGiffen had quit the clan several years ago because it was not radical enough to suit him. McGiffen called his group "The New Order," after a 1980s white supremacist group which made headlines for its crimes of armed robbery, counterfeiting and murder.

February 28, 1998, Massachusetts: U.S. marshals launch a long-awaited raid on the mansion of John Sweeney in Hamilton, Massachusetts, where Sweeney and his wife Rhetta had holed up for nine months in a stand-off over a $1.6 million bank loan. Authorities enter the house and arrest Sweeney, who surrenders peacefully, on contempt-of-court charges. Half a dozen supporters, including alleged militia members, who had been helping the Sweeneys, left willingly after being served with a court order to leave or be subject to arrest for criminal contempt.

MARCH

March 2, 1998, Washington: A federal judge hands down "exceptional sentences" to Veryl Knowles and

Charles C. Miller for their roles in a massive scheme to create and pass counterfeit money orders. The two "freemen" received sentences of eleven years and three months (for Knowles) and twelve years and three months (for Miller). Federal judge John Coughenour handed out particularly long sentences because he said he wanted to send a warning message to people who attempted similar schemes.

March 2, 1998, Ohio: Aryan Nations member Morris Lynn Gulett is sentenced to a year in prison after pleading guilty to a charge of aggravated assault on a police officer for an incident in which he purposely rammed his van into Dayton police officers trying to stop him for a traffic violation. As Gulett had already spent a year in jail awaiting trial and sentencing, the sentence actually means he will be freed from jail.

March 6, 1998, Illinois: A fourth member of the white supremacist group "The New Order," Glenn LeVelle Lowtharp, is indicted for crimes related to the group's various anti-government plots. Lowtharp helped turn rifles to automatic weapons for the group.

March 7, 1998, Illinois: Self-proclaimed Aryan Nations member Donald Young, a Springfield, Illinois, resident, is arrested after a car chase in connection with a series of telephone bomb threats. Police find two explosive devices in his car and one on a convenience store parking lot; Young admits to planting a bomb at Casey's General Store. He is charged with possessing incendiary devices, fleeing from an officer and criminal damages to property; additional charges are possible.

March 8, 1998, Texas: Jason Leigh, a Denton, Texas resident, attempts to take over the Veterans Affairs regional office in Waco. He crashes his vehicle into the office, telling authorities he is arms and possesses explosives, beginning a 14-hour standoff that lasts until his final surrender to police. At one point Leigh demands $1 million for an organization called "Save Our Soldiers," which apparently consisted only of Leigh. Leigh was obsessed with UFOs and a local newspaper editor characterized his anti-government views as similar to those of the Republic of Texas.

March 9, 1998, Washington, Montana: Federal investigators arrest white supremacist Kirby Kehoe in Springdale, Washington, on weapons charges. ATF agents seize grenades, tear gas machine guns and ammunition at Kehoe's residence and in a storage locker in Thompson Falls, Montana. Kehoe is the father of Cheyne and Chevie Kehoe, convicted criminals in connection with a shootout with law enforcement officers in Wilmington, Ohio, in February 1997 (see above). Chevie Kehoe is also under federal indictment in Arkansas on racketeering charges associated with the murder of an Arkansas gun dealer and his family, and other activities. The Kehoes had been allegedly attempting to establish an "Aryan People's Republic." Kirby Kehoe was indicted in 1997 in Spoke on various weapons charges. Additional firearms charges will be filed against him in a few days.

March 10, 1998, Idaho: Constitutionalist and tax protester Elaine Gott is sentenced to nine years in prison for her convictions on 23 counts of fraud, mail fraud, bank fraud and other charges. Gott, her husband George Michael Gott, and four other defendants, were involved in a number of activities designed to hide their income and file bogus liens against public officials and private individuals. All other participants but Gott's husband had been previously sentenced.

March 12, 1998, California: The leader of a militia group called the Southern California Minutemen Association is ordered to stand trial for a plot to use snipers to murder illegal immigrants at the U.S.-Mexican border. A judge rules that there is sufficient evidence to bring Alvin Ung to trial on thirteen felony counts, mostly various weapons and explosives charges.

March 12, 1998, Texas: Louis Ray Boudreaux, Jr., a "Christian Sovereign National of the Republic of Texas," is jailed on retaliation charges after sending a letter to state District Judge Lee Alworth threatening him with the death penalty for an act of "treason." Alworth's "treason" was to divide Boudreaux's property in a 1996 divorce case. Boudreaux faces a maximum ten year sentence if convicted.

March 13, 1998, Pennsylvania: Aryan Republican Army member Michael Brescia is sentenced to 57 months in prison for his role in an armed robbery designed to acquire funds with which to finance white supremacist activities. Brescia was one of five members of the gang which robbed 22 banks in the Midwest from 1992 to 1995. Also sentenced is Scott Stedeford, who receives a mandatory 20-year no-parole prison sentence. He is already serving a nine-year federal prison term on related charges.

March 14, 1998, Idaho: White supremacist Mathew Bracken of Sandpoint, Idaho, is arrested in western Washington while sleeping in a stolen car. He is jailed on suspicion of auto theft, possessing explosives and being a felon in possession of a loaded firearm. He had recently escaped from a Bonner County jail. He has an extensive criminal history, but police are not sure what he was planning to do with the bomb-making materials they found in the car.

March 16, 1998, Kentucky: Tony Gamble, Imperial Wizard of the KKK Tristate Knight Riders, is sentenced to 55 years in prison for raping and sodomizing two young girls.

March 16, 1998, Illinois, Ohio: Daniel Rick becomes the fifth person arrested in connection with a plot by the white supremacist group "The New Order" to carry out a campaign of armed robberies, assassinations, bombings and other crimes. He is held on felony charges of illegally possessing a machine gun and related weapons charges.

March 17, 1998, New York: Two former NYPD officers become the thirteenth and fourteenth NYPD members to be convicted in a long-lasting tax evasion scheme. Former officer Frank Sambula and former detective Barton Adams are convicted on 10 counts relating to tax evasion and conspiracy. Adams and Sambula sold tax evasion kits originating from extremist groups to other police officers, charging up to $2,000 per kit.

March 18, 1998, Michigan: Three members of the Michigan-based North American Militia are arrested for federal weapons violations, including possession of machine guns. The three militiamen, Ken Carter, Bradford Metcalf and Randy Graham, are alleged to have plotted to kill federal agents and bomb various targets, including the Battle Creek Federal center, a military hangar and a television station.

March 18, 1998, Florida: A 66-year old retired New York police officer is found guilty of driving with a suspended driver's license and failing to register his car by a Martin County jury which spent seven minutes deliberating. William John Rudge, a self-proclaimed "Freeman," defended himself, saying that he had "sovereign authority" to operate a vehicle in the U.S. without any restrictions from the state. Rudge's vehicle instead sported a homemade "Florida Republic" vehicle tag. The judge places Rudge on a one-year probation and fines him $400.

Circa March 18, 1998, Wisconsin: Militia leader Don Treloar of Ogdensburg, Wisconsin, is arrested by federal and local law enforcement officers for impersonating a federal official. Treloar had been masquerading as a "Special united States Marshal," which is one of several "patriot" groups that imitate valid law enforcement organizations (others include the Constitution Rangers and the Civil Rights Task Force).

March 19, 1998, Pennsylvania: Aryan Nations leader and "Aryan Republican Army" member Mark Thomas is sentenced to eight years in prison for his role in helping a white supremacist group plot and commit armed robberies to finance their crusade against the government. Indicted in early 1997, Thomas pled guilty and agreed to cooperate with authorities. This cooperation causes the judge to sentence Thomas to two years less than suggested by sentencing guidelines.

March 20, 1998, Oregon: Ronald A. Griesacker, known under a variety of other names as well, is arrested in Oregon on federal bank and mail fraud charges. Griesacker, a peripatetic figure on the extremist fringe, was associated with a wide variety of groups and activities, ranging from common law courts to the Republic of Texas to the Washitaw Nation, and had been long sought after.

March 20, 1998, Utah: Tax protester Fred Miller (see above) is sentenced to five years in prison for his tax protest activities which resulted in five felony convictions in January 1998. The state was willing to recommend probation had Miller simply filed tax returns, but Miller persisted in claiming he did not have to pay taxes.

March 24, 1998, Colorado: Colorado militiaman Ron Cole is sentenced to 27 months in prison for possessing four illegal machine guns (see above).

March 25, 1998, Washington: Federal authorities unveil four new charges against white supremacist Kirby Kehoe, accusing him of two counts of possessing unregistered firearms, one count of possessing a machine gun and one count of transportation of firearms while under indictment (see above).

March 25, 1998, Florida: Grant McEwan, a former millionaire and fugitive tax protester, receives a two year sentence on assorted charges of tax fraud, threatening IRS employees, filing bogus liens and bond jumping.

He was also given two years' probation and ordered to perform 50 hours of community service. The light sentence may have been due to cooperation offered by McEwan to authorities which led to the arrest of long-time fugitive tax protester Tupper Saussy, who had spent the last ten years successfully avoiding capture.

March 26, 1998, Minnesota, Iowa: Marvin Pullman of Elma, Iowa, and Milton Bigalk of Stewartville, Minnesota, are convicted on various charges related to tax protest activities. Pullman is convicted of conspiracy to defraud the government, possession of counterfeit securities and obstructing the IRS. Bigalk is convicted of making false claims and conspiring to defraud the government. Three other defendants have previously pled guilty. The tax protesters created a sham company called Freemen and Associates to try to hide offshore investments; they also used fraudulent trusts to hide money from the IRS.

March 26, 1998, Tennessee: Milford Dwayne Case is arrested by local and federal law enforcement officials and charged with soliciting to commit first-degree murder. Case is a member of a white supremacist group called the White Aryan Legion, but the alleged murder offer was apparently not racially motivated.

March 27, 1998, West Virginia: Floyd Raymond Looker, leader of the West Virginia Mountaineer Militia, is sentenced to 18 years in prison for his role in a 1996 plot to blow up the FBI's fingerprinting facility in Clarksburg, West Virginia.

March 31, 1998, Montana: Five Montana Freemen are found guilty of various charges in the first major trial of individuals involved in the 81-day standoff between the Freemen and federal authorities in 1996. Steven Hance, James Hance, John Hance and Jon Barry Nelson are convicted of being accessories after the fact to the armed robbery of an NBC television news crew, while the Hances are also convicted of being fugitives in possession of firearms. Elwin Ward is convicted of submitting a false claim to the IRS, but was found innocent of other charges. In a decision that dismayed some officials, the jury acquits Freeman Edwin Clark of all charges and frees him. The trial of the leaders of the Freemen begins in May 1998.

Notes

Chapter One. The Genesis of Bitter Air

1. Julian Hale, *Radio Power* (Philadelphia: Temple University Press, 1975), ix.
2. Michael Parenti, *Inventing Reality: The Politics of News Media,* 2d ed. (New York: St. Martin's Press, 1993), p. 69.
3. Ibid., p. 68.
4. Peter Laufer, *Inside Talk Radio* (New York: Birch Lane Press, 1995), p. 13.
5. Ibid., p. 15.
6. Ibid., p. 175.
7. Parenti, *Inventing Reality,* p. 217.
8. Laufer, *Inside Talk Radio,* p. 130.
9. Ibid., p. 138.
10. Frank Rich, "Journal," *New York Times*, June 5, 1997, pp. 1–30.
11. Anthony Violanti, "Air Power: Are Hate Media Poisoning America?" *Buffalo News,* May 7, 1995, Entertainment, p. q1.
12. Sean Paige et al., "Talking the Talk," *Insight* (February 9, 1998): p. 10.
13. From the syllabus for the Persuasion and Public Opinion course, Boston University, fall 1998.
14. Paige et al., "Talking the Talk," p. 10.
15. Ibid.
16. Sara Rimer, "Terror in Oklahoma: The Far Right, New Medium for the Far Right," *New York Times,* April 27, 1995, p. A1.
17. Ibid.
18. Ibid.
19. John F. Harris, "Clinton Says Talk Shows Not His Only Target," *Washington Post,* April 26, 1996, p. A14. President Clinton's address was on April 24, 1996.
20. David Tarrant, "Liddy Stands by His ATF Criticism," *Dallas Morning News,* April 20, 1995, p. 39A, cited in Cohen and Solomon, see n. 21.
21. Jeff Cohen and Norman Solomon, "Guns, Ammo & Talk Radio," in *Eyes Right! Challenging the Right Wing Backlash,* ed. Chip Berlet. (Boston: South End Press, 1995).
22. David Hinckley, "Nation Buffeted by Airwaves of Hate Talk," *New York Daily News,* April 27, 1995, p. 4.
23. Joseph T. Roy Sr., personal interview with co-author Robert L. Hilliard, Montgomery, Alabama, May 12, 1998.
24. James Latham, "Violent Words, Violent Actions," *Vista* (newsletter of Radio For Peace International), April 1995, p. 1.
25. "The Far Right Radio Review," rfpicr@sol.racsa.co.cr (Costa Rica).

26. Chip Berlet, "Who's Mediating the Storm? Right Wing Alternative Information Networks," in *Media Culture and the Religious Right,* ed. Linda Mintz and Julia Lesage (Minneapolis: University of Minnesota Press, 1998).

27. Mary Levin, *Talk Radio and the American Dream* (Lexington, MA: DC Heath, 1987), p. xiii

28. C. Richard Hofstetter et al., "Political Talk Radio: A Stereotype Reconsidered," *Political Research Quarterly* 47 (June 1994): 467.

29. Michael Harrison, telephone interview with Carla Brooks Johnston, June 24, 1998.

30. Howard Kurtz, *Hot Air* (New York: Basic Books, 1997), p. 3.

31. Interview with co-author Michael C. Keith, November 12, 1998.

32. Letter to co-author Michael C. Keith, October 22, 1998.

33. 8 FCC 333, January 26, 1941, "Mayflower Decision."

34. 13 FCC 1246, June 1, 1949, "In the Matter of Editorializing by Broadcast Licensees."

35. *Red Lion Broadcasting Co.* v *FCC,* 395 US 367, June 9, 1969.

36. H.R. 1934, 100th Cong., June 3, 1987.

37. FCC Memorandum Opinion and Order in Complaint of Syracuse Peace Council Against Television Station WTVH, 2 FCC Rcd 5043, 5057–5058, par. 98.

38. *De Jonge* v. *State of Oregon,* 299 US 353 (1937).

39. Ben Gross, *I Looked and I Listened* (New York: Random House, 1954), p. 68.

40. J.P. Dolan, "Hate Radio," review of *Radio Priest: Charles Coughlin, the Father of Hate Radio* by Donald Warren, *New York Times,* August 25, 1996. Sec. 7, p. 20.

41. Donald Warren, *Radio Priest: Charles Coughlin, the Father of Hate Radio* (New York: Free Press, 1996), p. 37.

42. Michael Kazin, "The First Radio Populist: A Lesson from the 1930s," *Tikkun* (January-February 1995): 37.

43. Warren, *Radio Priest,* p. 29.

44. Ibid., page number not available.

45. Nea Gabler, "Walter Winchell," *American Heritage,* November 1994, p. 96.

46. Hale, *Radio Power,* p. xv.

47. W.J. West, *Truth Betrayed* (London: Gerald Duckworth), 1987, p. 60.

48. James Wood, *History of International Broadcasting* (London: Peter Pereguinds, 1992), p. 50.

49. Masayo Duus, *Tokyo Rose, Orphan of the Pacific* (New York: Kodansha International, 1979), p. 98.

50. Warren Russell Howe, *The Hunt for Tokyo Rose* (New York: Madison Books, 1990), p. 5.

51. www.earthstation1.simplenet.com.Tokyo_Rose.html

52. Irving E. Fang, *Those Radio Commentators!* (Ames: Iowa State University Press, 1997), p. 6.

53. Ibid., p. 12.

54. Ibid., p. 6.

55. Michael Nelson, *War of the Black Heavens: The Battles of Western Broadcasting in the Cold War* (Syracuse, NY: Syracuse University Press, 1997), p. 44.

56. *Harper's Magazine,* November 1949, p. 579.

57. Fang, *Those Radio Commentators!,* p. 207.

58. Gini Graham Stott, *Can We Talk?* (New York: Insight Publishers, 1996), p. 197.

59. Ibid., p. 208.

60. Ibid., p. 206.

61. "Radio," *Time,* June 18, 1965, p. 26.

62. Ibid.

63. "Who's in Grant's Tomb?" *People Weekly,* August 19, 1996.

64. "Radio: The Hot-Hot Line," *Time,* June 12, 1995, p. 4.

65. Norman Goldstein, *The History of Television* (Surrey, England: Colour Library Books, 1991), p. 212.

66. Tom Shales, *Washington Post,* July 15, 1978.

67. Kenneth Jost, *The CQ Researcher,* Washington, DC, 1994, p. 363.

68. Patti Hartigan, "A war of words in cyberspace," *Boston Globe,* November 22, 1998, p. E2.

69. Maria Seminerio, "AOL Refuses to Remove KKK Site," *ZD Net,* April 8, 2997, p. 1.

70. *Web Communications,* "Censoring the Net—Disguised as Fighting Terrorism," p. 1, www.webcom.com/ezundel/english/alert/alert.G-7.html.

71. "Global Action Brief," October 15, 1997, http://www.xs4all.nl/felipe/germany.html.

72. "International Censorship Issues," www.efa.org.au/issues/censor/censs.html, October 16, 1997.

73. Ibid.

74. Sidney H. Schanberg, "How Dangerous Are Our Waves" (editorial), *Atlanta Constitution,* May 5, 1995, p. a3A.

75. Ellen Ratner, "After Oklahoma City: Talk Radio Responds, Our 'Back Fence,' " *Los Angeles Times,* April 27, 1995, p. 7.

Chapter Two. For Which They Stand

1. Promotional flyer on Bob Enyart, undated.

2. "Intelligence Project Documents Big Growth in Hate Groups," *SPLC Report* 28, no. 1 (March 1998): 3.

3. Internet printout, 1998; source undated.

4. Ibid. Guidebook appears to be published in 1993. Web address unavailable. The Horace Mann League, KH 414 Uno, Omaha, NE 68182–0162.

5. R. Simonds, "President's Report, National Association of Christian Educators/Citizens for Excellence in Education" (Costa Mesa, CA, 1993), p. 3.

6. Card distributed by Political Research Association entitled "Challenge the Promise Keepers," August 1997.

7. A "Dear Friends" letter from Jean Hardisty, executive director of Political Research Associates, November 28, 1997.

8. Southern Poverty Law Center, *Intelligence Report* (Winter 1998): 6.

9. Ibid., pp. 29–33.

10. "Terrorist Acts Drop But May Be More Deadly,"*ABI/INFORM* 16, no. 8 (August 1997): 9.

11. "3 Charged in Alleged Hate Conspiracy," *Los Angeles Times,* March 8, 1998, p. A17.

12. Leaflet and text from James Carville to specific addressees.

13. Chip Berlet and Margaret Quigley, "Theocracy and White Supremacy: Behind the Culture War to Restore Traditional Values," in *Eyes Right! Challenging the Right Wing Backlash,* ed. Chip Berlet (Boston: South End Press, 1995).

14. Ibid.

15. Jean V. Hardisty, "What Does 'Right Wing' Mean?" in *The Public Eye* (Political Research Associates), 1997.

16. Chip Berlet and Matthew N. Lyons, "Militia Nation," *Progressive Magazine,* date not available

17. Chip Berlet "Christian Identity, Survivalism & the Posse Comitatus: A New Face for Racism & Fascism," in *The Public Eye* (Political Research Associates), undated, 1997.

18. "Militia Planning to Wage War, Report Says," *New Orleans Times-Picayune,* May 4, 1996, p. A2.

19. "Militia Movement," Barefoot Bob, bobhard@nidlink.com, to Franco Berardi, August 31, 1996.

20. Ibid.

21. Ibid.

22. Ibid.

23. "The Threat of Anti-government Extremists," *False Patriots*, booklet, (Montgomery, AL: Southern Poverty Law Center, 1997), p. 74.

24. Ibid.

25. Ibid., p. 73.

26. Ibid.

27. Ibid., p. 72.

28. New World order response to an article in the *Toronto Star* of July 13, 1996, headlined "Terrorism—US Militia Movement Hitting New Highs—Public Anger, Arrests Haven't Deterred Anti-Government 'Citizen Soldiers,'" Internet: inforamp.net/-whitley.

29. *Congressional Record,* August 2, 1996.

30. "The Congresswoman from Texas Attacks 'Patriots' and the Militia," *New World Order Intelligence Report,* Internet: inforamp.net/-whitley.

31. Dave Zweibel, "Liberty Lobby Still Alive and Paranoid," *Capital Times,* August 16, 1996, p. 14A.

32. Internet, Nizkor Project, webmaster@nizkor.org, August 20, 1996.

33. Ibid.

34. Dave Zweibel, "Liberty Lobby."

35. Ibid.

36. Ibid.

37. Ibid.

38. Ibid.

39. Internet, Mark Rupert, "A Virtual Guided Tour of Far-Right Anti-Globalist Ideology." Six Web sites available at www.Virtual Tourists.com

40. Ibid.

41. Peter Cassidy, "The Rise in Paramilitary Policing," *CAG (Covert Action Quarterly),* undated (downloaded 1998), Internet: mediafilter.org.

42. Ibid.

43. Ibid.

44. Mike Trickey, "Five Years after Waco, Koresh Still Felt," *The Montreal Gazette,* February 3, 1998, p. A14.

45. Internet, Mark Rupert, "Virtual Guided Tour."

46. Jim Nesbitt, "Media-Conscious Militias Trying to Polish Image," *Cleveland Plain Dealer,* October 12, 1996, p. 2A.

47. Ibid.

48. Ibid.

49. James Ridgeway, "Freemen's Law: A Far Right Guide to the Constitution," in the *Village Voice,* April 16, 1996.

50. "Bioterrorism in Our Midst? Terrorists' Use of Biological Weapons," *American Society for Industrial Security Management* 41, no. 11 (November 1997): 12.

51. David Van Biema, "When White Makes Right: Skinheads Carve Out Their Niche in America's Violent Culture of Hate," *Time,* August 8, 1993, p. 40.

52. Stewart Bell, "Skinheads Tried to Recruit High-Schoolers," *Montreal Gazette,* April 28, 1998, p. F12.

53. *The War Ax,* published by the Georgia SS of America, 1993.

54. John Kifner, "Finding a Common Foe, Fringe Groups Join Forces," *New York Times,* 1998.

55. *New York Times,* April 29, 1995.

56. *USA Today,* January 16, 1996.

57. Judy L. Thomas, "Hunt for Terrorists Has Surged Since Blast: Oklahoma City Explosion Spurred Pre-emptive Strategy by FBI, Others," *Kansas City Star,* April 19, 1998, p. A1.

58. David E. Kaplan, Mike Tharp, Mark Madden, and Gordon Witkin, "Terrorism Threats at Home," *US News & World Report,* December 29, 1997/January 5, 1998.

59. Michael Reynolds, "Day of the Zealots: Militias," *Playboy,* August 1995, p. 56.

60. A "Dear Friends" letter from Jean Hardisty, executive director of Political Research Associates, November 28, 1997.

61. "The Religious Right," pamphlet, People for the American Way, November 7, 1997.

62. Clarence Page, "If the Brown Shirt Fits—Well, Wear It," *Rocky Mountain News,* January 4, 1996, p. 37A.

63. Robert P. Sigman, "Group Goes Too Far; Threats of Extreme Punishment Are Unacceptable," *Kansas City Star,* September 20, 1997, p. C6.

64. Southern Poverty Law Center, "Crackdown: Common Law Reels as 27 States Act," *Intelligence Report* (Spring 1998): 12.

65. Gayle White, "Q & A on the News: Christian Identity Movement: A Primer," *Atlanta Constitution,* March 6, 1998, News section, p. 10A.

66. Ibid.

67. Ibid.

68. Robert Marquand, "Hate Groups Market to the Mainstream," *Christian Science Monitor,* March 6, 1998, United States section, p. 4.

69. Jean M. Caldicott, "Lessons from Yesterday Provide Insight Today," *Tampa Tribune,* March 8, 1998, Commentary section, p. 3.

70. Chip Berlet and Matthew N. Lyons, "Militia Nation." *Progressive,* June 1995, p. 22.

71. Ibid.

72. "Rethinking Populism," in *The Public Eye* (Political Research Associates), Web site of Institute for Global Communication, 1997.

73. Ibid.

74. Ibid.

75. Chip Berlet, interview with Robert L. Hilliard, June 30, 1998.

76. Scott Powers, "Revolution Near, Militia Activist Says," *Columbus Dispatch,* November 4, 1996, p. 2C.

77. Ibid.

78. Brad Heavner, "Timeline of Far Right Activity," *VISTA* (newsletter of Radio For Peace International), April 1966.

79. Ibid.

80. John Sanko, "Bill Would Curb Militia Activities in Colorado; Opponents Fear Measure Would Infringe on Rights," *Rocky Mountain News* (Denver), February 13, 1998, p. 34A.

81. Mike McIntire, "Legislator Taking Look at State's Militia Law," *Hartford Courant,* February 10, 1998, p. A4.

82. Bruce Hoffman, "American Right-Wing Extremism," *Jane's Intelligence Review* 7, no. 7 (1995): 329.

83. Ibid.

84. Ibid.

85. Ibid.

86. Dick Foster, "Duke Has Apparently Left State; Ex-State Senator Moves; No News of Whereabouts," *Rocky Mountain News* (Denver), March 9, 1998, p. 5A.

87. Ibid.

88. "The 'Jew World Order,' " downloaded as part of "The Banned Media and Organizational List," September 9, 1995, 2d ed. Internet site address unavailable.

89. Ibid.

90. Thomas R. Eddlem, "Pending Legislation," Web page newsletter of the John Birch Society, October 21, 1997.

91. "White Supremacy in the 1990s," pamphlet. (Atlanta: Center for Democratic Renewal, August 14, 1994).

92. "Information," North Georgia White Knights, Internet: inform.htm, May 1998.

93. Charles Bosworth, "Tapes Detail Violent Plans of Hate Group, U.S. Says; Ex-Klan Leader's Lawyer Puts Different Spin on Talk," *St. Louis Post-Dispatch,* May 6, 1998, p. A1.

94. Evelyn Larrubia, "White Supremacists Plead Guilty to Shooting at Blacks," *Los Angeles Times,* April 28, 1998, p. B3.

95. Radio interview on "HateWatch" with Rev. Fred Philips, Internet: hatewatch.org, September 29, 1997.

96. "The Disease Is Hate," *Intelligence Report* no. 92 (Fall 1998): 2.

97. Ibid.

98. Ibid.

99. Laura Flanders, "The Video Strategy of the Fundamentalist Right," in *Extra* (newsletter of Fairness and Accuracy in Reporting [FAIR], June 1993).

100. Ibid.

101. "Another Far-Right Defection," *OutNOW* (gay newspaper of Silicon Valley and the Bay Area), August 19, 1997.

102. "The Heritage Front and the Canadian Far Right," Nizkor Project, Internet: webmaster@nizkor.org, September 3, 1996.

103. New World Order Intelligence Update, Internet: inforamp.net/-jwhitley, August 27, 1997.

104. Patricia Neill, "Mount Weather's Russian Twin." Internet: wanda@aol.com.

105. The New World Order Intelligence Update Web site, inforamp.net/-whitley. The original broadcast was June 20, 1997.

106. Ibid.

107. Chip Berlet, "Dances with Devils," *The Public Eye* (Political Research Associates).

108. Survival Enterprises, Internet: survival.simplenet.com/index.html, May 1998.

109. Ibid.

110. Review of *Millennium Rage: Survivalists, White Supremacists, and the Doomsday Prophecy* by Philip Lamy (Plenum Books, 1996), *Publisher's Weekly* 243, no. 45, p. 59.

111. Michael Barkun, "Militias, Christian Identity and the Radical Right," *Christian Century* 112, no. 23 (August 2, 1996): 738.

112. Chuck Harder, "For the People" radio program, June 20, 1998.

113. Bruce Hoffman, "American Right-Wing Extremists," p. 329.

114. "Paranoia as Patriotism: Far-Right Influences on the Militia Movement," the Nizkor Project, Internet: webmaster@nizkor.org, August 20, 1996.

115. Ibid.

116. Bob Hohler, "Texas Prison Is School for Hatred; Behind Bars, Jasper Suspects Were Free to Embrace Racism," *Boston Globe,* June 27, 1998, pp. A1, A4.

117. Craig Garrett, "Michigan Hate Groups on the Rise: Increase Is First since Oklahoma City Bombing. Terry Nichols Tied to Extremist Posse Comitatus," *Detroit News,* September 17, 1997, p. A1.

118. Ibid.

119. Graig Garrett, "Leader of Vigilante Group Denies Terry Nichols Link," *Detroit News,* September 17, 1997, p. C7.

120. Dave Daley, "Family Farm Preservation Members Guilty in Money Order Scam; Group Linked to Posse Comitatus Passed Millions of Dollars in Fake Notes to Attack Nation's Financial System," *Milwaukee Journal Sentinel,* December 7, 1996, p. 3.

121. "Hate Groups Are Increasing in the U.S.," *St. Louis Post-Dispatch,* March 4, 1998, p. A7.

112. Ibid.

123. Jim Leusner, "News Media Distort Image of Militias, 2 Leaders Say," *Orlando Sentinel,* June 15, 1996, p. A8.

124. Ibid.

125. Mark Potok, "Militant Militia Fringe Is Setting Off Alarms. Most Extreme Splinters Going Underground," *USA Today,* August 17, 1996, p. 4A.

126. Ibid.

127. Ibid.

128. Ibid., statement by Joe Roy of the Southern Poverty Law Center's Klanwatch.

Chapter Three. Lions of the Arena

1. "Jacor Sets Its Sights on Syndication," *Broadcasting and Cable,* June 9, 1997, p. 28.

2. "Internet Traffic Rapidly Increasing," Associated Press, April 15, 1998, Internet: nytimes.com/aponline/w/AP-exploding-internet.html.

3. National Alliance "American Dissident Voices" Broadcast Schedule, February 28, 1997.

4. Vincent Coppola, *Dragons of God* (Atlanta: Longstreet Press, 1996), p. 18.

5. "Who Rules America: The Alien Grip on Our News and Entertainment Media Must Be Broken," Internet: National Alliance Main Page, July 28, 1997.

6. Ibid.

7. Ibid.

8. Michael Barkun, "Militias, Christian Identity and the Radical Right," *Christian Century* 112, no. 23 (August 2, 1995): 538.

9. "Truth Radio," Internet: truthradio.com, May 1998.

10. "The Banned Media and Organization List," Internet: address unavailable, September 9, 1995, 2d, ed.

11. "Patriot Propaganda," in *False Patriots: The Threat of Anti-government Extremists* (Montgomery, AL: Southern Poverty Law Center, 1997), p. 15.

12. Leonard Greene, "Hate Radio Fans the Flames of Violence in U.S.," *Boston Herald,* April 26, 1995, p. 001.

13. Peter Baker, "Hillary Clinton Bemoans Influence of Right Wing Media," *Washington Post,* January 18, 1997, p. A11.

14. David Bianculli, "Disney Slips a Mickey to Hate Radio, or the Right to Free Speech, Depending on Whom You Ask," *New York Daily News,* April 23, 1996, p. 35.

15. Ibid.

16. Richard Wolf, "On the Radio, Conservatism," *USA Today,* August 14, 1996, p. 8A.

17. Jeff Cohen, and Norman Solomon, "Guns, Ammo & Talk Radio," *The Public Eye* (Political Research Associates, 1997), Internet: @igc (only partial address available).

18. "AM: These Airways Are Loaded," *New Orleans Times-Picayune,* September 19, 1997, p. L21.

19. "On the Air," in *False Patriots,* p. 19.

20. Internet: jwhitley@inforamp.net, November 8, 1997.

21. Al Brumbly, "Church Burnings Turn Up the Heat on Talk Radio,"*Dallas Morning News,* June 23, 1996, p. 8C.

22. Ibid.

23. Ibid.

24. Dusty Saunders, "Phony 'Christians' Love to Spout Their Bigotry on Radio Talk Shows," *Rocky Mountain News* (Denver), February 9, 1994, p. 16D.

25. Al Brumley, "Church Burnings," p. 8C.

26. Chip Berlet, excerpts from an interview with Grant Kester, March 1, 1995. Courtesy of Chip Berlet.

27. From a January 1, 1997 draft of Chip Berlet's "Right-Wing Alternative Information Networks" for *Who's Mediating the Storm?* a forthcoming anthology edited by Linda Kintz. Courtesy of Chip Berlet.

28. James Latham, "The Rise of Far-Right Hate Programming on the Short-wave Bands," *VISTA* (newsletter of Radio For Peace International), April 1994.

29. From a variety of sources, including Rogers Worthington, "Terror in the Heartland," *Chicago Tribune On-line,* April 26, 1995, and April 29, 1995; Jill Smolowe, "Radio Business Report," *Time, Inc., America Online,* May 2, 1995; Robert A. Massulo, "Short-wave Radio Still Best Link to Far-Reaching Places, People," *Sacramento Bee,* April 2, 1995, p. EN2.

30. Ibid.

31. Jean Marbella, "Paranoid Flock of Conspiracy Hunters Turns Short-wave Radio Far to the Right," *Baltimore Sun,* July 21, 1995, p. 1D.

32. Ibid.

33. *Global Community Forum* (Radio For Peace International), Internet: rfpicr@soil.racsa.co.cr, undated.

34. James Latham, "The Continued Growth of Far Right Radio," *VISTA* (newsletter of Radio For Peace International), October 1995.

35. John McPhaul, "Operator Alarmed by Racist Propaganda," *Tico Times* (San Jose, Costa Rica), April 28, 1995.

36. "Monitoring Group Detects Rise in Short-wave 'Hate' Broadcasts," *Minneapolis Star Tribune,* June 21, 1995, p. 11A.

37. Ibid.

38. James Latham, "Violent Words, Violent Actions?" *Far Right Radio Review* (Radio For Peace International) (April 1996): 2.

39. "Monitoring Group Detects Rise," p. 11A.

40. James Latham, "The Rise of Far-Right Hate Programming"

41. "ADV Needs Your Support," *Free Speech* (National Alliance) 1, no. 10.

42. Kevin Alfred Strom, "The FCC's Selective Persecution of Dissident Radio," *Free Speech* (National Alliance) 1, no. 9 (September 1995).

43. James Latham, "The Rise of Far-Right/Hate Programming."

44. Ibid.

45. Ibid.

46. Tyler Bridges, "N.O. Station Brings Nazis' Views to World," *New Orleans Times-Picayune,* April 29, 1995, p. A8.

47. Cheryl Heuton, "Main Street Media of Sarasota, Fla., Last Week Launched a Shortwave Radio Network," *Media Week,* 5, no. 3 (January 16, 1996): p. 8.

48. Deborah Amos, "Hate Groups Use Shortwave to Rant, Rave, and Recruit," transcript #1837.7, "All Things Considered," National Public Radio, May 4, 1995.

49. Tyler Bridges, "N.O. Station."

50. Kerry L. Lynch, "The Importance of Shortwave Listening: A Different Point of View." Internet: klynch@intrepid.net, October 1, 1996.

51. Steve McClellan and Harry A. Jessell, "Rightwing Shortwave Comes Under FCC Scrutiny; Oklahoma City Backlash Hits Airwaves," *Broadcasting and Cable* May 1, 1995, p. 6.

52. David Hinckley, *New York Daily News,* May 8, 1995, p. 62.

53. "Far Right Web Review" (Radio For Peace International), Internet: www.RFPI.com, 1997.

54. Ibid.

55. Tyler Bridges, "N.O. Station."

56. Rogers Worthington, "Far-Right Voice Loses Shortwave Radio Show," *Chicago Tribune,* April 29, 1995, p. 7.

57. Steve McClellan and Harry A. Jessell, "Rightwing Shortwave Comes Under FCC Scrutiny."

58. Tyler Bridges, "N.O. Station."

59. "Ripe for Recruitment," *Far Right Radio Review Update* (July 1996): 3.

60. Ibid.

61. Ward Harkavy, "Still Crazy After All These Years (The Names of the Patriots Have Changed, But Not Their Tune)," *Denver Westword,* July 4, 1996, Feature section.

62. "Ripe For Recruitment," p. 2.

63. Ibid., p. 3.

64. James Latham, RFPI, in a telephone interview with Carla Brooks Johnston, June 24, 1998.

65. Kerry L. Lynch, "The Importance of Shortwave Listening."

66. "News and Opinion Around the Dial," *Detroit News,* May 19, 1995, p. C1.

67. Ibid.

68. WWCR Press Release, undated.

69. Brad Heavner, "A Day on the Edge," *VISTA* (newsletter of Radio For Peace International), October 1996. Courtesy of RFPI.

70. "Radio Is Our Bomb." Internet: billy@dojo.ie, 1994.

71. Elizabeth Rathbun, "Little Radio Stations, Big Issues," *Broadcasting & Cable,* April 8, 1998, p. 57.

72. Ibid.

73. David Hinckley, "Little Guys Knocking Heads with FCC to Stay on Airwaves," *New York Daily News,* April 28, 1998, p. 75.

74. Howard Rheingold, "Pirate Radio or Community Communications?" Internet: hlr@well.com, 1994.

75. Ibid.

76. "NLNR 102.1 FM Mission Statement," flyer, undated.

77. Margot Hornblower, "Radio Free America," *Time,* April 20, 1998, p. 4.

78. Rob Patterson, "Radio Free Tejas; Right-wing Pirate Broadcaster Back on the Air," *Austin American-Statesman,* February 5, 1998, p. 19.

79. "Radio Free America Statement of Purpose," Internet: RF America Home Page, address unavailable, November 20, 1996.

80. "Micro-Radio in the U.S." Internet: sues@ricochet.net, July 24, 1996.

81. Bill Coats, "Jury Convicts Lutz Radio Broadcaster," *St. Petersburg Times,* February 26, 1998, p. 4B.

82. Bill Coats, " 'Pirate Radio' Debate to Air at Hillsborough Trial," *St. Peterburg Times,* February 23, 1998, p. 3B.

83. Lutz Community Radio flyer, with attachment entitled "Don't Let Them Take Your Guns Away," undated.

84. Ibid.

85. Michelle Bearden, "Pirate Radio Was Ministry," *Tampa Tribune,* November 29, 1997, p. 4.

86. Brad Heavner, "Far Right Programs Come and Go," *VISTA* (newsletter of Radio for Peace International), July 1995.

87. Ibid.

88. Mario Morrow, "The Beauty of Radio Talk Shows Is the Audience of Different Minds and Motives," *Detroit News,* March 11, 1998, p. S8.

89. "In Oakland County: Right-wing Group Speaks Out on Public Access TV," *Detroit News.* Internet: Detroit News Home Page (address unavailable), May 7, 1996.

90. Ibid.

91. "The Truth (as I see it)." Internet: the-truth.org, May 1998.

92. "Cable Show Creates Controversy," *Boston Globe,* March 1, 1998, p. B6.

93. "Jews Try to Stop Zundel TV Shows," *Montreal Gazette,* January 23, 1995, p. B1.

94. Ibid.

95. "Support the American Patriot Fax Network!" Internet: jwhitley@inforamp.net, February 1, 1998.

97. "Deceiving America: Communist Influence in the Media," New World Order Intelligence Report. Internet: jwhitley@inforamp.net, November 23, 1997.

97. "The Truth (as I see it)."

98. Matthew Kalman and John Murray, "New-age Nazism," *New Statesman & Society,* 8, no. 358, (June 23, 1995): 18.

99. Amy Harmon, "Bigots on the Net," in *What's Next in Mass Communications,* ed. Christopher Harper (New York: St. Martin's Press, 1998), p. 33.

100. Farhan Haq, "United States: 'Cyper-Nazis' Haunt the Internet, Group Warns," *Inter Press Service,* November 12, 1996.

101. Ibid.

102. Ian Harvey, "Monkeying with the Net; Censors Target Hate Literature, Bomb-Making Recipes," *Toronto Sun,* August 14, 1996, p. 41.

103. "Hate Groups Are Increasing in U.S., Report Says; Internet, Rock Music Are Blamed," *St. Louis Post-Dispatch,* March 4, 1998, p. A7.

104. Personal interview with Brian Youngblood, Montgomery, Alabama, May 12, 1998.

105. "Militants Multiplying," *Sacramento Bee,* March 4, 1998, p. A12 (from the report of Klanwatch and the Militia Task Force of the Southern Poverty Law Center).

106. Sudarsan Raghaven, "When It Comes to the Web, Much of the Hate Starts Here," *Philadelphia Inquirer,* January 5, 1998, p. A1.

107. "On-line Allies: At the Heart of the Patriot Movement is the Computer," in *False Patriots,* p. 16.

108. Ibid.

109. "Internet Music Aids 20% Rise in Hate Groups, Report Says," *Chicago Tribune,* March 4, 1998, p. 8.

110. "Terrorist Acts Drop but May Be More Deadly," *Facilities Design and Management* 16, no. 8 (August 1997): 9.

111. Internet: Web Review copyright @ Songline Studios, Inc. (no address).

112. Kevin Sack, "Hate Groups in U.S. Are Growing, Report Says," *New York Times,* March 3, 1998, p. A10.

113. "Internet Music, *Chicago Tribune,* p. 8.

114. Personal interview with Brian Youngblood, Montgomery Alabama, May 12, 1998.

115. Richard A. Serrano, "Internet Promotes a Surge in Hate Groups," *Los Angeles Times,* March 4, 1998, p. A10.

116. ALPHA HQ Web site, Internet: alpha.org, May 1998.

117. "Underground Software," Internet: undergroundsoftware.com, May 1998.

118. Patti Hartigan, "A War of Words in Cyberspace," *Boston Globe,* November 22, 1998, p. E2.

119. "Expose It—Criminalize It—Hack It." Internet: Web Review copyright @ Songline Studios, Inc. (no address).

120. "On-line Allies," in *False Patriots,* p. 16.

121. Patti Hartigan, "A War of Words in Cyberspace," p. E1.

122. World-Wide White Power. Internet: whitepower.com, May 1998.

123. Internet: webcom.com/ezundel/index.html.

124. John Olsen, "Computing and the Net; Hate to Say Goodbye," *Guardian* (London), April 2, 1998, p. 5.

125. William Bowie, "BC Tel Ponders Pulling Plug for Net for Hate Groups; Free-speech Advocates Watching Closely," *Ottawa Citizen,* April 8, 1998, p. E2.

126. "An E-mail Tactic Stirs U.S. Concern," *Boston Globe,* May 5, 1998, p. A28.

127. Beth Marklein, "Indiana Campus Latest Stung by Racist E-mail," *USA Today,* March 16, 1998, p. 2D.

128. Personal interview by Robert Hilliard with Joseph T. Roy Sr., Montgomery, Alabama, May 12, 1998.

129. Amy Harmon, "Bigots on the Net," p. 35.

Chapter Four. But Carry a Big Stick

1. William B. Falk, "Louder and Louder. Fifteen Years Ago There Were 82 All-talk Stations. Today There Are 1,308. A Look At How Talk Radio Has Elbowed Its Way Into Media Prominence," *Newsday,* May 29, 1996, p. B04.

2. Maclean Hunter, *Maclean's,* February 19, 1996, p. 50.

3. Rush Limbaugh, "How Dangerous Are Our Airwaves," *Atlanta Constitution,* May 5, 1995, p. 13A.

4. William Endicott, "Radio Talker Gets Defensive," *Sacramento Bee,* April 29, 1995, p. A3.

5. Arlene Levinson, "Silent Majority Speaks Up via Phone, Fax, E-mail, Talk Shows," *Houston Chronicle,* September 11, 1994, p. 8C.

6. William B. Falk, "Louder and Louder," p. B04.

7. Ibid.

8. Norma Greenaway, "Radio Ranter Outdoes Himself: Rush Limbaugh Corners the Market on Tastelessness," *Ottawa Citizen,* January 28, 1998, p. A8.

9. Thomas B. Rosenstiel, "Radio, TV Programs Become New Power in Political Game," *Los Angeles Times,* May 1992 [date, page not available].

10. Donella H. Meadow, "Talk Shows Don't Make Democracy," *Houston Chronicle,* February 21, 1993, pp. 1F, 4F.

11. William J. Bennett, "Bum Rush: Press Lunges at Limbaugh," *Wall Street Journal,* July 19, 1994 [page number not available].

12. Stephen Talbot, "Wizard of Ooze," *Mother Jones* (May/June 1995): 41.

13. Ibid., p. 42.

14. Ibid.

15. William B. Falk, "Louder and Louder," p. B04.

16. Stephen Talbot, "Wizard of Ooze," op. cit., p. 41.

17. Molly Ivins, "Lyin' Bully," *Mother Jones* (May/June 1995): 37.

18. Ibid., p. 39.

19. Statistics courtesy of Shane Media, Houston, TX.

20. Michael Rust, "Tuning to America," *Washington Times*, July 17, 1995, p. 11.

21. Jim Simmon, "Echo Chamber," *Houston Press*, June 29–July 5, 1995, p. 6.

22. From *The Way Things Aren't: Rush Limbaugh's Reign of Error* (New York: Foundation for Accuracy in Reporting, 1995).

23. William J. Bennett, "Bum Rush."

24. Jim Simmon, "Echo Chamber," p. 6.

25. "The MacNeil-Lehrer News Hour," April 25, 1995 (transcript #5213).

26. Ibid.

27. Kevin Berger, "Shortwave Rightists Make Liddy & Co. Seem Moderate," *San Francisco Examiner*, May 1, 1995, p. C1.

28. Donna Petrozzello, "Emotions Run High at Talk Radio Convention. G. Gordon Liddy Wins Freedom of Speech Award," *Broadcasting & Cable*, July 3, 1995, p. 26.

29. Ralph Z. Hallow, "No Liddy, No Williams at GOP Group's Dinner," *Washington Times*, May 3, 1995, p. A1.

30. Donna Petrozzello, "Emotions Run High," p. 26.

31. Michael Harrison, phone interview with Carla Brooks Johnston, June 24, 1998.

32. Donna Petrozello, "Emotions Run High," p. 26.

33. Jeff Cohen and Norman Solomon, "Spotlight Finally Shines on White Hate Radio," *Media Beat*, November 3, 1994.

34. Ibid.

35. Ibid.

36. Ibid.

37. Garry Wills, "Hate Radio Spreads the Decline of Civilized Talk," *Times Union* (Albany, NY), May 13, 1996, p. A7.

38. Jeff Cohen and Norman Solomon, "Spotlight Finally Shines."

39. Bob Enyart Live Page. Internet: [address unavailable], 1997.

40. Jeff Cohen and Norman Solomon, "Spotlight Finally Shines."

41. Garry Wills, "Hate Radio," p. A7.

42. Tom Gresham's Gun Talk, Internet: guntalk@guntalk.com, 1997.

43. Ibid.

44. Jim Asker, "Talk Radio Popularity Rise Crackles with Controversy," *Houston Chronicle*, June 11, 1989, p. 10A.

45. Kevin Berger, "Hate Radio," *San Francisco Examiner*, May 1, 1995, p. C1.

46. Ibid.

47. Ibid.

48. Timothy Egan, "Talk Radio or Hate Radio? Critics Assail Some Hosts," *New York Times*, January 1, 1995, Sec. 1, p. 22.

49. Glenna Whitley, "Big Talker," *Texas Monthly* (January 1995): 36.

50. Dan Sewell, "Talk Show Hosts Become Icons with Hot Air Rising Nationwide," *Houston Chronicle*, March 19, 1995, p. 12A.

51. "The McLaughlin Group: A Viewer's Guide" (Cultural Information Service, 1998).

52. "Liberty Lobby Endorses Buchanan," *Spotlight,* March 4, 1996, p. 19.

53. Carl T. Rowan, "Shame Talk Radio, But Don't Muzzle It," syndicated column in a number of newspapers, including *Washington Post* and *Houston Chronicle,* April 28, 1995.

54. Ed Shane, "Talk Radio." Unpublished paper, 1997.

Chapter Five. *Gott Mit Uns*

1. Anna E. Williams, "Citizen Weyrich: NET's Conservative Media Empire," *afterimage* (February/March 1995): 11–13.

2. Richard Vara, "Documenting the Rise of the 'Religious Right,' " *Houston Chronicle,* September 26, 1996, Religion section, p. 1.

3. Memorandum to Barry Drake et al. from G.A. Burns regarding WORD One-to-One, October 3, 1995.

4. Ibid.

5. General James M. Green, "Revolution!!" leaflet issued by the Aggressive Christian Missions Training Corps, Berino, NM, undated (received 1998).

6. Ibid.

7. General James M. Green, "It's War: Join the Army That Sheds No Blood," leaflet, Aggressive Christianity Missions Training Corps, Berino, NM, undated (received 1998).

8. Flyers, leaflets, and pamphlets received from the Kingdom Identity Ministries, 1997.

9. James Ridgeway and Leonard Zeskind, "Revolution USA: The Far Right Militias Prepare for Battle," *Village Voice,* May 2, 1995, p. 23.

10. Peter Klebnikov, "Time of Troubles," *Newsweek,* April 7, 1997, pp. 48–48B.

11. James Latham, "The Continued Growth of Far Right Radio," *VISTA* (newsletter of Radio For Peace International), October 1995.

12. Ibid.

13. ADL Report, "The Jubilee: New Voice of the Far Right," *US Newswire,* April 25, 1996.

14. Ibid.

15. Peter Klebnikov, "Time of Troubles," p. 48.

16. Christine J. Russo, "Bible Broadcasts: American Family Association," *afterimage* (February/March 1995): 5.

17. *American Family Association Journal* (March 1995).

18. Paul Holmes, "Natural Born Zealots," *Reputation Management* (July/August 1995): 9.

19. Ibid., pp. 9ff.

20. Richard Vara, "Baptists Target Disney," *Houston Chronicle,* June 13, 1996, pp. 1A, 20A.

21. Grant Kester, "Net Profits: Chip Berlet Tracks Computer Networks of the Religious Right," *afterimage* (February/March 1995): 9.

22. Diego Ribadeneira, "Black Religious Leader Faults Church's Treatment of Gays, Women," *Boston Globe,* May 30, 1998, p. B2.

23. Pat Robertson statement and map in mailing from Democratic National Campaign Committee, 1998, with letter signed by James Carville.

24. Mailing (letter) by People for the American Way, May 1998.

25. Estella Duran, "Ford Warns of Far Right: Says Extremists Hurt GOP Cause," *Boston Globe,* June 2, 1998, p. A3.

26. Jennifer Mears, "Focus on the Family's Dobson Has Long Reach Carrying into Politics," *Houston Chronicle,* February 4, 1996.

27. Ibid.

28. "Author Urges Baptists to Defend Morality" (Associated Press), *Boston Globe,* June 12, 1998, p. A21.

29. Diego Ribadeneira, "Southern Baptists Trumpet a Victory; Declaring Wives Must 'Submit'; Group Caps Conservative Takeover," *Boston Globe,* June 14, 1998, p. A16.

30. Vicent Coppola, *Dragons of God* (Atlanta: Longstreet Press, 1996), p. 18.

31. " 'God' Order Affirmed in Love Reference Library." Internet: updates@melvig.org, March 10, 1998.

32. Ibid.

33. Peter Klebnikov, "Time of Troubles," p. 48B.

34. Ibid.

35. Michael Barkun, "Militias, Christian Identity and the Radical Right," *Christian Century,* August 2, 1995, p. 738.

36. Ibid.

Chapter Six. High-Stepping for Hitler

1. Michael Fechter, "Neo-Nazi Group with Following in Tampa Poses Threat, ADL Says," *Tampa Tribune,* September 25, 1998, p. 1.

2. Ellen O'Brien, "Racist Fliers Distributed in Suburbs," *Boston Globe,* December 9, 1998, p. B5.

3. *Intelligence Report,* Southern Poverty Law Center, May 1996.

4. ADV promotional material describing some of Pierce's programs.

5. Rochelle Olson, "[Turner Diaries] Author Urges All to Think about Supremacist Stand," Associated Press release, date unknown.

6. Ibid.

7. This material and other material in this chapter, if not indicated otherwise, was downloaded from the National Alliance Internet Web site and includes publications and transcripts from American Dissident Voices broadcasts. The material covers the years 1993–1996.

8. ADV broadcast, May 29, 1993.

9. "New Studies Cast Doubt on 'Holocaust' Claims," ADV broadcast July 24, 1992.

10. "National Socialist Primer," in *Stormfront,* publication of the National Alliance, April 17, 1995.

11. Kevin Alfred Strom, "AIDS Secrets: What the Government and the Media Don't Want You to Know," ADV broadcast, July 10, 1993.

12. Kevin Alfred Strom, "The Beast as Saint: The Truth about 'Martin Luther King Jr.,'" ADV broadcast, January 15, 1994.

13. Ibid.

14. Kevin Alfred Strom, "My Political Education," ADV broadcast, June 19, 1993.

15. "The Roots of Civilization," ADV broadcast, August 28, 1993.

16. Ibid.

17. ADV broadcast, February 20, 1993.

18. "Treason Never Prospers," ADV broadcast, August 21, 1993.

19. National Alliance Internet flyer, undated.

20. "Freespeech," Internet: National Alliance Web site, undated.

21. "American Dissident Voices Broadcast Schedule," National Alliance Web site, February 8, 1997.

22. "The Wisdom of Henry Ford," ADV broadcast, September 25, 1993.

23. "Israel: Facing the Facts," ADV broadcast, October 23, 1993.

24. "Destructive Immigration," ADV broadcast, November 13, 1993.

25. "Why No Free Speech in Germany?" ADV broadcast, December 4, 1993.

26. Ibid.

27. Ibid.

28. "The New World Order, Free Trade, and the Deindustrialization of America," ADV broadcast, March 19, 1994.

29. "Survivalism: Response to Racial Chaos," ADV broadcast, May 1, 1993.

30. William L. Pierce, "Gun Control: Not What It Seems," ADV broadcast, January 29, 1994.

31. Kevin Alfred Strom, "The Only Way to a Better World," ADV broadcast, August 7, 1993.

32. "The Joys of Multiculturalism," ADV broadcast, January 8, 1994.

33. "A New Outlet for ADV," ADV broadcast, October 2, 1993.

34. Al-Moharer Al-Australi, Internet: ozemail.com.au/-fouad/index.html

35. Alpha, Internet: alpha.org

36. American Times Today, Internet: attoday.com

37. First Amendment Exercise Machine, Internet: bluemoon.net/-frenz

38. Fur Das Vaterland, Internet: concentric.net/-14words/odessa.html

39. Heritage Front, Internet: alphanetftc.com/-freedom/hflindex.html

40. Independent White Racialists, Internet: www2.cybernex.net/-odin

41. The Library, Internet: alpha.ftcnet.com/-ourhero

42. Nation of Europa, Internet: demon.com.uk/natofeur

43. National Alliance, Internet: natvan.com

44. The National Party, Internet: cyberg8t.com/natlprty

45. National Socialist Movement, Internet: pages.prodigy.com/white/nsm.htm

46. National Socialist Vanguard, Internet: alpha.org/nsv

47. National Socialist White People's Party, Internet: nswpp.or/ and capecod.net/-ndemonti

48. New Dawn, Internet: nb.net/-newdawn

49. NSADP/AO, Internet: alpha.org/nsdap/main/mainpage.html

50. Reichfreudigkeit, Internet: glasscity.net/users/stein/reich.html

51. Schutz Staffell/Computer Abteilung, Internet: flashback.se/-ssca/sscal.htm

Chapter Seven. In No One Do We Trust

1. T. Kirby, "Freemen Call In on Radio Talk Show During Mind Control Interview," Internet [address unavailable], March 23, 1996.

2. Ibid.

3. Sara Rimer, "Terror in Oklahoma: The Far Right; New Medium for the Far Right," *New York Times,* April 27, 1995, p. A1.

4. Bill Steigerwald, "Militias Utilize Up-to-Date Technology to Communicate Their Age-Old Beliefs," *Pittsburgh Post-Gazette,* April 30, 1996, p. A11.

5. Ibid.

6. Ibid.

7. Federal News Service, November 2, 1995

8. Ibid.

9. Sheila Wissner, "At Movement's Extreme, Conspiracy Theories Fuel Militias' Worst Fears," *Tennesseean,* September 5, 1995, p. 1A.

10. "The American Patriot Chat Room, Internet: micro.com/-pkb/chatroom.html, undated.

11. "Militias," Internet: alt.culture, undated.

12. Bruce Hoffman, "American Right-Wing Extremism," *Jane's Intelligence Review* 7, no. 7 (July 1, 1995): 329.

13. *ABC World News Tonight,* July 3, 1996, Transcript #6132–4.

14. Bennett Roth, "Militia Leaders Warn of Civil War, Claim Blast Story Is Untold," *Houston Chronicle,* June 16, 1995.

15. Daniel Junas, "The Rise of Citizen Militias," *Covert Action Quarterly* (spring 1995).

16. William F. Jasper, "The Rise of Citizen Militias: Are They a Threat to America or Essential to Its Security? *The New American,* February 6, 1995.

17. Jim Wade, "First Word." Internet: Indiana Militia Web site [address unavailable], undated.

18. Internet: Web site [untitled, address unavailable].

19. Kevin Flynn, "Cop-killing Divides Militia Movement," *Rocky Mountain News* (Denver), June 3, 1998, p. 8A.

20. Paul Brinkley-Rogers and Dennis Wagner, "Patriot Movement Gains Momentum, Desperation," *Arizona Republic,* April 14, 1996, p. A1.

21. Ibid.

22. Book review of *Dragons of God: A Journey Through Far Right America* by Vincent Coppola, in *Publishers Weekly* 243, no. 43 (October 21, 1996): 67.

23. "Reactionary Forces Link Up in Militias," Stop the Hate organization, Internet: info@stop-the-hate.org, February 1998.

24. James Risen, "Militias Rely on Networks of Fiery Right," *Los Angeles Times,* April 30, 1995, p. A1.

25. Ibid.

26. Ibid.

27. James Ridgeway and Leonard Zeskind, "Revolution U.S.A: The Far Right Prepares for Battle," *Village Voice,* May 2, 1995, p. 23.

28. Ward Harkavy, "Doom and Doomer; Dr. Norm and the Rest of Patriot Radio Face the Apocalypse. Now," *Denver Westword,* May 3, 1995, p. 15.

29. Ibid.

30. James Ridgeway and Leonard Zeskind, "Revolution U.S.A.," p. 23.

31. Ward Harkavy, "Doom and Doomer," p. 15.

32. Rogers Worthington, "Far Right Voice Loses Shortwave Radio Show," April 29, 1995, p. 7.

33. Ward Harkavy, "Doom and Doomer," p. 15.

34. Ibid.

35. Ibid.

36. Ibid.

37. Jason Vest, "The Spooky World of Linda Thompson; Her Videos Inflame the Militias," *Washington Post,* May 11, 1995, p. D01.

38. Ibid.

39. Ibid.

40. Ibid.

41. Ibid.

42. Ibid.

43. Ibid.

44. Ibid.

45. Ibid.

46. James Risen, "Militias Rely," p. A1.

47. Mark Tanner, "How the Media Misrepresent the Militia Movement," Internet: macktanner@adelph.com, undated.

48. Tom Kenworthy, *Washington Post,* June 30, 1998, p. A02.

49. Paul Brinkley-Rogers and Dennis Wagner, "Patriot Movement Gains Momentum," p. A1.

50. Ibid.

51. Azell Murphy Cavaan, "Profile in Courage Award Goes to Mont. Attorney," *Boston Herald,* May 30, 1998, p. 012.

52. "Kurt Saxon On Survival," *Kurt Saxon's Survivalist Web Pages,* Internet: kurtsaxon.com./cary/, March 18, 1997 and Atlan site: cary@halcyon.com, June 13, 1996.

53. Phone interview with Kurt Saxon by Michael C. Keith, March 18, 1997.

54. Kurt Saxon, "Can the Coming Dark Age Be Prevented? The Dictatorship of the Intelligensia." Internet: cary@halcyon.com, 1997.

55. Atlan Formularies catalogue, undated, received March 1997, from Alpena, Arkansas.

56. Ibid.

57. Ibid.

58. "Global Community Forum" (Radio For Peace International), Internet: rfpicr@sol.racsa.co.cr, 1997.

59. Kevin Carmody, "It's a Jungle Out There," *Columbia Journalism Review* (May/June 1995): 40.

60. Ibid.

61. Kevin Carmody, "Environmental Backlash—Big Bucks Behind It," *Sacramento Bee,* June 25, 1995, p. FO2.

62. Jonathan Alter, "The Age of Conspiracy," *Newsweek,* March 24, 1997, p. 47.

63. Chip Berlet and Matthew N. Lyons, "Pillars of Conspiracist Scapegoating in the U.S.," in *Too Close for Comfort* (Boston: South End Press, 1997). All material in paragraph from chapter 10.

64. William H. Freivogel, "King of Conspiracy Theorists," *Houston Chronicle,* May 14, 1995, p. 8A.

65. James Latham, "Violent Words, Violent Actions?" *Far Right Radio Review Update* (Radio for Peace International), April 1996, p. 2.

66. Chuck Harder, "For the People" broadcast, June 20, 1998.

67. "Our Mission Statement," Police Against the New World Order. Internet: police-against-nwo.com/mission.htpl, March 21, 1997.

68. "About Officer Jack McLamb (Ret.)," Police Against the New World Order, press release to all radio stations, Internet: police-against-nwo.com/mission.htlp, undated, downloaded 1997.

69. "Highest Decorated—Yet Most Fired Police Officer in Arizona History Takes to the Airwaves!" press release to all radio stations, May 1, 1995.

70. Sam Stanton, "For Some Fringe 'Patriots,' Uncle Sam Is Domestic Enemy," *Sacramento Bee,* May 7, 1995, p. A1.

71. Paul Brinkley-Rogers and Dennis Wagner, "Patriot Movement," p. A1.

72. "Tyranny Cannot Come to the Home of Any Free People Unless It Comes in Uniform," American Citizens & Lawmen Association. Internet: vdlm.com/public/acla/acla.htlp, March 21, 1997.

73. Written response from Jack McLamb, March 18, 1997.

74. "What Is the Center for Action???" Statement about Center for Action, founder Col. James "Bo" Gritz. Internet: bogritz.com, undated.

75. Thomas Halpern, David Rosenberg, and Irwin Suall, "Militia Movement: Prescription for Disaster," *USA Today* magazine, January 1996, p. 16.

76. "What Is the Center for Action???"

77. Thomas Halpern, et al., "Militia Movement."

78. Sara Rimer, "Terror in Oklahoma: The Far Right," p. A1.

79. James Latham, "Violent Words, Violent Actions?" *Far Right Radio Review Update* (Radio for Peace International), April 1996, p. 2.

80. Sara Rimer, "Terror in Oklahoma: The Far Right," p. A1.

81. James Latham, "Violent Words, Violent Actions?" Far Right Radio Review in *VISTA* (Radio For Peace International), April 1996, p. 2.

82. "Poisoning the Airwaves: The Extremist Message of Hate on Shortwave Radio," Research Report of the Anti-Defamation League, 1996, pp. 12–13.

83. Rogers Worthington, "Far Right Info Web: Rumors, Untruths," *Chicago Tribune,* April 26, 1995, News section, p. 15.

Chapter Eight. Up Close and Right

1. Chip Berlet, "Right-wing Alternative Media Networks," for *Who's Mediating the Storm?* January 6, 1997.

2. Loretta Ross, "White Supremacy in the 1990s," in *Eyes Right!* edited by Chip Berlet (Boston: South End Press, 1995), p. 169.

3. Ibid., p. 171.

4. Ibid., pp. 168–69.

5. "Robertson Warns over 'Gay Days,' " *Boston Globe,* June 10, 1998, p. A9.

6. Loretta Ross, "White Supremacy in the 1990s," p. 178.

7. Ibid., pp. 169, 170.

8. Ibid., p. 168.

9. "The New American Magazine," Knights of the White Kamellia home page, Internet: kwk@geocities.com, undated. The home page includes the following exhortation: "Stand Up for White Rights, White Pride, and a Future for Our Children, Join the Knights of the White Kamellia."

10. *Miami Herald,* March 18, 1995.

11. Robert Marquand, "Hate Groups Market to the Mainstream,"*Christian Science Monitor,* March 6, 1998, p. 4.

12. "RAHOWA. Cult of the Holy War." Internet: whitepride.com/rahowa/interview1.html, undated.

13. William Shaw, "Hate, Rattle, and Roll," *Details* (July 1995): 42.

14. "Resistance," Resistance Records. Internet: whitepride.com/rahowa/interview1.html, undated.

15. William Shaw, "Hate, Rattle, and Roll," p. 40.

16. Ibid., p. 39.

17. Ibid., p. 40.

18. Brian E. Albrecht, "Hate Speech; Across Ohio and Throughout the Nation, the Venom Is Spreading Faster than Ever," *Cleveland Plain Dealer,* June 11, 1995, p. 1A.

19. Brian E. Albrecht, "Language of Hate Is Spreading; Almost Invisible Anger Racing Through Media," *New Orleans Times-Picayune,* June 18, 1995, p. A1.

20. Doreen Carvajal, "Onetime Political Satire Becomes a Right Wing Rage and a Hot Internet Item," *New York Times,* July 1, 1996, p. D7.

21. Sarah Vowell, *Radio On: A Listener's Diary* (New York: St. Martin's Press, 1997), p. 81.

22. Ibid., p. 77.

23. Kenneth Stern, "Hate on Talk Radio," in *Inside Talk Radio: America's Voice or Just Hot Air?* edited by Peter Laufer (New York: Birch Lane Press, 1995), p. 217.

24. Loretta Ross, "White Supremacy in the 1990s," p. 177.

25. Ibid., p. 178.

26. "The David Duke International Internet Radio Show" home page. Internet: Can be downloaded from dspg.com, 1998. Duke has his own Internet address: duke.org.

27. Written response to Michael C. Keith from David Duke, July 2, 1997.

28. Adrianne Flynn, "Radio Show's Ties a 'Shock' for Salmon; Program Linked to Neo-Nazis," quoting journalist Steve McLemee. Publication source unknown, October 13, 1995, pp. B1–2.

29. Jean Marbella, "Paranoid Flock of Conspiracy Hunters Turn Shortwave Radio Far to the Right," *Baltimore Sun,* July 21, 1995, Features, p. 11.

30. Adrianne Flynn, "Radio Show's Ties."

31. Ibid.

32. Ibid.

33. Ibid.

34. "News and Opinion Around the Dial," *Detroit News,* May 19, 1995, p. C1.

35. Phone and mail interview with Tom Valentine by Michael C. Keith. Final commentary approved by Mr. Valentine on July 26, 1997.

36. Written statement from Dale Crowley Jr. to co-author Michael C. Keith, June 2, 1997.

37. Sobran, Joseph, "Laws—Too Many or Too Few?" *Capitol Hill Voice* (March–April 1997): 1.

38. Celeste Bailey, "Children Require Moral Education," *Capitol Hill Voice* (March–April 1997): 2.

39. Dale Crowley Jr., "Errors and Deceptions of Dispensational Teachings," *Capitol Hill Voice* (March-April 1997): 3.

40. Written statement from Dale Crowley Jr. to co-author Michael C. Keith, June 2, 1997.

41. Bill Briggs, "The World of Bob Enyart: Outspoken TV Broadcaster Steers Hard Right," *Denver Post,* May 17, 1995, p. F-01.

42. Ibid.

43. Ibid.

44. Ibid.

45. Letter from Leslie Jorgenson, *Mother Jones* (July/August 1995): 6.

46. Ibid.

47. Leslie Jorgenson, "Right-Wing Talk Radio Supports Militia Movement," FAIR, Internet: fair.org/fair/, April 21, 1995.

48. Ibid.

49. Ibid.

50. "Before They Were Patriots," in *False Patriots: The Threat of Anti-Government Extremists* (Montgomery: Southern Poverty Law Center, 1997), pp. 36–37.

51. "The Jubilee: New Voice of the Far Right," report of the Anti-Defamation League, April 24, 1996.

52. Ibid.

53. *False Patriots,* p. 51.

54. "The Jubilee: New Voice of the Far Right."

55. "Reverend Sharpton's Anti-Semitic & Racist Broadcasts," *Jewish Post of New York,* Internet: jewishpost.com, January, 1996.

56. Knowledge TV, 1996 (month and day unknown).

57. Letter from B. Eric Rhoads to co-author Michael C. Keith, June 3, 1997.

58. Victor Volland, "Group Warns of Hate on Internet," *St. Louis Post-Dispatch,* October 22, 1997, p. 08A.

59. "A Few Facts About the Institute for Historical Review," IHR, Internet: ihrgreg@kaiwan.com, 1997.

60. Ibid.

61. Victor Volland, "Group Warns."

62. "Statement of Purpose," Committee for Open Debate on the Holocaust," Internet: CODOHmail@aol.com, January 14, 1996.

63. "The Roots of Civilization," American Dissident Voices (The National Alliance), August 28, 1993.

64. "Mission Statement," The Zundelsite, Internet: webcom.com/ezundel/index.html, 1998.

65. Zundelsite, September 28, 1997.

66. "Table of Contents," Zundelsite.

67. "Ernst Zundel: German-Canadian Human Rights Activist," Internet: zundelsite.com, August 14, 1996.

68. "Good Morning from the Zundelsite," Internet: zundelsite.com, September 30, 1996.

69. Andrew Brown, "Internet Activists Foil Ban on Nazi Nerds on the Net," *Independent,* February 3, 1996, International section, p. 8.

70. Bill Dunphy, "Nazi Messenger Revels in Net," *Toronto Sun,* February 5, 1996, News section, p. 18.

71. Andrew Brown, "Internet Activists."

72. A.J. McIlroy, "New Moves to Curb Racists on Internet," *Daily Telegraph,* February 20, 1997, p. 5.

73. Greg Beck, "Focus on Social Issues: Project Uses History to Refute Anti-Semitic Internet Groups," *Orange County Register,* June 15, 1996, p. A16.

74. Zundelsite, July 7, 1997.

75. Zundelsite, July 13, 1998.

76. Charles Enman, "Group Supports Zundel's Net Freedoms. Rights Panel to Decide if Holocaust Denier Violating the Law," *Ottawa Citizen,* October 20, 1997, p. A6.

77. "Zundel Court Bid Fails," *Toronto Star,* May 8, 1998.

78. David Foster and Arlene Levinson, "Okla. Bombing Exposes Violent Fringe in U.S.: Right-wing Extremists Claim to Be Fed Up with Government," Associated Press report, *Houston Chronicle,* May 28, 1995, p. 52A.

Chapter Nine. Armed for the Right

1. "Far Right Radio Review," Radio For Peace International shortwave broadcast, December 6, 1997.

2. "Hate Radio Deserves Criticism," *Hartford Courant,* April 30, 1995, p. D2.

3. Joanne Ostrow, " 'Hate Radio' Boycott Plan Has Witch-Hunt Overtones," *Denver Post,* May 11, 1995, p. E-01.

4. Alan Dershowitz, "We May Learn All the Wrong Lessons from Oklahoma," *Times Union* (Albany, NY), May 1, 1995, p. A7.

5. David Hatch, "KKK 'Considered' Unfit to Be Sponsor," *Electronic Media* (November 1997).

6. "Religious Leaders Attempt to Calm Hate Talk on Radio," *Orlando Sentinel,* June 1, 1996, p. D5 (reporting on Conference of the Maston Colloquial at the Center for Christian Ethics in Orlando).

7. David Stout, "Terror in Oklahoma Radio; Some Rightist Shows Pulled, and Debate Erupts," *New York Times,* April 30, 1995, Section 1, p. 28.

8. Anthony Violanti, "Community Groups Unite to Combat 'Hate Radio' Trend on Talk Shows," *Buffalo News,* March 17, 1995, Television section, p. 13.

9. "Bell Fights Hate on Internet," *Pittsburgh Post-Gazette,* November 25, 1997, p. F1.

10. David Stout, "Terror In Oklahoma."

11. Bill Rodgers, "Radio Station Counters Extremists," *IAC Newsletter Database* (Electronic World Communications) 3, no. 81, May 3, 1995, ISSN 1074–3355.

12. From Radio For Peace International flyer received 1997.

13. "The Far Right Radio Review" (now the "Global Community Forum"), Radio For Peace International, Internet: rfpicr@sol.racsa.co.cr, 1997.

14. Ibid.

15. Ibid.

16. ADL press release on its publication, *Danger: Extremism, the Major Vehicles and Voices on America's Far-Right Fringe,* November 7, 1996.

17. Ibid.

18. Zundelsite.com, January 15, 1998.

19. Ibid.

20. Kevin Alfred Strom, "The ADL: America's Greatest Enemy, part 2," *American Dissident Voices* radio program, June 5, 1993.

21. *Frontline* (a publication of the Anti-Defamation League) (October/November 1995): 10.

22. Patti Hartigan, "A War of Words in Cyberspace," *The Boston Globe,* November 22, 1998, pp. E1–2.

23. Ibid., p. 1.

24. "Responding to Antigovernment Extremists," *False Patriots,* pp. 42–45.

25. *FAIR,* Internet: fair.org/fair/, February 19, 1998.

26. Ibid.

27. Political Research Associates publications, including "Unmasking the Political Right" (fifteen-year report), "PRA Annual Report" (for 1996), "The Right Facts" (pamphlet), received from PRA in June 1998.

28. "New Organization Forms, Launches Web Site," *Oasis,* Keeping Watch Coalition, Internet: kpwatch@aquilapub.com, February, 1996.

29. *CCO's Resource Guide,* pamphlet distributed by the Center for Campus Organizing (Cambridge, Massachusetts), received 1998, Internet: cco.org.

30. Center for Defense Information, Internet: cdi.org, December 14, 1997.

31. *Union-Tribune,* June 28, 1996, p. E1.

32. Ibid.

33. Interview with author/researcher Carla Brooks Johnston, June 18, 1998.

34. German National Socialist and Hammerhead Page, Internet: whitepower.com.germany/.

35. Becky Beaupre, "Hate on the Internet: Extremist Groups Find Forum on Web," *Detroit News,* February 13, 1997, p. C1.

36. Ibid.

37. Ibid.

38. Victor Volland, "Group Warns of Hate on Internet," *St. Louis Post-Dispatch,* October 22, 1997, p. 08A.

39. Becky Beaupre, "Hate on the Internet."

40. "Hate Radio: Confessions of an Ex-listener," abcdefg (A Basic Citizen's Definitive Electronic Freedom Guide), Internet: winn.com/abcdefg/ (Phillip Winn), 1997.

Index

301

About the Authors

Robert L. Hilliard is professor of media arts at Emerson College. He is the author or co-author of over a dozen books, including *Surviving the Americans: The Continued Struggle of the Jews After Liberation* (1997) and *Writing for Television and Radio,* the longest-in-print mass communication book by a single author and the most widely used text on that subject, in its seventh edition in 1999. Hilliard served in Washington, D.C. as chief of the Educational/Public Broadcasting branch of the Federal Communications Commission and as chair of the Federal Interagency Media Committee, reporting to the White House, among other positions. He has worked in commercial and educational television, radio, and theater as a writer, producer, director, and performer. Hilliard holds a Ph.D. from Columbia University.

Michael C. Keith is senior lecturer of communications at Boston College. He is the author of over a dozen books on the electronic media, including *Voices in the Purple Haze*, *Signals in the Air*, and the classic textbook, *The Radio Station*. In addition to *Waves of Rancor*, he has co-authored *The Hidden Screen* (to be published M.E. Sharpe), *The Broadcast Century,* and *Global Broadcasting Systems* with Robert Hilliard. He is also the author of numerous journal articles and has served in a variety of editorial positions, including that of coeditor of the M.E. Sharpe series "Media, Communication, and Culture in America." His work in education and the broadcast industry is extensive, and he is past chair of education at the Museum of Broadcast Communications. Keith holds a Ph.D. from the University of Rhode Island.